The Friendly Liquidation of the Past

Pitt Latin American Series

Billie R. DeWalt, *General Editor*

G. Reid Andrews, Catherine Conaghan,
and Jorge I. Domínguez, *Associate Editors*

The Friendly Liquidation of the Past

THE POLITICS OF DIVERSITY IN LATIN AMERICA

Donna Lee Van Cott

University of Pittsburgh Press

Published by the University of Pittsburgh Press, Pittsburgh, Pa., 15261

Copyright © 2000, University of Pittsburgh Press

Manufactured in the United States of America

Printed on acid-free paper

10 9 8 7 6 5 4 3 2 1

Library of Congress Cataloging-in-Publication Data
Van Cott, Donna Lee.
   The friendly liquidation of the past : the politics of diversity in
Latin America / Donna Lee Van Cott.
         p. cm. — (Pitt Latin American series)
      Includes bibliographical references (p.   ) and index.
      ISBN 0-8229-4126-0 (alk. paper) — ISBN 0-8229-5729-9 (pbk. : alk.
paper)
      1. Democratization—Bolivia. 2. Democratization—Colombia.
3. Multiculturalism—Bolivia. 4. Multiculturalism—Colombia. 5. Pluralism
(Social sciences)—Bolivia. 6. Pluralism (Social sciences)—Colombia.
7. Constitutional history—Bolivia. 8. Constitutional history—Colombia.
I. Title. II. Series.
JL2281.V37 2000
320.984'09'049—dc21

99-050676

Contents

List of Figures and Tables

List of Abbreviations

ACIA	Asociación Campesina Integral del Atrato, Integral Campesino Organization of the Atrato
ADM-19	Alianza Democrática M-19, Democratic Alliance M-19
ADN	Acción Democrática Nacional, National Democratic Action
AICO	Autoridades Indígenas de Colombia, Colombian Indigenous Authorities
AISO	Autoridades Indígenas del Sur-Oeste, Southwest Indigenous Authorities
ANC	Asamblea Nacional Constituente, National Constituent Assembly
ANUC	Asociación Nacional de Usuarios Campesinos, National Association of Peasant Producers
APG	Asamblea del Pueblo Guaraní, Assembly of the Guaraní People
API	Proyecto de Apoyo a Los Pueblos Indígenas, Project to Help Indigenous Peoples
ASI	Alianza Social Indígena, Indigenous Social Alliance
ASP	Asamblea por la Soberanía de los Pueblos, Assembly for the Sovereignty of Peoples
CEJIS	Centro de Estudios Jurídicos e Investigación Social, Center for Juridical Studies and Social Investigation
CEPB	Confederación de Empresarios Privados de Bolivia, Bolivian Confederation of Private Entrepreneurs
CIDOB	Confederación Indígena del Oriente Boliviano, Indigenous Confederation of Eastern Bolivia
CIPCA	Centro de Investigación y Promoción del Campesinado, Center for the Investigation and Promotion of the Campesino
COB	Central Obrera de Bolivia, Bolivian Workers Central

CONAPI	Comisión Nacional de Política Indígena, National Indigenous Policy Commission
CONDEPA	Conciencia de Patria, Conscience of the Fatherland
CPIB	Central de Pueblos Indígenas del Beni, Indigenous Peoples Central of the Beni
CRIC	Consejo Regional Indígena del Cauca, Regional Indigenous Council of the Cauca
CSCB	Confederación Sindical de Colonos Bolivianos, Syndical Confederation of Bolivian Colonists
CSUTCB	Confederación Sindical Unica de Trabajadores Campesinos de Bolivia, Bolivian Unitary Syndical Peasant Workers Confederation
CV	Comité de Vigilancia, Vigilance Committee
DDCP	Democratic Development and Citizen Participation
DGAI	Directoría-General de Asuntos Indígenas, Director-General for Indigenous Affairs
DMI	distrito municipal indígena, indigenous municipal district
ELN	Ejército de Liberación Nacional, National Liberation Army
EPL	Ejército Popular de Liberación, Popular Liberation Army; later changed to Esperanza, Paz y Libertad, Hope, Peace and Liberty
ETI	entidad territorial indígena, indigenous territorial entity
FARC	Fuerzas Armadas Revolucionarias de Colombia, Revolution-ary Armed Forces of Colombia
ICAN	Instituto Colombiano de Antropología, Colombian Anthropology Institute
ILO	International Labour Organization
IMF	International Monetary Fund
IU	Izquierda Unida, United Left
JAC	junta de acción comunitaria, community action junta
JAL	junta administrativa local, local administrative junta
JV	junta vecinal, neighborhood junta
LDA	Ley de Descentralización Administrativa, Law of Administra-tive Decentralization
LOM	Lex de Organización Municipal, Law of Municipal Organizations

LPP	Ley de Participación Popular, Law of Popular Participation
M–19	Movimiento 19 de Abril, April 19 movement
MBL	Movimiento Bolivia Libre, Free Bolivia Movement
MIC	Movimiento Indígena de Colombia, Indigenous Movement of Colombia
MIR	Movimiento de la Izquierda Revolucionaria, Movement of the Revolutionary Left
MITKA	Movimiento Indígena Tupaj Katari, Tupaj Katari Indigenous Movement
MNR	Movimiento Nacional Revolucionario, National Revolutionary Movement
MRTKL	Movimiento Revolutionario Tupaj Katari de Liberación, Tupaj Katari Revolutionary Liberation Movement
MSN	Movimiento Salvación Nacional, National Salvation Movement
NFR	Nueva Fuerza Republicana, New Republican Force
NGO	nongovernmental organization
OAS	Organization of American States
OBAPO	Organización de Barrios Populares, Organization of Popular Barrios
ONIC	Organización Nacional Indígena de Colombia, Colombian National Indigenous Organization
OTB	organización territorial de base, territorial base organization
PAE	programa de acción estratégica, strategic action plan
PAO	plan anual operativa, annual operating plan
PCN	Processo de Communidades Negras, Process of Black Communities
PDM	plan de desarrollo municipal, municipal development plan
PPM	planificación participativa municipal, participatory municipal planning
PROADE	Proyecto de Apoyo a la Descentralización, Decentralization Support Project
PRT	Partido Revolucionario de Trabajadores, Revolutionary Workers Party
PSC	Partido Social Conservador, Social Conservative Party

SAE	Sub-secretaría de Asuntos Etnicos, Subsecretariat for Ethnic Affairs
SAG	Sub-secretaría de Genero, Subsecretariat for Gender
SNAEGG	Secretaría Nacional de Asuntos Etnicos, de Genero y Generacional, National Secretary for Ethnic, Gender and Generational Affairs
SNPP	Secretaría Nacional de Participación Popular, National Secretariat for Popular Participation
UCS	Unidad Cívica Solidaridad, United Civic Solidarity
UDAPSO	Unidad de Análisis de Políticas Sociales, Unit for Social Policy Analysis
UDP	Unidad Democrática y Popular, Democratic and Popular Unity
UNDP	United Nations Development Programme
UP	Unión Patriótica, Patriotic Union
UPP	Unidad de Participación Popular, Popular Participation Unit
USAID	United States Agency for International Development
VAIPO	Vice Ministry of Indigenous and Original Peoples Affairs
VPPFM	Vice Ministry of Popular Participation and Municipal Strengthening

Foreword

This admirable volume illuminates a process of profound importance in the contemporary world. In different ways, the once dominant normative model of the nation-state as culturally united, whether in aspiration or reality, dissolves before our eyes in many parts of the world. The chronicle Donna Lee Van Cott provides of the constitutionalization of multiculturalism in Colombia and Bolivia in the 1990s has a comparative significance that extends far beyond these two Andes republics.

Yet the one-nation, one-people doctrine long had a powerful hold on the official mind and the popular imagination in these two countries, as in Latin America generally. Spanish colonial doctrine incorporated the conquered populations as subjects of the Crown, even though missions sought a separate zone of tutelage. At the same time, the reduction of large segments of the indigenous population to a reservoir of servile labor and the introduction of African slaves created a sharply stratified society. The high degree of racial mixing that occurred over time, and the social norms linking status to proportion of Spanish ancestry, created a singularly complex hierarchy that ranged along a color spectrum with somewhat fluid boundaries.

The nineteenth-century revolt of the mainland Spanish western hemisphere imperium introduced a new master ideology, the idea of the nation, whose carriers were the successor *criollo* elites. Outranked on the status ladder only by the narrow layer of *peninsulares,* freshly dispatched from Spain as a ruling class, the *criollo* revolutionaries seized the top rung, deploying a doctrine of state representing the citizenry as a universe of individuals joined by a common nationhood in construction. Meanwhile, everyday social reality continued to reflect the powerful inertial force of the norms of racial hierarchy.

Partly because the theory of sovereignty of the Latin American state drew upon ascendant concepts of the liberal state, these notions long remained uncontested at the normative level. The idiom of challenge of the vast inequalities in Latin American states found its sources in class rather than cultural theories of difference. Paradigmatic was the slogan of the Bolivian MNR in the 1950s, when it appeared as a radical challenger, labeling "Indian" a feudal concept, and insisting that the indigenous countryside find classification in class (campesino) terms. In some instances, the vocation of nationhood as a narrative of uniformity gave rise to doctrines of racial fusion *(mestizaje)*.

The hegemonic hold of such notions is reflected in the chapter on Latin American Indians in my own 1976 book, *The Politics of Cultural Pluralism*. This chapter, drafted in 1973, was not based upon field research but drew instead upon much of the extant anthropological literature and extensive consultation with Latin American specialists. The puzzle that led me to include the chapter was the absence of apparent cultural mobilization among the large Latin American indigenous populations, when such solidarities already demonstrated their central importance in Africa and Asia. The core of the explanation, it seemed to me at the time, was the potency of *mestizaje*, and the permeability of the racial boundaries. The Indian could choose the pathway of Ladinoization by a change of clothing and speech codes. Because social mobility appeared firmly tied to the racial hierarchy, the incentives to choose this pathway seemed strong for precisely those elements who (comparative analysis showed) were the critical agents of identity mobilization: the young, upwardly mobile people who might serve as cultural entrepreneurs and political brokers.

At the very moment the book appeared, the tides of identity history for indigenous populations were beginning to flow in a very different direction. The first of a new Indian activism dates from the beginning of the 1970s. Movements for indigenous rights were beginning to flow together on a global scale, and an international normative discourse rapidly took form. Indigenous aspirations found significant though incomplete codification in the 1989 ILO Convention (169), whose impact upon the two cases in this book Van Cott examines. The perils of political science masquerading as prophecy found eloquent illustration.

Another interesting 1976 book exploring a comparably fugitive racial identity among Afro-Latin populations by an African American scholar (Rout) had parallel findings, also subsequently confounded by a rise in black identity movements. Afro-Latin movements cannot base their claims for multicultural recognition on the same moral ground as do indigenous communities. However, as Van Cott well shows in this book, the constitutional acknowledgment of a multicultural reality, in a case such as Colombia, where the African ancestral strain is large, inevitably extends beyond the issue of the indigenous to other historically marginalized categories at the bottom of the racial hierarchy.

We are only at the beginning of the era of the politics of constitutional recognition of cultural diversity. The misadventures of my portrayal of Indian consciousness in Latin America as "fugitive ethnicity" should instruct us as to the vast uncertainties and accelerating changes in this epoch of globalization and communal mobilization. The dramatic constitutional changes Van Cott skillfully examines are both works in progress, far from fully rooted in the quotidian practices of political life. But they are probably irreversible; it is difficult to imagine a return to the premises of the "nation" as crucible of homogenization. In both countries, and in much of Latin America, a new chapter in the accommodation of diversity opens. This book is an invaluable preface.

Crawford Young
University of Wisconsin—Madison

Acknowledgments

Research for this book was made possible by grants from the J. William Fulbright Scholarship Board and the University of Tennessee, Knoxville, Cordell Hull Fund. I am grateful for both, and for the generosity of more than 120 Bolivians and Colombians who agreed to be interviewed for this project. I also would like to thank John Bailey, Gerardo Berthín, John Dugas, Eduardo Gamarra, Jonathan Hartlyn, Kevin Healy, Harvey Kline, José Antonio Lucero, Joanne Rappaport, Mark Warren, and the editors at the University of Pittsburgh Press for reading and commenting on all or part of the manuscript, and Willem Assies, Jean Jackson, Kathleen O'Neill, and Addison Smith for sharing and allowing me to cite their work in progress. Arturo Valenzuela kindly shared his files on the early stages of the reform process in Bolivia. Gerardo Berthín generously helped to arrange a quick research sortie in La Paz in 1998. I am grateful to them both.

The Friendly Liquidation of the Past

1 Democratization and Constitutional Transformation

IN 1991 AND 1994, respectively, Colombians and Bolivians undertook comprehensive constitutional reforms. In each country, the problem of exclusion generated crises that triggered the decision to reform the constitution. Similar crises came together in both cases: a representation crisis, generated by nonrepresentative political parties that monopolized access to the state; a participation crisis, owing to the absence of means for most citizens to participate in decision-making; and a legitimation crisis, arising from discriminatory access to the protection of the law and equal membership in the nation, and to the absence of effective bases of legitimation to unite and guide the political community. All three crises were rooted in centuries of extreme social inequality that underlay an exclusionary state. By the early 1990s, the crises had reached a critical stage. Efforts by political elites to reform the political system through ordinary politics failed repeatedly. Political elites and civil society organizations clamored for constitutional reform.

Public debates on constitutional reform in the 1990s provided an auspicious political context for indigenous peoples to frame their grievances in ways that resonated with reform-minded elites.[1] Constitutionalism is about limiting the power and reach of the state; indigenous organizations seek to delineate a sphere of autonomy where state power cannot penetrate. Constitutionalism is about establishing the rule of law and enunciating the rights of citizens under that law; indigenous organizations seek to redefine

1

the terms of their citizenship and to establish mechanisms to protect their individual and collective rights. Indigenous organizations seized the opportunity to act as *subjects* in the creation of the political regime, as opposed to the *objects* of legislation composed and imposed by a distant and hostile state. And this participation was important not only to them. Having been excluded from the process of constituting the states of Latin America, their inclusion in the reform processes afforded much needed legitimacy to the new constitutions. The highly symbolic act of constitution-making elevated a struggle for particular rights to the level of a discussion on the meaning of democracy and the nature of the state.

In the social movement literature, the intellectual and political activity in which indigenous peoples' organizations engaged is called "framing"—defined by Doug McAdam, John D. McCarthy, and Mayer N. Zald as "the conscious strategic efforts by groups of people to fashion shared understandings of the world and of themselves that legitimate and motivate collective action" (McAdam, McCarthy, and Zald 1996:6). Constitutions are themselves frames in the sense just defined. Indeed, constitution-makers were called "framers" long before the emergence of social movement theory. In the 1990s, indigenous peoples' frames resonated with the general public because their yearning for inclusion and citizenship rights was shared by other dominated social groups. They resonated with elites who also saw the contemporary crisis of governability (defined as the capacity of the state to make and execute decisions) as rooted in centuries of ineffective state- and nation-building.

The exclusionary state and political regime that threatens the region's democratization and political stability has deep roots in the colonial period. The colonial powers established a rigid race-based class hierarchy and concentrated productive resources in the hands of a tiny elite. This structure facilitated three hundred years of colonial domination, and the two hundred years of centralized, oligarchic rule that followed. Latin American states and societies were constructed through the conquest, domination, and exploitation of indigenous peoples. "National identity" was constructed by dissolving the legal basis of nonnational identities (the withdrawal of legal recognition for indigenous territories and communities, forced assimilation into the "national" culture, language, and faith), and by subjecting indigenous populations to a regime of legal tutelage and a racist ideology that supported elite claims to "national" ethnic superiority. Because contemporary power relations are rooted in these historical processes, the status of indigenous peoples always has conjured larger questions concerning the organization and power of the state (González Casanova and Roitman Rosenmann 1996:11–14; Roldán 1996:5).

A decade after most Latin American countries began their transitions from authoritarian rule, most are searching for institutional reforms to extend the benefits of citizenship and the market to a larger proportion of their populations and, thereby, to enhance the legitimacy and efficiency of the state and democratic regime. Intellectuals and a growing sector of the political elite increasingly view comprehensive political reorganization as vital to finally ending the colonial power relations and social structures in which contemporary crises and the region's external dependency are rooted (González Casanova 1996:32). The indigenous project of reconstituting relations between indigenous peoples and nonindigenous society—and a state built by the latter to dominate and exploit the former—is an alternative strategy for achieving this goal. Contemporary indigenous peoples' organizations propose to reconstitute Latin American states upon truly democratic institutions based in the recognition of ethnic diversity and respect for the free will of individuals and pre-constituted groups to form a common political community. This project is framed in terms of international law with respect to the rights of peoples for self-determination. It explicitly rejects the excluding states and societies that dominate the region and the fragile, manipulable legality upon which the dominion of the strong over the weak historically has been based (González and Roitman 1996:11).

The Bolivian and Colombian cases represent a phenomenon that has received scant attention in the democratization literature: the transformation of an unconsolidated democratic regime into a distinctly different model of democracy via a radical constitutional reform guided by normative criteria. The decision to expand the definition of democracy to include normative considerations occurs at a time when political scientists are converging on a minimalist, procedural definition and resigning themselves to expect limited results from democracy in developing countries (see Karl 1990:2; Mainwaring 1992:297; O'Donnell 1994a; Schmitter and Karl 1991:76). The normative transformation is not limited to the regime. To fully address the problem of exclusion, constitution-makers also found it necessary to transform the state, particularly with respect to its territorial organization and legality. In the years since the Bolivian and Colombian reforms were passed, neighboring states have adopted a similar set of reforms to cope with similar crises. They share an emphasis on recognizing ethnic and cultural diversity; on strengthening the protection of rights, the judicial system, and the rule of law; and on opening more spaces for popular participation in government.

Democratization and Constitutional Transformation

Democratization is the movement toward democracy, whether *from* an authoritarian regime or *within* an already democratic one. In a democratizing society decision-making becomes more inclusive and transparent; the legitimacy of democratic institutions increases and becomes more widespread; the interests and desires of an increasing proportion of the population are channeled more effectively through political parties and civil society organizations; civil society is increasingly autonomous, pluralistic, and organized; and the dominant political culture becomes more tolerant and solidary. Most of the democratization literature has focused on the initial emergence of a democratic regime or the transition from an authoritarian to a democratic one (see Huntington 1991; Karl 1990; O'Donnell, Schmitter, and Whitehead 1986; and Przeworski 1991). In order to measure the progress of these transitions, scholars turned in the 1990s to the study of democratic consolidation, the period following a transition from authoritarian rule during which newly adopted democratic rules and practices become institutionalized or habituated and democratic values become internalized (see Diamond et al. 1997; Gunther, Diamandouros, and Puhle 1995; Higley and Gunther 1992; Mainwaring, O'Donnell, and Valenzuela 1992; Rustow 1970). Scholars of the Latin American and post-communist consolidations have focused mainly on the establishment of the procedural, formal aspects of democracy, institutional choice, the effectiveness of political elites, and the technical competence of fragile state institutions in the context of a "double transition" toward democracy and market-oriented economics (see Haggard and Kaufman 1992, 1995; Lijphart and Waisman 1996; Mainwaring 1992).

To better understand why states are having trouble consolidating democratic institutions, some political scientists shifted their focus to normative issues. Two problems have received special attention: (1) the problem of legitimating a system theoretically based on equality in the context of worsening economic conditions and the increasing concentration of political and economic power (Castañeda 1996; Chalmers et al. 1997; Jelin and Hershberg 1996b); and (2) the gap between formal democratic procedures and rights and the effective exercise of citizenship and political rights by all sectors of society. Within the second area of study, Carlos Santiago Nino and Guillermo O'Donnell focus on the weakness or absence of a "rule of law" in Latin American societies and the resulting normative impoverishment of democratic institutions.[2] According to Nino, democratic consolidation stalls when constitution-makers fail to emphasize the moral (as opposed to the procedural) value of democracy. The primary requirement for securing the moral value of democracy is preservation of the rule of law, which requires empowering judicial institutions to respond independently to injustices and to reverse the delegitimation of mechanisms of representation and control caused by the marginalization of large sectors of society from effective democratic participation (Nino 1996:163–64). O'Donnell (1994b, 1997b, 1998) also emphasizes the legal dimension of citizenship, arguing that in most Latin American countries the state is unable to establish legality throughout its territory and for all social sectors, either because the laws themselves discriminate against certain groups, or because they are applied in a discriminatory or discretionary manner, or because ordinary citizens lack access to government bureaucracies or judicial institutions. Most legal systems in the region fail to play an important role in democracies—that of establishing "networks of responsibilities and accountability" within the state and between state and society. Following democratization, these problems actually were aggravated by the weakening of the state and the strengthening of rural elites at the same time that the rule of law was urgently needed to hold government accountable, protect the exercise of rights, and generate legitimacy for democratic institutions. Under such conditions, society perceives correctly that the state serves private interests rather than the public good.

I contribute to Nino and O'Donnell's efforts to address the normative roots of stalled democratization by identifying a type of democratization that represents a commitment to a set of democratic values with ethical content—a view of government that more closely approximates the indigenous cosmovision, in which politics is embedded organically in a larger ethical and cultural universe than the Liberal, Western constitutional tradition of Latin America. Constitution-makers make this commitment to values in search of a new basis for the legitimation of the state. Past sources of legitimation—the ability to improve material welfare, to protect the weak from the powerful—are decreasingly available to Latin American states in the late twentieth century. Recourse to traditional sources of state legitimacy (such as deriving the authority of the constitution from the divine will of God, as the Colombian constitution did until 1991) clashes with the need to modernize and secularize the state. Our cases are distinguished by a search for legitimacy derived from the protection of rights, particularly human rights.

As Ian Chambers observes, the problem of the state's legitimacy before its population is a global problem at the end of the twentieth century, particularly in multiethnic states with a tradition of excluding communal minorities. National-level constitution-making contexts are embedded as never before in the context of international human rights conventions, particularly with respect to the treatment of minorities. The legitimacy of states is measured in international fora against their own constitutions as well as international norms, particularly with respect to how they treat their most vulnerable groups (Chambers 1997:426–27). Thus, the decision to provide unprecedented recognition and rights to indigenous peoples is part of a larger effort to restore state legitimacy at home and abroad. Legal theorists will find it ironic that the state, the quintessential maker of law, must borrow legality from two sources—international law and the customary law of "primitive" indigenous communities—that are considered by some jurists to be "disputable or borderline examples of law," because they lack formal lawmaking and sanctioning structures and other features common to municipal or state law and because their force is primarily moral (Hart 1994:79, 216). Constitution-makers sought to infuse the new constitutions with moral content that would compel citizens to voluntarily obey the law out of acceptance of its principles rather than out of fear of punishment.[3]

I call this new type of democratization "constitutional transformation." I borrow the term from Istvan Pogany, who defines it as a genuine transformation of the character and habitual mode of operation of a society's political and legal institutions. In other words, constitutional transformation can be said to have occurred only where the process of constitution making results in the general and habitual application of the new constitutional norms. (Pogany 1996a: 568)

It is too early to say whether the institutional and normative changes attempted via constitutional reforms in Bolivia and Colombia have become habituated. In the interest of not inventing yet another term to describe democratization, I will use Pogany's term tentatively while associating it here with a set of factors specific to my cases. In my model of constitutional transformation, the multiple crises described above are brought to a head by an event or series of events that convinces political elites that their long-term interest in political and economic stability can be secured only by a radical revision of state and regime. The inability of the political class to achieve consensus on the reforms through ordinary politics generates a movement for constitutional reform. Thus, constitutional transformations are distinguished by the perceived necessity for radical constitutional change.

A commitment to normative transformation requires that constitution-makers reject a Liberal or purely legal understanding of constitutions and embrace their capacity to "embody the political aspirations of a people and serve as a means of integrating a fragmented society into a political community" (Elster, Offe, Preuss, et al. 1998:82). Ignoring the ethical and political nature of the constitution would lead constitution-makers to commit what Nino called the "fallacy of partial valuation," wherein systems of government are judged by norms of efficiency and stability while the values on which these norms depend are disregarded. As Nino, an advisor to the Argentine and Bolivian governments on constitutional reform, observed:

> The central value of a political system is its moral legitimacy—that is, its capacity for producing decisions that are morally justified and binding on those who are subject to them. Assuming that the system whose value is at stake is a democratic one, that value cannot be specified without articulating a normative conception of democracy. (Nino 1996:162–63)

Constitution-makers' emphasis on the normative roots of multiple crises— and on the need to build a new political order by imbuing political institutions with democratic values capable of legitimating the state and regime—generated a rupture with both countries' Liberal constitutional tradition. The prior tradition promoted a culturally and ethnically homogeneous vision of national identity based on the myth of a mestizo nation. The new model explicitly recognizes the failure of the creole nation-building project and begins a new one based on the veneration of ethnic and cultural diversity (E. Restrepo 1997:297–98; Stavenhagen 1996:142–43). In the old tradition, the state was the sole source of political authority. The new constitutions recognize the existence of indigenous peoples prior to the creation of the state and create spaces for the exercise of traditional authority. The old democratic model was representative and universalistic, and it recognized only individual rights. Both new constitutions recognize and promote spaces for the participation of citizens in decision-making fora, albeit with problematic restrictions (which are discussed in later chapters). All three types of collective rights—rights to self-government, special representation rights, and polyethnic rights (Offe 1998:123)—are recognized, alongside individual rights; collective citizen-subjects join individual citizens; and a uniform state structure is made more flexible in order to incorporate diverse ethnic political structures. The constitutional codification of group rights and exceptional state structures implies that Latin American constitution-makers expected these to be permanent features of their political systems.

In addition to improving our understanding of democratization in post-transition Latin American societies, Bolivia and Colombia represent real-life experiments in applying the ideals asserted by political theorists with respect to participatory democracy. According to this literature, participatory democracy connotes a democratic regime in which citizens are encouraged and empowered to take part in spheres of decision-making, expression, and deliberation at all levels of government, on all public issues, in state-sponsored as well as autonomous civil-society fora, apart from voting in periodic elections. The expansion of democratic participation does not imply the elimination of political representation—a system in which citizens choose authorized agents to deliberate on public issues on their behalf, subject to the approval of these citizens in periodic elections or other agreed fora. In Bolivia and Colombia, improving representation was a key goal of the new democratic model, and representation and participation were viewed as complementary.

Bolivia and Colombia are not unique in this respect. Most Latin American states are struggling with crises of representation resulting from problems of uneven modernity, weak political integration, and extreme inequality (described below). The representation crisis is manifest mainly in the failure of the region's political party systems to incorporate nonelite groups into the twentieth century. In contrast to the mass parties that evolved in western Europe, Latin American politics is dominated by unrepresentative, oligarchic, personalistic parties with weak roots in society, which obstruct the access of popular groups and peripheral populations (in most countries, the majority of the population) to political decision-making spheres (Calderón, Piscitelli, and Reyna 1992:25; Mainwaring and Scully 1995). Bolivian and Colombian constitution-makers aimed to improve representation along two dimensions. Along the "political" dimension, they created mechanisms to improve the accountability of representatives to voters in order to increase public confidence in democratic institutions. Along the "sociological" dimension, they tried to facilitate the election or appointment of representatives with the social and cultural characteristics of historically excluded constituencies. Such efforts commonly are justified by the contention that only members of one's own group can effectively represent one's interests (Pitkin 1967:214). Although this justification is debatable, it is certain that members of excluded groups perceive themselves to be represented more effectively when their representatives share characteristics upon the basis of which they have been excluded. Moreover, as Nicolás Lynch argues with respect to Peru, in countries where certain groups historically have been excluded, sociological representation may be necessary to realize effective political representation, since rigid ethnic and social hierarchies create a distance between representatives and represented that permits the former to act as if they were above public scrutiny (Lynch 1997:124, 133).

The Bolivian and Colombian cases are significant also because, as James Tully argues, the constitutional claims of indigenous peoples are an instructive lens for looking at contemporary constitution-making, since they question the Liberal principles of the Western constitutional tradition, which are often taken for granted as universal values. Most indigenous cultures do not value the ethos of private accumulation or individual achievement that underpins capitalist society. The good of the community is almost universally considered more important than the good of the individual, and consensus and conformity often are valued above the free competition of alternative ideas. Rather than conceptualize constitution-making as the coming together of atomized individuals into a political community, as Liberals do, indigenous peoples consider themselves already to be constituted as sovereign collectivities (Tully 1995:55; Díaz Polanco 1991). The type of horizontal recognition they seek is similar to the type of recognition that states extend to one another in the international system, in that they seek acknowledgment of their authorities, political structures, and justice systems.

Indigenous peoples also present particularly difficult problems for constitution-makers because of their extreme economic and political marginalization; their communal landholding systems, which conflict with Liberal individual property rights regimes; and the urgent threat they face of losing their cultures and, hence, their right to cultural membership. Their demand for the incorporation of ethnic authorities and structures into the state (conceded in both of our cases) presents a challenge for democratic theory because it creates an ambiguous sphere between state and civil society with uncertain consequences for the generation of political authority by the state and the oppositional role of civil society. In Habermasian terms, it raises the problem of the state's colonization of the lifeworld, which should be left free from interference from the bureaucracy and rationality of the state. For these reasons contemporary political theorists—including Will Kymlicka, Yael Tamir, Charles Taylor, James Tully, and Iris Marion Young—single out the rights of indigenous peoples as the most difficult challenge to the Liberal notion of democratic rights and the Western tradition of constitution-making. The added difficulty of accommodating the collective demands of indigenous peoples makes the Bolivian and Colombian reforms particularly instructive as "most-difficult cases" for cultural recognition within a political community.

The Bolivian and Colombian constitutions should be viewed within the context of a global reassessment of the ideal of the nation-state in the late twentieth century (C. Young 1993). The construction of national identity and unity around diversity opens a new era of "post-nationalist" constitutionalism. Post-nationalist constitutions reject universalistic notions of citizenship based exclusively on uniformly applied individual rights and emphasize multiple forms of citizenship through a variety of institutions and autonomous domains of sovereignty that maximize the effective participation of diverse groups (Habermas 1996:465).

The Fourth Wave: Constitutionalism in the 1990s

The creation of a new constitution, or the radical reform of an existing one, is a particularly intensive phase of democratization, when both the regime and the state are transformed in a short period of time in significant and presumably enduring ways. Constitutional politics absorbs the energies of a greater number of people in society than does ordinary politics. The stakes are higher because major changes will be made in a short period of time and the decisions made will persist in time to govern future deliberation.

The study of constitutions is enjoying a revival in political science in response to the wave of democratic transitions of the 1980s and 1990s and the frenzy of constitutional revision it spawned. Jan-Erik Lane refers to the period of constitution-making that began after the fall of the Berlin Wall in 1989 as the "fourth wave," a reference not to Huntington's periodization of democratic transition, but to three prior periods of intensive constitution-making: 1789–1799, 1914–1926, and 1945–1965 (Lane 1996:74). Since 1990, seventeen African countries have either written new constitutions or have dramatically changed existing constitutions, as have most of the post-communist countries of Europe and the former Soviet Union. Latin American countries replacing or reforming constitutions in recent years include Argentina (1994), Bolivia (1994), Brazil (1988, 1994, 1997), Chile (1989, 1994, 1997), Colombia (1991), Costa Rica (1996, 1997), Dominican Republic (1996), Ecuador (1996, 1998), Mexico (1994, 1995), Nicaragua (1987, 1995), Panama (1994), Paraguay (1992), Peru (1993), and Uruguay (1997). Comprehensive reforms were underway in Guatemala, Guyana, and Venezuela as this book went to press.

Prior to this fourth wave, the study of static, formal-legal arrangements initiated by Montesquieu's *The Spirit of the Laws* was perceived widely as moribund, a pursuit that by World War II social scientists had abandoned in favor of more dynamic sociological and economic approaches to understanding political behavior (Faúndez 1993:354–56; Wiarda 1992:139). The fourth wave, however, has inspired a number of books and journal symposia (see Elster, Offe, Preuss, et al. 1998; Elster and Slagstad 1988; Greenberg et al. 1993; Howard 1993; Landa and Faúndez 1996; *Political Studies* 1996; Preuss 1995). This wave is more interesting to political scientists because it is more *political* than previous waves. One reason is that constitutions have been used as tools for the articulation and assertion of rights by groups marginalized under authoritarian regimes. Constitution-making is an arena for the politics of multiculturalism and for contesting the "boundaries of the sovereign nation-state" (Bellamy and Castiglione 1996: 414).[4] Scholars are beginning to recognize that:

> Constitutions are important social realities in the contemporary world, whether in force or in suspense. They are important as transcendental justifications of political order. When suspended or breached in practice, as is often the case, they delegitimize governments and constitute normative assets for the opposition. (Arjomand 1992:40)

Just as the post–World War I and decolonization-era constitutional waves were entangled in issues of ethnic and group rights, the fourth wave ran headlong into a contemporaneous current that brought cultural pluralism back to center stage. The political reascendance of culture is the result not only of unresolved interethnic conflict, but also of three contemporary phenomena: rapid and massive population movements and dramatic demographic changes that alter the relative sizes of neighboring ethnic communities and have increased the pluralism of immigrant-receiving countries; the increased space for ethnic and cultural identities created by the collapse of state socialism in the 1990s; and the rapid penetration of formerly isolated rural and traditional areas by market capitalism, which has engendered a defensive intensification of spiritual, religious, and cultural identities and given rise to demands for greater political participation and group rights (C. Young 1993:18; Pogany 1996b). For these reasons, and because of the emergence of contemporary indigenous peoples' movements in the 1970s and 1980s, the discourse on cultural pluralism has penetrated the discourse on constitutionalism in Latin America for the first time.

Because most emerging democracies are ethnically diverse, they are having difficulty adapting Liberal constitutional values and institutions. The Western constitutional tradition lacks a conception of culturally alienated peoples or groups, having been developed to facilitate contestation within a culturally and socially homogeneous political community (that is, landed, educated Englishmen). In the West, constitutions were founded on far broader bases of social consensus and less severe social and economic inequalities than in the developing world (Ghai 1993:191). Their legitimacy is based in the respect for the law that permeates Western culture. Democratizing multiethnic societies are having to add to Liberal protections of individual rights and civil liberties the protection of positive and group rights, together with innovative modes of political participation to secure the allegiance of culturally distinct groups. Their solutions are influenced by international trends in political theory that emphasize the "politics of difference" or the "politics of cultural recognition" (see I. Young 1990; Gutmann 1994) and challenge the basic assumptions of the "modern" constitutionalism of the seventeenth and eighteenth centuries. Whereas modern constitutionalism sought strength and unity in uniformity (Tully 1995:16), the fourth wave seeks strength and unity in diversity—a motto encoded in both the Bolivian and the Colombian reforms.

The fourth wave of constitution-making was immediately preceded by a less dramatic increase in constitution-making in the 1980s, which Norberto Bobbio dubs the "new contractarianism." This increase was not merely the result of the technical need to devise new mechanisms of decision-making and power distribution for states undergoing a regime change. It reflected the dominance of two trends in existing, modern, capitalist democracies: the psychic need of societies passing through multiple upheavals for a symbolic act of renewal, and the tendency of collective decisions to be made "via negotiations which finish in agreements, in other words where the social contract is no longer a rational hypothesis but a practical instrument of government in everyday use" (Bobbio 1987:117, 132). The psychic need for a new social contract reflects the impotence of the state in the most advanced societies to meet increasing challenges of governability and the continuous need to legitimate and relegitimate the governmental bodies responsible for collective decision-making. This impotence is derived from the persistence of multiple centers of autonomous power that struggle to protect particular interests and insert these protections as clauses in the social contract. In recent years, the illusion of a state receiving obedience and loyalty from society in exchange for protecting fundamental civil and property rights, and capable of entering into and enforcing this contract, has become ever more evident as organized particular interests increase their autonomy relative to the state (Bobbio 1987:136; Offe 1996).

Latin American states share the problems endemic to modernity identified by European scholars, as well as a set of problems that are particularly intense in the region. They are unique in that "pre-modern," "post-modern," and "anti-modern" economic and cultural systems persist alongside modern democratic institutions and the rapid advance of the market. "Latin American modernity is therefore plural, contradictory, and uneven. Even today there are cultural matrices that are not of modern origin (indigenous and African) and large groups of people who are to a greater or lesser extent marginalized from the dominant circuits of material and symbolic production" (Escobar 1992:67). Indigenous peoples comprise approximately 10 percent of the region's population, ranging from less than 1 percent of the total population in Brazil, to approximately 30–45 percent in Peru and Ecuador, to more than 60 percent in Guatemala and Bolivia. More than 80 percent live in five countries that are the territorial heirs of the Incan, Aztec, and Mayan civilizations: Bolivia, Ecuador, Guatemala, Mexico, and Peru (Deruyttere 1997:2). Twelve language groups have more than one million members, which together constitute 73 percent of the region's total indigenous population.

Latin America's fragmented, uneven modernity also is attributable to the weak territorial integration of most countries, where mountain ranges, extensive rainforest, and desert expanses create natural barriers to political integration. Natural barriers were reinforced by political decisions to organize colonial and republican societies for export production, which tended to create pockets of capitalism and modernity where such activities were concentrated, leaving areas of feudalism and subsistence-economics where they were not. As Carlos M. Vilas observes, "A weakly integrated territory favors the regional or local persistence of social and political institutions and practices that officially do not exist from the point of view of the central authorities," presenting severe challenges for the even and nondiscriminatory extension of the rule of law or citizenship rights and the development of uniformly understood democratic values (Vilas 1997:13–14). The legacy of this lack of territorial and social integration, which favored the representation of groups and interests located in the pockets of modernity developed under export-oriented capitalism, is the representation crisis described above.

The historical development of Latin America as a region colonized for the extraction of natural resources and the enrichment of a tiny colonizing elite led to extreme inequality in the distribution of land, wealth, and income throughout the region. Structural inequality was perpetuated by government policies serving the landed, wealthy elite. Severe inequalities fostered and perpetuated political exclusion by increasing incentives for elites to maintain exclusionary politics while providing unusual opportunities to do so (Remmer 1985–1986:72–74). Historical inequality was exacerbated in the 1980s when international lenders required that Latin American governments slash social programs and public employment to avert fiscal catastrophe and debt default. As a result, income inequality worsened and the proportion of the population in poverty increased such that, at the beginning of the 1990s, 46 percent of the population lived in poverty (Vilas 1997:21).

The fourth wave of constitutional reform represents a significant change for Latin America, a region notorious for its disrespect for the rule of law (O'Donnell 1998) and the production of some two hundred mostly unimplemented constitutions in the one and a half centuries since independence. Whereas European constitutions historically have celebrated successful democratic revolutions (Preuss 1995:2), Latin American constitutions were created to protect the interests and preserve the domination of the elite. They tend to be replaced when a new faction of the elite seizes power, amid great fanfare about the birth of a new era, while in fact reflecting substantial continuity (Elazar 1985:236–37; Needler 1967:124). Elite invocations of political democracy, Liberalism, and constitutionalism have been "as frequent as they were empty" (Borón 1993:341–44), leading to the widespread mistrust of public institutions and a philosophical dualism in which norms and practices are kept separate. During the Liberal reforms of the late nineteenth century, most Latin American countries removed language recognizing the corporate rights of indigenous populations such as collective property rights, which were considered to be barriers to progress and national integration. References to indigenous peoples would not reappear until the 1970s, when a few charters began to recognize language and cultural rights (see chapter 9).

Despite this inauspicious constitutional legacy, the current wave of constitution-making in the region exhibits some salutary characteristics. The constitutions that codified transitions from military to elected civilian rule share an emphasis on promoting peace and development, restraining military authority, and respecting social and citizenship rights (Landa 1996:16). The newest Latin American constitutions exhibit five trends: (1) a propensity to create European-style constitutional tribunals (introduced in all the East European post-communist constitutions); (2) the introduction of new rights, including all three generations of human rights; (3) an increasing acceptance of binding international law, particularly with respect to human rights; (4) the incorporation of procedural figures and institutions to protect certain fundamental constitutional rights (such as the ombudsman and the writ of injunction); and (5) a concern for the better functioning of the judiciary to address endemic governmental corruption. Converging with and in some cases contradicting these trends is a shift in economic policy that promotes the shrinking and privatization of the state and its functions and the restriction of social and economic rights to conform to the new neoliberal economic model (García Belaunde 1996a:30–33).

The Bolivian and Colombian reforms exemplify these trends while breaking ground in the areas of recognizing ethnic diversity and expanding political participation. In both cases the prior, homogeneous, exclusionary model of national identity was judged to lie at the root of the failure of democracy. Thus, political reform was mixed inextricably with the process of defining a national identity that embraced society's linguistic and cultural diversity. The explicit recognition of this sociological fact "constitutes a genuine ideological rupture with the vision of the nation—and of society —constructed and propagated by elites at the beginning of the 19th century" and, thus, an opportunity for reconciliation and the mutual creation of a more viable national project (Gros 1997:24–25). The exceptionality of these two cases was the basis of their selection when this project was begun in 1996. They comprised the "most-changed end" of the constitution-making spectrum, the end where the most significant advances have been made in the promotion of participatory democracy and the recognition of ethnic diversity and special ethnic rights.[5] Other governments had passed constitutional provisions recognizing indigenous peoples' rights—such as Nicaragua in 1987 and Brazil in 1988—and with significant participation from indigenous peoples' representatives. But in these cases, governments made little attempt to implement the new rights and many of them have been overturned, particularly in Brazil where rural elites have blocked recognition of land rights.

Once the project had begun, several other Latin American states undertook radical constitutional reforms with provisions protecting ethnic rights similar to those of Bolivia and Colombia. The 1998 Ecuadorean Constituent Assembly and constitutional reforms currently under discussion in Guatemala and Mexico—pursuant to accords on indigenous rights between governments and armed rebels—are particularly interesting in this respect. Indigenous peoples are poised to play a prominent role in constitutional reforms under way in mid-1999 in Guyana and Venezuela. In fact, with the exception of Uruguay, whose indigenous population was nil by the end of the twentieth century, all Latin American states revising constitutions in the 1990s have incorporated parts of what I suggest is an emerging regional model of "multicultural constitutionalism." Thus, the motivation of this work has shifted from explaining the uniqueness of the Bolivian and Colombian cases to exploring trends that may have wider regional and global implications.

Aside from this erstwhile exceptionality with respect to multiculturalism and participation, our two cases shared additional features that made them ripe for comparison. The passage of both reforms within a three-year time span held constant temporal trends that might affect the content or process of constitution-making. As Latin American countries, both Colombia and Bolivia share a legal tradition derived from Roman law and French constitutionalism, presidential political systems, the political and intellectual influence of the Catholic Church, and a political culture characterized by "hierarchy, authority, personalism, family and kinship ties, centralization, the need for organic national unity, elaborate networks of patron-client relations, patrimonialism, and a pervasive pattern of vertical corporate organization" (Wiarda and Kline 1990:113). Both are Andean countries and share dramatic geographical variation presenting problems of national integration and identity. Both reforms followed more than a decade of organizing by some of the region's most mature indigenous social movement organizations.

Bolivia and Colombia are very different countries, however. Colombia has a population of thirty-five million; Bolivia's population of seven million is equal to the population of Colombia's capital, Bogotá. Colombia is predominantly urban, literate, and Spanish-speaking; Bolivia is predominantly rural, literacy is a serious problem, and two-thirds of the population is bilingual or even multilingual. Colombia is a middle-income country relative to others in the region; Bolivia is the poorest in South America, with high levels of extreme poverty and income inequality. This is chiefly because Colombia is rich in a variety of natural resources and situated on both the Caribbean and Pacific coasts, whereas Bolivia is one of two land-locked countries in a region highly dependent on international trade. The two also differ with respect to their ethnic composition. Colombia's Indians amount to less than 3 percent of the country's population; Bolivia has an indigenous population estimated at over 60 percent. Colombia has the second-largest black population in South America (29 percent); Bolivia's black population consists of an estimated thirty thousand people who are culturally assimilated into the Aymara indigenous group.

This dramatic variation in ethnic composition is theoretically and practically significant. It indicates that the insertion of ethnic recognition and rights in contemporary constitutional debates—and the resulting normative and transformative implications—need not be limited to those countries with proportionally large indigenous populations. This is because the pre-Columbian civilizations from which contemporary indigenous peoples descend played an important role in the history and culture of the region and in the construction of political and social institutions. Where they do not today have numerical weight, they retain sufficient symbolic weight to insert themselves in national debates on the construction of national identity and the transformation of state-society relations. They frame their alternative political projects by invoking the historical roots of the modern state in a history of conquest, violence, and domination. The Colombian case demonstrates that even minuscule indigenous populations can mobilize their striking visual images to gain press attention and public interest, construct alliances with sympathetic elites, and link their grievances to the problems of exclusion and intolerance that characterize late twentieth-century Latin American states and societies. At the level of the philosophy and rhetoric behind the new constitutions—constitution-makers' search for a new basis to legitimate the state and for new values to govern and orient a new voluntary political association—the proportion of the indigenous population does not matter. The point is to extend the political project to and defend the fundamental rights of all members of the community. The Colombian case falsifies Claus Offe's hypothesis that the larger the ethnic group (the greater its size, visibility, and territorial concentration), the more successful it will be in its struggle for rights, since Colombia's is among the least numerous and most territorially dispersed indigenous populations in Latin America (Offe 1998:137).

Nevertheless, the types of rights claimed by indigenous movements in

Bolivia and Colombia have different chances of elite acceptance and political, territorial, and social implications, depending on the size of the indigenous population. Guaranteed proportional representation for Indians in the Colombian Senate was achieved relatively easily because it has no significant impact on the operations of the institution, the dynamics of the political party system, or the prevailing racial hierarchy. In Bolivia and Guatemala, elites consider such an idea to be extreme and palpably undemocratic, given the majority status of the indigenous population, although some Indian activists in both countries have proposed that congressional representation be based proportionally on ethnicity (Sieder 1999:116n8). The proposition that the state's territorial-administrative organization should be adjusted to allow for anomalous units based on ethnicity has a different meaning in countries such as Bolivia or Guatemala, where indigenous peoples constitute a majority and inhabit a majority of the territory, than it does in countries such as Colombia or the United States, where the indigenous population is relatively small and their territories—while extensive—are relatively isolated and more easily incorporated within a predominantly uniform scheme (Sieder 1997:4). Creating an office within the state to address the grievances of and coordinate state policy toward indigenous peoples seems appropriate for countries where they are a numerical minority and otherwise would have little chance of influencing state policy. Where the population is a majority, an office for indigenous peoples seems inappropriate—or at best temporary—since, in an ethnic democracy, we would expect to see indigenous peoples occupying a majority of elected and appointed government positions. For this reason, in fact, Mayan Indians are protesting the Guatemalan government's proposal to create an indigenous secretariat or ministry (Plant 1998). When we are dealing with a numerical majority, "special" programs or projects are inappropriate. Directly addressing the exclusion of a marginalized majority requires us to think in terms of a comprehensive reform of the state and political regime (Vadillo 1997b:333).

A Three-Phase Model of Constitutional Transformation

The process of constitutional reform has a decisive impact on the resulting text by providing varying opportunities for different actors to affect the outcome (Franco and Valderrama 1990:35; Martínez-Lara 1996:1). A constitution that is drafted by a small group of ideologically homogeneous actors with common interests will be more coherent than a charter that results from negotiation among many actors with diverse interests. A constituent assembly (the most common method in Latin America)[6] will lead to a more thorough reform with a more indeterminate outcome. A process controlled by the national Congress will tend to produce a more piecemeal, partial, and predictable reform. For this reason, decisions about the mode of reform are not made casually (McWhinney 1981:27). The process chosen also will affect the degree to which political actors and the general public consider the result to be legitimate. This is crucial when regime (re)legitimation is a primary goal of constitutional reform.

The legitimacy of the reform process may be even more important than the resulting text in cases where a cathartic political exercise is more critical than institutional reform, as Javier Martínez-Lara argues with respect to Brazil's 1987–1988 constituent assembly (1996:8, 38). The participatory nature of the process was crucial in the Colombian context because several armed guerrilla groups had proposed a participatory, pluralistic constituent assembly as a condition of their demobilization and reintegration into civil life. Diverse political actors concurred that legitimate institutions and norms would result only from a participatory process. A participatory process also may have a pedagogical effect. In a country where the people rarely have been invited to participate in deliberations on issues of public concern, the generation of an open and participatory process of deliberation fosters a transition from a passive and subservient to an active and participatory political culture.

By contrast, in the Bolivian case, in light of a long history of puppet constituent assemblies convoked to legitimate de facto executives, as well as a desire to keep disruptive actors from derailing the process, a majority of political elites believed that greater legitimacy would accrue to the constitution if it was reformed according to the legally prescribed method, even though these rigid requirements had been imposed by a military regime to perpetuate its rule. This reasoning explains the choice of most European post-communist governments to reform communist-era constitutions according to the rules contained therein rather than to succumb to the temptation of a constituent assembly, which might have provided a public celebration of the democratic revolution. Following legal procedures represented a reaction to the lawlessness and hypocrisy of the communist regimes (Preuss 1995:8–9).

Focusing on the constitutional reform process has methodological advantages. It enables us to isolate actors and variables that were important at different phases of the reform and to suggest hypotheses about the political conditions necessary for constitutional transformation. Toward that end, I divide the process into three more-or-less discrete phases, with the understanding that these will sometimes overlap (see figure 1).

The first phase, the constitutional conjuncture, encompasses the set of political conditions that led to the decision to transform the democratic regime via constitutional reform. The political moment that marks the beginning of this phase is the convergence of the crises of representation, participation, and legitimacy, which generates calls for state and regime reform. This phase may be compared to Dankwart Rustow's "preparatory phase" of democratic transitions, in which inconclusive and protracted struggles lay the groundwork for a regime transition (1970). Rustow's only background condition for this transition is national unity, whereas in my model national unity is a *goal* of constitutional transformation and its *absence* a key root of the crises generating calls for reform. My constitutional conjuncture also is comparable to Keith G. Banting and Richard Simeon's

FIGURE 1
Phases of Democratization

Van Cott	Rustow	Banting and Simeon
Phases of Constitutional Transformation	Phases of Democratic Transition	Phases of Constitution-Making
Initial Condition:	*Initial Condition:*	*Initial Condition:*
Unconsolidated democracy	*National unity*	*Existing state*
	Preparatory phase	Mobilization of interests
Constitutional conjuncture	Decision phase	Decision-making stage
	Habituation phase	Ratification stage
Creative phase		Legitimation stage
Implementation phase		

first phase of constitution-making, in which interests begin to mobilize and countermobilize and actors begin to frame constitutional proposals in more precise terms (Banting and Simeon 1985a:18–19). In my model this idea-generating and proposal-defining activity continues into the creative phase.

My second analytically distinct phase, the creative phase, encompasses formal constitution-making procedures and the formal and informal negotiations and pacts that facilitate agreement on specific issues. Banting and Simeon call this the "decision-making stage," which they distinguish from a separate, subsequent "ratification stage." As they observe, most constitutional reform attempts do not reach this stage because reform proponents usually are unable to force constitutional reform onto the political agenda with sufficient force to elicit a response from the political system. Attempts may become stalled for years if elites are unable to agree on a reform project that is worth the sacrifice of vested interests (Banting and Simeon 1985a:19). My creative phase differs from the "decision phase" of Rustow's model, and from the "transition phase" described by Guillermo O'Donnell, Philippe Schmitter, and Laurence Whitehead (1986), because the stakes are different. In my model actors choose among *democratic* institutions and structures; the choice of authoritarian institutions or structures is precluded. Military figures are not major actors, so there is no need to appease "hard-liners" or the military to avoid a reversion to authoritarian rule. Thus, my creative phase lacks the heightened sense of panic, confusion, and uncertainty that characterizes transitions from authoritarian to democratic rule. The overriding consideration of most actors is the protection or enhancement of their personal chances (or those of their party or movement) of attaining access to government power and resources through electoral or other *democratic* means (Dugas 1997:75).

Edward McWhinney identifies five possible procedures for constitutional reform: the constituent assembly, parliamentary enactment, an expert commission, executive diplomacy (mostly used in federal systems), and the popular initiative via petition and referendum. Because it confers the greatest amount of political legitimacy on the resulting text, McWhinney proposes that the ideal procedure is a constituent assembly that maximizes opportunities for public participation in and scrutiny of the reform process (McWhinney 1981:27–33). This option is most viable when a public consensus on the need for and direction of constitutional change exists. This option was chosen in Colombia, where a broad public consensus on the need for constitutional reform emerged in 1990. In Colombia the creative phase is delimited neatly by the election of the National Constituent Assembly on December 9, 1990, and the promulgation of the new charter on July 5, 1991. In Bolivia, where the public mood had not aligned as decidedly with the preponderance of elite opinion on either the need for or the direction of constitutional reform, constitution-makers rejected this option (McWhinney 1981:134–35). The Bolivian reforms combined a technical commission under the direction of political leaders with a great deal of elite pact-making, managed by the Bolivian president, prior to the formal congressional enactment of the reforms. Because of the staged nature of the reforms, the delimitation of the creative phase in Bolivia is messier. It begins with the negotiation of a Law on the Necessity for Constitutional Reform toward the end of the Paz Zamora regime in 1993 and ends with the legislative approval of the Law of Administrative Decentralization during the Sánchez de Lozada administration in 1995.

My third phase, the implementation phase, encompasses the executive, legislative, administrative, and judicial actions that transform the constitutional text into policies, statutory laws, and institutions. During the implementation phase, new democratic institutions and norms are fragile and amorphous and actors and institutions can play a decisive role in their establishment and consolidation—or in their neutralization and distortion. Although civil society and international actors may influence this process significantly, our attention is focused mainly on the state during this phase. If the reforms themselves originated elsewhere in society, it is always the state that coordinates the implementation of a constitutional reform. The constitution itself operates as an independent variable by helping to generate its own legitimacy and by providing tools for the mobilization of political and social interests. At the same time, the charter formally represents the principal dependent variable of the implementation phase, the emerging democratic model. This period precedes Rustow's "habituation phase," in which political actors and common citizens begin to practice the new norms and experience new institutions, although there is likely to be some overlap with respect to the implementation of specific provisions of the constitutional reforms; that is, while citizens are becoming habituated to some new institutions, other institutions are only beginning to be established.

Political Elites and Social Movements

In both the cases examined here, two actors—one emanating from the highest stratum of elite power (the president) and another from the sphere of subaltern social movements (indigenous peoples' organizations)—were crucial to moving the constitution-making process forward and to constructing frames of meaning that injected the normative dimension into the new democratic model. As in democratic transitions, in cases of constitutional transformation, elites are mainly responsible for the negotiation of pacts that make the transition or transformation possible. Social movements play the crucial role of challenging "dominant discourses on politics and development," mediating between political parties and communities, placing new issues, ideas, and institutional alternatives on the democratization agenda, and "appropriat[ing] and reconfigur[ing] the state's democratic discourses on rights, citizenship, and 'nation'" (Alvarez and Escobar 1992:327). Latin American social movements in the post-transition era are demanding that civilian constitutional regimes undergo a second or third political transition to achieve a superior quality of democracy (Hochstetler 1997:200–201). They are focused in particular on strengthening the regime of rights and destroying the monopoly of the region's political party systems on channels of representation to the state (Calderón, Piscitelli, and Reyna 1992:29).

I synthesize discourse- and identity-based approaches with resource mobilization theory in order to portray the multidimensional nature of social movement activity (Cohen 1985; Foweraker 1995:3). Indigenous movements are strategic political actors with a "strongly institutionalist" orientation, that is, a desire to transform political institutions and their relationship to them (Foweraker 1995:64). But they are equally involved in the recuperation, affirmation, construction, and reconstruction of collective identities. The fact that identities are not primordial—that they are constructed through internal and external contestation, often for strategic purposes—does not diminish their "reality" or internal resonance for members of the group. In the 1980s and 1990s, indigenous organizations throughout Latin America presented to allies and adversaries an objectified indigenous identity based on a relatively consistent set of cultural traits that were chosen for their genuine resonance within the indigenous population as well as their suitability for attracting support from external allies (Gros n.d.:19). These include traits such as "non-materialist and spiritual relation to the land, consensual decision making and communitarianism," and aversion to disproportionate accumulation within communities (Assies 1998:4; see also Roldán 1996:6). Once rights have been codified, indigenous organizations must continuously objectify and "perform" their identities (Gros n.d.; Jackson 1999) in order to prove their "Indianness" to the state and to nongovernmental organizations (NGOs) that expect the beneficiaries of indigenous policies to fit a particular definition. In some cases a complex culture must be "simplified and folklorized to make it easier for outsiders to understand" (Jackson 1995:15). As organizations construct language-group-level identities, they must simultaneously construct national and transnational, pan-Indian identities, all of which are mobilized in different political spheres. The resulting identities and cultures are neither spurious nor contrived, since all cultures are to some extent invented, particularly in contexts where ethnicity is highly politicized. They seem less "authentic" to us only because their mutation is more recent. As Jean E. Jackson observes, the search for authenticity and accuracy in culture is misguided (1995).

A systematic comparison of the actions of key actors during the three phases of reform in both countries enabled me to generate a set of hypotheses about political conditions that contribute to constitutional transformation (see figure 2). These are not meant to be mechanically predictive. Other conditions may be more important in other cases.

The Constitutional Conjuncture

During the constitutional conjuncture, if the following conditions are present, then the constitutional reform will advance to the creative phase. First, multiple conjunctural crises converge, motivating political elites to search for solutions. A catalytic event, or series of events, generates momentary consensus among a preponderant sector of political elites that urgent reforms cannot be made through ordinary politics. In terms of the social movement literature, this catalyst alters the "political opportunity structure." It momentarily opens the political system to outsiders by lowering the costs of

FIGURE 2
Conditions Contributing to Constitutional Transformation

Constitutional Conjuncture	Conjunctural crises converge
	Catalytic event occurs
	Presidential leadership with convincing electoral victory and programmatic mandate
	Strong regional or national ethnic organizations mobilize
	Ethnic and elite discourses on causes of crisis are linked
Creative Phase	Presidential leadership continues
	Phase does not exceed first two years of new president's term
	Neoliberal economic model not threatened
	Procedural and substantive legitimacy acquired
	Ethnic rights linked to elite goals
	Relevant international conventions signed
Implementation Phase	Constitution perceived as legitimate
	Institutional guardian of constitution emerges
	Civil society organizations mobilize to defend and demand implementation of new rights
	Ethnic groups mobilize around new rights

collective action or by raising the costs of inaction; by shattering elite unity; and by injecting instability into political alignments, making alternative alignments possible and influential elite allies available to challenging groups (Tarrow 1998:77–80; McAdam 1996:27).

The constitutional conjunctures in both Bolivia and Colombia were characterized by a severe crisis of representation. The representation function had been monopolized by party-based systems of clientelism that were exceedingly corrupt, even by Latin American standards. The representation crisis was compounded by a participation crisis resulting from the lack of spaces for common citizens to participate in decision-making or to influence politics through their actions. These regime crises contributed to and were exacerbated by a crisis of the state, a crisis of governability. The state was unable to make and execute decisions because it lacked both the legitimacy and the authority to secure compliance from citizens and rival power enclaves, as well as the efficiency and rationality to increase economic growth and redistribute it equitably (Offe 1996:4, 9; Santana Rodríguez 1996:52–53). The result was extreme political instability, manifested in Colombia as a prolonged, multisided war between armed groups and the state. In Bolivia, political instability was manifested in different ways: as a series of fragile, opportunistic political alliances within the equilibrated six-party system; and in direct, often violent, confrontations between the state and highly mobilized social forces unrepresented by the party system. The need to replace authoritarian patterns of conflict management that had failed to provide durable political stability motivated a search for a new model of democracy in both countries. This search was expressed repeatedly as a search for a better fit between state and society.

In their study of constitutional reform in industrialized countries, Banting and Simeon found that the existence of a general crisis may be necessary to provide a sufficient mood of urgency to galvanize a decision to initiate constitutional reform. Elites must believe that the costs of failing to reform will be higher than maintaining the status quo, even if their particular interests are somewhat disadvantaged by the reform. Consensus among elites that reform is urgently necessary must be stronger than disputes among elites over specific constitutional provisions (Banting and Simeon 1985a:20). The Bolivian and Colombian cases confirm this finding. In both cases political elites perceived restoring legitimacy and governability to the political system to be crucial to the future success of any individual government or political party.

The next necessary condition for the advancement of the constitutional reform is for a presidential candidate to generate and lead a pro-reform coalition that places radical constitutional reform on the political agenda. I stipulate that this must be a presidential candidate because in systems barring reelection, such as our cases, only at the beginning of a term does a president have sufficient political capital to lead a comprehensive reform. Where reelection is allowed, this stipulation would no longer hold. In our two cases, both presidents had campaigned on the issue of radical institutional reform, enabling them to credibly claim a popular mandate for their vision of constitutional reform. Both won by substantial margins—Gaviria with more than twice the votes of his closest competitor; Sánchez de Lozada, with the widest victory margin since the military annulled the 1980 elections—providing an electoral mandate as well. These auspicious conditions appear to be converging again in Venezuela. As this book went to press, Venezuelan president Hugo Chávez was awaiting the start of a constituent assembly, the convocation of which had been his principal campaign issue. Chávez also has an electoral mandate, having trounced his opponents in the 1998 election by the largest victory margin in forty years of democracy. According to the Caracas daily *El Universal:* "The election of Hugo Chávez alone seems to have consolidated the collective conviction that a Constituent Assembly in Venezuela is the only road to renovate institutions, give 'legitimacy' to public powers, and conform a new political pact with new protagonists."[7] Chavez is poised to dominate the reform process: assembly candidates supporting him won 121 of the 128 seats in the July 1999 elections.

Finally, ethnic organizations capable of articulating the constitutional claims of their constituents must already exist at the regional or national level. Ethnic leaders and their advocates must link their grievances to the discourse of political elites on constitutional reform. In Bolivia and Colombia, contemporary indigenous political organizations began to form in the 1970s. During the fifteen years preceding the reforms, they educated society about the injustices they had suffered and continue to experience. They called repeatedly for recognition of indigenous authorities, languages, territorial rights, customary law, and political structures. Mobilization by indigenous organizations around the problem of exclusion during the constitutional conjuncture fostered a special emphasis on tolerance of minorities and respect for minority rights during the creative phase, when indigenous and nonindigenous actors presented the marginalization of Indians as a visible symbol of the exclusion of nontraditional political groups. At the symbolic level, the indigenous movements linked the constitutional reform process to a historical search for national unity and identity, which had failed because elites had tried to impose an artificial, homogeneous identity. They suggested that the solution to the crises of state and regime lay in the creation of a more viable national project, one that recognized the "pluricultural and multiethnic" reality of society. They demanded that this reality be reflected in the structure of the state.

In Colombia, indigenous leaders themselves inserted their demands into the national debate on constitutional reform through their participation in the National Constituent Assembly. In Bolivia, where the dialogue on constitutional reform was less participatory, indigenous organizations and the intellectuals associated with them influenced the thinking of political party leaders through their participation in a series of intensive dialogues on the reform of the state sponsored by partisan, academic, and not-for-profit organizations in the early 1990s. They also articulated their ideas in widely circulated legislative proposals. As the quincentenary of the conquest approached in 1992, Bolivia's two regional indigenous confederations framed alternative constitutional projects purporting to construct a multiethnic and pluricultural state. This rhetoric was adopted by several nonindigenous political parties during the 1993 presidential campaign. By the time the reform process had begun, political elites were professing ideas about ethnic diversity that had seemed extremist only five years earlier.

The Creative Phase

During the creative phase, if these conditions are present, then the constitutional reform will be completed. First, the president must continue to provide effective, coherent, and consistent leadership. As Scott Mainwaring observes, leadership (presidential or otherwise) usually is a residual category in analyses of democratization because it is "difficult to formulate non-tautological rigorous arguments" about its effects (Mainwaring 1992:331). To avoid this problem, I define presidential leadership as the effective performance of the following functions: putting the topic of constitutional reform at the center of the political agenda; offering reform alternatives in order to generate public debate; building elite consensus on the necessity, scope, and procedure of reform; moving substantive and procedural consensus toward final agreement; and generating public support for the constitutional reform process and its results. The president is best able to exercise this leadership if the creative phase does not exceed the first two years of the president's term, when his or her political influence, public support, and ability to devote sustained attention to the reform is greatest. Banting and Simeon observe that the maintenance of the pro-reform coalition during the creative phase is far from a foregone conclusion. Most constitutional reform attempts fail to reach the decision-making stage or become mired in protracted disagreement because elites cannot reach consensus on the need for or direction of reform. The Belgian debate on regional authorities and the recent Canadian constitutional reform attempt are good examples (Banting and Simeon 1985a:19–20). The longer the creative phase is delayed, the more likely it is that temporarily weakened vested interests will recuperate their strength and co-opt or derail the reform process, or that the crises that galvanized the pro-reform coalition will lose their urgency. As Richard Gunther cautions, based on the experience of the 1977–1978 Spanish Constitution, the constituent process must not be allowed to linger too long, since, once agreements are made public, vested and particular interests will have time to mobilize against them and representatives will have to worry about maintaining the support of their constituencies, providing an incentive to adhere to rigid positions. In addition, granting rights to one group may create a demonstration effect, causing other groups to mobilize for similar rights, as occurred in Spain with respect to Andalusia's demands for the same autonomous rights granted to Euskadi (Gunther 1985:65–66). Thus, the president can play a decisive role by facilitating elite pacts and quickly moving the creative phase to a conclusion before the risks of reform appear to outweigh the costs of maintaining the status quo.

Both Colombian President César Gaviria and Bolivian President Gonzalo Sánchez de Lozada were intimately involved in negotiations among political elites on the process and scope of constitutional reform, even prior to taking office. Once inaugurated, both immediately prioritized constitutional reform, investing a significant portion of their personal prestige and energy in the process. Both presidents wielded the exaggerated powers of the Latin American presidency vis-à-vis the legislature and judiciary in an effort to leave an indelible mark on the substance of the reforms, to sustain the pro-reform coalition, and to deflect efforts by vested interests to derail reform. Gaviria's most important leadership activity was to build consensus among feuding groups within the constituent assembly. In Bolivia, the role of the president in defining the reform agenda and in sustaining the pro-reform coalition was more important: a consensus on the scope and direction of reform did not exist, the correlation of political forces in favor of democratic transformation was neither as solid nor as broad as in Colombia, and no coherent grassroots movement for radical structural reform had emerged comparable to Colombia's student movement. Rather than fostering consensus through lengthy private and public deliberations, Sánchez de Lozada used secrecy, patronage, and the prerogatives of his office to exclude, silence, and neutralize the entrenched opposition. One important reason that both presidents were able to prevent powerful private sector elites from mobilizing against the democratic reform was that neither reform program threatened the neoliberal economic model. In fact, this model was strengthened in both cases.

During this phase, the reforms themselves must obtain substantive and procedural legitimacy. Substantive legitimacy means that the reforms agreed upon respond to popular and elite aspirations. Procedural legitimacy may be derived either from the strict legality of the reform process or from the extent to which all sectors of society and political interests perceive their interests to have been represented in the constitutional deliberations. The unprecedented openness and transparency of the Colombian creative phase generated considerable procedural legitimacy for the product of that reform, together with the substantive legitimacy conveyed by the extent to which the 1991 Constitution fulfilled the aspirations of Colombians for greater participation and the protection of rights. In Bolivia, the reform obtained procedural legitimacy by following the legally prescribed route. Although the exclusion of popular sectors and the political opposition from the process initially generated considerable skepticism and even outright hostility toward the reform, this was mitigated by the substantive legitimacy the reform generated by embodying long-standing popular demands and addressing elite concerns.

Finally, ethnic organizations and their advocates must effectively link their constitutional claims to those of political elites. Arguing particular interests in terms of universal appeals is a strategy common to constitutional debates. This strategy is particularly important in Latin America since ethnic minorities in that region cannot wield the threat of competing loyalties to a neighboring state, which was a potent threat during post-communist European constitutional debates (Elster, Offe, Preuss, et al. 1998:77, 88). In Colombia and Bolivia the linkage of indigenous and elite goals operated in both directions. Elites used the demand of indigenous organizations and communities for greater political and administrative autonomy to buttress their argument for radical municipal decentralization. Indigenous organizations' call for recognition of their traditional authorities, governing structures, and customary law furthered the goal of the Gaviria and Sánchez de Lozada administrations to extend the territorial presence of civil authority and the rule of law. In Colombia, indigenous constituents Lorenzo Muelas and Francisco Rojas Birry successfully argued that the inclusion of Indians —widely considered to be the most marginalized group in Colombian society—would ensure the inclusion of other marginalized groups. Thus, in neither case can we explain the codification of unprecedented indigenous rights provisions solely as the result of pressure from indigenous organizations. In both cases political elites were convinced that adopting the multiculturalist reforms would improve the legitimacy and governability of the state while lifting the psychic burden on state and society of a homogeneous national identity with no basis in reality. They also sought to improve the image of their states abroad—stained in the 1990s by superlative levels of political corruption, drug trafficking, extreme poverty, and (in the case of Colombia) violence. By joining the wave of industrial democracies that had embraced multiculturalism as state policy, political elites cast themselves as modernizing reformers and champions of human rights.

One of the reasons that indigenous organizations were relatively more successful than other civil society organizations in achieving special constitutional rights is the greater strength of indigenous identity as a mobilizing tool. This strength is based on the historical tie to territory of indigenous identity in Latin America and the enormous historical legitimacy of indigenous peoples' claims, which are backed up by documentation, archeological artifacts, and living cultural and social systems (Archila 1995:280). Strong identity enabled indigenous organizations to maintain their struggle in the face of intimidation and violence and, at times, without much support from other sectors. Indigenous communities' fervent desire for autonomy makes the development of clientelist and corporatist relations more difficult for self-interested indigenous leaders to reconcile with movement goals (M. Medina 1996:29). In addition, in both cases they had the support of a relevant international convention to frame and buttress their arguments. In 1989, the International Labour Organization revised its 1957 convention on the rights of indigenous peoples to remove assimilationist and paternalistic language that indigenous peoples found offensive. The revised convention embodies many of the aspirations of Latin American indigenous peoples with respect to protecting their autonomy from intrusions by the state and private actors and requiring that states consult with indigenous organizations and communities on policy issues affecting them. As is more fully discussed in chapter 9, ILO Convention 169 (1989) provided both a model of state-indigenous relations and, once ratified, a tool for indigenous organizations to use to press for constitutional reforms. Colombian President Gaviria signed ILO Convention 169 on March 4, 1991, during the National Constituent Assembly. Bolivian President Paz Zamora did the same on July 11, 1991, two years prior to the commencement of the creative phase. What had seemed to me to be an interesting transnational twist to the two cases appeared to be a strong regional trend after ILO Convention 169 came to play an influential role in the subsequent Ecuadorian and Guatemalan reforms.[8]

The Implementation Phase

Once the implementation phase was under way, the sense of urgency that had characterized the first two phases dissipated, and issues that had been put on the back burner began to claim presidential attention. Meanwhile, policy and administrative choices that disappointed some supporters brought the presidential honeymoon to an end. Once this occurs, an actor or institution must emerge within the government to assume the role of guardian of the constitutional reform and to defend it from counterreform efforts.

Realizing that post–constituent assembly elections might return traditional politicians to a legislature that acquired new powers under the 1991 constitution, President Gaviria prioritized the early implementation of autonomous democratic institutions designed by constitution-makers to guarantee the constitutional contract from within the government. The most important of these were the Constitutional Court, the People's Defender (ombudsman), and the Fiscalía General, an independent prosecutorial agency atop the judicial branch.[9] When the legislature and executive were unwilling or unable to pass legislation implementing fundamental constitutional rights, Colombia's Constitutional Court developed judicial standards to facilitate their immediate exercise. In addition, the Constitutional Court and the Fiscalía General generated legitimacy for the new charter by defending the rights of the powerless against the powerful, eroding, if only slightly, the prevailing regime of arbitrariness.

The importance of constitutional courts to democratic transitions has been demonstrated in post-communist Europe, where they are held in high public esteem because they tend to rule in favor of citizens' rights against the abuses of government (Schwartz 1993:167). "The record so far—and it is still very early—indicates that these courts will do whatever they can toward maintaining a free constitutional democracy and rule of law. And this could be a very great contribution indeed" (1993:195). In Hungary, for example, the constitutional court has "proved strong enough to issue judgments counter to parliamentarian majorities even on extremely divisive issues, and thus preserved the supremacy of the constitution over the vacillations and power plays of the everyday political business" (Elster, Offe, Preuss, et al. 1998:283). Independent constitutional jurisdiction is particularly important in fragmented political systems, where the rights of social groups and institutions tend to conflict (1998:102–05), and in post-communist countries where the executive can dominate a quiescent legislature (Pogany 1996a)—an observation that travels well to Latin America's exaggerated presidential systems. With respect to eastern and central Europe, Pogany concludes:

> The potential importance of the region's Constitutional Courts also derives from the numerous interpretative problems thrown up by the new or revised constitutions, and by the need to vet existing laws and administrative regulations to ensure their conformity with the new Constitutional norms. Constitutional Courts are thus of critical importance in securing a transition to genuinely democratic, constitutional rule. (Pogany 1996a:581)

On the other hand, politically compromised courts in Slovakia and Romania make consolidating democratic institutions more difficult. This is the case in Bolivia, where judicial appointments still are determined by political party affiliation. Sánchez de Lozada postponed implementation of Bolivia's judicial reform (for reasons discussed in chapter 7). Lacking independent judicial institutions to act as institutional guardians of the constitutional reform, the Bolivian president depended on a coalition of actors mostly external to the state to deflect attacks from counterreformers. This coalition consisted mainly of international donors, the Catholic Church, civil society organizations, and the armed forces. The pressure of these actors was helpful at critical moments, but their efforts were neither as dramatic nor as legitimating as the actions of the Constitutional Court and the Fiscalía General in Colombia.

With or without an internal institutional guardian, effective civil society pressure is necessary during the implementation phase. It is more likely to emerge and be sustained if the reforms enjoy broad public legitimacy and promise tangible benefits. Ethnic organizations must mobilize to defend their new rights and insert themselves in the implementation process to ensure that the unique multicultural character of the reform is developed so that it may lend credibility to the constitutional project's promise of inclusion and participation. The active participation of indigenous leaders in politics following both reforms helped to convey the impression, if not the reality, that a new democratic era had dawned. Moreover, as Christian Gros argues, the existence of mobilized indigenous peoples' organizations provides Latin American states with an interlocutor to negotiate the implementation of the principles of decentralization and democratic participation (Gros 1997:38).

Organization of the Book

The three phases of constitutional reform in Colombia are discussed, sequentially, in chapters 2 through 4. Three chapters on the Bolivian reforms follow. The two chapters on the creative phase—chapters 3 and 6—conclude with a discussion of the reforms in light of theoretical debates on ideal frameworks for promoting participatory democracy and recognizing diversity. In chapter 8, I compare the measurable results of the reforms thus far and assess the prospects for constitutional transformation in each case. In a concluding chapter, I consider subsequent constitutional reforms that also emphasized the recognition of cultural and ethnic diversity and the protection of rights and suggest that a regional model of "multicultural constitutionalism" is emerging.

Part I

In a country without history and without respect for it, dominated by a mentality of miracles and lotteries, institutionalism,
under the form of constitutional reformism, seems at times to
be a magic expedient for the immediate solution of all of the defects in the political and social structure, like a substitute for revolution. Only the lack of collective memory makes it possible
that we forget how many times this semantic constitutionalism
has served to sweep away the exigencies for change of a civil society too fragmented and disorganized to be able to express co-
herently and continuously its pressures and demands.

—Iván Orozco Abad

Political life proceeds through a series of conflicts which are
never definitely resolved, and whose temporary resolution
comes about through provisional agreements, truces, and those
more durable peace treaties called constitutions.

—Norberto Bobbio

2   From Chaos to Catharsis

The Struggle for Constitutional Change

THE 1991 Colombian Constitution replaced the 1886 charter, which was imposed by Conservative President Rafael Nuñez following the military defeat of the Liberal Party. As had become the pattern, the 1886 Constitution favored the interests of the party that had been victorious in battle and it marginalized the losers (Angarita 1994:23–40). The Conservative and Liberal Parties, formed in the 1840s, have dominated Colombian politics since that time, creating subcultures so mutually antagonistic and deeply rooted in society that they have been compared to ethnic or religious segments. Prolonged periods of interparty violence engendered sufficient hatred and resentment to solidify loyalties based on inherited party identification (Hartlyn 1988:25–27, 45). In 1910, a country tired of civil war held its first truly bipartisan, indirectly elected constituent assembly, which trimmed back the authoritarian excesses of the 1886 text and codified rights for political minorities. But these rights were not respected for long, and the bloody legacy of the Thousand Days War (1899–1902) was surpassed in the 1940s and 1950s by a decade of interparty warfare known as La Violencia (the violence). The assassination of Liberal leader Jorge Eliécer Gaitán on April 9, 1948, during a period of popular protest and rioting in the capital of Bogotá, lit the fuse that ignited La Violencia. An estimated 150,000 to 200,000 people died in the carnage that convulsed the next decade.

One legacy of La Violencia was the emergence of Liberal guerrilla armies throughout the countryside, where the state had little presence. The guerrillas attracted bandits and revolutionaries eager to take advantage of the absence of government authority. The threat of mounting social unrest in the countryside convinced elites to seek accommodation through an "intra-elite" and "anti-popular" consociational pact that alternated power between the two parties in order to avoid prolonged military rule or social revolution (Munck 1998:28). The military junta that overthrew the Rojas Pinilla military government in May 1957 decreed a set of constitutional reforms that included the National Front pact, which was approved by popular referendum on December 1, 1957. Under the pact, between 1958 and 1974 the presidency was alternated, and cabinet, legislative, and judicial posts were distributed evenly. The constitutional reforms included many institutional rigidities that future generations would endure, including an article prohibiting future referenda, whose legitimacy would become the focus of political and juridical debate in the 1980s.

The National Front pact eliminated the key trigger for interparty violence (the tendency of the party in power to completely exclude the other from government and access to patronage), assured the parties' monopolization of power and resources, and enabled elites to forestall social revolution and lasting military rule. Because the consociational pact did not establish bipartisan decision-making institutions, Congress was consistently deadlocked and distracted by issues of regionalism and patronage. A small cupola of party elites reached important decisions through ad hoc summits, inhibiting the development of effective state power (Hartlyn 1988:92). The Colombian state never fully penetrated society, and its presence in rural areas has been represented mainly by military and police forces; in their absence (and elsewhere with their collaboration), rural elites maintain order.

The regime never established legitimacy throughout the population because of its narrow social base and the restriction of competition to the two elite-based parties in the face of pressures to open the system to emerging social forces in the 1960s and 1970s. Until the 1991 reform, the only legitimate channels to the state were through the traditional political parties, a typical weakness of the consociational regime type. Extra-partisan demands were ignored or treated as problems of public order, that is, through the imposition of states of siege and campaigns of repression. Thus, although the elite domination of policy enabled Colombia to develop one of the most stable and well-managed economies in the region, the price of this stability was the inability to adapt to changing social conditions and open up the political system to popular groups (Hartlyn 1988:144).

According to Colombian social scientists, not only did the consociational pact prevent the creation and consolidation of democratic state institutions, it prevented the emergence of a civil society or public sphere. Miguel Eduardo Cárdenas argues that the oligarchy historically had backed a policy of violence against the majority of the population in order to maintain a culture of submission and prevent the emergence of autonomous organizations. This strategy—in particular, the systematic elimination of popular leaders—prevented the emergence of a democratic elite. The complete domination of the state by the oligarchy blurred the lines between public and private spheres and prevented the achievement of an agrarian reform or social revolution. Pro-democracy activist Libardo Sarmiento also blames the weakness of civil society, the lack of social cohesion, and the absence of respect for the rule of law on the systematic repression of popular organizations by the oligarchy and the state. He notes a pattern in Colombia of intense social conflict followed by reform, which is then followed by violent counterreform. The result is the absence of a public sphere and also a civil society marked by extreme fragmentation, particularly among popular organizations that urgently need alternative mechanisms of representation and spaces for dialogue (Santana Rodríguez 1996:55).[1]

The National Front began to fall apart in the 1970s in anticipation of the pact's expiration. Legislative parity was eliminated and competitive presidential elections were resumed in 1974. Cabinet and public sector parity was maintained until 1978, after which the constitution called for "adequate and equitable" representation of the opposition. This parity was observed until 1986, when the Conservatives refused the seats they were offered in the Liberal Virgilio Barco government. The National Front was also enervated by societal changes emerging in the 1970s. During that decade, rural violence increased as landowners and state security forces worked together to counter the growing guerrilla insurgency. The main guerrilla groups were the ELN (National Liberation Army), a pro-Castro group formed by university students in 1964; the communist-party-allied FARC (Revolutionary Armed Forces of Colombia), formed in 1966; the smaller EPL (Popular Liberation Army), a pro-Chinese group formed in 1974; and the M-19 (April 19 Movement), formed by socialists protesting the theft of the April 19, 1970, presidential election from the National Popular Alliance (Kline 1999:18). Landowners and security forces also repressed the increasingly radical peasant and indigenous movements, which seized hundreds of thousands of hectares of land from rural elites in the 1970s. Urban unrest also increased. Spontaneous, multi-class alliances led civic strikes protesting the failure of local and national government to satisfy popular demands. In order to quell the escalating popular mobilizations and to stall the further deinstitutionalization of the regime, the Conservative Misael Pastrana government imposed a state of siege throughout most of the country in 1971. In 1976 the Liberal López Michelsen government extended the state of siege to the entire territory and expanded military powers over the public, inspiring the first serious Colombian movement to investigate human rights (Buenahora 1991:95). During the López Michelsen government, the axis of political violence shifted from conflict between Liberals and Conservatives to violent altercations between the closed, bipartisan system and those it excluded (Hoskin 1991:26). By the 1980s, the decline in public identification with the Liberal and Conservative Parties, and the refusal of traditional politicians to open the system or to address the impunity of state-sponsored human rights violations, had caused a precipitous decline in regime legitimacy.[2]

The Emergence of Ethnic Movements

After independence from Spain in 1819, the population's ethnic heterogeneity and the absence of Colombian national identity inspired an intellectual tradition that sought the answer to the nation's problems of endemic violence, civil war, and ungovernability in Colombian national character. This intellectual tradition contrasts unity, uniformity, and strength with disunity, diversity, and weakness. Although other aspects of Colombian character have been probed, the predominance of the mestizo (mixed Amerindian, European, and African heritage), the persistence of ethnic enclaves, and the territorial dispersion of the population have come under particular scrutiny. The constitutional discourse on collective identity that would emerge in the 1990s, and its association with efforts to remove obstacles to the foundation of a modern democratic regime, are part of a long-standing Colombian intellectual tradition (Urueña 1994:5–25; Pabón Tarantino 1993:161–208; Padilla 1996:81).

Colombia's population of almost thirty-five million is composed of the descendants of Europeans, African slaves, and Amerindian tribes. The largest ethnic group is mestizo, roughly 70 percent of the population, depending on how ethnic minorities are defined. As in other Latin American countries, elites have promoted a myth of an original, hybrid nation of mestizos in which cultural, ethnic, and regional differences are submerged. The myth obscures the reality of a racial hierarchy in which progress is achieved through whitening (Wade 1993a:18–19). After Brazil, Colombia has the largest proportion of black population in South America, with estimates ranging from 14 percent to 30 percent of Colombia's total population. Higher figures tend to include more of the mulatto population. Blacks are concentrated in urban areas and in the Pacific Coast region, where they form 80–90 percent of the population (Arocha 1992a ; Sánchez, Roldán, and Sánchez 1993:116–20).

The legal distinction of the Afro-Colombian population ended on January 1, 1852, after which slaves formally became Colombian citizens. Colombia is similar to the United States with respect to the conceptualization of "blackness" as a racial category whose members experience some (highly contested) degree of racial discrimination (Asher 1998:37–38; Wade 1993a: 344–45). But there are important distinctions as well. First, in Colombia, there are multiple types of black or Afro-Colombian identity, which vary according to region and income level. In the Atlantic Coast region, black identity was constructed through the pre-independence practice of *cimarronaje*—the escape of slaves from plantations and the construction of black or multiracial fortified refuges *(palenques)* (Wade 1993a:53–54, 87–89). In the predominantly black Pacific Coast region, black *ethnic* identity is relatively recent, dating to emancipation in the early nineteenth century and the creation of new settlements along rivers penetrating the Pacific Coast near former mining centers. Here black community identity first developed an attachment to a specific territory. In these remote areas, blacks were able to preserve and invent cultural practices and forms of social organization derived from African cultures and distinct from the wider society. There is a distinct population of Raizals inhabiting the San Andrés, Providencia, and Santa Catalina archipelago. Raizals are descendants of English Puritan colonists, West African slaves, and Jamaican immigrants, who, over centuries, developed a distinct culture characterized by Protestant religion, English language, and customs that combine European, Caribbean, and African traits (Orjuela 1993:150). Black identity as a political category owes its construction to university-educated urban intellectuals influenced by the U.S. civil rights movement. But many blacks reject the idea of a distinct black identity, preferring to identify themselves simply as Colombians or, as do Colombians of all races, by their region (Wade 1993a).

Unlike in the United States, those of mixed parentage with relatively light skin have the option of escaping the black category and the negative social consequences attached to it (Wade 1993a:326). Because lighter-skinned blacks may escape the category and because there are multiple ways of being black in Colombia, there is less of a basis for political solidarity among the black population:

> The very structure of the black category and its relationship to the non-black world is an obstacle. The boundaries of the category at a national level, whatever their relative clarity in the Chocó or in Medellín are fuzzy and shifting; opportunities for escape from blackness exist and are made the most of by some blacks, and whatever the personal motives involved, these strategies are frequently understood as a rejection of blackness by some other blacks. (Wade 1993a:325–26)

The ambiguity of black identity in Colombia "undermines the *politicization* of race in the public arena" (Wade 1993a:346). The question of whether black ethnic identity exists became a national political issue during the 1991 National Constituent Assembly and subsequently, as black organizations mobilized to interpret their ambiguous new constitutional recognition.

According to the 1993 census, 2.7 percent of the population, around 972,000 people, consider themselves indigenous (Padilla 1996:93). The diverse and widely dispersed indigenous population is comprised of eighty-one distinct ethnic groups, speaking sixty-four languages, with the largest concentration in the southwestern departments of Cauca and Tolima, along the Pacific Coast, and in the Amazon, where close to 36 percent of the indigenous population resides.[3] In three Amazonian departments (Guainia, Vichada, and Vaupés), the indigenous population is the numerical majority. Their remote location and the recognition of their territories and authorities in colonial law, which persisted after independence, enabled indigenous groups to survive into the mid-twentieth century. Although the population is minuscule, its territorial presence is considerable. Even before the 1991 reform, about 84 percent of the indigenous population lived on reserves totaling 27.8 million hectares, comprising 24 percent of the total national territory.

Territory always has been the key point of conflict between the indigenous and nonindigenous populations, particularly in the southwestern department of Cauca, where landownership is extremely concentrated. In the 1960s, economic change and demographic pressures accelerated land conflict. Although indigenous organizations at the local and regional levels exist today throughout the country, those with a national presence by the time of the constitutional reform were based in the Cauca. In the 1960s Cauca Indians mobilized to demand government compliance with Law 135 of 1961, which called for the expansion of Indian *resguardos* (communally owned lands with specific legal rights) according to the cultural, social, and economic development necessary for the survival of the indigenous communities, and Law 89 of 1890, which returned to indigenous communities communal lands that legitimately belonged to them according to their titles and possession (CRIC 1981; Padilla 1996:81–82).[4]

The legal persistence of Law 89, of the *resguardo* and *cabildo* (legally recognized governing councils of the Indian *resguardos* dating to the colonial era) sets Colombia apart from most other Latin American states. It represents the preservation of some aspects of Spanish legal philosophy from the sixteenth and seventeenth centuries with respect to the rights of peoples as the basis for Indian law, which were not swept clean by Liberal, positivist reforms in the late nineteenth century. This would partially explain the ease with which at least a sector of legal and political society accepted the idea of anomalous administrative-territorial units and group-specific rights in the 1991 Constitution. Roque Roldán identifies a number of other explanations for Colombian political elites' greater and earlier receptivity to indigenous grievances. First, although Indians comprise a tiny proportion of the population, they always have held a distinguished place in the national imagination, and they have enjoyed the most extensive individual and collective rights of any identified group in society. It is widely perceived that their protection is a fundamental responsibility of the state. Second, along much of the country's frontiers indigenous communities represent the only effective human presence. "Backing these populations juridically, economically, and technically, as the new Political Constitution attempts, in order that they assume the responsibility as Colombians and as Indians, to administer and defend their own territories, represents a necessary option and the only one possible" (Roldán 1997:236). Third, by the late 1980s, because of the efforts of the national and international environmental movements, a sector of Colombian elites perceived Indians to possess valuable specialized knowledge and modes of production compatible with the country's rich and diverse but increasingly threatened biological diversity. Some constitution-makers would perceive Indians to be valuable partners in protecting the fragile ecosystems they inhabit. Finally, political elites would be receptive to indigenous constitutional aspirations because of their unceasing capacity and willingness to defend their legal rights, their forms of social organization, collective lands, and cultural traditions (Roldán 1997:234–36).

On February 24, 1971, 2,000 mostly Páez and Guambiano Indians representing ten *cabildos* formed the Regional Indigenous Council of the Cauca (CRIC) to further the struggle to recuperate indigenous ancestral lands. The CRIC worked separately and in conjunction with the now independent campesino organization ANUC (National Association of Peasant Producers), which had been created by the government in 1967 to control peasant mobilization (Posada E. 1998:154). Local authorities responded to the subversive meeting, and to recent land invasions involving more than 15,000 families occupying 350 haciendas, by imprisoning the Toribío *cabildo* that had hosted the meeting and intensifying repression of the peasant movement. In the early 1970s a sector of the Cauca indigenous movement split from the CRIC. This sector organized according to ethnic group and strove to assert the legitimacy of traditional ethnic authorities and their historic rights as peoples under Colombian law. In 1977, it established the Governors on the March, which later changed their name to Southwest Indigenous Authorities (AISO) (Gros 1988:241–53).

In 1982, the CRIC helped found the National Indigenous Organization of Colombia (ONIC) to coordinate the movement and establish a presence in Bogotá. During the 1980s, while continuing to repress rural political mobilization, the Belisario Betancur (1982–1986) and Virgilio Barco (1986–1990) governments opened a dialogue with the Indian movement and facilitated its consolidation as a counterpoint to the influence of guerrillas in the countryside. Both governments intervened to create millions of hectares of *resguardos*. A decree was passed guaranteeing the right to bicultural, bilingual education, although funding never materialized (Gros 1993:13). The high level of mobilization and organization that the Cauca-based indigenous rights movement had achieved by the 1980s enabled Indians to educate the Colombian public about the situation of the nation's indigenous population, to sensitize senior government officials to indigenous constitutional claims, to earn representation for both tendencies of the movement in the 1991 National Constituent Assembly, and to help set the terms of the debate on pluralism and recognition of diversity during the constitutional reform process.

During the 1980s black activists in the Pacific Coast region formed their own grassroots organizations with support from local Church officials and representatives of European development NGOs, following the successful example of the indigenous movement. Collaboration between black and indigenous organizations had begun with the land struggles of the 1970s and expanded in the late 1980s and early 1990s, inspiring blacks to claim legal status for their communities comparable to that of Indians. Diverse black organizations used the political opening created by the pending constitutional reform to make a bid for recognition as an ethnic group for the first time. At pre–constituent assembly planning meetings held in August 1990, they debated alternative reform proposals and formed a National Coordinator for Black Communities to articulate a common voice, although efforts to build a consensus on black rights were overcome by the diversity and fragmentation of the organizations. Nevertheless, the constituent assembly process enabled a sector of the black rights movement to shift the center of gravity of black politics from the traditional black politicians' equal-opportunity agenda toward ethnocultural claims reminiscent of the indigenous movement's ethnicity-based collective-rights agenda (Friedemann and Arocha 1995:68; Grueso 1995:3–5; Grueso, Rosero, and Escobar 1998:199; Sánchez, Roldán, and Sánchez 1993:177–80; Wade 1993a:116–17, 353–54).[5] As Kiran Asher argues, black activists chose to replace a negative, derogatory *racial* identity associated with discrimination and marginalization with a positive *ethnic* identity derived from newly valued "black cultural practices, traditions, rituals, values, and the history of resistance against slavery and racism" (1998:37–38).

The Constitutional Conjuncture

The proximate cause of the destabilization of the Colombian state was increasingly brazen attacks by drug cartels on Colombian institutions and officials and the offices of newspapers critical of the cartels. These attacks answered a Barco government crackdown on the Medellín cartel and included a spate of car bombings in Medellín and Bogotá in the fall of 1989 that left hundreds dead and wounded. In the seven years prior to the 1991 National Constituent Assembly (ANC), the drug cartels murdered Colombia's justice minister, attorney general, and 120 judges and magistrates for investigating acts of violence attributed to the cartels (Buenahora 1991:107). Added to this were hundreds of civilians who got in the way of car bombs, were blown out of the sky, or who were eliminated in "social cleansing" campaigns by the cartels' private death squads. The purpose of these attacks was to paralyze the justice system and to intimidate the public and public officials into outlawing the extradition of Colombian nationals (Buenahora 1995:33–34; Bushnell 1993:264; Kline 1999:46–47).

As John Dugas argues, the war between the drug cartels and the state made apparent the corruption and inefficiency of the state and focused rising public discontent on the bipartisan, clientelist, and exclusive nature of the regime. It also demonstrated the impotence of the state and its institutions vis-à-vis the cartels. Added to this was the public disgust generated by the failure of the government to prosecute mounting human rights abuses and an escalation in the violent attacks by guerrilla groups and paramilitaries—mostly against each other, but with significant collateral damage. By 1990 violence had reached unprecedented levels: every twenty-four minutes a murder (10,488 in the first seven months of 1990); every seven hours a kidnapping; every twelve hours a terrorist act (Echeverri de Restrepo 1993:465). Murder became the leading cause of death in Colombia. As the crime rate escalated, the justice system's capacity to apprehend and prosecute criminals appeared to be declining (Kline 1999:155).

The Colombian state and regime faced a serious legitimacy crisis. Its most important cause was the government's lost monopoly over the legitimate use of force (Pabón Tarantino 1993:166). This was compounded by the delegitimation of the state's use of force, attributable to a systematic pattern of human rights abuses linked to the military and police. The state could no longer protect citizens from the violence of non-state actors, from the extra-constitutional violence of the military against the civilian population, or from non-state armed organizations linked to and tolerated by the state. By the time the constituent assembly was convened in 1991, the critique of the militarized state extended even to its creators. As the delegates of the Social Conservative Party (the old Conservative Party was renamed in 1987) argued in their joint proposal during the general debate:

> The Colombian state has lost the capacity to preserve social order and to impose respect for the law. It governs praetorianly, nobody pays attention to justice, it is the peace of the bodyguards, the Congress is repudiated by public opinion, the political parties are discredited, the electoral system debased by manipulation and fraud, weakening the political will. (Echeverri de Restrepo and Orejuela Díaz 1995:95–96)

The legitimacy of the regime also was threatened by the tendency of the neoliberal economic model to aggravate income inequality and increase poverty (Murrillo 1993:10). During the 1980s, as inequality and poverty increased, government spending on education, housing, health, and social security declined (Echeverri de Restrepo 1993:35). At the time of the constituent assembly, approximately 50 percent of Colombians were living in absolute poverty. These economic dislocations made more apparent the extreme concentration of wealth, productive resources, and positions of authority in the hands of a small elite, and the extent to which this elite ruled in its own economic interest. The concentration of power and wealth traditionally has been so extreme in Colombia that political positions are monopolized by the same individuals or families for years, resulting in a near total lack of elite rotation (Echeverri Uruburu 1990:22, 37).[6] In the past, this political elite had maintained legitimacy by managing a prosperous and stable economy (Munck 1998:28); the dislocations caused by the implementation of the new economic model called into question its competence. The growing perception of an incompetent and greedy elite was aggravated by daily revelations of its corruption: At the end of 1990, Colombia's solicitor general was processing 49,155 disciplinary actions and launching 50 new administrative investigations each day against officials suspected of corruption. That year the *Economist* named Colombia one of the world's five most corrupt countries (Buenahora 1991:98–99).

As in previous periods of crisis, intellectuals and political leaders suggested that the problem lay in the poor fit between the country's centralizing, repressive institutions and a dispersed heterogeneous population. Not only were Colombian state institutions incapable of solving the country's grave problems, many perceived their exclusivity and obsolescence to be the root cause of these problems. Public figures proposed a sweeping constitutional reform to adjust institutions to reality. The surging movement for a constituent assembly was an explicit indictment of the political class, their self-perpetuation through the pervasive clientelism institutionalized by the National Front, and their incapacity to make necessary reforms. The petition for a constituent assembly presented to President Barco in February 1990 explicitly justified the call for a constituent assembly on the basis of the "incompetence of the political class to provide a response to the grave problems of the country."[7]

Attempts to reform the constitution were not new. They had begun in earnest following the dissolution of the National Front. In 1977, Liberal President Alfonso López Michelsen attempted to convoke what became known as "the little constituent assembly." The Colombian Supreme Court struck down the effort on May 5, 1978, arguing that Congress did not have the power to delegate its constitutional faculties. The following year, Liberal President Julio César Turbay Ayala secured congressional approval of constitutional reforms contained in Legislative Act No. 1 of 1979 via the constitutionally indicated congressional route. The Supreme Court overturned the legislation on November 3, 1981, citing problems of form. During 1984 and 1985, Conservative President Belisario Betancur attempted to revive Legislative Act No. 1 of 1979, but was blocked by Congress and the military. Betancur, however, did achieve passage of the 1986 municipal reform—the only constitutional reform since 1968 to avoid the axe of the Supreme Court.[8] The 1986 municipal decentralization introduced the direct popular election of mayors in 1988, as well as a number of mechanisms to facilitate local citizen participation upon which the 1991 Constitution would build, such as the local administrative junta, the local referendum and plebiscite, the participation of consumers on the governing boards of public services agencies, and sectorally organized participation committees (Hoskin 1991:28; Velásquez 1992b:60). These three failures generated a current of opinion that argued that a constituent assembly must be convoked to resolve a stalemate between the two traditional parties and to resolve the institutional deadlock between the executive and the Supreme Court.

A constituent assembly was proposed not just to undertake the urgent task of designing new institutions. It also was expected to provide a forum for national reconciliation between what Colombian commentators called "the political country" and the "real country." A serious obstacle existed to this solution, however: The convocation of a constituent assembly was unconstitutional. Under Article 218 of the 1886 Constitution the only method to reform the constitution was the approval of a legislative reform act by two successive legislatures. On this basis, the constituent assembly option was opposed by prominent conservative legal scholars and traditional politicians. Former president Turbay Ayala, for example, declared a plebiscite on the question of a constituent assembly to be "constitutional demagogy." While opponents argued the illegality of the plebiscite on constitutional reform, proponents dismissed such arguments as smoke screens used to obscure the vested interests and privileges likely to be eliminated by a reform of Congress and the judiciary (Echeverri de Restrepo 1993:88).[9]

The convocation of a constituent assembly as a path toward national reconciliation and institutional renovation became a central issue on the national political agenda in 1987, when, on June 7, the Supreme Court ruled on the legality of the convocation of the 1957 plebiscite that approved the National Front and prohibited future plebiscites and referenda. In the years that followed, this decision would be cited as the legal basis for convoking a constituent assembly in apparent violation of Article 218. The Court argued:

> When the Nation, in the exercise of its sovereign and inalterable power, decides to pronounce itself on the constitutional statute that has reigned over its destiny, it is not nor can it be submitted to the juridical normativity that precedes that decision. The primary constituent act exceeds all types of delimitation, even when established by the prior juridical order and, therefore, is immune to all types of judgment that pretend to compare it to precepts of that order. (Cited in Echeverri de Restrepo 1993:91; translation by the author)

In a January 12, 1988, letter to the Bogotá daily *El Espectador,* Liberal President Virgilio Barco proposed that a plebiscite on the question of derogating Article 13 of the plebiscite of 1957 (prohibiting future plebiscites and referenda) be included in the March elections in order to eliminate the constitutional obstacle to the convocation of a constituent assembly or the submission of a constitutional reform to popular referendum. Barco's letter echoed a 1987 proposal by ex-president Lleras Restrepo, which *El Espectador* had endorsed. The letter indicated a reversal of Barco's opinion, expressed in his inaugural speech in 1986, that constitutional reform was unnecessary, demonstrating, perhaps, the extent to which public order had deteriorated in the intervening years, and the mounting consensus that the crisis of order was related to the inadequacy of political institutions. It also reflects the influence of an original legal argument contained in a memorandum drafted in 1988 by constitutional advisor Manuel José Cepeda (*El Tiempo,* December 9, 1990, 3A). Barco's letter and the legal memorandum on which it was based, which was circulated by the press, sparked a national debate on the issue.

Congressional Conservatives blocked the March plebiscite. On February 20, 1988, Barco signed an accord with Conservative leader Misael Pastrana to appoint an Institutional Readjustment Commission composed of leaders of the Conservative and Liberal Parties to craft a constitutional reform, which, following congressional approval, would be submitted to a popular referendum. On that occasion, Barco described a political crisis that he believed could only be resolved through constitutional reform:

> Our democratic institutions have continued to lose legitimacy. Faith in judges has been eroded. The credibility of the Congress has deteriorated. The people despair of public administration. Few believe that the oversight agencies are really looking out for the good performance of the State. With the referendum, the time has come to bring back legitimacy to the actions of the State and its institutions. (Cited in Dugas 1998:28)

The February 20, 1998, accord was overturned by the Council of State on April 4. Barco then presented a constitutional reform proposal to Congress on July 27, 1988, in accordance with Article 218 of the constitution. His new government minister, César Gaviria Trujillo, negotiated legislative approval of a reform package that affected 180 constitutional articles but did not include the normative themes that would become the hallmark of the new charter or the extensive reforms of the legislature and judicial system that analysts deemed necessary (*El Tiempo,* December 9, 1990). While the reform awaited action in the next legislative period, in October 1988, the Supreme Court ruled that the president is not authorized to call a referendum and that only Congress can reform the constitution.

The assassination of the popular young Liberal Party presidential candidate, Senator Luis Carlos Galán, on August 18, 1989, revived the constituent assembly proposal. Galán, the leading candidate, had embodied popular aspirations for democratic reform, particularly among the young. Eight days later more than twenty thousand students participated in a silent march protesting his assassination.[10] This event marked the beginning of a student-led movement that collected thirty-five thousand signatures on a petition calling on President Barco to convoke a constituent assembly. The shocking death of the charismatic "crusader against corruption and political clientelism" shook privileged university students out of their characteristic apathy (Dugas 1998:25) and struck a common chord: it seemed to symbolize the deaths of hundreds of judges, politicians, journalists, and common citizens. As Jaime Buenahora observes, finally "there was true national indignation" (1991:108–09). The students' call for a constituent assembly was soon seconded by the country's major newspapers, *El Tiempo* and *El Espectador,* and by César Gaviria, who replaced Galán as the Liberal Party's presidential candidate. Gaviria would be the first candidate to publicly promote the convocation of a constituent assembly. In addition to his association with the government's pending constitutional reform project, as Galán's successor in the progressive wing of the Liberal Party, Gaviria was best positioned to promote a popular democratic initiative that emerged as a result of Galán's murder (Carrillo 1994:194).

The climate of violence and panic escalated when, on December 6, 1989, the cartels car-bombed the headquarters of the Department of Administrative Security, killing sixty-three and injuring six hundred (Kline 1999:50). The cartels intensified their violent attacks in response to the government's crackdown following Galán's murder, in an effort to intimidate Congress into voting to outlaw extradition. The Extraditables, as they called themselves, used a campaign of violence, payoffs, and threats to successfully pressure the lower chamber to include the prohibition of extradition in a referendum scheduled for January 21, 1990, on the Barco government's constitutional reform package. To prevent the cartels from launching a new wave of violent intimidation against the public, President Barco reluctantly canceled the referendum. The student movement and political commentators used the apparent weakness of the majority of Congress before the Extraditables to prod the national conscience, awaken indignation against the political class, and establish a connection between popular frustrations with the infiltration of the political class by the cartels and the necessity for institutional reform (Buenahora 1991:14). They discredited the Congress, which had also lost prestige because of its high rates of absenteeism and nepotism and the conspicuous abuse of public funds for clientelist relations and exotic foreign trips (Kline 1999:164–65). Throughout the constitutional reform process, Congress would be attacked as a symbol of what was wrong with Colombian democracy. The discrediting of this institution, the only entity legally empowered to reform the constitution, intensified the drive for a constituent assembly (Buenahora 1991:125; Carrillo 1994:181; L. Restrepo 1991:53).

As contemporary social movement theory explains, the students "framed" (McAdam, McCarthy, and Zald 1996:7–17) the convocation of a constituent assembly as the only possible solution to the problem of the political crisis generated by the vast gulf between the Colombian state and society while assigning blame to the traditional political class for failing to address the inadequacy of political institutions. The students' analysis was not original; they articulated an argument that had been prominent for more than a decade among political analysts.[11] The students' innovation was to publish this "frame" as a petition in *El Tiempo* on October 22, 1989, calling on President Barco to convoke a constituent assembly and urging readers to sign and mail the petitions to the students (Dugas 1998:27–32). As Sidney Tarrow observes, the trigger for this frame—the death and funeral of an important public figure—has historically been a common trigger for traditional social movement activity under conditions of repression (1998:36).

In an article published in *El Tiempo* on February 6, 1990, Fernando Carrillo—a law professor at the private university that was the base of the student movement at this time, and an adviser to the students—proposed the inclusion of a "seventh ballot" during the upcoming elections (in addition to the six planned official ballots for a variety of offices) on the convocation of a constituent assembly. On March 11, 1990, during local, regional, and congressional elections, students organized the ballot initiative, with support from the media—in particular from the daily *El Espectador* (whose director, Guillermo Cano, had been murdered by the drug cartels in 1985, and whose offices had been bombed by the cartels) and from *El Tiempo* (which had opened its editorial pages to the student movement). Both major newspapers printed sample ballots prior to the elections for readers to cut out and cast with their official ballots. Roughly two million voters added seventh ballots, including hundreds of thousands of homemade, handwritten versions, to indicate their support for the convocation of a constituent assembly (Dugas 1998:16).

While the country waited for the government to act on the results of the seventh ballot, two more presidential candidates were assassinated. The first, on March 22, 1990, was Senator Bernardo Jaramillo Ossa, the second Patriotic Union (UP) presidential candidate to be assassinated (the first, Jaime Pardo Leal, was murdered in 1987). The party retired from the presidential campaign. The loss to the party was added to the more than one thousand UP militants assassinated since its founding in 1985 by a coalition of leftist groups that included the Communist Party and affiliates of the FARC guerrillas (Hoskin 1991:30).[12] The second assassination occurred on April 26, 1990, when Carlos Pizarro Leongomez, presidential candidate of the Democratic Alliance M-19 (ADM-19) was gunned down on a flight from Bogotá to Barranquilla.[13] The ADM-19 was the party of the M-19 guerrillas, which had negotiated the movement's demobilization and entry into politics the month before. The ADM-19 replaced Pizarro with Antonio Navarro Wolff, the M-19's number two, who still bore the scars of a nearly successful attack on his life during unsuccessful peace negotiations with the Betancur administration.

The violence and kidnappings perpetrated by the drug cartels against state and civil society targets continued. The most grotesque acts of violence became routine. Amid a mounting crisis of institutional legitimacy and public insecurity, the moving courage and optimism of the student movement, the rhetoric of the presidential candidates (all of whom now supported the ANC), and the hyperbole of the press, the constituent assembly appeared to be the country's only hope.

The purpose of the seventh ballot had been to create a "supra-constitutional" political fact that would enable pro–constituent assembly forces to argue credibly that the people themselves were convoking the assembly under their primary constituent powers, since the Supreme Court had ruled that no government entity was empowered to do so (Carrillo 1994:191). Using the seventh ballot as his legal justification, President Barco decreed that a plebiscite be conducted during the May 27, 1990, presidential elections and directed the Registrar to tabulate the results. This decree (Decree 927) resulted from talks in April conducted by Barco's government minister, Horacio Serpa, with the presidential candidates of the Liberal, Social Conservative, National Salvation Movement (MSN, a rival new conservative party), and ADM-19 parties. With the exception of the Social Conservative Party (PSC), the four parties agreed to support the inclusion on the presidential ballot of a question with respect to the convocation of a constituent assembly. They failed to agree on the mechanisms for convoking and regulating the assembly, on the subject matter of the reforms, or on any other questions to be put to voters.

In order to provide the initiative a stronger legal foundation, the decree was issued under Barco's state-of-siege powers, in force since 1984, as a measure intended to "maintain institutional order." This argument was supported by the public statements of several guerrilla leaders that they would lay down their arms if a constituent assembly were convoked. Barco provided further proof of the connection between the demobilization of the guerrillas and the convocation of a constituent assembly on May 23, 1990, when he announced that he had begun peace talks with three guerrilla groups —the EPL; the Revolutionary Workers Party (PRT); and the Quintín Lame, a mostly Páez sector of the Cauca indigenous movement with close ties to the M-19, which had been founded in the early 1980s in response to assaults on indigenous communities from multiple sources.[14] Two days later, the Supreme Court upheld both arguments: that the seventh ballot represented the will of the people in favor of a constituent assembly; and that its convocation was a question of public order falling under the president's state-of-siege powers. The text of the plebiscite offered by the government read as follows: "In order to strengthen participatory democracy, would you vote for the convocation of a Constitutional Assembly, with representation of the social, political, and regional forces of the Nation, integrated democratically and popularly, to reform the Political Constitution of Colombia?" On May 27, 1990, more than five million people (86.6 percent of voters) voted yes, with 39 percent of registered voters participating. Thereafter, the national debate began in earnest over the procedures for conforming and operating the ANC and the scope of issues to be discussed.

Liberal Party candidate César Gaviria won the presidential election with

47 percent of the vote—more than twice the total of his closest competitor, Alvaro Gómez Hurtado of the MSN. The ADM-19's Navarro Wolff finished third, with 12 percent. Gaviria immediately began working to create consensus among the four major parties (those winning at least 5 percent in the March elections), the Liberals, the two conservative parties, and the ADM-19, on the substantive scope and procedures for the ANC. The 5 percent minimum cruelly excluded the UP, which had withdrawn from the presidential elections after two of its presidential candidates were murdered but which had a greater presence in Congress than the ADM-19, and contradicted candidate Gaviria's public statements that the UP, as well as sectors of civil society, would be represented in the preparatory commission on the convocation of the ANC (Echeverri de Restrepo 1993:75–77).

Gaviria was inaugurated on August 7, 1990. That month the four parties signed two accords on the scope of issues to be discussed, the composition of the ANC, and the requirements for membership, based on proposals made in July by then-president-elect Gaviria. A key purpose of the accords was to allay the fears of traditional party leaders that their powers would be usurped by an unprecedentedly powerful ANC. The government and parties agreed that the ANC would not revoke the mandate of the sitting legislature, that delegates could not run for Congress for eight years, and that the ANC would be popularly elected—presumably providing an arena in which the parties enjoyed a comparative advantage. According to constitutional adviser Manuel José Cepeda, the government also attempted to provide thematic limits for the constitutional deliberations—not to close off discussion of problematic issues but, rather, to provide clear guidelines with respect to what might happen within the ANC in order to lessen the fears of the political elite.[15] Decree 1926, containing these understandings among the parties, was promulgated by President Gaviria on August 24, 1990. Although these closely held negotiations secured elite support for the constituent assembly, legal and political analysts criticized the political parties' domination of the process and, in particular, the autonomy with which President Gaviria appeared to be controlling the scope and procedure of the ANC (Buenahora 1991:186–87).

Decree 1926 marked the first appearance of ethnic minorities' interests on the reform agenda. In addition to pressures from indigenous organizations, this appearance also may be attributed to the insertion by anthropologists of ethnic issues into peace talks between the M-19 and the government in 1989 as a contributing factor to violence in Colombia (E. Restrepo 1997: 310–11). Following talks with indigenous and other groups that were not signatories to the four-party accords, the decree incorporated "the recognition of the multiethnic character of the nation, respect for indigenous authorities and culture, and indigenous communities' property rights to *resguardo* lands."[16]

As had President Barco in issuing Decree 927, Gaviria issued Decree 1926 under his state-of-siege powers as a means of restoring public order, arguing that only the transformation of public institutions through legitimate means could do so. As evidence, the administration noted that several armed groups had signaled their intention of laying down their arms in exchange for participation in the ANC. On this point, the Supreme Court concurred. But the Court took the government's popular sovereignty argument further, striking down limits on the scope of the ANC that the political parties had tried to impose and declaring unconstitutional the article of Decree 1926 that required ANC candidates to put up five million pesos (about five thousand U.S. dollars) to show their seriousness, which the Court found to violate the principle of equality.

The ANC would not have taken place without the favorable decisions of the Supreme Court on the legality of Decrees 927 and 1926. At the time, several commentators used the arguments of Rousseau and Condorcet with respect to the primary constitutive power of the people, which, they argued, was prior to any written constitution or law and, thus, could not inhibit the constitutive power of future generations (Buenahora 1991:149; Angarita 1994:36). What gave force to these theoretical arguments was the unique fact that in the Colombian case, through the seventh ballot, the "autonomous and sovereign people" was not just a theoretical construct but a tangible political actor.

Not everyone bought this line of reasoning, however. As the country prepared for the ANC, traditional legislators prepared an alternative constitutional reform, and representatives of powerful economic interests and prominent figures within the Liberal and Conservative Parties argued the illegality of any constitutional reform method other than the congressional route specified in Article 218 (Echeverri de Restrepo 1993:133). Former president Alfonso López Michelsen, then leader of the Liberal Party, argued that the concept of the "primary constituent" was intended to be an abstraction and not be pushed to an illogical extreme and confused with a political fact. Far from autonomous actions of the collective will, he argued, the student movement and the two votes in favor of the ANC on March 11 and May 27 were provoked and led by the Barco government: "In all of this, more than a primary constituent, I see a bit of 'bonapartism.' To take as given that an induced vote is a manifestation of the primary constituent is like pretending that Rousseau's social contract is registered in a notary."[17]

According to Manuel José Cepeda, Barco's constitutional adviser, three factors were equally important in convincing the Supreme Court to rule as it did: (1) the weight of the legal argument developed by the government with respect to the sovereignty of the people; (2) the sharp increase in violence in the late 1980s; and (3) the pressure on the Court exerted by the student movement, the press, and public opinion. It is impossible to separate the juridical argument from the rising tide of violence, because the juridical argument was made credible by the environment of political crisis and political pressure in which it was made. The Court also was influenced by a popular argument for the convocation of an ANC that was derived from a definition of the constitution as a peace treaty, a concept taken from the writings of Norberto Bobbio.[18] The Supreme Court even cited Bobbio in its review of Decree 927. The idea of a constitution as a peace treaty has long roots in Colombia, since many charters and comprehensive reforms were enacted to end political violence.

Despite the considerable public consensus on the need to convoke the constituent assembly, not all Colombians shared the same expectations. The Left sought peaceful social transformation; the middle class sought the moral redemption of the existing political class (Buenahora 1991:157). Both sought the transition from a *representative* model, which was considered incapable of sustaining the legitimacy of Colombia's institutions, to a *participatory* model, in which citizens would be able to participate directly in decision-making. The process leading to the convocation of the constituent assembly was widely viewed as proof that such a regime was possible (Cepeda 1995b:3). There also was broad public agreement that the success or failure of the ANC depended on the composition of its members. But there was no consensus on how to choose delegates to the ANC or on the appropriate number to choose. The process for conforming the ANC and its general procedural orientation were to some extent predetermined by the ballot initiative cited above, which stipulated that representatives would be chosen "democratically and popularly," that they would represent the "social, political and regional forces of the Nation," and that the purpose of the reform was to "strengthen participatory democracy." These guidelines, however, are open to multiple interpretations. One could argue either that "democratically and popularly" requires that all delegates be elected rather than appointed, or that the representation of diverse "social, political and regional forces" requires some type of corporate allocation of seats. The idea of corporatist representation raised the difficult questions of how many seats each group would get, how their representatives would be chosen, and what to do about unorganized sectors of society (Buenahora 1991:175–78; Franco and Valderrama 1990:41). In the end, seventy constituents were elected from lists presented by parties and social movements through a single, national circumscription. In addition, guerrilla groups involved in the peace process that had laid down their arms were allowed to send representatives.

A two-stage process of preparation for the ANC began in late 1990. First, between September 30 and November 15, a series of working groups were held throughout the country to receive citizen proposals. Citizens and municipal authorities organized 1,579 working groups throughout the country, of which 840 were organized by mayors and 286 by social movements. Forty indigenous *cabildos* (about one-third of the total) and a variety of social organizations also submitted proposals (Buenahora 1995:47; República de Colombia 1991a:655, 1991b). The government established twenty-nine commissions and subcommissions, corresponding to each chapter of the constitution, to organize and summarize the 110,340 proposals submitted by Colombians. A separate commission was established for "mechanisms of participation," which included a subcommission on participatory democracy. These met between October 30 and November 30.

The commission on human rights established a subcommission on "equality and multiethnic character" composed mainly of Indians and experts on indigenous issues, with lesser representation from the black organizations and academics. According to participants, the subcommission focused more on indigenous peoples than on Afro-Colombian issues, a pattern that would continue during the constituent assembly. In participant Raúl Arango's words, "The black problematic had not yet arrived."[19] According to Jaime Arocha, a scholar of black movements who participated in the subcommission, despite their assurances that they would give the rights of blacks equal weight, once elected to the ANC indigenous delegates continued to distinguish the greater scope of indigenous rights from that of "other ethnic groups," a distinction that is apparent in the written proposals presented by the delegates, in particular those of Lorenzo Muelas (Arocha 1992b:47). Similarly, the pre-ANC political accords noted the need for recognition of indigenous rights and a special code of laws for the Raizals but included no mention of blacks as a distinct group.

On December 9, 1990, Colombians voted for or against the convocation of the ANC. Those voting in favor chose delegates from 119 lists representing 788 aspirants. That 80.6 percent voted for the convocation of the ANC was not a surprise. The surprise was that only 26 percent of fourteen million Colombians eligible to vote—just under three million voters—did so, when polls had predicted better than 70 percent participation. Only twenty-five successful candidates won more votes than the amount of null votes cast (24,467). The poor turnout put in question the legitimacy of the ANC and its delegates while appearing to bolster the legitimacy of the National Congress, which had been elected by eight million voters.[20] Speaking for the traditional political class, former presidents Alfonso López Michelsen (Liberal) and Misael Pastrana Borrero (Conservative) argued that the high abstention indicated that the majority of Colombians were satisfied with the 1886 Constitution. Other explanations offered for the abstention included the short (forty-day) campaign period; fear of election-day violence; the fatigue of voters, who already had participated in two elections in 1990; the lack of understanding by the majority of the public of the importance of the ANC or the complex issues involved (a theory bolstered by the more than seven hundred thousand blank votes deposited on the question of the convocation of the assembly); and the lack of motivation for supporters of the two traditional parties, since delegates had no patronage to disburse and were prohibited from running in the next elections (Buenahora 1991:359–63; Echeverri de Restrepo 1993:450; L. Restrepo 1991:59; Revista Foro 1991a:1–2).[21]

Doubts about the legitimacy and representativity of the ANC were offset by the diversity of groups represented and the clear break with bipartism. As the election campaign progressed, political parties had increasingly seized the initiative from civil society and won sixty-five of seventy seats in the assembly. This was principally because of the fragmentation and diversity of interests within civil society—the student movement alone offered twenty-nine lists for the ANC elections—as well as the unequal distribution of campaign financing and free media time, which strongly favored the four parties to the August accords.[22] Liberal Party candidates won the most votes, with 34.7 percent (twenty-four seats), using a strategy of thirty-six lists with regionally strong candidates. But the traditional hegemony of the National Front parties was shattered by the success of the unified ADM-19 list, headed by Antonio Navarro Wolff, which finished second with 26.7 percent (nineteen seats) and finished first in nine departments. This impressive showing for the new party was less than the 43 percent predicted by polling. As the weekly *Semana* observed: "No country in the world had delivered so much power in so short a time to forces that had just finished being the enemy" (October 30, 1990, 28). Navarro attracted the most votes of any single candidate or list, followed by former MSN presidential candidate Alvaro Gómez Hurtado, with 15.7 percent, suggesting a polarization of preferences between the leaders of the Left and Right opposition (Dugas 1993a:47). The three conservative parties together garnered 27.7 percent of the vote (twenty seats), with eleven for the MSN, five for the PSC, and four for independent conservative leaders loosely allied with the latter. Rounding out the list of delegates, the beleaguered UP won two seats and social movements won five: two for evangelical Christians, two for indigenous parties, and one for the student movement list led by Fernando Carrillo.[23] The seventy elected delegates were joined by four representatives of guerrilla movements involved in peace talks with the government. Two voting seats were allotted the EPL—which demobilized prior to the start of the ANC, changing its name from the Popular Liberation Army (Ejército Popular de Liberación) to Hope, Peace and Liberty (Esperanza, Paz y Libertad). The Quintín Lame and PRT each received a seat without voting rights, because of the smaller size of these movements. The country's largest guerrilla movements, the FARC and the ELN, never joined the peace process and were not represented. The FARC had asked for at least twenty delegates and had unleashed acts of violence in the months leading up to the ANC elections.[24] Efforts on the part of a peace commission composed of constituents to negotiate with the remaining guerrilla groups and include them in the ANC ultimately failed.

3 "The Friendly Liquidation of the Past"

Colombia's 1991 National Constituent Assembly

CONSTITUENTS MET, following the December 9, 1990, elections, to ne-gotiate the rules for governance of and deliberations within the National Constituent Assembly (ANC) and to consolidate their resistance to the set of rules that the Gaviria government was trying to impose. After the Liberal Party lost its battle to exercise a hegemonic presidency of the ANC, delegates elected the leaders of the parties with the three largest delegations —Horacio Serpa (Liberals), Antonio Navarro Wolff (ADM-19), and Alvaro Gómez Hurtado (MSN)—to be co-presidents of the ANC. They assigned the presidencies and vice presidencies of five thematic working commissions to the smallest parties.[1]

These decisions with respect to leadership were truly innovative for Colombian democracy. They demonstrated in practice the new philosophy of pluralism and respect for minorities that had characterized the debate on the ANC, in contrast to a political tradition of intolerance and irresponsi-bility on the part of governing majorities. They also set the tone for the de-liberations, which would be characterized by a lack of ideological conflict and a tendency toward pragmatism. The accords on the regulation of the ANC, signed on February 11, 1991, also prefigured what would become a common strategic alignment on procedural questions when consensus could not be reached: the ADM-19 and MSN, forming an absolute majority to-gether with most of the independent minority forces, against the Liberals and the PSC, who were usually in the minority on procedural questions. The ANC was a radically different forum from Congress, where the Liberals and PSC held 80 percent of the seats (Buenahora 1995:46–49).

Pursuant to the February 11 accord, proposals for reform could be presented by the delegates, by the highest bodies of the branches of government—for example, the Supreme Court, the constitutional committees of the Senate and House of Representatives, the Ministry of Government—as well as national-level civil society organizations and associations, universities, and guerrilla organizations involved in the peace process. Even some international organizations, such as Amnesty International, were allowed to present proposals. These were distributed to the appropriate commission and published in the *Gaceta Constitucional*, established by the ANC to disseminate the text of proposals, transcriptions of plenary and commission debates, as well as general news about the proceedings. In addition, the ANC's information and press office broadcast a daily nationwide radio report.

The ANC opened on February 5, 1991, amid concerns for the safety of the delegates, many of whom had received death threats. Only days before, the public had learned of the death on January 25 of journalist Diana Turbay, daughter of the ex-president, who had been kidnapped by drug traffickers months earlier and was killed in a confused attempt by the police to free her. A special police district was created to encompass the headquarters of the ANC and 250 police officers were assigned to protect the 74 delegates. Metal detectors and electronic surveillance equipment checked for bombs and a private security company searched visitors. As a mood of expectation charged the capital on the first day of the ANC, nine departments suffered more than fifty major guerrilla actions—an unprecedented level of guerrilla terrorism. The attacks were, in part, retribution for the government's attack on FARC headquarters on December 9, 1990, the day of the ANC elections, an attack that turned out to be a strategic mistake on Gaviria's part. Aside from being a military failure, it made it more difficult to incorporate the major guerrilla groups into the constituent assembly process. As the ANC opened, President Gaviria continued to try to negotiate a means through which the country's largest guerrilla organizations could participate. According to Kline, Gaviria's team feared that if it conceded too many seats (together with those the ADM-19 was projected to win through elections), the guerrillas might dominate the assembly (Kline 1999:ch. 6).[2]

The first month of the ANC was devoted to oral presentations of general proposals and philosophies. During the February 13–24 General Debate (which was actually a series of individual presentations), sixty-one delegates offered their views on the new constitution. The most common topics were congress, peace, and extradition, with all speakers in the first days linking the constituent assembly to the search for peace. These orations enabled delegates to assess the conceptual orientations of their colleagues and to begin to form alliances and adjust their proposals (Buenahora 1995:52). Five working commissions convened between February 12 and May 15, with the most intensive sessions being held in April and May. Their work was divided as follows:

Commission 1: rights, principles, participatory democracy, electoral system, political parties

Commission 2: territorial organization, municipalities and departments, indigenous territories

Commission 3: government and congress, public force, international relations

Commission 4: administration of justice

Commission 5: the economic regime, social policy, environment

Each constituent was allowed to join the commission of his or her choice, creating imbalances in commission membership. The resulting distribution of political forces on the commissions is noteworthy. No commission had a majority of any party. The largest commission, number 5, with eighteen members, attracted eight Liberals and six conservatives of various stripes, balanced by four representatives of the ADM-19. This predominance of traditional forces facilitated the strengthening of the neoliberal economic model[3] and the modernization of state fiscal powers; it also left the traditional forces in the minority on Commissions 1 and 4, and evenly balanced with nontraditional forces on Commission 3. On Commission 2, which dealt with territorial organization, the conservatives—the traditional defenders of centralization—had only two representatives, which eased the way for decentralization proposals.

Between April 30 and June 23, 1991, delegates made speeches and offered written projects with respect to specific articles of the constitution. This first plenary debate was to have ended in late May, in order to leave the month of June for the second debate. (Under the rules of the ANC, each new article of the constitution must be approved during two plenary debates.) However, the emergence of a number of auxiliary issues, such as ongoing negotiations with guerrilla groups, lengthened the first debate until June 23.[4] Proposals approved in the first debate went to a codifying commission composed of delegates with legal training, where, between June 23 and 28, they were revised and prepared in legal language for revoting in the second plenary session. That session began on June 28 and lasted only six days. Particularly contentious issues, such as the territorial rights of indigenous peoples, were saved till the second plenary debate, where they received less discussion because of time pressures. For this reason, rather than the simple majority required for passage in the first debate, during the second debate passage required a qualified majority.

Despite the polarization of Colombian politics at the time of the ANC, voting records demonstrate considerable consensus.[5] Of all articles approved in the first debate, 94 percent passed with 80 percent of the votes, and 43 percent (192/449) were approved unanimously (Dugas 1993a:69). According to PSC delegate Augusto Ramírez Ocampo, the greatest substantive consensus among the delegates was on the need to create a strong charter of rights, duties, and guarantees of the person and the citizen. Delegates acknowledged the problem of human rights and the extent to which this had become a point of national shame (Ramírez 1991:4). A related goal on which there was broad consensus was the need to make deep reforms in the justice system, from the penal code to the organization of its institutions. There was also consensus on the need to adopt more mechanisms for participatory democracy. The section on participatory democracy, and all of the mechanisms for making it effective, were approved by consensus, "which is highly significant, given the magnitude of the institutional transformation that this implied" (Cepeda 1993:xi–xii; translation by the author).

The most controversial issues were the extradition of Colombian nationals, the administrative expropriation of property, the creation of the *Fiscalía General*[6] and the Constitutional Court, and the dissolution of the sitting Congress and convocation of new congressional elections following the ANC (Angarita 1994:39). The recognition of collective property rights for black communities also polarized the assembly: in an effort to block this measure the MSN abstained from voting; the majority of the Liberals and the ADM-19 voted to approve, although the measure split the leadership of these groups. It was eventually slipped back in and approved as Transitory Article 55 (see below). Most proposals were voted on publicly, but thirty-three proposals were submitted to secret ballot, including the potentially life-threatening extradition issue (Cepeda 1993:20–21).[7]

The fragmentation of the major parties and the strong presence of non-traditional forces within the ANC meant that no group could control the agenda or determine the results. This led to the equitable division of power within the ANC and an effort to reach consensus while giving minority forces considerable leverage to form voting alliances. Most constituents shared with the country the sense that Colombia had reached a turning point and that the ANC had the opportunity to effect a durable, positive change. The spirit of reconciliation that characterized the ANC—symbolized by the harmonious cooperation of two of the three co-presidents (former M-19 guerrilla Antonio Navarro Wolff and Alvaro Gómez Hurtado, who was kidnapped and held by the M-19 from May 29 to July 20, 1988)— also inspired delegates to seek consensus, as did the presence of three indigenous delegates.[8] Observers singled out the presence of indigenous delegates among the most prestigious politicians in the country as proof that Colombians, divided by violence and inequality, could live together in peace and work toward a new social compromise:

> In a moment in which the country had been beaten down by violence and disorder, putting all its hopes in the renovation of its institutions, the presence of elected Indians at the side of other representatives of the guerrillas and civil society was offered to Colombian eyes as the tangible proof that it was possible to live together. It was the dreamed-of reality of a country that respected differences, hospitable, tolerant. The Constituent Assembly demonstrated, through its internal composition, that the separation between the real country and the formal country—so denounced as an essential ingredient in the restricted democracy that prevailed in the country—was not as insuperable as it had seemed. (Gros 1993:9; translation by the author)

The indigenous delegates represented the two main branches of the indigenous movement. Francisco Rojas Birry, an Emberá Indian from the mostly black department of the Chocó, represented the Colombian National Indigenous Organization; Lorenzo Muelas Hurtado, a Guambiano leader from the Cauca, represented the Southwest Indigenous Authorities; and Alfonso

Peña Chepe, a Páez and also from the Cauca, joined the ANC in April to represent the Quintín Lame guerrillas. Rojas Birry was vice president of Commission 1, which included the political process, democratic participation, and the electoral system, as well as the discussion of the multiethnic and pluricultural nature of the country; Muelas was vice president of Commission 2 (on which the Quintín Lame delegate, Alfonso Peña Chepe, also served), which covered territorial reorganization and regional and local autonomy, another key set of indigenous demands.[9]

The indigenous candidates had placed nineteenth and twenty-seventh among the seventy delegates elected from 119 lists, an enormous surprise given their lack of resources and campaign experience, the minuscule size of the indigenous population, its low level of voter registration, and the distance of indigenous communities from polling places. The success also surprised the indigenous organizations, which had asked for guaranteed seats in the ANC on the assumption that their electoral efforts would fail. The Indians' electoral success has been attributed to the effective organization and steady growth of the Indian movement as well as the support received from nonindigenous urban voters. Indigenous leader Jesús Avirama cites the widespread disaffection of the popular classes with traditional politics, combined with a positive image of the Indian as the honest outsider (Avirama and Márquez 1994:85; Gros 1993:11, 15). One significant factor in the support achieved from nonindigenous sectors was the ample and positive media attention they received, which compensated for their lack of resources.[10]

No delegate from the black organizations was elected to the ANC because of a lack of financing, the weak politicization of blackness in general, lack of support from other sectors, and fragmentation among the Pacific Coast black communities. Manuel José Cepeda recalls that black organizations were less well organized than were indigenous ones at the time of the ANC. Even the tiny and remote Raizal population was better organized.[11] Some blacks reported voting for Rojas Birry or candidates of the Left, believing them to be better able to defend their interests than less-experienced black candidates (Asher 1998:47). The one Afro-Colombian elected, ADM-19 delegate Francisco Maturana, resigned on May 1 to fulfill commitments to the Spanish soccer team he coached; he was replaced by the next candidate on the ADM-19 list, who did not happen to be black. To compensate somewhat for the absence of blacks, the ANC leadership appointed black jurist Jacobo Pérez Escobar to the highly visible role of secretary-general of the assembly. Within the ANC the interests of blacks were defended mainly by Rojas Birry, the indigenous delegate from the predominantly black Chocó, and by sociologist Orlando Fals Borda, who, together with Rojas Birry and two other delegates chosen by the three ANC presidents, drafted and presented the only article specifically addressing the aspirations of the black communities (Pérez Ariana 1996). The indigenous delegates maintained close contact with Raizal and black organizations and included black activists within their teams of advisors.

The dramatic increase in pluralism in the ANC, symbolized by the presence of indigenous delegates and ex-guerrillas, was also marred by the small number of female delegates. Only four women were elected: labor activist Aida Abella (UP); lawyer and academic Helena Herrán (Liberal Party); poet María Mercedes Carranza (ADM-19); and lawyer, academic, and democracy activist María Teresa Garcés Lloreda (ADM-19). This poor showing can be attributed to the failure of the weak, diffuse feminist movement in Colombia to launch a successful candidate, as well as the failure of political parties (other than the ADM-19, which placed women sixth and seventh on its single list) to promote female candidates.

Alliances and Strategies

On the eve of the ANC, President Gaviria was poised to play a major role in the proceedings. Since his election, he had been the most important protagonist in the assembly preparations: negotiating the accord on ANC procedures with the major parties; overseeing the formulation of the legal argument that would assure the constitutional legality of the convocation of the assembly; providing a substantive proposal as a basis for debate; promoting citizen participation in the ANC elections and preparatory work; and negotiating with three guerrilla groups to lay down their arms and join the assembly. Once the ANC began, the president's leadership was vital, given the divisions within the traditional parties and the fragmentation and inexperience of nontraditional forces. The government's formal role was negotiated during the January negotiations on ANC rules of procedure. In order to prevent the government from dominating the process, the regulations stipulated that the government's proposals would be channeled to the ANC through Minister of Government Humberto de la Calle (Echeverri de Restrepo and Orejuela Díaz 1995:14–20).

After some initial problems resulting from heavy-handed attempts to control the agenda, the team headed by De la Calle became an important actor. De la Calle's low-key approach gained the government the confidence of most constituents (Dugas 1993a:55). President Gaviria continued to play an important role by resolving disputes and keeping the process on track. For example, he intervened personally to secure the agreement of the Liberal delegation to the idea of a collegial presidency that had been proposed by the other parties. He brokered the crucial tripartite deal that suspended the terms of the congress elected in 1990, prohibited ANC delegates from running in the next congressional elections, created a new Constitutional Court, and nixed the proposal of submitting the final text to a popular referendum (Dugas 1997:372; Lleras de la Fuente et al. 1992:20, 29–31). Those negotiations excluded the PSC and some of the Liberal Party leadership and circumvented the valid forum for such accords. The leaking of a tentative agreement to the press provoked a crisis within the Liberal Party, which almost led to their withdrawal from the tricephalous ANC presidency. It did result in the resignation of Conservative leader and ex-president Misael Pastrana, who referred to the pacts negotiated by the president as "dictatorship by agreement."[12] A final pact among the party leadership (the Casa de Nariño Political Accord) was signed on June 8, 1991. Thus, in addition to an open and pluralistic process of debate on the constitutional reform, a parallel process of elite pacts secured agreement on important procedural and substantive issues. In some cases, the constituents were not aware that these negotiations were taking place until they were leaked to the press.[13] Some observers argue that the exclusive nature of these pacts severely impaired the participative and deliberative nature of the assembly and, thus, the democratic character of the resulting constitution (Mejía Quintina and Formisano Prada 1998:62). As with the failure to include the FARC and ELN, these pacts presented serious birth defects for the new democratic order. Such inquietudes must be balanced against the possibility that without a certain amount of elite pact-making the constitution might not have been reformed.

On balance, the Gaviria government's efforts to shape the 1991 Constitution must be judged a success. It was most often part of the winning Liberal/ADM-19 voting alliance, and 85 percent of the Gaviria administration's proposal is included in the 1991 Constitution (Cepeda 1992a:appendix 2). Gaviria received a thunderous ovation from delegates assembled for the signing of the new charter and accolades from the press and public since that time.

The strategies and alliances of the various delegations within the ANC also contributed significantly to the mood within the ANC and the final outcome. These were derived from the fact that the two parties that had monopolized Colombian politics lacked a voting majority and were internally fragmented. The twenty-four Liberal delegates got to the ANC on twenty separate lists, following a strategy of promoting regionally strong candidates. Adding to the resulting incoherence of the Liberal Party as an actor within the ANC was the division of its leadership among Horacio Serpa, head of the Liberal delegation, César Gaviria, the Liberal president, and ex-president López Michelsen, head of the Liberal Party. Liberal Party fragmentation was demonstrated by the Liberals' voting record, which exhibited the lowest level of party loyalty in the ANC. Liberals offered eight separate global reform proposals (aside from the government's) and forty-three partial proposals—by far the most numerous offering of any party (Cepeda 1993:xi).

The most common voting alliance to form within the ANC was the forty-three-vote bloc formed by the Liberal Party and the ADM-19 in opposition to the loose alliance between the two conservative parties. The ADM-19 delegation was characterized by the diversity and independence of its members, who mixed cohesion on procedural issues with greater independence on substantive questions (Dugas 1993a:51). It included six former guerrillas, three Liberals, three Conservatives, and three labor activists. Despite this diversity, the ADM-19 exhibited the greatest cohesion and party discipline, which may have been due to the popularity and talents of its leader, Navarro Wolff, whom fellow delegates voted the most outstanding member of the assembly (Cepeda 1993:ix). The leadership and efficacy of Navarro Wolff and his party were apparent outside the assembly as well, with 70 percent of Colombians polled saying that he had done the best or the most in the ANC.[14] In addition to the nineteen seats won by the unified ADM-19 ticket, the party could count on the solidarity of the two indigenous delegates, the two UP delegates, as well as the four representatives of demobilized guerrilla groups (only two of whom could vote). In the context of fragmentation and open division in both the Conservative and Liberal groupings, this leftist block of twenty-seven out of seventy-four delegates enabled Navarro Wolff to have a say in all procedural and substantive decisions—as well as the opportunity (subsequently squandered) to position himself for the next presidential elections.

The ADM-19 was the linchpin of another key alliance within the ANC. It often joined with the MSN to counteract the Liberals' hegemonic pretensions, to promote more inclusive procedures, and to lay the groundwork for their political aspirations following the ANC. The MSN alternated between a strategic alliance with the ADM-19 on ANC governance and a programmatic alliance with other conservatives. Bitterly disappointed by its exclusion from the collegial presidency of the ANC, the PSC declined to accept any leadership position within the ANC.

Despite the minuscule size of its delegation, the indigenous movement also played a significant role in setting the mood and determining the results of the ANC. The ANC coincided with preliminary planning meetings for a hemisphere-wide protest organized by indigenous organizations to counter official quincentenary celebrations planned for 1992. Favorable publicity surrounding these events generated public sympathy for indigenous peoples immediately prior to the ANC. This political capital was useful to the indigenous delegates during the deliberations. As Gaviria's constitutional advisor recalls: "Once in the Constituent Assembly, their status grew. They became symbols. They represented more than their constituency: they represented tolerance and pluralism, a rediscovered national identity, historic reconciliation, justice, and the feeling that past grievances should be redressed" (Cepeda 1995c:105; translation by the author). Their novelty and distinctive appearance earned the indigenous delegates more than their share of press coverage, which they used to raise public awareness of issues of concern to indigenous communities outside the sphere of constitutional reform, particularly with respect to human rights. Publication by *El Tiempo* and *El Espectador* of numerous photos of the indigenous delegates amplified their importance within the ANC. The media made such a celebrity of Rojas Birry he won a seat on the Bogotá city council after the ANC. He was elected to the Senate in 1998.

Armed with this public sympathy, the indigenous delegates accomplished their goals within the assembly in a variety of ways. They made oral presentations to the assembled delegates, which were printed in the *Gaceta Constitucional* and picked up in the national press. In these presentations and in their written proposals the indigenous delegates argued repeatedly that the road to national unity and identity, consensus and reconciliation, was through recognition and protection of ethnic and cultural diversity. In social movement theoretical terms, the indigenous delegates "framed" their constitutional rights agenda in ways that resonated sympathetically with elites and the general public. Although they were only marginally part of the framing activity that put the convocation of a constituent assembly at the center of the nation's political agenda, by the time the ANC opened, indigenous organizations had developed their own frame linking the country's desperate need for institutional renovation to the problem of the exclusion and domination of disadvantaged groups. This frame had been developed through fifteen years of grassroots organizing and a year of intensified internal debates prior to the ANC, which allowed the indigenous organizations to construct a coherent frame that resonated with their members. For example, delegate Rojas Birry linked the Indians' goal of inserting a special chapter on ethnic rights in the constitution with the ANC's emphasis on reconciliation and participatory democracy:

> This is the best reason for ethnic groups to contribute to defining the future of the nation, so that we may assume the collective responsibility and solidarity of constructing a new nation, free of poverty, fear, and desperation. To the loss of values, to the progressive disintegration and crisis of Colombian society, it is necessary to respond by reforming the very bases of national identity: strengthening the ties of solidarity that have as a fundamental motive the respect for diversity, the recognition of difference, and the connection among them through participation. That connection must have as its motive the respect and recognition of our culture, of our ways of life. Our ways of life must be respected by the authorities and by all people: if not, the very values proclaimed by the new constitution (peace, liberty, equality) will be made null. The road to a democratic and pluralistic society requires the recognition and effective respect of ethnic and cultural diversity. (Rojas Birry 1991a:14; translation by author)

The frame was so successful that other delegates echoed the conceptual link between the recognition of indigenous rights, the creation of an effective new rights regime, and the peaceful building of consensus. As one UP delegate explained: "Now there is no reason to go to the mountains [as guerrillas] because the Indians are protected, the disadvantaged have their social protection" (cited in Kline 1999:168). President Gaviria and his advisors offered the protection of the rights of ethnic minorities as emblematic of the new regime of rights protection. Since the violation of fundamental rights was a principal cause of the violence that pervaded Colombian society, the protection of these rights, he argued, would help stop the violence. The Indians' frame, thus, resonated with the parallel framing efforts of Gaviria and his constitutional advisors. Following years of indigenous mobilization, a sector of the Liberal Party was receptive to the indigenous-rights agenda. Language similar to that in the article recognizing the "multiethnic and pluricultural character of the people," which was approved in the assembly by a 64-0 vote (with six abstentions) had been included in the Gaviria government's original proposal. Liberal president Virgilio Barco, Gaviria's predecessor, had promoted Colombia's signing of ILO Convention 169 on the rights of indigenous and tribal populations (signed by Gaviria during the ANC). The broad set of rights it contained provided a basis upon which indigenous delegates could make claims. After fifteen years of grassroots mobilization and public education—particularly through the framing activity developed around the Five Hundred Years of Resistance Campaign—indigenous peoples and cultures enjoyed a reservoir of public sympathy and admiration such that, in President Gaviria's opinion, no one in the ANC opposed granting some form of recognition.[15]

In addition to underscoring the government's emphasis on normative themes, recognition of indigenous rights furthered substantive goals. For example, recognizing indigenous authorities and territories implied a dramatic extension of the reach of a historically weak state into areas long dominated by extralegal authorities. Granting indigenous jurisdiction fosters the allegiance of indigenous authorities to the state while helping to establish the state as the source of authority. Recognizing indigenous customary law dramatically extends the reach of the rule of law, filling a geographically huge vacuum of legality.[16]

Individually or in coalition with others, the indigenous delegates signed ten reform proposals. These proposals shared a demand for various things:

recognition of the multiethnic and pluricultural character of Colombia; recognition of the political, administrative, and fiscal autonomy of ethnic territories; state protection for ethnic cultures and languages; greater representation of indigenous peoples in political bodies at all levels; participation in economic policy and planning decisions; and the inalienability of communal land rights. The most controversial ethnic rights proposals were those having to do with territorial rights, indigenous special legal jurisdiction, the status of native languages, and the scope of the national indigenous electoral district for the Congress. Agreement was reached on all these issues. Myriam Jimeno, who chaired the preparatory subcommission on multiethnicity, attributes this success to the indigenous delegates' early preparation, which included active participation in many state-sponsored and independent fora. Jimeno recalls that this process of "decanting" the indigenous proposals was enormously important in their refinement: it enabled the delegates to arrive at the ANC with viable proposals and with strong, informed support from their constituents. Once the ANC opened, they could focus on building alliances with other delegates.[17] The most successful alliance was formed with the ADM-19, which consistently voted with the indigenous delegates on their controversial territorial claims. Aside from the philosophical affinities between the indigenous delegates and the ADM-19, the M-19 guerrillas had enjoyed friendly relations with the sector of the Cauca indigenous movement represented by delegates Rojas Birry and Peña Chepe.

As Dugas argues, "external" framing processes usually are directed at the media, which have the resources social movements lack to disseminate the frame widely (1998:10). The indigenous delegates made dramatic appeals to the media and mobilized their organizations to sponsor demonstrations and public relations activities in support of their reform proposals. They maintained teams of experts to elaborate proposals and handle public relations. Political elites also used the news media to manipulate the significance of the indigenous delegates' presence in the ANC for their own purposes. Editorialists used the example of the inclusion of Indians in the ANC to demonstrate the representativeness of the body; to deflect charges that the ANC lacked legitimacy because of low turnout in the ANC elections; to demonstrate the link between the newfound heterogeneity of the political scene and the more participatory democratic model that the country sought; and to demonstrate the revolutionary nature of the constitutional reform (e.g., *El Espectador,* December 13, 1990).

Black organizations to a limited extent were able to take advantage of the political opportunities generated by the successful framing and alliance activities of the indigenous movement. But they were not as successful. Black organizations had weaker "mobilizing structures"—"those collective vehicles, informal as well as formal, through which people mobilize and engage in collective action" (McAdam, McCarthy, and Zald 1996:3). As Tarrow observes, "The most effective forms of organization are based on partly autonomous and contextually rooted local units linked by connective structures, and coordinated by formal organizations" (1998:124)—a good description of the Colombian indigenous movement in 1991. Black organizations had weaker and more contested collective identities, were less rooted in cultural traditions, and were less well connected to each other. In addition, the diverse black organizations could not agree among themselves on a legitimate frame, nor could they produce a frame with strong resonance among Afro-Colombians, because of the great diversity of experience and the absence of strong collective identity among this population. The frame that did emerge gained little sympathy from potential political allies or the media.[18]

The press generally ignored the activities staged by black activists and rarely ran photographs of or interviews with their leaders. One exception was coverage of the black organizations' May 22, 1991, occupation of the Haitian Embassy and several government and Church offices in Bogotá and major cities in the Chocó. The occupations were staged to provide a platform for insisting that their demands for the recognition of blacks as an ethnic group and their right to collective property be considered by the ANC. These protests and others had little impact. According to black activist Zulia Mena, Rojas Birry was responsible for convincing delegates to approve Transitory Article 55, with respect to black communal land rights, just minutes before the close of the assembly. He and Muelas threatened not to sign the charter unless it was approved.[19]

In sum, the constituent assembly provided a fortuitous "political opportunity"[20] for the already organized and mobilized indigenous movement to frame its particular grievances in more universalistic terms. Many of the movement's principal grievances could be linked conceptually or practically to the broad array of institutional questions encompassed by a wide-open constitutional reform process. Its challenges to the legitimacy of relations between the state and indigenous peoples struck a nerve in the context of a severe legitimacy crisis widely attributed to the lack of fit between state institutions and society. The indigenous movement was in a more mature stage of development at the time of the ANC than the black movement, was more capable of autonomous interaction with its environment, and was thus less susceptible to political opportunities in its environment than was the nascent black movement (McAdam, McCarthy, and Zald 1996:17–18).

The last few weeks of deliberations were hectic, as delegates rushed to meet the July 4 deadline, after which the assembly would be legally dissolved. During the last week of the ANC, Gaviria's Office of Indigenous Affairs worked full-time to resolve what had become a "crisis" between the government and the indigenous delegates, who threatened not to sign the final text of the constitution if their demands with respect to territorial rights were not included. Their refusal to sign would have impugned the legitimacy of the reform process, appearing to imply that the rights of the most excluded Colombian social group had been trampled upon.[21] On the last day of the assembly, accord was finally reached on the creation of special indigenous territories with a range of self-government rights, and on a more ambiguous and weaker set of black territorial rights. In order for the controversial articles to be passed, the language was deliberately left vague, with specifics left to statutory legislation. It would prove to be a hollow victory, as the lack of consensus on this issue would impede the full implementation of indigenous and black territorial rights.

On July 4, 1991, President Gaviria lifted the state of siege that had been imposed throughout the country in 1984, and the assembly elected a thirty-six-member Special Legislative Commission, or "mini-congress," to advise the president on legislative issues until December 1, 1991, when a new legislature would be seated. Colombian television covered the closing of the ANC, airing the speeches of President Gaviria and the three presidents of the ANC, and the procession of delegates that took turns signing as their colleagues applauded. Among the most loudly applauded that day were the three indigenous delegates and Gaviria's point man in the ANC, Humberto de la Calle.

Given the effort by the Gaviria government to promote every possible means of citizen participation in the constitutional reform, it seems incongruous that the resulting text was not submitted to a popular referendum—as the student movement, among others, had insisted.[22] The referendum had been nixed as part of the June 7 pact that dissolved Congress. The government fought to avoid a referendum on the new constitution for three reasons. First, Gaviria's team worried that low voter turnout might delegitimate the new charter; there had been three elections the previous year, resulting in some voter fatigue, indicated by a downward trend in turnout in 1990. Second, the team knew that referenda on broad projects such as constitutions had a high statistical likelihood of failure, as had occurred recently with Canada's Meech Lake Accord. Finally, Gaviria did not want to delay the implementation of articles of the constitution that were to become effective immediately and provide vital protections of rights and checks on government corruption.

The Constitutional Reforms

The new Colombian constitution was received with some trepidation both within and outside Colombia. The charter was immediately criticized for its excessive length, its inelegant and inconsistent language, for several contradictions and ambiguities, and, most vociferously, for the inclusion of diverse populist offerings and regulations that constitutional scholars considered best left to statutory law. Constituents defended the regulatory nature of the charter as being necessary to ensure that the revolutionary new order would be implemented by the counterrevolutionary political class, as well as to ensure that the most important provisions of the charter would enter into force immediately. Colombian constitution-makers rejected the view of many contemporary jurists and political theorists that the sole basis of political solidarity in the constitution should be the creation of rights and the mutual acceptance of procedures (Habermas 1994:125–39). The majority of constituents concurred that a strictly procedural charter would not inspire the patriotism or feeling of community necessary to establish a viable democratic regime. Colombians, thus, created a document permeated by ethical content.

The public was satisfied by the ceremony and hyperbole that accompanied the signing of the charter and the well-publicized fact that the charter had emerged as a result of consensus rather than imposition by stronger over weaker forces. Many public figures expressed their conviction that it represented a clear break from the bipartisan past, had cleared away many of the excesses and opportunities for corruption in the legislature, had strengthened and reformed the judiciary, and conveyed the yearnings of the Colombian people for peace, justice, and reconciliation (Dugas 1993b:24; Lleras de la Fuente et al. 1992:26).[23]

Participatory Democracy

The creation of a more participatory democracy was the sole substantive constitutional mandate provided by the seventh ballot. It is not surprising, then, that participatory democracy was widely extolled by constituents as the "cement of the entire structure" (Dugas 1993b:27). The word "participation" or "participatory" is invoked to modify "democracy" in the preamble and in Article 1, which describes the form of the regime and state (republican, unitary, decentralized, *democratic, participatory,* and pluralistic). In addition, Article 2 identifies fostering participatory democracy as a fundamental purpose of the state:

> The basic purposes of the state are to serve the community, promote the general prosperity, and guarantee the effectiveness of the principles, rights, and duties established by the Constitution, *facilitate participation by all in decisions affecting them and in the economic, political, administrative, and cultural life of the nation,* defend national independence, preserve territorial integrity, and ensure peaceful coexistence and the efficacy of a just order. (my emphasis)[24]

The participatory nature of the regime is further specified in Article 3, which observes that the people exercise their sovereignty through their representatives *and directly,* and in Article 40, which provides all citizens with the "right to participate in the makeup, exercise, and oversight of political power." Article 40 also specifies the activities and fora through which citizens exercise this right: voting and being elected; plebiscites and referenda; political parties and movements; the recall of municipal, departmental, and national representatives (except the president); the institution of criminal proceedings in defense of the constitution and laws; and in the performance of public functions and occupation of public positions. A new inserted title—Title 4, "Democratic Participation and Participation by Political Parties"—established all forms of direct democracy: elections, plebiscites, referenda,[25] popular consultations, open meetings, legislative initiatives, and recall (note the redundancy with respect to Article 40). As Benjamin Barber advises for the creation of "strong democracy," the direct democracy mechanisms are established not in isolation, but as part of a comprehensive effort to foster citizen involvement in a broad range of public decision-making activities (Barber 1984:263).

The constitution also created spaces for participation of civil society in governmental decision-making spheres. At the national level, sectoral and functional organizations such as ecological, ethnic, and social groups may participate in development-planning through their representatives on the National Planning Council (art. 340). Chapters regulating the various agencies and functions of the state also recognize the citizens' right to participate in decision-making. For example, the chapter on the Fiscalía General (Ch. 1, Title 10) provides for the law to "organize forms and systems for citizen participation, making it possible to monitor public management at the various administrative levels and its results."

Participatory democrats consider the creation of spheres for citizen participation in local government to be a vital part of the establishment of a participatory democratic regime. Only at the local level is it feasible for citizens to participate actively in decision-making on a regular basis and reap the transformative benefits of participation. In Colombia, the division of municipalities into *comunas* (in urban areas) or *corregimentos* (in rural areas), and the creation of directly elected local administrative juntas (JALs) for each, facilitate local participation. The JALs actually were created in 1987 as part of the municipal reform to replace weaker community action juntas (JACs), which had been established in 1958 by the first National Front government to reduce the cost of social programs (Archila 1995:271).[26] Although the JALs had raised expectations among civil society leaders in the late 1980s, they soon fell into disrepute because they proved unable to represent local interests and were overwhelmed by internal partisan conflicts and clientelism (Jaramillo 1996:40–51; Velásquez 1996:41). The intent of constitution-makers was to increase the political autonomy of the JALs and prevent their continued operation as patronage mechanisms. Toward this end, the constitution gave them the following rights and duties: "participation in the preparation of municipal plans and programs for economic and social development and public works"; monitoring and supervising the provision of municipal services and the investment of public funds; presenting investment proposals to the municipal, departmental, or national authorities; distributing the resources allocated to them in the municipal budget; and performing duties assigned by the municipal council or other local authorities (art. 318).

Although Colombia remains a unitary rather than a federal state, the 1991 Constitution strengthened the decentralization begun in 1986 by introducing the direct election of departmental governors, transferring administrative responsibility for many social programs to municipalities, and distributing unprecedented levels of financial resources for their management.[27] The distribution of this income among the country's more than one thousand municipalities is determined according to a formula that weighs total population, percentage of the population living in poverty or with unmet basic needs, the tax and administrative efficiency of the municipality, and "demonstrated progress in the quality of life" (art. 357). Departments and municipalities are also entitled to keep revenues from their own taxes and properties.

The 1991 Constitution promotes more tentatively the establishment of participatory spheres outside the state. For example, note the use of the word "may" in Article 57, which stipulates that "the law *may* establish the stimulus and means through which workers participate in the management of their enterprises" (my emphasis). Article 39 declares that the internal structure and functioning of labor and social organizations must operate according to democratic principles, but the inclusion of political parties in this article is noticeably absent (Restrepo Londoño 1996:30–31).

The participatory measures cited above and the recognition of participation as being among the highest-ranking fundamental principles in the constitution affirm the main themes of contemporary participatory democratic theory. Like participatory democrats, Colombian constitution-makers equated participation with the active involvement of common citizens in decision-making and envisioned this participation as central to the effective operation of government (Barber 1984; Pateman 1970; Vilas 1997:20). Participation in decision-making was viewed as conducive to societal reconciliation because it demonstrates to participants that all interests were considered and enables individuals to accept collective decisions that may not conform to their own personal interests—a crucial function in societies such as Colombia riven by social, cultural, and economic cleavages (Pateman 1970:25). Participation in decision-making provides an escape valve for societal pressures by making people aware of the scarcity of resources to satisfy competing demands and the necessity for compromise (Nino 1996: 52–53). Finally, and perhaps most important given the absence of social cohesion in Colombian society, participation plays an integrative function by inculcating a sense of belonging to a community through the regular interaction of diverse individuals in search of a common public good (Barber 1984; Pateman 1970:27).

Colombian constitution-makers also embraced the transformative effects that participatory democrats promote to improve the quality of individuals' lives, as well as the quality of democracy (Pateman 1970:22; Tocqueville 1988). The constitutionally mandated teaching of the constitution in all public and private educational institutions and the Gaviria government's Workshops for a New Citizen (a series of educational workshops conducted to teach citizens about their new constitutional rights) were designed to promote the transformation of Colombia's passive, submissive, individualistic citizens into an active, participatory national political community. Like participatory democrats, Colombian constitution-makers viewed participation as having a pedagogical function: to teach people to be concerned with the interests of others and the public good in general, which constitutional authors envisioned as being vital to the struggle against the multiple forms of violence and injustice that threatened the democratic regime.

As participatory democrats advise, the 1991 Constitution fosters autonomous civil society organizations, which prepare citizens for the exercise of the vote on important national issues (Pateman 1970:110; Tocqueville 1988). To promote a vigorous civil society, Article 103 instructs the state:

> Contribute to the organization, promotion, and training of nongovernmental professional, civic, union, community, young people's, benevolent, and public service associations without detriment to their autonomy, the intention being that they should constitute democratic mechanisms for representation in various bodies that may be established for participation, dialogue, control, and supervision in connection with public administration.

The constitution also empowers "social movements or significant groups of citizens" to register candidates for electoral office (art. 108). This is a significant advance and one that was denied social movements and civil society organizations in Bolivia. State financing for electoral activities is provided to parties and movements with legal status (achieved by gathering fifty thousand signatures, receiving that many votes, or achieving congressional representation in the previous election), and retroactively to parties, movements, and "significant groups of citizens" who obtain a minimum number of votes. Legally recognized parties and movements also have access (albeit minimal) to state-owned media.

One important aspect of democratic participation that Colombia's constitution-makers did not address was the problem of extreme economic inequality, which democratic theorists since Rousseau have viewed as inimical to the free and effective exercise of participation (Barber 1984:146; Pateman 1970; Putnam 1993:104–05). Aside from redistributing resources from the center to the periphery, the constitution makes no effort to redress extreme economic inequalities, which are without a doubt among the root causes of violence in Colombia.

Ethnic Recognition and Rights

According to Manuel José Cepeda, President Gaviria's constitutional advisor, the recognition and protection of ethnic rights are pillars of the new participatory democratic model. Protecting the rights of marginalized ethnic groups brings democracy to the bases and incorporates the most excluded sectors into the system. It is thus fundamental to the establishment of a more participatory regime.[28] In addition to facilitating in practice the incorporation of marginalized sectors, the public and official recognition of minority rights sends an important message to all formerly excluded groups that the era of exclusion and marginalization is over. The expression of a new multiethnic national identity symbolizes the inclusion of all disaffected political minorities into a more tolerant, pluralistic national political community. Only a national community—not an atomized set of particular interests and dispersed, competing power centers—was considered capable of resolving the grave problems challenging the Colombian state and society in the late twentieth century.

In addition to the unprecedented recognition of specific indigenous and black community rights outlined below, the new constitution makes it a duty of the state to "promote the conditions for real and effective equality and [to] adopt measures favoring groups which are discriminated against or underprivileged" (art. 13). Equality is promoted in two distinct ways: through the proscription of all forms of discrimination and through special measures to empower marginalized and disadvantaged groups to participate in political life. In so doing, constitution-makers made an argument for group-conscious policies similar to that of Iris Marion Young: A disadvantaged social group merits special group-conscious policies because its oppression by a dominant culture renders "its own experience invisible," which can only be remedied "by explicit attention to and expression of that group's specificity," and because such policies may be necessary "to affirm the solidarity of groups, to allow them to affirm their group affinities without suffering disadvantage in the wider society" (I. Young 1990:173–74). The constitution identifies indigenous peoples as the most deserving of disadvantaged social groups while acknowledging lesser rights for Pacific Coast blacks and Raizals. As Young notes, and the constitution affirms, indigenous peoples are a special case justifying a distinct legal status amounting to something akin to dual citizenship, because of their constitution as peoples prior to the creation of the state (1990:181). Not only does this status offer tangible protections and benefits, but it provides an important *symbolic* good, by affirming the version of history and their place in it long advanced by indigenous peoples and satisfying their psychic needs for recognition and identity.

Indigenous delegates failed to achieve a separate, comprehensive statement of ethnic rights. Cepeda recalls that the government wanted to avoid creating a "juridical ghetto" that would isolate and stigmatize Indians and other groups. This was vital to the government's project of recognizing diversity and bringing all Colombians into its vision of the nation. In retrospect, ex-delegate Francisco Rojas Birry does not consider the lack of a separate statement of indigenous rights to present any obstacle for indigenous peoples to exercise their rights. Similarly, indigenous delegates fought unsuccessfully for the explicit recognition of indigenous rights as collective rights. Again, because the government wanted to avoid creating rights that might be construed as divisive, the only collective rights acknowledged as such are those that may be enjoyed by all Colombians, such as environmental and consumer rights. Nevertheless (as will be discussed in chapter 4), the Constitutional Court has interpreted indigenous and black rights as collective rights, with the justification that this is the only way to fulfill the state's duty to foster and protect all forms of diversity.[29]

In Article 7, "The State recognizes and protects the ethnic and cultural diversity of the Colombian Nation." This achievement cannot be attributed solely to the efforts of the indigenous delegates, since similar language had been included in the Gaviria government's Decree 1926, which codified the understanding among the major parties prior to the ANC with respect to the content of the reforms. This accord also recognized indigenous authorities and cultures, the right to bilingual education, and indigenous property rights in *resguardo* and reserve lands. The indigenous delegates' key achievement in the constituent assembly was the institutionalization of the presence of Indians as a group with special rights in Colombian society. They are mentioned no fewer than twenty times throughout the constitution (Sánchez, Roldán, and Sánchez 1993:23, 66). More important, and for the first time in Colombian history, the constitution now recognizes the collective and inalienable nature of the country's existing *resguardos*. The recognition of the territoriality of indigenous communities (their *pre-constitutional* jurisdictional and autonomy rights over their traditional lands, as opposed to property rights), together with a share of state resource transfers, provides the material basis for the exercise of the Indians' right to difference under the constitution. The perception of indigenous territories as jurisdictions allows for the exercise of indigenous customary legal systems (to the extent they are not contrary to the constitution and laws) (art. 246), as well as the exercise of self-government rights by indigenous *cabildos* or other native forms of self-government. Provisions in Article 329 allowing for the consolidation of reserves into indigenous territorial entities (ETIs) created the possibility of forming vast autonomous regions in some areas. In addition, the constitution prohibits the exploitation of natural resources in native territories in any manner that harms the cultural, social, or economic integrity of indigenous communities, requiring such exploitation to be planned and implemented with the participation of representatives of the affected communities (art. 330). This provision is extremely important, because the ownership of subsoil resources such as petroleum was retained by the Colombian state under the new charter. The demand for recognition of indigenous rights over subsoil, water, and air space contiguous to their territories was the only aspiration that indigenous delegates failed to secure.

Article 171 created a national two-seat senatorial district for Indians, even though Indians had proved their electoral prowess in the ANC elections. The possibility of special black representation in the lower house was provided by Article 176, through which "the law may establish a special election district [yielding a maximum of five representatives] to ensure participation in the House of Representatives by ethnic groups, political minorities, and Colombians residing abroad." Ethnic minority representation complements a wider effort to increase the electoral chances of representatives of dispersed religious groups, political minorities, and peripheral regions through the creation of a national senate district.

Lesser rights were codified for the Afro-Colombian and Raizal populations, reflecting delegates' larger concern for promoting equality and environmental protection, rather than their recognition of blacks or Raizals as possessing special rights. Cepeda argues that the lesser recognition of the rights of Afro-Colombians is attributable to Colombians' perceptions that they are more integrated into society than indigenous peoples and that black Colombians do not suffer discrimination. While the public and fellow delegates perceived the Indians to be conciliatory, they considered black organizations to be "belligerent" (Cepeda 1995c:107). The lesser recognition of rights for blacks confirms Offe's proposition that the "willingness of majorities to grant group rights to minorities is contingent upon both properties of the minority in question and properties, perceptions and considerations of the majority" (1998:137). However, the Colombian experience disconfirms Offe's hypothesis that "those minorities who are most similar and show the greatest affinity with the majority in terms of cultural (phenotypic, ethnic, linguistic and religious) traits will be given priority in the granting of group rights" (1998:138). Blacks received lesser rights because of their greater assimilation into Colombian culture; greater rights for Indians were justified precisely by their extreme cultural alienation.

Transitory Article 55 recognizes the collective *property* rights of black communities in the lands they inhabit in the Pacific Coast riverine region, and calls on the state to respect their traditional culture and distinctive identity and to promote their economic and social development (Orjuela 1993:153). The rights addressed to this geographically specific population may be applied in other parts of the country where black communities exist in similar circumstances. Article 310 calls for a law to be devised to limit the rights of population movement and residence and to regulate the use of land and ownership of property for the purpose of preserving the cultural identity of the Raizal population in the Archipelago of San Andrés, Providencia, and Santa Catalina, to preserve its natural environment, and to guarantee the representation of Raizal communities in the archipelago's departmental assembly.

The constitutional rights regime is strengthened by the explicit constitutional incorporation of the principles of international human rights law. Also significant are constitutional measures to enforce both individual and collective rights. A new legal mechanism—*acción de tutela,* or the writ of protection (art. 86)—empowers citizens to appeal for immediate court action when their fundamental constitutional rights are violated and no other judicial means are available. By defending fundamental rights, the writ of protection is the crucial mechanism through which the 1991 Constitution helps to "construct legitimacy through the exercise of authority" (Cepeda 1992b:33).

Many Latin American constitutions have established constitutional courts devoted strictly to the study of constitutional questions and ombudsmen for the defense of human rights since the transitions to democracy of the 1970s (García Belaunde 1996a:30).[30] They were incorporated into most post-communist constitutions of eastern and central Europe, as well (Schwartz 1993). The Colombian constitution includes both: constitutional review was shifted from the Supreme Court to the newly created Constitutional Court, and the figure of the People's Defender (art. 282) was established in the autonomous Public Ministry to act as an institutional tool for the defense of constitutional and human rights. These new mechanisms would become central to the development and defense of ethnic rights in the constitution. As Kenneth Baynes argues, Liberal democratic guarantees of equal rights and special rights protecting cultural identities are insufficient to sustain democratic discourse in a multicultural political community. In such societies, state and society must endeavor to propagate a "militant tolerance" of diversity (Baynes 1992:64). The Constitutional Court would come to exemplify this "militant tolerance."

The Colombian constitution fully embraces neither the communitarian nor the traditional Liberal positions with respect to the rights of cultural communities. Instead, the text reflects the approach of Will Kymlicka (1989) and Yael Tamir (1993) of recuperating from the Liberal tradition the valorization of cultural membership as a necessity for the full realization of the Liberal vision of equality. However, on certain issues the constitution strays into the sphere of communitarianism, to assign rights directly to communities rather than to individuals, and to allow certain conditions under which cultural community rights may prevail over the freedom of individuals—for example, by recognizing the prevalence of the customary law of unacculturated indigenous communities. Colombian constitution-makers' inclination to support the "cultural survival argument" of communitarians —the idea that cultural associations merit protection apart from the rights of their members in order to ensure the survival of the culture in the face of internal and external threats—would be affirmed by the Constitutional Court, which has attempted to provide concrete guidelines for the harmonization of conflicting liberal and communitarian norms. The "cultural survival argument" is vehemently rejected by most political theorists claiming any ties to the Liberal tradition, including Kymlicka and Tamir.

Conclusion

The principal goals of the new constitution—making democratic institutions more participatory in order to establish governmental legitimacy and restore order; creating stronger, independent judicial institutions to fight arbitrariness and injustice, decentralizing administrative functions and political powers to improve the efficiency and penetration of public services —were conducive to claims for ethnic inclusion and participation in decision-making and for improved access to public services for Indians settled in peripheral areas. The more participatory conception of democracy sought by the Gaviria administration, the ANC delegates, and the majority of the public and the national cohesion necessary to collectively confront multiple crises required a more inclusive definition of the nation and a greater sphere of protection for minority rights to ensure the equal participation of all Colombians. The indigenous delegates helped the Gaviria administration and nontraditional forces in the ANC to successfully make the case that the only viable democratic regime for the country was a radically more participatory model, based in protection of fundamental rights. But not all indigenous aspirations were fulfilled. Those that conflicted with the goals of political elites represented in the ANC were either excluded or phrased in ambiguous language.

The 1886 Constitution had been created by eighteen relatively homogeneous delegates in eight months, following previously approved guidelines. The 1991 Constitution, in contrast, was drafted by seventy-four diverse delegates in four months. With no prior agreement with respect to the philosophical thrust of the document, the delegates considered 131 reform projects emanating from the delegates and the government, and around 200,000 proposals from municipalities and civil society groups that were generated during the working tables at the end of 1990 or were presented during the ANC. As President Gaviria observed, there are few countries that could argue as convincingly that their constitutions resulted from a collective creative act or represented a consensus of opinion among such a diverse and representative constituent body (República de Colombia 1991b:367–71).

4 Implementing the 1991 Colombian Constitution

The Rise of Rights and the Victory of Violence

T HE POLITICAL context for implementing the 1991 Constitution was mixed. The public mood was euphoric, heated by the adulatory media coverage surrounding the signing of the constitution. Determined to prevent their work from becoming a dead letter, the constituents had included a clause requiring the study of the constitution in all public and private educational institutions and directing the state to disseminate its text. National newspapers published the complete text, together with numerous articles explaining the implications of the reforms and their development by the government. A television-based public information campaign disseminated information about the constitution, particularly about the writ of protection. During the 1991–1992 academic year, the Superior School of Public Administration conducted 140 workshops on topics such as constitutional law, community participation, and municipal government, involving more than 7,835 Colombians from eleven departments. The Director-General for Indigenous Affairs (DGAI) commissioned the translation of the charter into seven major indigenous languages and collaborated with the National Organization of Colombian Indians on educational programs targeting the indigenous population. As a result of these targeted efforts, the indigenous population achieved a basic, general understanding of their constitutional rights.[1] Similar efforts were carried out by churches and grassroots organizations in the Pacific Coast region to educate Afro-Colombians about their rights.

As a result of these campaigns, for the first time the constitution became a topic of public conversation, rather than the specialized interest of legal scholars and judges. After a year of education on the content and implications of the reforms, 52 percent of Colombians held a favorable opinion of the constitution and roughly the same number believed it an improvement on the 1886 text. As the reforms became effective and information about them was disseminated, public opinion toward the constitution improved to 66 percent in 1994, the last year the government requested polling.[2] Public satisfaction with the constitution, however, was reduced by the return to pre-ANC levels of narco-terrorism and guerrilla violence and increased poverty and unemployment resulting from Gaviria's neoliberal economic policies and a recession that continued into 1999.

Implementation Efforts of the Gaviria Administration

President Gaviria's immediate priorities were to reform the judicial branch and to strengthen the institutions protecting citizens' rights. This entailed establishing new institutions such as the Constitutional Court, which Gaviria dubbed the "soul of the Constitution," its "guardian and protector"; the Office of the People's Defender (human rights ombudsman); and the Fiscalía General de la Nación,[3] an autonomous monitoring and prosecutorial agency atop the judicial system (Cepeda 1992a:376–79). Implementing legislation also was required to activate the constitution's direct democracy and citizen participation mechanisms and to modify the Procuraduría General de la Nación (national prosecutor's office) and move it from the judicial branch to the autonomous Public Ministry alongside the People's Defender. The new role of the Procuraduría General is to safeguard the independence and integrity of the judicial system, to protect the interests of the nation from abuses by public officials, and to work with the People's Defender to protect human rights. The office exercises a horizontal control function over the Fiscalía General and the entire judicial branch (Angel 1993:113–14).

The new justice minister, ex-constituent Fernando Carrillo, worked under intense pressure to prepare legislation implementing the judicial reforms prior to the installation of the new Congress on December 1, 1991. Strong, independent judicial institutions were vital to the constitution-makers' goal of establishing a regime of rights and providing nonviolent means of conflict resolution. On the basis of the experience of other countries, Gaviria and Carrillo were aware that if the judicial reforms were not institutionalized early, they might not be implemented at all. Aware of the possibility that the traditional political class might be resurrected in the October elections, the government worked around the clock to pass implementing legislation during the term of the special legislative session composed of ex-ANC delegates. Carrillo and the mini-congress also established the new office of the Fiscalía General, which would prove to be one of the most important new institutions by courageously denouncing links between drug traffickers and political institutions—an act that would have been unthinkable from anywhere in the prior government structure—while improving the efficiency of law enforcement. During its first year in office, the Fiscalía handled 186,000 of the 325,000 cases it inherited (Kline 1999:173). Because the office was born in the constituent assembly, like the Constitutional Court, its actions reflect legitimacy on the constitution as a whole.[4]

Implementation of Democratic Participation

The 1991 Constitution provides a wide array of opportunities for the insertion of individual and community participation in public policy-making and administration. The charter conceptualizes participation in three ways: as a fundamental principle, as a right and duty of citizens, and as a mechanism at the disposal of citizens (Posada E. 1998:157). Civil society leaders and social scientists have observed that the constitution's rhetorical emphasis on fostering participation has been contradicted by legislative provisions and government policies restricting access to effective participation: relegating it to voice without vote, confining it to implementation rather than the design of policies and programs, removing all possibility of citizen input in certain "off-limits" areas. In particular, citizen participation has been altogether removed from the spheres of macroeconomic policy-making and the deliberations of the National Congress (see, for example, Orjuela E. 1998; Mejía Quintina and Formisano Prada 1998; Posada E. 1998). The absence of participation and transparency in these two spheres is especially troubling given the origin of the Colombian state's legitimacy crisis in the incompetence, corruption, and partisanship of the Congress and the inability of the economic model to provide material well-being to the majority of the population.

The legislative and executive restrictions placed on the implementation of the direct democracy mechanisms contained in the constitution typify this counterreformist syndrome. During the assembly debate on the direct democracy mechanisms, delegates had expressed concern that political instability might result if they were too easy to use. Thus, the constitution itself established strict requirements to regulate their use. These restrictions were further increased by the president and Congress. For example, the original proposal of the Gaviria government to regulate the direct democracy mechanisms, fashioned in consultation with NGOs and social movements, included provisions to regulate the democratic participation of civil society organizations in the formulation of social policy. As ex-constituent María Teresa Garcés Lloreda recalls, the first post-ANC Congress further restricted the use of the direct democracy mechanisms, which were not regulated until the Samper administration, and removed the civil society aspects from the law:

> The original idea was to unite both aspects, because it seemed to us that in order to promote political participation we had to give more possibilities for nongovernmental organizations, social movements, with the consideration that isolated people could not do anything, and in Colombia there is very little tradition of participation and association. There is no organized civil society. So the object was to give civil society the tools to organize itself. But we were not able to get Congress to approve this aspect of the proposed law because there were a number of objections from members of Congress who complained that if they gave such importance to NGOs and social organizations, they would reduce the importance of political parties. And finally they were able to bury this aspect of the law.[5]

The direct democracy mechanisms would not be regulated until the Samper administration. The Gaviria government also restricted the scope of participation rights in the constitution. For example, under Article 278, the state was to create spheres for the participation of citizens and social organizations in decision-making and to promote the formation of citizens' oversight groups *(veedurías ciudadanas)* to oversee the investment of public funds. In the opinion of Inés de Brill, president of the Colombian Confederation of NGOs, although the Gaviria administration was committed to the establishment of the political participation mechanisms, it was less willing to open spaces for autonomous participation of civil society groups in public policy-making; spaces for participation created by law were obstructed in practice by government ministries.[6]

Implementing Ethnic Rights

The Gaviria administration responded to the demand of national indigenous organizations for participation in the development of their new constitutional rights by creating, within the DGAI, the National Commission on Indigenous Policy (CONAPI) on March 10, 1992. The most important and divisive issue CONAPI would consider was legislation implementing the new indigenous territorial regime. At the end of 1993, after a year and a half of intense negotiations and more than one hundred consultations with indigenous communities, the Gaviria administration achieved consensus on the issue with and among indigenous representatives. It appeared to be moving toward presentation to Congress when Vice Minister of Government Héctor Riveros was replaced and the project was stalled. Gaviria's indigenous affairs director, Luis José Azcárate, recalls that President Gaviria was supportive of the legislation but by the second half of his term had become distracted by more pressing problems, which enabled government functionaries and legislators representing the traditional political class to stall the establishment of the ETIs.

Other factors also were important. First, the unity of the indigenous movement dissipated following the ANC, when new opportunities for political office generated tensions within the leadership of the indigenous organizations and among organizations mobilizing for the 1991 congressional elections. Three indigenous political parties contested those elections: ONIC and Colombian Indigenous Authorities (AICO), the two organizations represented in the constituent assembly, and the Indigenous Social Alliance (ASI), a new party created by CRIC.[7] AICO and ONIC launched candidates in the special indigenous circumscription created by Article 171 of the constitution; ASI followed CRIC's long-standing policy of working in solidarity with other marginalized sectors and launched its candidate in the national circumscription, hoping to build on the urban base of popularity that indigenous leaders had gained during the ANC. Their expectations were fulfilled. In 1991, Colombians elected three indigenous senators and two indigenous representatives to the lower house, doubling the votes received by indigenous candidates in the ANC elections, with most votes coming from non-Indians in the major cities (Gros 1993:19–21).

In addition, the weak consensus on the ETIs within the ANC left the Indians without committed allies during the implementation phase. As Héctor Riveros and César Gaviria recall, during the ANC the government and the political parties lacked the information to evaluate the territorial demands of the better-prepared indigenous delegates. They resolved the impasse on this issue by incorporating vague language and postponing the specifics to statutory legislation. The implementation of the ETIs raised the thorny problem of land redistribution and territorial claims in a country with extreme inequality of land distribution, as well as the question of proprietary claims on valuable natural resources such as oil, gold, and timber on indigenous lands. It also raised the question of self-determination and indigenous authority in the one-quarter of Colombian territory belonging to Indians.

Colombian elites are particularly sensitive to threats to the country's territorial integrity in light of the painful loss of Panama and contemporary territorial disputes with Venezuela and Nicaragua. Establishment of ETIs would have required the adjustment of electoral districts for the lower house of Congress and departmental assemblies, upsetting the delicate partisan balance of power (Cepeda 1999:63). For all these reasons, President Gaviria recalls, while the entire process of approving the constitution's implementing legislation was difficult, the government encountered its greatest challenge in securing approval for the new territorial regime.[8]

In contrast, Government Ministry officials concur that significant progress was made on the constitution's mandate to create space for dialogue on indigenous policy through the various commissions created at the local, departmental, and national levels. For the first time, indigenous organizations and the state shifted from confrontation to reconciliation and dialogue. But, outside of the creation of some ethno-education programs and the participation of indigenous communities in a greater share of state resources through transfers to resguardos, there was little substantive progress made during the Gaviria administration because of divisions within the indigenous movement, the scarcity of resources, the lack of interest and goodwill on the part of some ministries, and frictions within the departmental governments.[9]

Even less progress was made toward implementing the constitutional rights of black communities. This reflected the lack of awareness on the part of government officials and the general public about the situation of the black communities. It also resulted from divisions within the black organizations—mainly between those pursuing increased participation for blacks in traditional politics and proportional access to state resources and those pursuing more "ethno-cultural" goals linked to identity, territory, and autonomy (Asher 1998:59–60)—as well as the fragmented black movement's lesser capacity to pressure the government or attract the media.[10]

Pursuant to Transitory Article 55, the Gaviria administration established a Special Commission for Black Communities to draft a proposed law implementing black constitutional rights on August 11, 1992, after considerable government delay. Parallel to the Special Commission discussions, as they had during the constituent assembly, black organizations sponsored a series of National Assemblies of Black Communities (July 1992, May 1993, September 1993) with the goal of crafting and monitoring the implementation of a consensus legislative proposal. Divisions among the diverse organizations prevented the achievement of consensus, but a draft black rights law was produced at the May 1993 meeting and formed the basis for negotiations between the black organizations and the government. Black Liberal senator Piedad Córdoba de Castro subsequently presented a version of this text to the Colombian Congress. Two important results of the September 1993 assembly were the establishment of a new black organization, the Process of Black Communities (PCN), to coordinate the efforts of 120 grassroots organizations to effect the implementation of black constitutional rights; and the effective distancing of this grassroots ethno-culturalist tendency from traditional, integrationist black politicians. Most black politicians and elites opposed the codification of special rights for blacks "not only because they feel that the law treats them like 'Indians' but because they want to integrate and be treated as regular Colombians—that is, they do not want to be singled out as an 'ethnic minority' at all" (Grueso, Rosero, and Escobar 1998:207).

Black representatives immediately clashed with the government on the definition of the "black communities" to which the constitutional rights would apply, a definition on which the constitution itself was ambiguous. Even among black organizations and anthropologists close to them there is a lack of consensus on this definition: Whether black communities exist in fact or only in the minds of some intellectuals; whether black cultural identity is rooted in a common history or is a project-in-progress, toward which black organizations should strive; whether black identity preceded the 1991 Constituent Assembly or was constructed subsequent to the creation of constitutional rights on the basis of which claims to cultural rights could be made; and whether it is better to speak of black cultural *identities* in the plural, to recognize a diversity of cultural experiences. Black organizations argued that the definition should include the entire black population; the government worked to limit its scope to the minority that lived in rural, traditional communities in the Pacific Coast lowlands (Asher 1998:54; Foro de ICAN 1993).[11] Black organizations engaged in a struggle with the Colombian state and among themselves to construct a legal definition of Afro-Colombian identity that would reflect their particular histories and realities and would support social, political, and economic reforms favorable to their constituencies (Asher 1998:7). Another obstacle to the implementation of black constitutional rights was the fact that the Pacific Coast black communities are located in one of the world's most biodiverse zones. State and private development interests in the biodiverse region of the Pacific Coast have impeded implementation of Transitory Article 55, since plans to complete the Panamerican highway threaten indigenous and black communities' chances of titling lands that lie in the path of the project, as well as the survival of already titled communities (Pardo-Rojas 1994; Wade 1993a:145).

The key piece of legislation developing black constitutional rights is Law 70 of 1993. (A separate 1993 law implemented the constitutional rights of the Raizal population.) According to Senator Córdoba problems with the elaboration of Law 70 began with the imprecision of Transitory Article 55 and its eleventh-hour approval during the assembly. The article failed to develop the cultural implications of the rights conferred and did not represent a clear commitment from the government to the assertion and protection of black cultural rights. The government failed to support her efforts to implement the constitutional commitment (art. 176) to provide two seats in the House of Representatives for representatives of the Pacific Coast black communities.[12] The minister of interior (the Ministry of Government became the Ministry of Interior on June 22, 1995) at the time did not accept the idea of the black seats, arguing that there were already two blacks in the House. In fact, for the past forty years blacks have held elected and appointed offices in the Pacific Coast—as mayors and in the police, in the departmental assembly, and in a variety of other state offices (Wade 1993a:116–17). The problem constitution-makers sought to remedy was not the exclusion of blacks as a racial or ethnic group from public office but, rather, the poor representation of certain rural black communities (Vásquez 1996:205–06). The two congressional seats eventually were inserted (as Law 70, Article 66) in time for the 1994 elections. On September 26, 1996, the Constitutional Court eliminated the electoral circumscription for black communities in the House of Representatives on the grounds that this statutory law had not been submitted to prior review by the Constitutional Court, as required by Article 153 of the constitution. In February 1997, Senator Córdoba submitted a legislative proposal to save the circumscription, but it was not approved.[13]

Despite the disappointment of black activists with the results of their negotiations with the government on the implementation of black community rights, activist Libia Grueso concludes that the process of exchange and debate fostered by the government was extremely worthwhile. It contributed to the generation of self-esteem among blacks (an important step in the development of a successful social movement) and significantly diminished the invisibility of black communities in the eyes of the government, which, following several years of debate, had a far better understanding of the conditions and diversity of the black communities. The difficult process of pressuring a disinterested government bureaucracy to pay attention to their demands helped the black organizations and grassroots movements to "construct a form of organized expression" with respect to the ethno-territorial problematic based on the recognition of the right to difference, "giving to the revindications of the black community a political connotation that until then had been confined to the plane of social demands" (Grueso 1995:5–6). Black organizations have stronger grassroots links than ever before: in 1997 there were more than eighty black organizations in Colombia, most of them created after 1991 and located in the Pacific Coast (Wade 1993b:182). The idea of black ethnic identity is more widely accepted among the black and nonblack populations (Wade 1993a:356–58). The processes leading up to the ANC in 1991, the assembly itself, and the efforts to implement black rights which followed, constitute the generation and consolidation of a new paradigm of ethnic difference that facilitated the first expression of an Afro-Colombian political project (E. Restrepo 1997:312).

Counterreform

Seven months after the new constitution was signed, President Gaviria's approval rating was 78.8 percent, with most respondents polled (53.6 percent) naming the constitutional reform as his greatest achievement.[14] But Gaviria's popularity and his progress in implementing the political reforms began to slip by the end of 1992. This decline is attributable to an intense battle with a Congress bent on its own interpretation of the constitution; a bruising conflict with the state telecommunications company; the failure of peace negotiations with the guerrillas; the escalation of drug and guerrilla violence; the demoralizing prison escape of drug cartel leader Pablo Escobar on July 22, 1992; and the unemployment and poverty generated by the government's structural adjustment program. The second half of Gaviria's presidency was consumed by these issues, leaving the implementation of the constitution in the hands of a legislature that had not been politically renewed, as constituents had hoped when they suspended the 1990 Congress. Throughout 1992, Congress declined to discuss statutory laws on citizen participation, political parties, or territorial organization. As a result, the Gaviria government was required to concentrate more on lobbying and negotiating to save the government's legislative proposals from substantial modifications and to get the Congress to act on important legislative projects (Revista Foro 1992b:1–3; Murrillo and Ungar 1996:59–60).

Implementation Efforts of the Samper Administration

In contrast to President Gaviria's impressive electoral mandate, his successor from the Liberal Party, Ernesto Samper, narrowly won a run-off election in 1994 to gain the presidency. After his inauguration on August 7, 1994, Samper was immediately beset by accusations by the losing candidate, Conservative Andrés Pastrana, that his election campaign knowingly accepted money from the Cali drug cartel. Added to the distractions was an increase in guerrilla and other forms of political violence and a mounting fiscal crisis. Thus, Samper's ability to focus on and to mobilize the bureaucracy in support of the implementation of the constitution was severely impaired. Staying in office absorbed an increasing amount of the president's energy. As a result, the implementation of the democratic reforms remained in the hands of a legislature that, following the 1994 elections, resembled even more the pre-ANC Congress (Murrillo and Ungar 1996:62).

Implementing Democracy Rights

Law 134 of 1994, approved early in the Samper administration, implemented the direct democracy mechanisms described in Article 103 of the constitution: the referendum, legislative initiative, revocation of mandate, plebiscite, popular consultation, and *cabildo abierto*.[15] In addition to placing excessive restrictions on the exercise of these mechanisms, the law is problematic with respect to another concern of participatory democrats: It fails to link political and social participation.[16] Aside from noting the right of civil society organizations to form vigilance committees, it leaves the development of the rights of civil society organizations to a future ordinary law. The Constitutional Court later ruled that the failure to develop statutory law with respect to the participation of civil society contradicts the constituents' clear intention to strengthen civil society and stimulate citizen participation in public management and its oversight. A civil society law approved by the government in consultation with civil society organizations in October 1996 awaited congressional action in late 1997, leaving existing norms with respect to the vital role of civil society in the realization of participatory democracy dispersed among more than a dozen laws. Although Pilar Gaitán and Ana María Bejarano cite half a dozen ordinary laws that incorporate a component of citizen participation, a number of important instruments in the constitution to facilitate popular participation and to hold government accountable have yet to be developed legislatively, and many commissions established to promote popular participation do not meet (Gaitán and Bejarano 1994:33).[17] Legislation implementing participatory mechanisms consistently subordinates participation to representation. Where citizens are permitted to participate in public service delivery, it is only with respect to implementation of policies designed elsewhere (Posada E. 1998:158).

In the latter half of 1996, the Samper government established an Interinstitutional Participation Committee (CIP) to enable ministries with responsibility for citizen participation to coordinate their efforts. After a year-long struggle by the Colombian Confederation of NGOs, five civil society leaders were allowed to serve on this committee. Its importance is questionable, however, since government participants are from low levels of the administration. Originally under the direct responsibility of Samper's vice president, Humberto de la Calle (Gaviria's representative before the ANC), the CIP was downgraded after de la Calle's resignation on September 10, 1996. It is seldom convened, and most tasks for which it was responsible have not been carried out. The Fund for Citizen Participation—created pursuant to the constitution's Article 103 to "finance programs that make effective citizen participation through the diffusion of its procedures, the training of the community for the exercise of the institutions and mechanisms recognized in this law, as well as the analysis and evaluation of participatory and communitarian behavior"—also has been a disappointment. It lacks resources and has failed to establish objective and transparent criteria by which to evaluate submitted proposals. According to De Brill, the main obstacle to the fund's education and training activities is the resistance to the idea of participation among government officials, who do not want to let go of their control over the design and implementation of policy.[18]

The Samper administration also secured legislative approval of Law 130 of 1994, which regulates political parties and movements pursuant to Articles 107–12 of the constitution. The statute provides state subsidies for political parties and movements, campaign financing, and access to government-controlled media and allows the National Electoral Council to establish limits on spending and to require reports from candidates on their sources of campaign funds. Since financing and media access are allocated according to existing representation in Congress or votes received in a prior election, the measures tend to favor larger parties. Law 130 does not require the internal democratization of political parties and movements, as many observers had hoped (Ungar 1995:113).

In addition to the problems discussed above, advancement of the democratization project also was sidelined by a lack of institutional coordination. The Interior Ministry was absorbed by its own structural transformation during Samper's term and unable to fulfill its responsibilities with respect to policy or to fund its increasing responsibilities, which include the offices of indigenous and black community affairs and the Citizen Participation Fund.

Implementing Ethnic Rights
The indigenous movement's 1991 electoral success resulted in the proliferation of indigenous party lists in the 1994 elections, when eight lists were

offered: three within the special indigenous district and five in the national district. As a result of this fragmentation, only the two most popular lists in the special indigenous district gained office.[19] In order to recuperate the unity and focus of the national indigenous movement, which had been harmed by factionalism and the distractions of electoral campaigning, the national indigenous organization ONIC renounced its party registration and bowed out of electoral politics. During the Samper government, ONIC struggled to establish its place in the state-indigenous dialogue following poor relations with the Gaviria administration, which tended to deal mainly with indigenous senators and congressional deputies. As Tarrow explains, following a "cycle of contention" such as the constituent assembly, a demobilization phase typically sets in. Factionalism occurs as those willing to compromise with state authorities or work through elected office or newly created spaces for dialogue differentiate themselves from activists preferring to maintain a more confrontational stance. Moderates seek to institutionalize the movement and relations with the state (Tarrow 1998:148–49). At the end of the twentieth century, Colombia's indigenous social movement was struggling to harmonize three competing social movement models identified by Dieter Rucht: the grassroots, informal network of local indigenous organizations and authorities; the interest-group model characterized by lobbying (ONIC); and the party-oriented model of the three indigenous parties (Rucht, cited in Dugas 1998:9).[20]

The Samper government failed to advance the constitutional agenda of ethnic rights and, in some respects, reversed the gains of the Gaviria administration. It terminated both CONAPI and the indigenous human rights committee. Indigenous activists, anthropologists, and international organizations sharply criticized Samper's DGAI, Gladys Jimeno, for her lack of experience with indigenous policy issues, for the poor lines of communications she established with indigenous organizations, and for her strategy of working with traditional community authorities and marginalizing the national and regional indigenous organizations from policy decisions and government programs. They contend that Jimeno's policy of excluding the national organizations has been a conscious attempt to weaken them and to use government and international resources to reward favored local and regional groups. This sort of strategy is described by McAdam, McCarthy, and Zald: "The presence of extremists encourages funding support for the moderates as a way of undercutting the influence of the radicals" (1996:14). According to Jimeno, the DGAI adopted the policy of working directly with communities or individual ethnic groups because the national indigenous organizations were not representative of the diverse indigenous population. Representatives of the multilateral Indigenous Peoples Fund observe that it has been common practice for governments reluctant to relinquish control over international funds to refuse to work with adversarial indigenous organizations on the grounds that they are not representative.[21]

The deterioration of state-indigenous relations has not been entirely Jimeno's fault. Her criticism of the representativity of the national and regional indigenous organizations has some validity, and ONIC's president, Abadio Green, adopted a confrontational stance, in part to counter the emergence of a state discourse less favorable to indigenous grievances. Jackson notes that a "new indigenous discourse is emerging in the national arena" which accords greater cultural authenticity and, thus, political legitimacy to traditional community authorities (Jackson 1999). This discourse puts the organizations into competition with the communities they claim to represent. It forces ONIC, for example, to argue that traditional community authorities are less competent than ONIC staff, which conflicts with its own line in favor of strengthening traditional authorities. Indigenous peoples' professional organizations are vulnerable to criticism, since the state and political elites can criticize the large indigenous organizations without suffering charges of Indian-bashing if they can hold up weak and fragmented indigenous authorities as more "authentic." As Jackson observes, this exacerbates the indigenous movement's leadership and representation dilemma: the more skilled and experienced its leaders become the less culturally "authentic" they appear to their own constituency and other actors. Moreover, while effective policy intervention requires a presence in national institutions, indigenous identity and authenticity are derived not from membership in the aggregative, artificial category of Indian but from membership in a particular indigenous community and language group (Jackson 1999; Iturralde 1997a:360).

According to indigenous Senator Lorenzo Muelas, the Samper government ignored indigenous proposals with respect to the Territorial Organization Law and failed to consult with indigenous communities and organizations on the pending Law of Frontiers, as required by law. Congress failed to take action on four successive drafts of legislation to establish the ETIs. In an effort to pressure the government to establish the constitution's indigenous territorial rights regime, on June 25, 1996, ONIC, other indigenous organizations, and the indigenous senators launched a series of mobilizations demanding that the government take action under Transitory Article 56 of the constitution, which authorizes it to take necessary measures to ensure the proper functioning of ETIs pending the promulgation of statutory legislation. The unity and public unanimity of indigenous organizations during this uprising demonstrated the maturity of the movement and its capacity to mobilize effectively on the national level, despite the problems within and among the organizations discussed here (Valencia 1997:265). The indigenous organizations and the government signed accords on August 9, 1996, which, among other things, reestablished the Gaviria-era commissions that the Samper government had dismantled. Indigenous representatives on the commissions claim that the government has failed to fulfill its commitments under the accords. According to anthropologists at the state's anthropology institute the project to implement the ETIs is dead.[22]

In 1994, President Samper established the Office of Black Communities and Ethnic Collectivities in the Government Ministry, pursuant to a provision inserted by Senator Córdoba in Law 70. Although Córdoba considered the mere creation of such an office to be a significant achievement, she was disappointed that a political ally of the government rather than someone with experience in the black rights movement was chosen to head the office. According to the office's director, Jenny de la Torre, rather than the defense of particular rights, the role of her office is "the recuperation of the spiritual values of the African peoples." Since it opened, the office has worked mainly on ethno-educational programs for black communities, the education and training of the Community Councils established in 1996 to oversee the land-titling process, and the development of the Samper government's policy with respect to the ethnic recognition of the black communities—a policy that had not been approved in February 1997.[23]

At a March 1995 government-sponsored conference on the implementation of Law 70, Vice Minister Juan Carlos Posada aired his concern that spaces for dialogue and participation created by the consultative commissions had been overtaken by a "permanent sense of conflict among the diverse organizations, groups and political forces," which was impeding productive working relations between the state and black communities. To clarify problems identified during the conference, in October 1995 the government issued Decree 1745, which further regulated Law 70 with respect to collective land titling and called for the establishment of democratically elected "community councils" to receive the titles and act as interlocutors with the government. The creation of the councils has generated conflict within the communities, because they emerge as rivals to existing councils of elders or other traditional authorities, and because the establishment of legitimate authority has been difficult owing to the destruction of traditional African forms of authority during centuries of slavery.[24]

In the judgment of black grassroots activist Carlos Rosero the key obstacle to the participation of black communities in the state's spaces for dialogue and participation is the great distance between the communities and those who purport to represent them (1996:180–81). In the impoverished Chocó region, political office and public service agencies are the main source of employment for the educated elite. With the country's smallest electoral population, the Chocó receives only a tiny portion of the national budget. These conditions of resource and status scarcity induce intense competition among educated blacks, while the economic dependence of the region renders insignificant the few government programs that are designed and implemented (Wade 1993a:117–19). The endemic problem of political conflict and frustrated professional aspirations has been aggravated in the Pacific Coast by the advance of narco-traffickers and by a guerrilla war in the northern part of the Chocó that intensified in the mid-1990s. These problems are compounded by a culture of political passivity in the communities that has been attributed to the self-serving and clientelistic behavior of black politicians and grassroots leaders and to the failure of black organizations to prioritize satisfaction of the communities' immediate basic needs. Although clientelism is pervasive among politicians in the Chocó, accusations of greed and venality spring also from a culture of equality and disdain for hierarchy and authority among the Pacific Coast black population. Those who rise through education to positions of prestige in the region are resented and suspected of achieving at the expense of others; those who leave in pursuit of opportunities are seen as traitors (Wade 1993a:324–25). An additional obstacle to substantive progress through implementation of Transitory Article 55 has been the low level of literacy and education among the rural black population, which the government has tried to address through training and education programs sponsored by the Office of Black Communities and the Education Ministry (Pérez Ariana 1996:98–109).[25]

The Growing Scandal and Samper's Counterreform

Declining public confidence in the government plummeted after a Liberal-dominated House of Representatives (the only government body constitutionally empowered to investigate the president) absolved President Samper of wrongdoing in a drug-money scandal connected to his presidential campaign. The scandal toppled Defense Minister Fernando Botero and tainted three other cabinet ministers charged with accepting illicit campaign contributions from the Cali cartel or covering up the scandal. Throughout 1996, 55 percent of Colombians polled believed the president could not be trusted and should resign; 52 percent opposed the House's exoneration of Samper; 80 percent believed that drug trafficking had infiltrated all major sectors of society, including politics and the economy.[26] One salutary result of the drug-money crisis was the unprecedented response of civil society organizations, which, in April 1996, formed a Citizens Monitoring Commission to follow the investigation and generated a process of "participation and collective deliberation" designed to "teach, for the first time and in a pedagogical manner, this type of exercise of participation."[27] The establishment of the commission followed a number of civil society actions staged to ensure that the scandal be adequately prosecuted and to demand public access to information on the investigations conducted by Congress and the comptroller general.

Although he was not implicated in the scandal, Humberto de la Calle resigned as Samper's vice president in September 1996 and urged the president to do the same for the good of the country. Carlos Lemos Simmonds, an ex-constituent and firm traditionalist warmly welcomed by the counterreform faction of the Liberal Party, replaced him.[28] De la Calle partially blames Samper and government minister (and former ANC copresident) Horacio Serpa for facilitating the resurgence of the traditional class and encouraging its drive to weaken the constitution. He believes the counterreform effort also indicates that consensus was weak on the rules of the game codified in the 1991 Constitution and that the government has failed to integrate into that consensus the powerful forces that did not participate in the ANC—the traditional politicians of the National Congress, the drug traffickers, and the active guerrilla movements.[29]

The Samper administration began work on a constitutional reform proposal emphasizing political party reform in May 1995. The opposition denounced the effort as a smoke screen to deflect attention from the drug-money scandal and the rampant corruption of the political class. Congress responded by establishing its own commission to study a broader array of state reforms, providing an opportunity for traditional politicians dissatisfied with the 1991 Constitution to propose ways to reverse its most offensive provisions, in particular, to tame the renegade Constitutional Court (*El Espectador*, Feb. 16, 1997:3a; Molina García 1996:3–4). On August 13, 1996, one month after the House exonerated Samper, the president sent Congress a constitutional reform project. Among the useful reforms proposed was the internal democratization of political parties, whose absence from the 1991 Constitution was seen as a major flaw by many analysts, as well as the total public financing of presidential campaigns, an effort to avoid the type of scandal that had destabilized the Samper government. Another interesting proposal was the obligatory vote, for a period of twelve years, in order to address the decline in voting since 1991. In order to lighten the severe backlog that had arisen in the court system, particularly at the highest levels, because of the public's enthusiastic exercise of the writ of protection and to eliminate contradictions among the findings of the higher courts, the project proposed the restriction of the writ of protection from use by the Supreme Court and from use against judicial sentences.

Democracy activists criticized the remainder of Samper's reforms as authoritarian. For example, Samper called for the removal of the Constitutional Court's control over the president's powers to impose states of exception.[30] Samper also sought to expand the powers of the police and military to fight corruption, crime, and impunity, rather than to address the source of these problems: the lack of public confidence in the security forces and justice system. Democracy activists complained that Samper's reforms restricted democratic representation and participation, restored electoral advantages to the traditional parties, and fostered clientelism. For example, Samper proposed the modification of the national senatorial district—which had provided unprecedented opportunities for political, religious, and ethnic minorities and eroded the powers of local and regional traditional party elites—on the grounds that it had denied representation to half the departments in the country. He proposed changes to the electoral calendar in order to unify national, departmental, and local elections. He argued disingenuously that electoral unification would help to consolidate local political movements and improve voter turnout. The measure had been proposed by the traditional parties, who would be the clear beneficiaries, since it increased their ability to influence all three levels of elections through clientelist incentives and to improve congressional representation through linkages to popular local candidates. Finally, the counterreform demonstrated a clear tendency to reverse the process of decentralization. Carlos Lleras de la Fuente, who had represented the Conservative MSN in the ANC, characterized Samper's reform as

> a type of rubbish behind which are hidden the political interests of a corrupt political class that is encrusted in the Congress of the Republic and which appears to be led by the Minister of Interior. . . . To try to reform something like 12 percent of the Constitution without consulting the people, almost behind their backs in the midst of a public order situation where people are preoccupied by the guerrillas, by coca trafficking, and by a series of problems of violence, seems to be irresponsible. (Cited in Jacinta Lizarazo 1996:4)

According to Manuel José Cepeda, "the counter-reform proposal does not seek to construct consensus, but to destroy it. It is a constitutional reform generated in opposition to the values of constitutionalism" (Cepeda 1997:15).

In early February 1997, the government withdrew the reform project from congressional consideration, in recognition of the vehement opposition of minority congressional parties and the press, as well as its imminent nullification on technical grounds by the Constitutional Court (it had been approved in the House without a quorum). Moreover, as the Congress's legal advisers informed Samper, the reform failed to incorporate the participation of citizens' organizations, as the constitution requires. The government announced it would seek a new reform project that would be the fruit of extensive negotiations among all political forces, but the opportunity receded as the 1998 presidential elections approached.[31]

The Role of the National Congress

Prior to entering into force, many aspects of the new constitution required implementing legislation, which subsequently must be reviewed by the Constitutional Court. As President Gaviria and many constituents had feared, the new Congress did not make faithful implementation of the constitution a priority. In the year following the ANC, Congress focused mainly on its own internal regulation and tax reform; the following year, congressional debates focused mainly on the escape of drug cartel leader Pablo Escobar. By the end of 1992, Congress had completed only 20 percent of the legislation required to implement the constitution's citizen participation mechanisms, one of the most popular aspects of the charter. Legislative activity was more vigorous the following year. By mid-1993, 80 percent of the statutory legislation to develop fundamental constitutional rights had been completed (Ungar 1995:107, 111).

Ungar cites the failure to renovate the composition of Congress as a main reason for the delay. The weakness of the independent parties and rules that facilitated bipartisan clientelist practices had allowed the traditional parties to recuperate their pre-ANC strength. Of 102 senators elected in the first elections following the ANC, 52 had served in the Senate dissolved by ANC delegates; only 40.3 percent of representatives in the lower house had not served in the prior legislature. Nontraditional forces, which were so important in the ANC, were less numerous and more isolated in the new Congress (Ungar 1995:104–05, 122). María Teresa Garcés Lloreda, who was among the ANC delegates in favor of prohibiting the delegates from running for congressional office as an ethical lesson for the country in self-sacrifice for the collective good, believed in 1997 that this had been a grave error, since it impeded the badly needed renovation of Congress.[32]

The swift resurgence of the traditional parties enabled them to launch a counterreform effort almost immediately. The effort ultimately failed. This counterreform attempt called for the elimination of the People's Defender, the limitation of the powers of the Fiscalía General, and the reestablishment of corrupting congressional prerogatives that had been eliminated by the 1991 Constitution. Elizabeth Ungar concludes that, rather than becoming an instrument for the establishment of governability and the implementation of the constitutional reform, the National Congress continued to impede the recuperation of the legitimacy of democratic institutions while eroding the fragile public belief in the benefits of the new constitution and the constitutional reform process (Ungar 1995:114–17).

The congressional representation of ethnic minorities since the ANC has been mainly symbolic rather than substantive. The indigenous senators and deputies are a small minority and have made mistakes as they learn to operate in a complex new environment. Indigenous senators have lost prestige amid charges of co-optation and corruption. Like their colleagues, indigenous politicians must satisfy their constituencies' demands for patronage and public works by cooperating with the government and traditional parties on close votes. To do so, they must avoid the political confrontation necessary to realize the greater goal of indigenous self-determination. The three indigenous senators during the 1991–1994 term successfully fought for legislation securing constitutionally mandated resource transfers to indigenous *resguardos,* which have been fundamental in endowing local *cabildos* with the resources to negotiate development policy with municipal governments. But they and those that followed failed at their greatest challenge— passing statutory legislation to create the ETIs and to secure their autonomous administration with respect to property rights, administration of justice and resources, and development policy (Rappaport and Dover 1996:23). As observed above, this may have been an impossible task, given the lack of consensus on these rights within the ANC itself and the firm congressional resistance since then.

After the passage of Law 70, black congressional representatives focused on inserting articles benefiting Afro-Colombians into various legislative proposals. Their achievements were hampered by their small numbers and their disinterest in working together. Given the lack of specificity with respect to the definition of black communities, and the general ignorance of black culture and identity, black representatives had to promote legislation based on more general constitutional principles of ethnic and cultural diversity (art. 7), pluralism (art. 1), equality of opportunities (art. 13), access to culture (art. 40), and participation (art. 2).

The Role of the Justice System

Because the movement for constitutional reform in 1990–1991 was in significant part a movement for justice, the reform of the judicial branch and the creation of new justice institutions have been crucial in gaining the confidence of the public in the new democratic regime. In the opinion of Fernando Carrillo, the establishment of new judicial institutions and mechanisms for the defense of rights was the most important result of the popular movement for a constituent assembly that he helped lead (1994:196–97).

No institution has been more important than the Constitutional Court in this regard. Through its rulings on concrete cases with respect to virtually all of the constitution's fundamental rights, in only its first year the court gained prestige among the Colombian people as a defender of the rights of the common citizen. That year the court issued 95 sentences of constitutionality and 210 revisions with respect to writs of protection (about half were conceded), providing a considerable body of jurisprudence for lower courts and legislators. In so doing, according to President Gaviria, the Constitutional Court helped to resolve one of the key problems giving rise to the spiral of violence that led to the ANC: arbitrariness, lodged in a disrespect for rights (Cepeda 1992a:385–91). Among its most important decisions are those that reduced impunity for human rights violations perpetrated by agents of the state. For example, an August 5, 1997, decision (C-358/97) limited the jurisdiction of military courts over military personnel accused of human rights violations and common crimes.

The Constitutional Court supports the democratization process by ensuring that "procedural rules and conditions of the democratic discussion and decision are satisfied," by protecting the autonomy of individuals so that they can contribute to the democratic process, and by making democratic decisions efficacious (Nino 1996:200). The Court has stepped in where the constitution is ambiguous or vague, usually interpreting the text in a spirit favorable to the protection of diversity and the opening of spheres for participation. For example, it has tried to fill the legal vacuum on the rights of civil society, which it interprets as a key protagonist in the establishment of participatory democracy.[33] The Court also has provided crucial institutional resistance to counterreform efforts. It curtailed congressional efforts to restrict citizen participation by striking down a provision in the statutory law implementing the direct democracy mechanisms that would have required prior judicial review. The Court also struck down language in the statutory law on political parties and elections that restricted the use of public campaign financing to those parties with congressional representation.

The writ of protection, the citizen's primary defense against the violation of fundamental constitutional rights, was among the first articles of the constitution to be implemented by the government during the tenure of the Special Legislative Commission. As critics feared, its establishment inspired an avalanche of complaints, which quickly began to stress the country's overloaded justice system. By mid-1993, sixteen thousand writs of protection had been presented to the Colombian courts; by mid-1996 more than one hundred thousand citizens had exercised the writ of protection (Pinzón 1993:35; Bernal 1996:18).[34] Court rulings have affirmed the negative right to equal treatment as well as the positive fundamental rights of vulnerable groups. Special attention has been paid to women, ethnic minorities, the mentally and physically handicapped, prisoners, domestic workers, homosexuals, and adolescents. The Court has established a practice of accepting cases only when a power inequality exists that places the fundamental rights of the weak in immediate peril, earning it a reputation as a defender of the powerless (Cepeda 1995b:17).

The indigenous population has been the object of some of the Court's most innovative rulings. As of 1999, more than thirty-seven rulings considered the issues of pluriculturalism, indigenous constitutional rights, and indigenous jurisdiction, an accumulated jurisprudence on the issue that is far more extensive than in any other Latin American country (Cepeda 1999:56; Gaviria Díaz 1998:134). The Court has tended to rule in favor of indigenous claims against the private interests of other Colombians, such as logging firms or missionary settlements, and has used both constitutional and international law in its rulings, in particular ILO Convention 169. When the Court has ruled against indigenous communities, it has done so in light of countervailing fundamental rights or public interests, such as the need to install radar at an airport situated adjacent to an indigenous reserve in order to fight drug trafficking. The court has upheld the fundamental right to the integrity of a community, establishing a precedent for the protection of collective rights, even though only individual rights are listed as fundamental rights. As Cepeda observes, "A judicial instrument conceived to protect individuals, according to the liberal tradition, was transformed into a tool to protect communitarian rights, according to the traditions of the ethnic minorities themselves" (Cepeda 1995b:18–19, 1995c:111). The Court also has protected the right of indigenous communities to collective property, to collective subsistence, and to the maintenance of cultural and ethnic diversity—both as a right of indigenous communities and as a mandate of the state to protect all kinds of diversity for the benefit of all Colombians. In Cepeda's accounting, twenty-three rulings have favored the indigenous community, six have favored an indigenous community member, six have gone against the community, and two have equally balanced community and noncommunity interests (1999:56).[35]

Among the most important constitutional rights gained by indigenous communities is the right to judge civil and criminal matters within indigenous territories according to indigenous law. The "Special Indigenous Jurisdiction" (art. 246) represents the culmination of a long struggle by Colombian indigenous communities and organizations for recognition of indigenous law and jurisdiction (Vásquez 1997:253). It is worth examining this right at some length. As Interior Minister Horacio Serpa observed at a government-sponsored conference on the topic, the articulation of special indigenous jurisdiction with Colombian law is one way that the plural nation is constructed "with regard to themes like the public and the private, the scope of state autonomy and that of indigenous peoples and territories, and the rights and duties of citizens and of national public and indigenous authorities" (Serpa 1997:22; translation by author).

In the absence of implementing legislation, in a 1994 decision (T-254) the Constitutional Court developed a standard for implementing this right. First, cultural traditions are to be respected, depending on the evaluating court's judgment with respect to the extent that those traditions have been preserved. That is, the more contact an indigenous community has had with Western culture, the less weight may be given to its cultural traditions. Critics contend that this gives courts the impossible task of measuring a concept as complex as cultural assimilation. Second, the decisions and sanctions imposed by indigenous tribunals must not violate fundamental constitutional rights or the international human rights incorporated therein. Finally, the Court established the supremacy of indigenous customary law over ordinary civil laws that conflict with cultural norms, and over legislation that does not specifically protect a constitutional right of the same rank as the right to cultural and ethnic diversity. A 1996 decision (T-496) extended the territorial scope of indigenous jurisdiction beyond indigenous territories in cases where a judge deems the cultural alienation of an indigenous defendant to warrant it.

In order to prepare Colombian courts for the challenge of applying the new standard, the government commissioned a study of the legal systems of twenty indigenous ethnic groups. Anthropologists have criticized the project for imposing Western positivist categories and concepts onto more flexible, oral traditions that defy such categorization, and for separating the practice of customary law from the fabric of indigenous society. Nevertheless, the process of anthropological recuperation and systematization has assisted indigenous communities that have not recently or consistently practiced their tradition of customary law in recuperating these traditions —a task that has become a priority within the indigenous movement.

The issue of special indigenous jurisdiction became national news in early 1997 when a conflict erupted between the Páez *cabildo* of Jambaló, Cauca, and seven indigenous defendants banished from the community, stripped of their political rights as Indians, and sentenced to varying numbers of lashes with a leather whip. The sentence, announced by *cabildo* authorities on December 24, 1996, followed the defendants' being convicted of publicly linking the town's indigenous mayor, Marden Betancur, to the paramilitaries and, thus, inspiring the Cacique Calarcá front, an indigenous sector of the ELN, to kill him on August 19, 1996. One of the accused, Francisco Gembuel, a Guambiano Indian living in the Páez community who received the harshest sentence, filed a writ of protection with a local court to prevent its fulfillment. The lower court ruled that the defendants had been denied the opportunity to defend themselves, that the judges in the case were biased, and that the whipping constituted torture and, therefore, was illegal under international law. A new investigation and trial were ordered. A higher court affirmed the ruling following an appeal by the Páez cabildos, adding that corporal punishment, even if it did no permanent physical harm, violated the defendants' fundamental constitutional rights.

The case gained international attention when Amnesty International accused the *cabildo* of condoning torture and, thus, violating international law. The case quickly became controversial within the indigenous movement as well, particularly in the Cauca, since the accused and the murdered mayor belonged to rival political factions of the regional indigenous organization CRIC and had been engaged in a hotly contested 1994 electoral battle for the mayorship of Jambaló. The local custom, after an election, is for the lesser political offices to be distributed among the losing factions; but in this case, all offices were taken by Betancur's winning slate, which escalated rather than lessened the hostilities. Páez leader Jesús Piñacué, president of the CRIC, publicly took the side of his political constituency in the *cabildo* against that of his rivals, thus disobeying the decision taken by the CRIC executive board (and the traditional practice of the organization) to remain neutral and seek reconciliation in such cases. (A former candidate for vice president and senator, Piñacué was accused of using the issue to gain national media attention. In fact, the following year he won election to the senate in the national circumscription with the highest placement ever of an indigenous candidate in nationwide balloting.) Gembuel's supporters note that the Jambaló *cabildo*'s ruling violated Páez norms of procedure—a claim sustained by a confidential memorandum to Piñacué from Carlos Perafán, an expert on Páez law and director of the government's project to codify indigenous law.[36] This is a serious issue, since one of the most important reservations that legal scholars have with respect to recognizing oral justice systems is the difficulty of ensuring that sentences are not arbitrary while allowing for the flexibility of justice as inextricably embedded in dynamic cultures. Gembuel's supporters also claim that Gembuel and his followers were persecuted because they are political rivals of the *cabildo* leadership, and that Piñacué exceeded his authority by becoming involved in the capture and judgment of the accused.

The Jambaló *cabildo* ultimately prevailed. On October 15, 1997, the Constitutional Court ruled that indigenous authorities could order the public whipping and expulsion of community members who violate indigenous laws. In his decision, Magistrate Carlos Gaviria Díaz concurred with the Páez Cabildo Association of the North that the intention of the whipping was not to cause excessive suffering but, rather, to represent the ritual purification of the indigenous violator and the restoration of harmony to the community. The extent of physical suffering was ruled insufficient to constitute torture. Gaviria concluded with the observation that only a high degree of autonomy would ensure cultural survival. This decision strengthens the autonomy of indigenous jurisdiction with respect to the standard devised by the Court in 1994. Not only were corporal punishment and expulsion ruled constitutional, but the Court in the Jambaló case applied its decision to a community whose level of cultural assimilation is relatively high. This would appear to lower the burden of proving cultural "purity" on the part of indigenous authorities. The decision also contributes to the inconsistencies demonstrated by the Constitutional Court in developing and applying special ethnic and fundamental constitutional rights—inconsistencies and contradictions that the magistrates themselves admit, and which reflect their lack of experience with the issues and categories presented by the constitution with respect to ethnic rights and the internal normative contradictions of the constitution itself (Gaviria Díaz 1997:162; Mosquera de Meneses 1997:282; Santos 1997:203). The Court has fluctuated between a vision that seeks a consensus on minimal universal norms and that restricts the exercise of indigenous jurisdiction accordingly, and a vision that fully recognizes an intangible sphere of ethnic diversity whose integral nature precludes restriction (Angarita 1998:111–12; Esther Sánchez 1997:291–92). With respect to the customary law issue, Magistrate Gaviria attributes the Court's vacillations to the ambiguous language of Article 246 (1998:134).

The larger impact of the Jambaló dispute is the alarm it generated within the indigenous movement over the intrusion of the state in what indigenous activists considered to be internal indigenous affairs, and the negative image of Indians, portrayed by the press as violators of human rights. In addition, the Jambaló case illuminated the extent to which indigenous culture and authority are internally contested. As a result, there has been an effort within indigenous organizations to recuperate knowledge of their justice systems, to strengthen traditional authorities, and to devise indigenous remedies for resolving disputes between the *cabildos* and the accused—for example, by establishing an indigenous institution to review controversial decisions so that Indians need not resort to nonindigenous courts.

The Constitutional Court has produced fewer rulings with respect to the rights of Afro-Colombians, reflecting their lesser set of rights in the constitution as well as their lesser experience before the courts. Three cases are interesting. In the first, the Court ruled against a private logging company in the Chocó and in favor of the right to cultural identity and collective property rights of black communities over areas that had not yet been legally titled as black collective lands. In the second, the Court upheld the special rights regime established by the constitution for the Raizal population, whose cultural integrity and autonomy are threatened by unmanaged immigration, development, and tourism. This case was also notable because the Court invited Raizal organizations to present their views of the matter to compensate for their lack of representation in the ANC (Cepeda 1995c:

115–16, 125–26). Finally, the Court ruled that blacks in the Atlantic Coast city of Santa Marta, although they are not organized according to the constitution's narrow definition of a black community, are entitled to the protections and positive measures extended to ethnic groups under the constitution by virtue of their having been victims in the past of social marginalization, "which has had negative repercussions on their access to economic, social, and cultural opportunities." The ruling is significant for Colombia's blacks because it expands the scope of the population protected under the constitution; it explicitly applies to blacks—as a racial as well as an economically disadvantaged group—the constitutional right to equality, as well as the state's duty to "adopt measures favoring groups which are discriminated against or underprivileged"; and it affirms the general interest of the public in promoting equality. The decision emphasized the socioeconomic marginalization of blacks while maintaining a sensitivity to the possibility that blacks would recuperate Afro-Colombian cultures on the basis of anthropological information and follow the path of indigenous peoples toward the (re)construction of ethnic identity.[37] Thus, it appears that at least a portion of the Court was receptive to the constitutional rights "frame" projected by the ethnoculturalist sector of the black movement.

As Cepeda argues, the Court's development of ethnic rights in the constitution has compensated for the weakness of ethnic actors in the legislative and political arenas and frustrated the efforts of legislators and the executive to stall the implementation of these rights or restrict their scope. The Court's actions have been particularly important in areas where implementing legislation has been stalled, since the Court has demonstrated a willingness to protect constitutional rights even in the absence of statutory legislation. For this reason, Cepeda argues that the Court's development of ethnic rights has had an impact beyond ethnic minorities, in that it has affected the general development of constitutional law and the role of the judicial branch (Cepeda 1995c:123). The example set by the Court in protecting the rights of society's most vulnerable groups has inspired other sectors to seek protection in the courts—a radical advance in a country where power relations have traditionally been based on force and privilege rather than rights. One measure of the writ of protection's success is its high public approval rating (see table 1). The problem remains that the Court can only affirm rights; it has no implementation or sanctioning powers.

TABLE 1

Favorability and Credibility of Institutions, October 1996 (in percentages)

Institution	Favorable/Unfavorable	Credibility/Noncredibilty
Writ of protection	80/13	83/16
Fiscalía General	76/17	78/22
Catholic Church	72/25	71/28
Media	68/26	68/30
Armed forces	62/32	58/40
Presidency	51/45	46/52
Congress	37/50	37/61
Guerrillas	6/90	6/92

Source: Napoleon Franco poll, 490 interviews, October 6, 1996.

Given the Constitutional Court's success in defending the rights of the weak, it is no surprise that the powerful have attempted to restrict its powers. Members of Congress and two national newspapers have accused the Court of assuming the powers of a constituent assembly and have called for its abolition and the return of judicial review to the Supreme Court. (Actually, the Constitutional Court has consistently rejected legislation expanding its review powers.) A June 1995 congressional effort to "pack" the Court with six new appointees and to require a two-thirds majority for the invalidation of statutory laws, treaties, and amendments narrowly failed. Another attack on the Court came in March 1997, when the Court struck down the state of economic emergency declared by President Samper, a decision Samper declared politically motivated. Interior Minister Horacio Serpa immediately submitted to Congress a constitutional reform proposal to exclude all questions concerning states of exception from the scope of the Court's review powers. Some politicians compared the president's actions to those of Guatemalan President Jorge Serrano, who in 1993 tried to dissolve Guatemala's Constitutional Court. But a sector of Congress received the proposal warmly; some legislators even called for the elimination of the Court. The Council of State and the Supreme Court submitted their own joint constitutional reform initiative, which proposed confining the use of the writ of protection to lower courts, and prohibiting its use to challenge judicial sentences, except in extreme cases.[38]

The People's Defender

The other institution that has performed the role of guardian of constitutional rights is the People's Defender (ombudsman) within the autonomous Public Ministry. The office is intended to function much differently than its Swedish ancestor, whose role is not political or adversarial and is primarily confined to correcting errors and sorting out largely procedural complaints brought by individuals against public administration and the courts. The Swedish ombudsman represents the Rikstag and does not take sides in disputes.[39] In Colombia, in contrast, its mission is to promote public knowledge of the constitution's fundamental rights and to bring claims in Colombian courts against state agencies on behalf of individuals or groups whose fundamental rights are violated.

The office includes a Delegate for Ethnic Minorities, who works with ethnic organizations to formulate grievances in legal terms to pressure or prosecute the offending government agency. The most famous case the Delegate has prosecuted is the U'wa Indians' objection to the Environment Ministry's February 3, 1995, decision to grant an environmental license to Occidental Petroleum to explore for oil in its traditional territory. The Delegate argued on behalf of the U'wa that the Environment Ministry violated their constitutional right to participation by issuing the license without effectively consulting tribal authorities. On February 3, 1997, the Constitutional Court ruled (5-4) in favor of the U'wa. The Court agreed that the U'wa had not been adequately consulted because the series of meetings organized by the Environment Ministry and the oil company in January 1995 failed to respect the U'wa's cultural mechanisms for decision-making and were not conducted in good faith—conditions required by the constitution and the statutory law creating the Environment Ministry. This ruling followed a similar one by the Superior Court of Bogotá on September 12, 1995, which had been overturned by the Colombian Supreme Court on October 19, 1995. The Superior Court ruling was significant in its own right, since, in addition to defending the U'wa's constitutional right to life, it was the first time "that an administrative decision [was] held to violate the rights of participation in decision-making processes. The idea of participatory democracy, the core of the new Constitution, began to bite, in spite of the general skepticism about its feasibility" (Cepeda 1995a:10–11). But the U'wa victory did not stand. One month later Colombia's Council of State, which has ultimate authority over questions of administrative procedure, ruled that the consultations were proper and the environmental license legal. In 1998 the Constitutional Court again supported an indigenous community against the government by declaring unconstitutional Decree 1320 of July 1998, which regulates the procedure for states to consult with indigenous and black communities.[40]

The U'wa case illuminates a major weakness in the Samper government's strategy to construct the multicultural state envisioned by the constitution. As government anthropologist Miguel Vásquez argues, the operationalization of the mechanism of prior consultation is the chief mechanism through which indigenous-state relations and the "interculturality" of the state project are negotiated and jointly constructed (1997:264). The failure of state agencies to converge on an effective operational definition of the term is, thus, troubling. Equally troubling is the Constitutional Court's failure to define the parameters of the constitutional right to "participation"—a right that is crucial to the conceptual and practical construction of a multicultural state, given the greater problems members of marginalized cultures face in securing effective representation and access to decision-making fora (Santos 1997:203).

The U'wa case also illuminates the obstacles that Colombia's indigenous peoples face in pressuring the government to implement ILO Convention 169 on the rights of indigenous and tribal peoples with respect to territorial and natural resource rights. This convention commits signatories to consult with indigenous communities and authorities on decisions with respect to "the formulation, implementation and evaluation of national and regional development plans and programs that may affect them directly" (art. 7), and to "establish or maintain procedures with a view toward consulting the interested peoples, in order to determine if their interests would be prejudiced and to what extent, prior to undertaking or authorizing any program of prospecting or exploration of the resources existing on their lands" (art. 15). According to Senator Muelas:

> The government has said that there are two things that cannot be discussed with the indigenous: land and natural resources. The rest the government is willing to discuss: education, health, etc. For this reason we are blocked, because for the Indians, life is rooted in the land. . . . One of the justificatory arguments of the Westerners for this is that the indigenous are against devel-

opment. But there is no real effort on the part of the West to understand the indigenous system. . . . Indians do not oppose development but, rather, ask for respect from the West for their forms of thinking, for their difference. Indians are also a non-renewable natural resource.[41]

Civil Society Efforts to Affect Reform Implementation

Civil society organizations contributed to the development of the constitution in three ways: disseminating information about the reforms; monitoring reform implementation; and improving the institutional capacity of community and sectoral organizations. According to Fernando Carrillo, citizens' organizations emerged in the 1990s for the first time in an effort to defend the 1991 Constitution. Although they have had little impact on government actions, they have helped to generate an understanding among political elites and sectors of the general public that civil society organizations have a legitimate role to play in balancing the power of the state and the market, a concept heretofore alien to a region whose public space has traditionally been dominated by the state and concentrated economic interests. Organizations like Viva la Ciudadanía constitute the minority of civil society that is practicing the new participatory, active political culture that the constitution was designed to support.[42] Viva la Ciudadanía formed part of the coalition of pro-democracy groups that established a Citizens Monitoring Commission in April 1996 to monitor the official investigation into the Samper drug-money scandal. In addition, invoking Article 270 of the constitution, which authorizes Colombian citizens to oversee public administration, in 1996 Viva la Ciudadanía helped to organize a national network of citizens' observer groups. Its impact has been modest because of the magnitude of the political crisis in Colombia and the far greater cohesiveness and resources of the political parties, the state, and private economic interests.

Conclusion

Factors in addition to those identified above also have impeded the faithful implementation of the constitution. First, in addition to the drug-money scandal, in 1997 the Fiscalía General was investigating 518 (roughly half) of the country's mayors for administrative wrongdoing, and the Procuraduría had suspended from office 6 of 33 departmental governors under investigation for irregularities with regard to the administration of the national lottery.[43] Endemic corruption absorbed scarce resources and counteracted efforts elsewhere to legitimate the new democratic regime.

Worsening economic conditions also inhibited the capacity of the Gaviria and Samper governments to address one of the major sources of conflict giving rise to the spiral of violence that spawned the 1991 ANC: extreme inequality of wealth, landholding, and income and massive amounts of urban and rural poverty. President Andrés Pastrana—who defeated Liberal candidate Horacio Serpa in a June 21, 1998, runoff—inherited "soaring unemployment and gaping government budget deficits" and has promised continued austerity.[44] The new economic model emphasizes privatization and market forces and has led to increased unemployment and the reduction of public social spending—factors that have weakened the ability of disadvantaged sectors to exploit the political opening.

> This restructuring is interrelated with a profound crisis of legitimacy and leadership suffered by the state and political regime in the last three decades.... This situation is reinforced by the neoliberal nature of the new model, whose excluding character and emphasis on reducing public spending limits the possibilities of elites to make alliances with other social sectors. (Orjuela E. 1998:56–59; translation by the author)

The political inclusion promised by the constitution has been impeded by the exclusion generated by macroeconomic policies and by the exclusionary manner in which the economic model was adopted and implemented (1998:60; Mejía Quintana and Formisano Prada 1998).

Finally, important perpetrators of the violence—the guerrillas, the paramilitaries, peasants, and the drug cartels—were not successfully incorporated into the constitutional debate and, thus, were not signatories to the "peace treaty." It is tempting to wonder whether the incorporation of the FARC and ELN into the ANC process might have resulted in a more effective and legitimate peace treaty. It is possible that, had the two groups demobilized in 1991, a main source of violence in Colombian society—and the rationale for the fastest-growing source (paramilitaries)—would not be present today.

Part II

Occasionally, it becomes sufficiently urgent to alter constitutional practice to maximize its moral legitimacy—either in
relation to the recognition of substantive rights or in relation to
the improvement of the democratic method—that one must
risk the continuity of the practice. On other occasions, it is so
important to prevent a break in the continuity of the practice
that we must permit solutions that are less satisfactory from the
moral point of view, although in the long run they are justified
on the basis of other moral considerations.

—Carlos Santiago Nino

To me it doesn't matter what color the cats are, only that they
catch rats.

—Gonzalo Sánchez de Lozada

5   The Struggle for Stability

The Bolivian Constitutional Conjuncture

F ROM A DISTANCE, the Bolivian process of constitutional reform could not be more different from the Colombian process. There was no National Constituent Assembly, no moment of national catharsis after the birth of a new order. The Bolivian reform process consisted mainly of closed-door negotiations among political party chiefs and deliberations among technical experts. The results were delivered piecemeal through a series of legislative packages over a four-year period. Yet the Bolivian process is similar to the Colombian in important respects. Gonzalo Sánchez de Lozada, as leader of the National Revolutionary Movement (MNR) Party and as the president presiding over the reforms, performed a role similar to that of Colombia's César Gaviria: he put radical constitutional reform on the political agenda, proposed substantive alternatives, forged elite consensus, and promoted the result to the public. As in Colombia, the indigenous movement and its advisors would play a major role in the constitutional reform by linking the indigenous agenda for recognition and rights to problems of weak national integration, fragile institutional legitimacy, and extreme inequality that troubled elites.

At the time of independence in 1825, Bolivia was the most predominantly Indian (73 percent) of the American republics, and its social and ethnic stratification was among the most rigid (Klein 1992:123). Bolivian society was really two societies: one Spanish, one Indian. Today Indians comprise

66 percent of the total population of about seven million, the largest proportion in South America (Psacharopoulos and Patrinos 1994). Since 1976, the majority of Bolivians speak Spanish, although many also speak indigenous languages. Four million speak either Aymara or Quechua, or both; and two hundred thousand speak one of thirty lowland languages. Indians are widely dispersed throughout the country, with approximately half living in communities on traditionally claimed lands; another 3 percent living as colonists in agricultural frontiers; and the remainder settled in cities, particularly in the Aymara migrant city of El Alto, which is perched above La Paz. Approximately thirty thousand Afro-Bolivians, descendants of slaves brought to work in the mines, are assimilated into the highland Aymara community and are considered an "indigenous people" by the state's office of indigenous affairs (República de Bolivia/VAIPO 1998:35).

Contemporary relations between the state and indigenous populations are rooted in Bolivia's 1952 social revolution. During the military government of 1946–1952, the political system rapidly disintegrated in the face of growing labor militancy. In 1951 the military forcibly prevented the MNR from assuming power following a landslide electoral victory. In April 1952 the MNR armed Indians and workers and overthrew the military government. The party rewarded Indian campesinos by abolishing *pongueaje* (the exchange of labor for the use of a small plot of land), supporting the campesino-led process of forced recuperation of communal lands, and enfranchising the illiterate. Supported by the national labor federation, the Bolivian Workers Central (COB) peasants organized their own militias and attacked the hacienda system. The MNR propagated a dense network of syndical unions to co-opt and control the campesino vote. In some areas, the MNR built on the structures of approximately 140 Andean *ayllus,* traditional native communities with discontinuous territories allowing economic production at different ecological levels. In other areas, where social organization may have been less structured, the MNR imposed the syndical structure. Elsewhere, the MNR co-opted independent campesino *sindicatos,* which were first established in the highlands by Quechua ex-combatants following the Chaco War (Ticona 1996:6). Campesinos are organized into local *sindicatos,* provincial *sub-centrales,* and *centrales,* which are joined in federations, usually at the departmental level. The MNR established a Ministry of Campesino Affairs and banned the term *"indio,"* effectively transforming ethnic collective social actors into an economic class and subordinating this class through corporatist ties (Assies 1998). The ethnic dimension of campesino identity would not be recuperated on a widespread basis until the early 1970s.

Once indigenous communities regained their lands, they became the conservative anchor of the MNR, acting over the next twenty years as a counterweight to the radical COB. After the military overthrew the MNR government of Víctor Paz Estenssoro in 1964, it inherited the allegiance of the peasantry by maintaining support for agrarian reform and co-opting the upper levels of the syndical structure (Albó and Barnadas 1990:243–64). General Hugo Banzer's military regime continued to support agrarian reform but, after 1971, worked to reduce the importance of Indians in national politics and to suppress their autonomous organizations. By this time many campesino *sindicatos* had joined the Independent Campesino Block, which had been established by disaffected campesino leaders in 1967 to protest a new tax on campesinos.

The Emergence of Independent Indigenous Organizations

An autonomous Indian leadership emerged within the peasant unions in the late 1960s. By the 1970s dramatic gains in literacy and access to formal education had fostered the emergence of a small Indian intelligentsia, particularly among the Aymara—by 1976, literacy had reached 67 percent of the school-age population (Klein 1992:265). Through the use of familial and community networks, and radio programs that linked the Aymara countryside and urban settlements, urban intellectuals engaged in a conversation with their rural counterparts in the burgeoning independent campesino movement. In 1973 Aymara students, intellectuals, clergy, and campesino leaders published the Manifesto of Tiwanaku, in which they denounced the economic and cultural oppression of the indigenous population and urged them to unite and liberate themselves. The manifesto provided the ideological foundation for an indigenous movement based on the then novel combination of the cultural-subordination discourse of Indian intellectuals and the existing leftist discourse of economic and political oppression. Between 1973 and 1979, Aymara intellectuals disseminated the manifesto throughout the Andean region and established a dense network of hierarchically arranged autonomous campesino organizations (Calla 1993; Hurtado Mercado 1995: 127–54; and Ticona, Rojas, and Albó 1995). The dissemination of the Manifesto of Tiwanaku represents the beginning of the framing process in Bolivia in which indigenous intellectuals and social movement organizations proposed as the solution to chronic political instability and endemic poverty an alternative model of state-society relations based on recognition of ethnic difference.

The 1974 government massacre of unarmed Quechua campesinos protesting agricultural policies at a roadblock near Cochabamba had a profound impact hundreds of miles away on Aymara intellectuals, who organized the Tupaj Katari movement in 1976 (Rivera 1987:144–46). The "Kataristas" shifted the political allegiance of the campesinos from the MNR and the military to the labor movement. In the process they transformed the labor movement by supplanting the waning influence of the miners and contributing a distinctive cultural analysis to its class-based rhetoric and syndical mode of organization (Rivera 1991:22). Several Katarista political parties emerged in the 1970s. They splintered along personalist and ideological lines throughout the 1980s until there were at one time more than ten Katarista parties. Kataristas considered the Bolivian state to be the enemy, which had made of Indians stateless nations and foreigners within their own ancestral territory. The Katarista parties sought not to join the political party system, considered a foreign imposition, but to replace it with a radically restructured multicultural, multilingual, and multinational Bolivian state that respects Indian autonomy. Rather than the Bolivian flag, these parties flew the Aymara *wiphala* and invoked the protection of indigenous deities and historical figures (Albó 1994:60; Hahn 1992:11; Le Bot 1988:229–31; Rivera 1987:156–57).

Taking advantage of the new democratic political environment and the surge in ethnic awareness stimulated by the Kataristas, in the 1980s the campesino movement expanded throughout the highlands. Katarista leaders formed the Bolivian Unitary Syndical Peasant Workers Confederation (CSUTCB) in 1979 at a conference organized by the COB to unify the fragmented and conflictive campesino movement and replace the government-controlled organization. The creation of independent, ethnically oriented confederations harks back to pre-Hispanic times, when diverse ethnic confederations existed in the central highlands (Izko 1993:193). The CSUTCB was the key instrument in the 1970s and the first half of the 1980s for placing the idea of "pluriculturality" on the political agenda and introducing the concept of "unity in diversity" into a wide range of political tendencies. In the late 1980s and early 1990s the concept was incorporated into the political discourse of the Left (mainly within the Free Bolivia Movement [MBL], a leftist political party formed in the mid-1980s), the emerging populist parties (most notably Conscience of the Fatherland [CONDEPA], a populist party formed in 1989 by media celebrity Carlos Palenque), and even of traditional parties such as the MNR, which was struggling to attract the ethnically diverse urban migrant population of La Paz. After 1985, the idea of ethnic and cultural diversity increasingly would be politicized as it was juxtaposed with the homogenizing, individualistic thrust of the neoliberal economic model (Calla 1992:50–54).

After 1985 the dynamism in the indigenous movement shifted from the highland-syndical wing of the indigenous movement to the lowland ethnic organizations (Calla 1993:56, 70–71). In the 1980s, Indians in the Amazon and Chaco began to form their own organizations to defend their territories and natural resources against increasing incursions by the expanding economic elite. Following a series of preliminary encounters, in 1982 the Indigenous Confederation of Eastern Bolivia (CIDOB) was formed to provide a united front against timber companies encroaching on lowland indigenous territories. In 1999 CIDOB represented twenty-eight local and regional organizations. In contrast to the CSUTCB, the Amazon groups originally did not demand access to state power or to become part of the official political system. They demanded that the state recognize their traditional territories and their autonomy within them. Amazon Indians are not campesinos but, rather, hunter-gatherers and artisans. They did not benefit from the 1952 or later agrarian reforms and so lack a history of loyalty to the MNR, the labor movement, the Left, or any other representative of the formal political system (Hahn 1992). The lowland movement constructed a frame based on a different experience of interaction with the state that competed with the Katarista discourse.

In 1990 a regional member organization of CIDOB, the Benian organization Indigenous Peoples Central of the Beni (CPIB) sponsored a March for Territory and Dignity, from Trinidad, the capital of the Beni. Seven hundred marchers left Trinidad on August 15 on a thirty-five-day, over-three-hundred-mile journey up rugged terrain to La Paz, which sits at four thousand meters (Albó 1996a:15). After arduous negotiations, the Indians were able to secure their main goal: a set of presidential decrees that titled in their names more than two million hectares of land, and a moratorium on timber harvesting in indigenous territory. Subsequent government actions brought the total to nine territories encompassing almost three million hectares (Ticona, Rojas, and Albo 1995:72). But the March for Territory and Dignity would take on greater importance. It had a dramatic impact on the awareness of the political class concerning the indigenous problematic; it made a national figure of CPIB leader Marcial Fabricano; and it provided a critical opportunity for organizing within the lowland indigenous movement and for coordination between the eastern lowland and western highland indigenous movements. The 1990 March for Territory and Dignity enabled both indigenous movements to disseminate their grievances through the mass media, which covered the march in detail. The comportment of the marchers and the justness of their grievances gained the movement important allies among the political elite.

On the date that the territorial decrees were issued the government announced the creation of a commission to draft a Law of Indigenous Peoples of the East and Amazon, which included representatives of CPIB and other indigenous organizations. This effort came to nothing, but President Jaime Paz Zamora did make a concerted effort to raise the profile of indigenous issues in Bolivian political circles and internationally. In addition to bringing the multilateral Indigenous Peoples Fund to La Paz, he was among the first Latin American presidents to sign and secure ratification of ILO Convention 169 on the rights of indigenous and tribal peoples. As in Colombia, the ratification of this international convention provided a basis upon which indigenous organizations could devise their own legal proposals and demand the fulfillment of their rights (Albó 1996b:337).

The Transition from Authoritarian Rule

Exhausted by the incompetence and corruption of the military government, in 1978 Bolivians began a tortuous transition to civilian rule, which was less a triumph for democracy than the disintegration of the armed forces as an institution (Lazarte 1991:588). Adding to the political chaos was the collapse of the economy, which, because of the mismanagement and corruption of the military regimes, had been recording negative growth rates since 1978. By the time of the transition, the national debt had spiraled out of control (Klein 1992:266–68). The disastrous economy and the unprecedented brutality and corruption of the García Meza regime galvanized the commitment of the business elite to restore democratic politics. The democratic era finally dawned in Bolivia in 1982, when a newly elected Congress selected as president the plurality winner of the 1980 elections, Hernán Siles Zuazo, leader of the leftist Democratic and Popular Unity (UDP) coalition. The election ended an era of instability marked by more than 170 coups d'état since Bolivian independence in 1825. The UDP's base of support was in the intellectual Left, the Bolivian Communist Party, and the labor movement. The redistributive demands of this constituency were not realistic in light of the urgent need for fiscal austerity and structural adjustment. Declining agricultural and mineral production—combined with Siles Zuazo's poor management and political skills—aggravated the situation, siphoning credibility from the government. By 1985 annual inflation topped the 8,000 percent mark, and Siles was forced to resign the presidency and convene early elections (Klein 1992:269–73).

An alliance between the MNR and General Banzer's center-right National Democratic Action Party (ADN) governed Bolivia between 1985 and 1989, led by longtime MNR caudillo Víctor Paz Estenssoro—his fourth and last stint as president of Bolivia. The MNR-ADN government was able to restore economic stability and serve out its term by imposing a drastic but effective structural adjustment program. The structural adjustment most severely hurt the Bolivian labor movement, whose militant vanguard was destroyed by the dismantling of the state mining companies. An estimated 40–45 percent of state miners and factory workers were fired between 1985 and 1987, accordingly reducing the size of the most politicized sectors of the labor movement (Calla 1993:73).

Amid the decline of the two traditional corporate actors in Bolivian politics—the labor confederation and the armed forces—in the 1980s, new civil society actors confronted the state directly. The principal actors in the new "informal politics" were the reorganized campesino and indigenous movements; local and departmental civic committees, among the few refuges for citizen protest during the authoritarian regimes of the 1970s; and business organizations, particularly the Bolivian Confederation of Private Entrepreneurs (Gamarra and Malloy 1995:411; Laserna 1997:11). The civic committees, which emerged in the 1970s, are the political expression of elite interests in the departmental capitals. They demand improved public services in urban areas and greater political and administrative autonomy for the departments and, hence, the departmental capitals where their constituents are based (Urioste and Baldomar 1996:31–32). Because the main constituency of the civic committees is the business sector, the civic committees overlap to some extent with the private sector organizations.

Constitutional Reform in Bolivia

The 1967 Bolivian Constitution, the country's fifteenth, had been promulgated by General René Barrientos, who overthrew the MNR government that had led the 1952 revolution. Following the established pattern, the de facto executive's constitution was sanctioned by a puppet constituent assembly. Bolivia has a long history of constituent assemblies, usually convoked by dictators to legitimate and institutionalize their rule. Constituent assemblies or national conventions previously, since 1826, had spawned fourteen new constitutions. Only the 1826 Constituent Assembly, however, merits the name, as the other fourteen were convoked by de facto executives to legitimate nondemocratic regimes (Galindo de Ugarte 1991). As in Colombia, Bolivia's constitutional history reflects the country's origin as a federation of states and the struggle between forces for centralization and decentralization. If one includes major constitutional reforms (as opposed to wholesale constitutional replacements), the average life span of a Bolivian constitution is eleven years, two months—not surprising for the most unstable political regime in South America (Harb and Moreno 1996:20). Nevertheless, some of Bolivia's most eminent constitutional historians argue that Bolivia really has had only one constitution—the 1826 Bolivarian text —whose structure and spirit were retained through the 1967 reform. Indeed, the 1967 version contains 111 of Bolivar's 157 articles (Galindo de Ugarte 1991:63–68). This essentially Liberal, centralist tradition was left behind by the 1994 reforms, inspiring some to refer to the post-1994 era as the "Second Republic" (Molina and Arias 1996:11).

Bolivia's 1967 Constitution contains rigid provisions for constitutional reform similar to the restrictions in Colombia's 1886 charter. Articles 230–31 require that constitutional reform be conducted via congressional promulgation of a Law of Necessity for Constitutional Reform that specifies the scope of the reform and must be approved by a two-thirds vote of this and the subsequent legislature. The 1967 Constitution—still in force—provides no means for its complete reform or replacement, only its modification. These rigid requirements have antecedents dating to the 1826 version; until 1994, they were systematically ignored. As in Colombia prior to 1991, Bolivia's constitution prohibits the popular referendum, although it was used once by a de facto executive in 1931. Article 4 states that the people deliberate and govern only through their representatives, effectively proscribing direct participation.

Three years prior to the Colombian Constituent Assembly, however, Bolivian proponents of an extra-constitutional method of comprehensive political reform based their arguments on the same Rousseauian and Sieyésian arguments as their Colombian colleagues, arguing that the constituent power of the people is omnipotent and, thus, cannot be constrained by the 1967 charter (Urcullo 1993:115–20). In the years leading up to the 1993–1994 reforms, this argument was adopted by the president of the Supreme Court and by the leftist MBL, which viewed the Colombian experience as a positive example. Surprisingly, popular organizations did not support the MBL campaign for a constituent assembly, fearing that any opportunity during the current neoliberal climate for elites to tamper with the gains made by campesinos and workers in the 1952 revolution, codified in the 1967 charter, would yield unfavorable results.[1] As a result, the sole "bottom-up" impetus for constitutional reform in the mid-1990s came indirectly from efforts to design a multicultural state promoted by the indigenous and campesino movements.

After the return to elected government in 1982, political elites began to suggest constitutional reforms to respond to the severe crisis of governability and economic stability that accompanied the difficult transition, as well as the problem of building and consolidating democratic institutions under a constitution created and imposed by a military regime. Social scientist Carlos Toranzo categorizes the structural and political pressure for constitutional reform in Bolivia as "the accumulation of problems." These consisted of rapid, unplanned urban migration and the concurrent depopulation of rural areas; the economic and political marginalization of the 42 percent of the population continuing to reside in rural areas; the lack of a national economic market to integrate producers and consumers; the absence of state services and authority in the majority of the territory; the fragmentation, clientelism, weak institutionalization, and lack of representativity of the political party system; as well as the second-highest poverty rate in the Western Hemisphere.[2] Although this set of problems did not engender the severe crisis of order and violence that distinguish the Colombian case, they generated interrelated crises of representation, participation, and legitimacy.

As in Colombia, during the 1980s and 1990s, Bolivian intellectuals argued that the political regime suffered from the lack of a pact between society and state—an argument with roots in Bolivian political thought dating to the writings of René Zavaleta in the 1960s and 1970s. Political scientist Jorge Lazarte argued at a forum in 1991:

> A State that can only produce compliance with its decisions by society through force is undoubtedly unable to produce consensus; the history of the country is a revelation of this impossibility. In general, there has been a fracture between the State and society or, said in another way, between the principles of legitimacy used by the State before a society that has not assimilated them. (Lazarte 1992:10; translation by author)

As in Colombia, in Bolivia the state was seen correctly to represent the private interests of a particular minority rather than the public interest (Lazarte 1992:11). As in Colombia, the problem of the state was tied to the imposition of a homogeneous national identity without basis in the actual ethnic, cultural, and regional diversity of Bolivian society. An interesting argument by Javier Sanjinés linked the absence of state legitimacy to a "crisis of sociocultural motivation" in the Habermasian sense. In societies as intensely stratified as Bolivia's, which reproduce relations of domination, it is impossible for most citizens to participate in the public sphere in the public discourse necessary to legitimate democracy. Added to this structural inadequacy is the neoliberal transformation of the Bolivian state after 1985 and its subjugation since the 1950s to international economic entities (the IMF, World Bank, USAID), leaving the state even more indifferent to, and impotent to regenerate, the bases of its own sociocultural legitimation. In this context, society is left susceptible to the "therapeutic theatre" of populism, to demagogy, and political vehicles willing to wield a socioculturally derived legitimating discourse and able to create alternative public spheres (Sanjinés 1992:75–86).

The "multicultural" aspects of the constitutional reform had little basis in existing policy. The 1967 Constitution made no reference to indigenous peoples or ethnic minorities, referring only to community lands and campesino syndicates. Ordinary legislation referring to Indians in force in the 1980s pertained primarily to the lowland indigenous population; it recognized the existence of indigenous customary law, declared the Indians not responsible for their actions because of their primitive state, and placed them under the protection of the state. The recognition of diverse indigenous cultures and authorities was the product of a rich debate during the 1980s among the Left, popular organizations, anthropologists, and Indian intellectuals on an alternative conception of a "pluricultural" Bolivian society and state, which might be achieved in the future through a comprehensive constitutional reform. Thus, the framing process that resulted in the insertion of multicultural and indigenous rights issues into the constitutional reform debate was a result of both autonomous efforts by indigenous organizations and interactions between these organizations and nonindigenous intellectuals aimed at identifying the sources of Bolivia's chronic political instability and at proposing a solution.

An early and influential example of the pluricultural state frame is the 1983 Political Thesis of the CSUTCB, published following its second national congress. The thesis calls for the establishment of a plurinational and pluricultural state in which the diversity of indigenous cultures and authentic forms of government are recognized and freely developed, as well as the provision of education in indigenous languages (CSUTCB 1983). The concept of a pluricultural state had been introduced in the CSUTCB's first Political Thesis in 1979 and was developed and radicalized through intensive debate among campesinos and intellectuals after the transition from military rule in 1982. It would ultimately penetrate the thinking of the highest levels of politics in Bolivia (Ticona 1996:14). In 1983 the CSUTCB proposed a Fundamental Agrarian Law that envisioned the radical transformation of the juridical, political, and administrative structure of the Bolivian state, and a radical break with the capitalist economic model. The central pillar of the proposal was the recognition of campesino communities as the principal form of social organization and the basis of campesino self-government. In 1984, the project was formally presented to Congress, where it was considered in committee but never brought to a vote. In 1985 it was presented to President Siles Zuazo. Neither he nor his successor, Víctor Paz Estenssoro, considered the proposal. A coauthor of that proposal was Aymara intellectual Víctor Hugo Cárdenas, who would become the first indigenous vice president in 1993 and a major participant in the 1993–1996 constitutional reform.

As in other countries of the Americas, in the early 1990s, Bolivia's campesino and indigenous movements prepared an organized, preemptive response to officially sponsored celebrations of the quincentenary being planned for 1992. As part of these efforts, the CSUTCB called for a new political constitution that would incorporate the history, authorities, and autonomy of the campesino majority into a "multinational and pluricultural state." The latter is defined as a state "with the right to participate, representative of the Original Nations, mestizo and black peoples, mutual respect among nations and classes, with equality of conditions, a state directed by the oppressed and exploited" (De la Cruz Willka 1992:17–18). The CIDOB developed its own institutional reform proposal, in light of the failure of the government-sponsored effort to draft a Law of Indigenous Peoples following the 1990 indigenous march. In 1992 CIDOB presented a proposed Indigenous Law, based on ILO Convention 169, signed by Bolivia on July 11, 1991, which called for recognition of the juridical personality of indigenous peoples and protected their collective rights, including recognition of their forms of government and social organization and customary legal systems, the right to preserve and develop their culture and ethnic identity, the right to hold land collectively, the right to "cultural, political, and administrative autonomy within their territorial jurisdiction," and the right to participate in politics. The Paz Zamora government never seriously considered the proposal, which was presented to Congress in 1993. The CIDOB proposal was considered by the Sánchez de Lozada government, and many of its key points were incorporated into the 1994 constitutional reform.[3]

Another important inspiration for the 1994 reforms was a series of workshops beginning in 1988 organized by the Center for the Investigation and Promotion of the Campesino (CIPCA). The workshops aimed to stimulate a broad dialogue on "the restructuring of the Bolivian state and society from the campesino and indigenous perspective" as an alternative to a state considered to be "colonialist and anti-campesino" and to projects of the traditional Left and the labor movement. Many of the most important figures involved in the 1993–1996 constitutional reforms took part. The volume resulting from the workshops (CIPCA 1991) offered a vision of radical decentralization based on the autonomy of local community governments comprised of campesino and indigenous organizations. These local community organizations would be linked through their autonomous regional federations to a multinational state congress. CIPCA proposed a corporatist, sectoral scheme of representation that would all but dispense with political parties and state and regional levels of government, while shifting the bulk of government policy decisions to sectoral organizations. Political parties would play a role only in the popular and direct election of the president.

This vision differed from the department-based decentralization schemes being proposed at the time by the civic committees. Traditional political analysts vilified CIPCA's proposal for dismissing the role of Bolivia's admittedly weak and unrepresentative political party system in democratic representation (Molina M. 1997:19). The CIPCA model would represent one pole of a critical debate that would later take place within the team working on the Law of Popular Participation, between a conception of participatory democracy that envisioned a central role for functional organizations and one that prioritized local, territorially based civil society organizations.

The CIPCA proposal was more extreme and baroque than a proposal formulated at the same time by the leftist MBL party in consultation with campesino organizations. Both models were based on the recognition of the juridical personality of indigenous and campesino communities and the radical expansion of the participation of these communities in the design and execution of social policy. MBL congressional deputy Miguel Urioste recalls that the proposal was an attempt to incorporate and make viable many of the aspects of the CSUTCB's 1983 proposed Fundamental Agrarian Law, including the demand for recognition of the identity, authorities, and jurisdiction of indigenous campesino communities, which had been the most important demand of highland Indians since the late nineteenth century. The MBL's proposal envisioned what Urioste calls a "tree of popular participation" to be constructed by social organizations within civil society, disconnected from the municipality and the state structure. By 1991 the municipality had become the space where civil society organizations interacted with the state. That year Urioste presented the Law of Communities to the lower house of Congress, where the justice and constitution commission declared it unconstitutional.[4]

As these efforts to articulate an alternative, "multicultural" model of the Bolivian state advanced, a parallel debate developed on the best way to decentralize the state to improve its efficiency and responsiveness to societal demands. Departmental elites, represented by the civic committees, advocated a department-based scheme that would heighten their political power and control over resources. Meanwhile, a small group of intellectuals argued that the municipality, an entity already recognized by the constitution, was the ideal space to articulate the diversity of Bolivia's civil society with the uniformity of the state apparatus (Molina M. 1997:23–24, 28).

In the late 1980s, Carlos Hugo Molina, a Santa Cruz law professor and legal advisor to CIDOB, became one of the most important advocates of municipal decentralization. The departmental decentralization movement was strongest in the prosperous and politically independent department of Santa Cruz. In 1986, Molina began to publish a series of articles in the local press arguing that municipal decentralization was the only viable route for a unitary country like Bolivia. Molina's writings were a direct response to politicians and civic leaders in Santa Cruz who were advocating department-based decentralization. It was also a critique of President Paz Zamora's January 1990 proposed Law of Organization of Departmental Governments (Molina S. 1994:7; Molina M. 1997:65). In 1991 the municipalization idea gained the support of two political parties—CONDEPA and the MNR. Both controlled important municipalities in the country and saw in the scheme a way to enhance their ability to effect change in opposition to the central government (Molina S. 1994:7).

The Constitution by Pact: The Paz Zamora Era Reforms
The constitutional reforms enacted in 1994 brought to fruition a process of reform that began in 1982 with the transition from authoritarian to elected civilian government and advanced with the installation of the new economic model by the MNR-ADN government (1985–1989). The MIR-ADN

government (1989–1993) revived the political and institutional reforms that had been put on hold during the economic crisis. Political reform became urgent in 1989 because of the drain on regime legitimacy caused by the ascension to the presidency of the third-place presidential candidate and the resulting inability of the government to lead the major structural reform considered necessary by most political elites.

Under Article 90 of the 1967 Constitution, in the event no party wins an absolute majority in presidential elections (a likely outcome in Bolivia's fragmented multiparty system), the National Congress chooses among the top three contenders. In this manner, Jaime Paz Zamora from the Movement of the Revolutionary Left (MIR), who finished third with 19.6 percent of the votes, assumed the presidency in 1989. Paz Zamora made a deal with second-place finisher Hugo Banzer of the ADN (who had 22.7 percent of the vote) to form a governing coalition that left first-place winner Gonzalo Sánchez de Lozada (with 23.07 percent) out of the government. As a result, Paz Zamora lacked the popular support necessary to build on the regime and state reforms of the Paz Estenssoro government.

Paz Zamora was in an even weaker position to lead a major structural reform than was Chilean President Salvador Allende in the early 1970s. Allende had been harshly criticized for trying to impose a major structural reform after having won only 37 percent of the vote. Compared to Paz Zamora, Allende at least had the advantage of having won first place. The weakness of Paz Zamora's mandate, his poor political skills, the fragmentation of the party system, and the militancy of civil society organizations such as the COB required the president to engage in extensive negotiations in order to further any legislative projects. An example of this syndrome of protracted negotiations and policy stalemate is the three-year failed effort to pass a decentralization law in consultation with the civic committees. In a country as fragmented, heterogeneous, and polarized as Bolivia, the achievement of absolute consensus is enormously difficult. President Paz Zamora's inability to lead was accentuated by the bicephalus nature of his presidency—a result of the programmatically illogical pact with the ADN's General Banzer that sent Paz Zamora to the presidential palace (Molina M. 1997:128–38, 430).

To address the weak legitimacy of his government and the democratic regime, Paz Zamora sought to reform Article 90. His agreement to a reform of the provision that had allowed him to gain the presidency generated a climate of trust in which the constitutional reform project could move forward. Paz Zamora, the ADN, and the MNR reached accord on electoral reform in February 1991. But because Paz Zamora lacked public support or political clout, more far-reaching structural reform had to wait. According to Paz Zamora's minister of the presidency and chief constitutional advisor, Gustavo Fernández Saavedra, the legitimacy crisis caused by Paz Zamora's thin electoral mandate was not the only catalyst to constitutional reform. Reform also was motivated by a conflict between the Supreme Court and the National Congress.

A group of MIR and ADN legislators—acting independently of the government and party leaders—had begun a series of politically motivated attacks on the MNR-dominated Supreme Court. As Eduardo Gamarra observed at the time: "This dispute has evolved into the gravest constitutional crisis facing Bolivia since the transition to democracy as the remaining four members of the Supreme Court attempt to administer justice while two thirds of their members are suspended" (Gamarra 1991:81). The judicial system was also in crisis because of the government's indictment of eight Supreme Court magistrates on charges of lying and the inability of the government to move forward with their cases or suspend the proceedings. In addition, constitutional problems arose in the 1991–1992 trial of ex-dictator General Luis García Meza, tried in absentia for crimes committed during his regime. Thus, an additional priority of the constitutional reform was the creation of professionalized judicial institutions independent of partisan control.[5]

In the absence of a steady, focused effort from President Paz Zamora to generate consensus among opposed political and social forces on the necessity and scope of constitutional reform, deliberations intensified within civil society and among intellectuals and the political parties. The legislature, the Supreme Court, national and international institutes and development agencies all sponsored a variety of fora to discuss alternatives. In response to pressure from these sectors, in June 1991 President Paz stated his intention to convoke a constituent assembly during national elections scheduled for 1993. According to Fernández, Paz Zamora never intended to convoke a constituent assembly. Within the MIR there was great trepidation about the danger of doing so, since the assembly would have unlimited power. Fernández, who had been ambassador to Brazil during its 1988 Constituent Assembly, and who had followed the process in Colombia, had fresh in his mind the many difficulties that had arisen in both cases. Aside from the political risks of a constituent assembly, Fernández and his MIR colleagues wanted to avoid the overly detailed character of both the Brazilian and the Colombian constitutions, which tends to result from negotiations among many particularistic interests.[6]

By the end of 1991, the political consensus in favor of a constituent assembly had shifted to a preference for employing the constitutionally prescribed route, that is, a law approved by two successive legislatures. Sánchez de Lozada's advisors and a majority of constitutional scholars vehemently opposed convoking a constituent assembly, arguing that Bolivia's new legal order must be grounded in a legally sanctioned process (Urcullo 1993:120–24). Proponents of the constituent assembly option could not argue as persuasively as their Colombian colleagues had either that the state and regime were so decomposed as to be considered "unconstituted" or that the "sovereign people" had in any way made evident their wish to reconstitute the Bolivian state. In Bolivia there was no spontaneous popular movement in favor of a constituent assembly, comparable to Colombia's student movement, that could provide political leaders with a "political fact" as potent as the "seventh ballot." This difference explains the choice of Bolivians to deviate from the Colombian example and past Bolivian practice.

Sánchez de Lozada's Constitutional Reform Project
Electoral reform was the principal motivation for constitutional reform for MNR party chief Gonzalo Sánchez de Lozada, who sought a mechanism to avoid a repeat of the 1989 presidential outcome, which had nullified his plurality victory. In the spring of 1991, the Fundación Milenio, a policy institute founded by Sánchez de Lozada in 1990, organized a project to elaborate a new constitution. With funding from the U.S. National Endowment for Democracy, the collaboration of Georgetown University, and the advice of a team of national and international political scientists and legal experts that included Carlos Santiago Nino and Juan Linz, the Fundación Milenio convened a series of seminars to develop viable alternative proposals for constitutional reform.[7] The consultants looked at a variety of constitutions and reform experiences, including the Colombian, which had concluded one

month before their first meeting. According to Bolivian consultant Fernando Aguirre, the Colombian and Brazilian constitutions were considered to represent poor examples, because of their excessive length and overly regulatory nature. The international and national consultants worked on all aspects of constitutional reform. Among their most important contributions were concepts and structures with respect to the recognition of indigenous authorities and modes of social organization, popular participation, decentralization, and a proposal to divide the entire territory into municipalities. The Fundación Milenio team had hoped to introduce the beginnings of the municipalization scheme into the constitutional reform but were concerned that there would be too much opposition from advocates of department-centered decentralization. Its final proposal did not include direct democracy mechanisms, which had been so important in the Colombian model. According to Juan Cristóbal Urioste, these were associated in the minds of the national consultants with authoritarian dictators and plebiscitarian politics, not with democracy. Similarly, later drafts of the proposal omitted the phrase "the people deliberate and participate directly in decision-making via means established by this Constitution."[8]

Sánchez de Lozada's announcement of his constitutional reform project, and the urging of international consultant Arturo Valenzuela, finally moved Paz Zamora to seriously address the constitutional reform issue in mid-1991. This decision also may have been influenced by the closing of the Colombian National Constituent Assembly in early July 1991, which was reported favorably in the Bolivian press. Following a congressionally sponsored seminar on constitutional reform in the fall of 1991, the six main political parties (and the Bolivian Confederation of Private Entrepreneurs) signed an accord promising to forge consensus on a constitutional reform proposal by August 1992. The parties declared their consensus on the following constitutional issues: the strengthening of the regime of individual rights and guarantees and the broadening and deepening of the democratic system; the need to take into account the rights of indigenous peoples and to conserve the natural environment; and the necessity of establishing the institutional and political independence of the judicial system. Disagreement persisted on important issues, including the process through which reforms should be made. The ADN, MNR, MIR, and CONDEPA supported the constitutionally defined route, whereas the MBL, UCS (United Civic

Solidarity; a recently formed populist party with growing representation in local government), and Supreme Court chief magistrate Edgar Oblitas called for a constituent assembly and/or a referendum. On July 9, 1992, eight of nine political party leaders signed an accord indicating their agreement to work on ten substantive themes, including constitutional reform. The need for such accords demonstrates the difficulty of undertaking institutional reform under conditions of party fragmentation and ineffective executive leadership.[9]

In August 1992, the Fundación Milenio sent its final proposal to political party chiefs and to the new Commission for Reform of the Constitution. The foundation's executive director described the proposal as follows:

> This proposal seeks to deepen the democratic process and the modernization of the country. In this context, special emphasis has been put on the consideration of themes that are fundamental to today's societies, such as human rights, the governability of the political system, the Constitutional Tribunal, the People's Defender, the environmental theme, the promotion of a democratic process of discussion and decision making, and the search for consensus in the designation of authorities crucial to the good functioning of the country. In sum, we have sought to design the framework for making Bolivia a more just, democratic, participative, and modern nation, and to give her the means with which to face with greater vigor the challenges of the 21st century.[10]

Thereafter, using the Fundación Milenio's proposal as a basis for discussion, Sánchez de Lozada negotiated directly with Banzer and Paz Zamora. Realizing that there was not enough time prior to the end of the legislative term to launch a comprehensive reform, the leaders decided to proceed only where substantial consensus existed and to defer action on controversial issues. In the end, four issues were chosen: the judicial reform; the reform of Article 90, governing the election of the president; the reform of Article 60, to elect half the seats in the lower house through single-member district; and administrative decentralization, beginning with the municipalization of the entire territory.[11]

Unexpected time remained prior to the end of the legislative session, enabling the party chiefs to work on a few other issues. These included the question of recognition and rights of the indigenous population. The Fundación Milenio team had prepared constitutional modifications with respect to this theme, which is addressed in Articles 1 and 171. Their work coincided with an awakening among the political elite to the importance of addressing the constitutional claims of the indigenous movement. President Paz Zamora had just issued decrees titling land to lowland indigenous peoples and had campaigned to establish the multilateral Indigenous Peoples Fund and base it in La Paz. Mainstream intellectuals and the political elite had been discussing the cultural and social origins of the institutional crisis since the 1990 March for Territory and Dignity and were receptive to cultural approaches to its resolution. Gustavo Fernández recalls that the 1990 march constituted a turning point in the Paz Zamora government's understanding of the ethnic question.

The government's first reaction was to respond in a classic policing fashion, to detain and disperse the marchers. But the Presidential Ministry prevented that response, arguing that the march had deep roots in Bolivian history and society and must be allowed to continue. According to Fernández, the march "allowed the country to discover itself" and brought to public consciousness an agenda of cultural identity and territory that was distinct from the campesino demands of the past, and that laid the basis for the recognition of the pluricultural nature of Bolivian society in the 1993 Law of Constitutional Reform.[12]

In addition, Iván Arias argues that in the early 1990s the Bolivian elite feared that an Indian-based guerrilla movement might emerge in Bolivia if an effort was not made to address the Indians' reasonable demands—a concern based on misguided conclusions about the origins of the Shining Path movement in the Indian highlands of neighboring Peru. These fears were stoked by the emergence in Bolivia between 1987 and 1990 of a variety of tiny armed movements taking Katarista-sounding names. According to Arias, the political class decided not to follow the Peruvian path. This decision created a "social disposition" to be receptive to the indigenous movement's demands.[13] In a 1993 interview Gonzalo Sánchez de Lozada explained the importance of having chosen Aymara leader Víctor Hugo Cárdenas as his running mate, observing that Cárdenas's presence on the ticket indicated to Bolivians that they need not fear an uprising like the Shining Path's in Peru, because this government would respect linguistic and cultural diversity (Mesa Gisbert 1993:229).

As the Paz Zamora government was developing its first policies in favor of indigenous demands, the national consultants on the Fundación Milenio team were taking up the ethnic issue under the direction of Carlos Hugo Molina, the municipalization advocate who had worked in the late 1980s as an advisor to CIDOB. As in Colombia, a main goal of the recognition of indigenous authorities was to extend the authority of the state and the rule of law to previously vacant terrain, which in Bolivia covered a majority of the territory. Juan Cristóbal Urioste recalled:

> We realized that it would have been impossible to govern these areas if there had not been a special law for the Indians, as there always had been in the colonial era. We did not have very much time, so we basically took it from the Colombian constitution, although, in Colombia, this was always treated in terms of minorities. In our thinking, we focused on the idea of authorities elected by the communities who could exercise administrative and jurisdictional functions.

The issue was a new one for Sánchez de Lozada, who was more familiar with the highland campesino problematic. Nevertheless, according to Molina, he was receptive to both the cultural and the territorial issues being raised by the lowland organizations. Despite the elite predisposition to address the indigenous organizations' demands, the ideas proposed by the Fundación Milenio consultants were controversial and there was a great deal of opposition, particularly from President Paz Zamora. Thus, the original language with respect to indigenous rights was significantly reduced by the time it entered the 1993 Law of Necessity of Constitutional Reform. But the germ of the idea remained—the formal recognition of indigenous authorities and the creation of an institutional linkage between indigenous authorities and territories and the state.[14]

In March 1993, the ordinary session of Congress having adjourned, President Paz Zamora convened an extraordinary session to deliberate on the government's proposed Law of Necessity for Constitutional Reform. Contemporaneous newspaper accounts report that members of Congress were furious about having received the text only minutes prior to the scheduled debate. This insult caused some to walk out in protest, which cleared the way for its approval without modification. The law had been negotiated among the three party leaders (whose parties had the two-thirds of votes necessary for approval) without consulting opposition parties or sectors of civil society, causing a senator from one of the three parties to quip, "The table is set; everything has already been cooked."[15] The press and public had no knowledge of the law until the Senate passed it on March 23. The project was then left to await consideration by the new legislature, to be seated in August.

This methodology of reforms by pact, negotiated in secret and pushed through the legislature via a voting majority, would continue to characterize the constitutional reform during the following administration, as Sánchez de Lozada attempted to outmaneuver the opposition. The most important opposition to the Law of Necessity came from the country's strongest civic committees in Cochabamba, Santa Cruz, and Chuquisaca, whose leaders argued that the reform did not go far enough in the area of departmental decentralization. The civic committees would continue to lobby for greater decentralization throughout the Sánchez de Lozada and Banzer administrations.

Conclusion

In his second run for the presidency, Sánchez de Lozada chose as his vice presidential running mate Víctor Hugo Cárdenas, an Aymara linguist and leader of the Katarista movement since 1978. Cárdenas represented the largest Katarista party in Congress between 1985 and 1989, Tupaj Katari Revolutionary Liberation Movement (MRTKL), and was its presidential candidate in 1989. The controversial choice capitalized on the growing popularity of indigenous themes in the early 1990s. Although militants within the MNR came to see the wisdom of the alliance, Cárdenas's former colleagues condemned him as a traitor (Albó 1994:65–68).

In May 1993 Sánchez de Lozada presented the MNR-MRTKL's Plan for Everyone *(Plan de Todos)*, which set forth the candidates' vision for political reform. The plan had benefited from discussions with the Fundación Milenio constitutional reform team, which had functioned between 1990 and 1992 as a sort of think tank in which a dialogue on constitutional reform among various parties and political tendencies matured. The team's ideas and suggestions were incorporated by other parties, such as CONDEPA, which included Carlos Hugo Molina's decentralization model in its electoral platform (Molina M. 1997:179–80). In the lofty language typical of a campaign document, the Plan calls for the modernization of the state, the reactivation of the moribund economy, the veneration of the country's cultural diversity, the construction of a stable legal order, and the transformation of the nation via a democratic revolution at the municipal level. Although the concrete mechanisms of what would become the Law of Popular Participation had not yet crystallized in early 1993, the Plan locates the space for popular participation in the municipality through the operation of "legitimate and authorized" civil society organizations, which may include native authorities and organizations, and new specialized committees. The goal of the participation of popular organizations in government is not solely to make social policy implementation more efficient but also to empower the people to control state resources and, thereby, to progressively improve social equity. The Plan proposes that state services be provided through community-based committees for each sector, which would decide their own priorities, make proposals, and oversee their execution by local government—an idea based on the experience of popular health committees during the MNR-ADN government. The Plan conceives of representative and participatory democracy as complementary, mutually reinforcing systems articulated in the municipality, as in the MBL's Law of Indigenous and Campesino Communities. The MNR-MRTKL campaign disseminated the Plan widely through the media. It was debated in the press and in a variety of public fora. Thus, Sánchez de Lozada could later argue, as had Gaviria in Colombia, that the people had given him a mandate to expand popular participation in government.

In the June 1993 elections, Sánchez de Lozada and Cárdenas won 35.6 percent of valid votes in a field of fourteen candidates—fourteen percentage points more than the runner-up ADN-MIR ticket, and the widest victory margin of any candidate since the military annulled the 1980 elections. The decisive victory gave Sánchez de Lozada's MNR a majority 17 of 27 seats in the Senate, and 51 of 130 seats in the Chamber of Deputies. Although Cárdenas was not wholly responsible for the decisive win, many analysts attributed to Cárdenas the ticket's win in the majority Aymara department of La Paz, which the MNR had not carried since the democratic transition. Thus, despite the small size of his party, Cárdenas's contribution to the electoral victory gave him considerable influence as the new government entered office in August 1993 (Albó 1994:72). However, in order to ensure the passage of his legislative agenda, Sánchez de Lozada invited the MBL and

UCS to join the government, an alliance that weakened the influence of Cárdenas in the coalition.

The size of Sánchez de Lozada's electoral victory is significant. Carlos Hugo Molina observes that had Sánchez de Lozada not won such a convincing electoral mandate, he would have been required to negotiate extensively with opposition parties—the methodology that had frustrated comprehensive reform during the weak Paz Zamora government. Had this been the case, Molina doubts that the Law of Popular Participation would have emerged as it is—or at all.[16] In addition to his decisive electoral victory and substantive mandate, and his more effective leadership style, Sánchez de Lozada would benefit in his first year in office from the widespread public sentiment that he should have been president in 1989–1993. His effective management of economic reform as planning minister under the MNR-ADN government (1985–1989) gave the public high expectations of his postponed presidency (Molina M. 1997:153).

6 Imposing Democracy

The Sánchez de Lozada Reforms

T HE CREATIVE PHASE of the constitutional reform resumes on the eve of the Sánchez de Lozada–Cárdenas inauguration in the summer of 1993. The MNR-MRTKL partnership has been expanded to include the MBL and UCS and assure a voting majority in both houses of Congress. The 1993 Law of Necessity of Constitutional Reform has been passed by the previous legislature and awaits approval by the new one. But this package of reforms by pact represents only the first stage of the constitutional reform. As Jan-Erik Lane observes, a constitution is not solely the written document that bears the name; it includes the customs, conventions, and statutes that complement a country's formal constitution (Lane 1996:8–9). In addition to the reforms contained in Law 1585, the Sánchez de Lozada administration passed two statutory laws that profoundly realigned the relationship between state and society and, thus, should be considered an extension of the constitutional reform. These are the 1994 Law of Popular Participation (LPP) and the 1995 Law of Administrative Decentralization. The latter reforms were not included in the Law of Necessity itself because there was insufficient consensus on these measures in 1993 among the three major parties and insufficient time to flesh out these concepts or to work out an agreement prior to the end of the Paz Zamora term.[1]

Sánchez de Lozada used his decisive electoral victory and working legislative majority to outmaneuver reform opponents within and outside his own party. He astutely sequenced the reforms such that less radical changes would provide the basis for later projects and would defuse or deflect opposition. He and his team worked in strict secrecy so that opposition forces were unable to anticipate assaults on their particular interests until it was too late to derail them. Thus, while the constellation of forces in favor of democratic reform was perhaps not as solid as it had been during Colombia's National Constituent Assembly, Sánchez de Lozada skillfully managed the opposition, enabling the reforms to pass. As Sánchez de Lozada later described the process:

> I really admire the capacity of this country to resist change. . . . I was obsessed—I am monomaniacal—with the termination of the great reforms. I knew that if these were not finished [earlier], later it would have been much more difficult. It is the same when a sick person is given a dose of penicillin; half-measures can cause the appearance of antibodies . . . in general, changes generate antibodies, resistance . . . I wanted to finish everything before this resistance became too strong. For that reason the government has been imposing, if you wish, vertically.[2]

The exclusionary, managed, top-down process of democratization can be attributed to the fact that there was no coherent political movement for the radical transformation of state-society relations from below, apart from the weak indigenous organizations and the writings of politically impotent intellectuals. The structural adjustment of the 1980s and the international decline of socialism had crippled and shrunk the Left. The vast majority of civil society organizations capable of articulating aggregated demands in the public sphere supported the retention of the corporatist model that perpetuated their role as political intermediaries and recipients of patronage. Peak organizations representing popular sectors, the most important being COB and CSUTCB, were in a state of severe crisis because of the neoliberal reforms of the previous governments, as well as internal contradictions within their leadership, structure, and mission. They proved unable to block the state-led reform or to articulate a viable alternative.

Behind Closed Doors: Drafting the Law of Popular Participation (LPP)

Prior to the inauguration of President Gonzalo Sánchez de Lozada and Vice President Víctor Hugo Cárdenas on August 6, 1993, the president-elect convened a group of trusted politicians and independent technical experts to begin to flesh out the popular participation concept. The group included Cárdenas, MBL leader Miguel Urioste, and Carlos Hugo Molina. According to Urioste, it was during this period that the MBL's idea of recognizing social organizations and community authorities and jurisdictions was wedded to the Fundación Milenio municipalization scheme. Contemporaneously, the amorphous plans of the president-elect were debated by international advisors, including Harvard's Jeffrey Sachs, who had helped Planning Minister Sánchez de Lozada devise a successful anti-inflation scheme during the Paz Estenssoro administration. Technical experts at the World Bank, the Inter-American Development Bank, and the United Nations Development Programme, all of whom had major aid programs in Bolivia, also contributed ideas (Molina M. 1997:182–83). Bilateral development agencies, particularly from the United States, Germany, and Switzerland, offered suggestions and reviewed the progress of the plan with a view toward supporting its implementation.[3]

As one of the poorest countries in the Western Hemisphere, Bolivia has long been among the largest recipients of international aid. As a result, international aid agencies have had considerable leverage in proposing and implementing economic and social policy. International advisors strongly supported expanding popular participation through radical decentralization and giving local communities control over development design and implementation—ideas that had been popular in international development and democracy-promotion circles for more than a decade. The enthusiasm of these foreigners would lead opponents of the plan to surmise (incorrectly) that the plan was concocted by international agencies and imposed on the Bolivian government. Actually, international experts were more interested in copying the plan and applying it elsewhere. The LPP was the product of the convergence of international trends in development theory and practice, the example of municipal decentralization schemes in Argentina, Chile, Colombia, Mexico, and Peru, as well as sui generis ideas inspired by the ethnic and social diversity of Bolivian society.

The 1993 Law of Necessity of Constitutional Reform had been conceived primarily as a political negotiation rather than a technical problem. The reverse was true of the LPP. Sánchez de Lozada already had made the decision to dramatically increase popular participation in government and to decentralize economic resources and administrative and political power. The question was how to achieve this within Bolivia's legal and political framework. Some advisors argued that a new regime to increase popular participation must be created through a highly participatory process, preferably through the convocation of the popular sectors. But the president's more technical vision prevailed.[4] One participant recalled that the president had expressed the desire to craft an immediate and irreversible "shock plan" to address the political crisis, along the lines of the economic shock plan he had helped devise in 1985. At the outset, Sánchez de Lozada was committed to two key principles: that the political and economic decentralization be radical, and that it be irreversible. He was flexible with respect to the technical means of achieving this (Molina M. 1997:194–202; Archondo 1997:10).

During the first week of the new administration, a Popular Participation Unit (UPP) was established within the new Ministry of Human Development, under the direction of Carlos Hugo Molina. Molina reported directly to "super minister" Fernando Romero, a politically independent banker and the president's top advisor. Sánchez de Lozada's preference for hiring highly trained technical experts and politically independent intellectuals began during his tenure in the Paz Estenssoro administration. This preference came back to haunt him and the LPP during the latter half of his administration. Over the next few weeks, Molina hired economists to work on the economic and financial aspects of the law, and lawyers and social planners to flesh out the municipalization scheme and address legal barriers that emerged as the plan progressed. A crucial task of the UPP was collecting data, since at the commencement of its work the Bolivian government did not even know how many municipalities existed in the country, and the limits of many territorial entities were disputed or undefined.

Interviews with participants paint a picture of a highly dedicated staff committed to the reforms they were designing and convinced that they were effecting transcendent change. The LPP's official history (Molina M. 1997) refers to the "exalted ambience" of this "heroic" period, a reference to the paltry budget of four hundred thousand U.S. dollars allocated to the project, as well as the long hours invested by UPP staff. Some team members worked without salary for months. Evening and weekend meetings were common. UPP staff member Rubén Ardaya recalls frequent meetings with the president from 5:30 p.m. until midnight. Pampered Bolivian technocrats endured these hardships in order to inhale the rarified air of the utopian project. The environment was highly charged by the horizontal and approachable nature of Molina's leadership, the youth and optimism of the team, the opportunity to work directly with the president, and the lack of confining limits on the team's utopian dreams (Molina M. 1997:190–93; Ardaya 1996:125–43).[5]

On October 18, 1993, the National Commission on Popular Participation was established to provide a forum for high-ranking representatives of a carefully chosen cohort of the political spectrum to air their views to the president on the plan as it took shape. The commission included the government's three "super ministers," representatives of the government coalition in Congress, independent consultants from the Fundación Milenio project, and senior UPP staff. Members of an interministerial technical committee participated in these higher-level meetings when issues requiring their expertise were discussed. After its first meeting, with the vice president presiding, the commission was chaired in the Presidential Palace by the president himself. Sánchez de Lozada's famed good humor, openness to ideas, philosophical digressions, and personal charm enchanted and inspired participants to search harder for creative solutions to seemingly insurmountable conundrums (Molina M. 1997:166, 194; Archondo 1997:11). The president's leadership style was to assign a diverse group of people to develop multiple alternatives; then he would consider the merits of each alternative and make his choice.[6] Although the president was strong enough to impose his final decision, he was open enough to new ideas that on several occasions persuasive arguments prevailed over his personal preferences. One of the most common criticisms of Sánchez de Lozada throughout his term was his tendency to want to make every minute decision himself. Critics insist he spent too much time working on the design of the reforms—an estimated three hundred hours of the president's time was spent in meetings on the LPP—and not enough on selling them to panicked opponents during a time of rapid structural change and great uncertainty. The failure of his strategy to sell the reforms to a doubting domestic audience resulted in abysmal public approval ratings at the end of his term and the MNR's loss in the 1997 elections, despite the international prestige of the reforms and the strength of the Bolivian economy (Gamarra 1997:2).

One of the few issues settled was that the municipality would be the basis of a radical economic and political decentralization effort. The municipality already existed in Bolivian law, which conferred on it some measure of autonomy. As of 1987, municipal mayors and councillors were elected directly. If the municipality could be generalized throughout the country, rather than confined to a few urban areas, it would be close to the people, in particular, the 42 percent of the population living in rural poverty. Large areas of Bolivia actually lacked local authorities with ties to the national government, partly because of the extreme dispersion of Bolivia's population: 36 percent of Bolivians live in communities of less than 250 inhabitants (Molina S. 1996b:9).

Most of the estimated sixteen-thousand-plus hours of discussion on the LPP focused on a small set of contentious issues. These were the unit of territory upon which the municipalization of the country would be based; whether the collective subjects envisioned for the law would be territorial or functional organizations, or a combination of both; the functions of these organizations vis-à-vis the municipal governments; and the mechanism for distributing resources to municipalities. With regard to the first issue, the team settled on the provincial section (Bolivia's nine departments are divided into provinces, which are divided into sections). At the time there were approximately 305, which was thought to be a workable number.[7] The second issue was more difficult. All participants agreed that the purpose of the law was to articulate civil society to government at the community level and that the existing dense network of community civil society organizations should be incorporated into the plan. The germ of this idea was available in the MBL's proposed Law of Indigenous and Campesino Communities, whose most recent draft identified the municipality as the space for linking community organizations to local government. The question was of which existing organizations would represent civil society. Horst Grebe, a senior advisor in the Human Development Ministry, recalls that the participants in the UPP and in the National Commission could be arrayed on a spectrum between those advocating purely territorial representation and those advocating a purely corporatist, functional scheme. Sánchez de Lozada was closer to the purely territorial scheme; politicians associated with the traditional parties and labor unions, such as Miguel Urioste and MNR Senator Torres Goitia, were more insistent on including the unions, business associations, and civic committees. In practice, at the local level the distinction was moot, since a community-based campesino organization was at the same time a territorial unit and a functional organization. The difficulty came at the higher organizational levels.

The debate between functional-corporatist and territorial representation was highly ideological. In Bolivia's political tradition, corporate representation is associated with the rejection of the Liberal state and its individualistic, territorially based scheme of representation and homogeneous conception of citizenship. The Left has traditionally defended the right of groups to be represented before the state according to their position in the economy—a representation that the Liberal state has denied. From a Liberal perspective, however, corporate representation was viewed as undemocratic and even fascist. Corporatist organizations had become bloated with militants dependent on kickbacks. The division within the National Commission on this question fractured more or less along this ideological divide (Molina M. 1997:214). As the work progressed, influential Liberal voices within the team—the president, in particular—worked to rid the plan of the higher-level functional organizations, leaving only their community-level expression. According to his advisors, Sánchez de Lozada intended to marginalize functional organizations like the civic committees, which he considered undemocratic and with whom he had experienced difficult relations in the past.[8]

Ultimately, territorially based social organizations—specifically, indigenous and campesino communities and urban neighborhood committees *(juntas vecinales)*—were designated as the sole subjects of the LPP and given the generic name of territorial base organizations (OTBs). In defining their functions, the team began with the concept of "social control" *(control social)*. The term "social control" may convey an intention to control society in a top-down fashion, but the term is meant to imply the bottom-up oversight of government by the people, in the absence of a Spanish equivalent for the English word "accountability." Under the LPP, community organizations would provide the checks and balances to inefficiency, corruption, and abuses of power at the local level that the division of powers of government played at the central level. In a country where the judicial system barely functioned, at any level of government, this seemed like the most natural option. It was through consideration of this mechanism of social control that the link between the representative/state-centered system of government and the participatory or direct/community-centered system of social organization was finally discovered (Molina M. 1997:218).

This link was the oversight committee *(comité de vigilancia)*, an entirely new entity in Bolivian politics with greater structure, powers, and control over resources than the citizens' observer committees or local administrative juntas of the Colombian constitutional reform. The oversight committees would be composed of representatives of the OTBs in a given municipality, chosen according to local custom. They facilitated Sánchez de Lozada's goal of decentralizing real power to the community level, as opposed to merely opening space for toothless consultation. For this power to be made real, resources must be channeled to the communities, which led to the next difficult question: how to release the majority of government co-participation (revenue-sharing) resources so that they could be more evenly distributed throughout the country, particularly to needy rural areas. Pursuant to the Law of Tributary Reform (Law 843 of May 1986), 75 percent of revenues went to the central government, 10 percent to the municipalities, 10 percent to departmental development corporations, and 5 percent to public universities. Because municipal revenues were distributed to the cities in which the source of revenue was domiciled, 90.8 percent went to only three cities—La Paz, Santa Cruz, and Cochabamba (collectively known in Bolivia as the "central axis")—even though the populations of the departments in which those three cities are located represented only 68.1 percent of the total in 1992 (Galindo Soza and Medina 1996:99; Archondo 1997:13–14). Not only was this grossly regressive, the scant resources destined for the majority of the country's new municipalities would not be sufficient to support the new responsibilities they were to receive under the LPP. Some change in the scheme of revenue distribution was urgently needed, which required the UPP team to convince the president to significantly alter one of the most successful laws he had designed as planning minister.

Once the president had been convinced to alter the co-participation formula, it was decided that funds would be distributed according to population, a formula that did not provide extra resources to areas and groups that needed them, as the Colombian municipal decentralization plan does. The president chose to distribute resources according to population for two reasons. First, there was no consensus on the exact formula for calculating inequality or deprivation, a formula that could be jiggled to advantage particular municipalities or departments. Second, the creation of this mechanism would require at least several months of work to gather the necessary data, choose from a range of measures, and calculate the appropriate amount of resources to be distributed. In order to avoid such a delay, and the possible political manipulation of the distribution mechanism, the team chose the path of least resistance—distribution according to population.[9] Employing the per capita distribution formula, the UPP team found that the amounts destined for the poorer departments increased by more than 1,000–2,000 percent and generated a more equitable distribution of income between the central axis (now to receive 32 percent of resources) and the remainder of the country (to receive 68 percent), and within and among the country's nine departments (Molina M. 1997:225; Archondo 1997:13–14). To the dismay of the civic committees, which enjoy formal representation within the departmental development corporations, the 10 percent of national revenues that had been channeled to these notoriously inefficient and corrupt corporations were transferred to the municipalities, in order to increase the flow of resources to the central axis and avert their organized opposition to the plan, while still reducing their *proportion* of state revenues.

At the end of November 1993, after four months of private discussions, the process of reform opened up dramatically when the seventh draft of the proposal was leaked to the Santa Cruz Civic Committee. The outraged civic leaders accused the government (correctly) of secretly trying to undo the progress already negotiated on decentralization—a reference to the department-centered legislative proposal passed by the Senate at the end of the Paz Zamora administration. A great deal of the team's energies were now diverted to involving the civic committees in specious debates long enough to allow the team to continue its work in peace (Molina M. 1997:204–05; Archondo 1997:10–11; Ardaya 1996:128). Once the project was made public, the government was forced to engage in multiple consultations to deflect criticism that it was drafting a law of popular participation via a completely nonparticipatory process. The president threatened to severely sanction future leakers and ordered all copies of the project but one to be destroyed following each meeting. No further leaks occurred. Sectors of the president's own party were excluded from the negotiations because of their resistance to structural change. After January 9, 1994, the primary political forum for discussion of the draft law became the president's cabinet. Some opposition remained within the cabinet, particularly from the traditional wing of the MNR, which feared that the decentralization of resources would weaken the party's control over the politically determined distribution of state resources, and would also disadvantage the city of La Paz, the home of senior MNR officials in the Ministry of Hacienda. Of course, these changes were much the point of the reform. The resistance of the centralized government bureaucracy to any diminution of its policy-making or resource-distribution prerogatives required the continual intervention of the president.[10]

In general, sectors considered to be incapable of good faith negotiations, whose political posture or ideology was confrontational and extreme, were excluded. The confrontational posture of many popular organizations was a legacy of decades of military rule and government domination and neglect. It was inconceivable to many civil society leaders that the government was working on a plan to benefit the people rather than to control and manipulate them for political gain. The ingrained skepticism and confrontational posture of civil society were most pronounced within the labor sector, a legacy of the brutal suppression of labor by a succession of military and elected governments and the collapse of the UDP government coalition in 1985, of which the labor movement had formed a part. During the debate on popular participation, the national labor organizations were confronting the government on labor and social policy, and their leaders were unwilling to exchange extremist bargaining positions in favor of workable solutions. The labor sector had suffered a decline in support from its base because of its inability to deliver substantive gains and the rise of representational alternatives, such as the traditional *ayllu* authorities and populist political parties, like CONDEPA and UCS. Thus, in retrospect, close advisors to these groups defend the government's decision not to negotiate directly with the civic committees and the labor movement. As consultant Laurent Thévoz observed, it was not a question of negotiating certain offending details, but of the realization, or not, of a project to which the government had already committed itself (Molina M. 1997:206). Moreover, Rubén Ardaya argued, those organized interests that demanded greatest participation in the drafting process—the civic committees and the labor confederation—were among the least democratic and most oligarchic in the country. However, even though the labor movement and civic committees as institutions were formally excluded from the drafting process, individuals representing these constituencies were privately, informally consulted.[11]

Incorporating Marginalized Groups

Political elites accorded the ethnic issue an unprecedented amount of discussion and legitimacy. The two agencies responsible for adding a sensitivity to the country's ethnic and cultural diversity were the Office of the Vice President and the new National Secretariat for Ethnic, Gender, and Generational Affairs (SNAEGG). Sánchez de Lozada created the SNAEGG within the Human Development Ministry to provide a higher profile for diversity issues and to provide an agency for the vice president to staff with loyal MRTKL militants. Indigenous peoples' issues previously had been handled in the Campesino and Agricultural Affairs Ministry by a weak Bolivian Indigenist Institute. This institutional change marks a shift away from the MNR's economicist view of Indians and toward a view of indigenous peoples as a distinct social group whose concerns, like those of women, children, and the elderly, should be treated transversally. Rather than hire cronies from his party to staff the office, however, Cárdenas hired politically independent professionals. Neither Secretary Ramiro Molina R. nor Subsecretary for Ethnic Affairs Luz María Calvo was even indigenous.

Cárdenas had been expected to play a major role in the design of the LPP. Instead, the politically cautious vice president increasingly distanced himself from the project as it progressed. According to Ramiro Molina, Cárdenas preferred to leave technical questions to the SNAEGG and to focus instead on a more political, diplomatic role within the small group working on the LPP. Although Molina credits Cárdenas with having earned in this way the confidence of the president, Cárdenas's failure to coordinate with the SNAEGG left its politically inexperienced and independent staff without policy direction or political protection. Cárdenas's senior advisor, Iván Arias, attributes this reticence to concern on the part of the vice president and his staff that they were being used to provide information on the indigenous population and its aspirations that might ultimately be used to control and manipulate this sector. Having already been bitterly criticized for selling out the Katarista movement to join the government, Cárdenas took care not to associate himself too strongly with the project until it had received broad public support.[12]

According to Arias, there was nothing in the LPP that had not been suggested by civil society organizations and intellectuals in the years prior to the Sánchez de Lozada administration. Even the municipal participatory planning methodology already had been elaborated by NGOs during the 1980s. Sánchez de Lozada's innovation was his willingness to incorporate existing ideas and popular practices into public policy. What is remarkable is that only a few years earlier the same ideas had been considered subversive, unconstitutional, and even communist. Arias believes that the combination of Víctor Hugo Cárdenas, who had a positive and moderate public image, with the neoliberal president made it possible for radical, revolutionary ideas to be injected into public policy debates. The involvement of the president alone in the scheme would have raised doubts among the popular sectors; the vice president's support alone would have raised doubts among the traditional political class.[13]

The SNAEGG was responsible for defining the subjects of the LPP and harmonizing the role of indigenous communities and authorities with the revised version of Article 171 of the constitution, which recognized the political autonomy and public character of these entities. According to Alcides Vadillo Pinto, a SNAEGG legal advisor, the first drafts of the LPP included no references to indigenous peoples or to incorporating their communities as subjects of the law. After several meetings with UPP staff, indigenous communities were recognized as one class of territorially based organization. At this point in time, Vadillo recalls, the UPP was quite closed to outsiders, so the influence of the SNAEGG at this early juncture was decisive. His office also worked on incorporating the diverse structures and norms of indigenous communities into special Indigenous Municipal Districts (DMIs), and on inserting indigenous planning methodologies and organizational structures into the law's methodology for promoting popular participation in local development planning. Secretary Ramiro Molina and indigenous organizations had pushed for a more expansive recognition of the territoriality of indigenous communities and ethnic groups. This idea was vehemently opposed by a large contingent of Sánchez de Lozada's close advisors from the department of Santa Cruz, where powerful interests opposed the territorial aspirations of indigenous peoples. In the end, indigenous organizations had to settle for the recognition of the communities and save the territoriality issue for the congressional debates on the reform of Article 171 and the proposed agrarian law.[14]

The Ethnic Affairs Subsecretariat also convened indigenous organizations to discuss the evolving participatory regime. It held three open meetings with lowland indigenous organizations with the collaboration of CIDOB and conducted three seminars with leaders of the *ayllus* of Norte de Potosí. Vadillo believes the indigenous organizations had the greatest impact on the law through these meetings by making government staff aware of the diversity of indigenous organizational and authority structures and persuading them of the need to create a flexible law to allow multiple interpretations for key concepts. UPP technical staff also met separately with leaders of CIDOB and CPIB (the Beni confederation) on several occasions to discuss the progress of the plan and with highland campesino syndicates that were independent of the national confederation, which publicly opposed the plan. In the end, several of their suggestions were incorporated, and these ethnic leaders were among the staunchest supporters of the law.

CIDOB offered several alternative proposals and resubmitted its draft Law of Indigenous Peoples. Ramiro Molina chose not to recommend submitting the latter to Congress, because the LPP and other projects being prepared at the time actually provided a more far-reaching vision of a multiethnic state than the CIDOB proposal. In addition, in Molina's view, in a country with an indigenous majority it made no sense to have a special law for indigenous peoples; it would be more logical and have a greater impact to consider questions of ethnicity, culture, and gender as a fundamental component of each of the new constitutional reform projects. CIDOB president Marcial Fabricano believes that the CIDOB proposal—with the exception of its most important components (explicit recognition of indigenous territorial jurisdiction and control of natural resources)—provided the basis for much of the Sánchez de Lozada administration's constitutional reform as it affected indigenous peoples. From his point of view, however, the government did not sufficiently discuss the new laws with CIDOB. As a result of the close cooperation enjoyed by CIDOB in the design of important legislation (such as the LPP, educational reform, and agrarian law), as well as the institutional support channeled from international development agencies to CIDOB by the SNAEGG, the government would be able to count on its staunch support for the LPP at a time when the campesino confederation CSUTCB was denouncing the law as a trick to co-opt and subjugate the indigenous and campesino population.[15]

The work of the Subsecretariat of Ethnic Affairs on the LPP was conducted in conjunction with the reform of Article 171. A reform of that article, recognizing the authorities and organizational structure of indigenous and campesino communities, had been included in the 1993 version of the Law of Necessity of Reform of the Constitution. Further emendations were made during the Sánchez de Lozada administration. The Subsecretariat hired Colombian government anthropologist Raúl Arango to redraft Article 171 and adjust the Colombian scheme to the distinct demographic reality of Bolivia. In particular, the Subsecretariat wished to address the silence of Article 171 with respect to the status of indigenous territory. It did so in two ways. It alerted the country's indigenous organizations to this omission and encouraged them to mobilize politically behind this issue, and it worked with Fabricano during the week when the article was discussed in Congress to lobby political leaders to incorporate language protecting the traditional territories of the indigenous population as territorial jurisdictions, not merely as property. In the end, however, there was no absolute majority on the territorial question. An intermediate solution recognized the property rights of indigenous communities in their *tierras comunitarias de origen* (original community lands). The territorial issue would be taken up again in 1996 during the debate on agrarian reform.

In marked contrast to the government's sensitivity to ethnic diversity, the gender issue was pushed through the back door by a few determined female government officials. "Officially, we never saw the draft of the law," recalls Sonia Montaño, a prominent Bolivian feminist and the first Subsecretary of Gender in the Sánchez de Lozada administration. With no high-ranking female political leader on the National Commission on Popular Participation, with only one female staff member in the UPP (Verónica Balcazar), and in the absence of a women's movement able to mobilize support behind issues of gender equity as the indigenous movement had done with respect to ethnic rights, the insertion of gender sensitivity in the LPP was fraught with difficulty. The staff of the SNAEGG ethnic affairs division had been consulted on the LPP from the beginning of the drafting process. Montaño, however, did not see a draft until the beginning of February, after a previous version had been leaked to the Santa Cruz Civic Committee. The women's input was facilitated by Miguel Urioste. Since Urioste was forbidden to give her a copy of the current draft, Montaño had to view the document on his office computer. In addition, UPP economist Verónica Balcazar kept Montaño and her group informed of the status of gender issues in the proposal (Montaño 1997).[16]

Montaño quickly formed a small coalition composed of women from her office and members of the congressional commission on women. There was no time to incorporate the views of campesino and indigenous women, who would be most affected by the law. She worked secretly, since, as a government official, she was forbidden to discuss the law publicly (and officially had not even seen it). Montaño and her group suggested several changes. They asked that the LPP include a mandate for the promotion of gender equity in the functioning of the law, and for sanctions in case this was not achieved. They suggested that gender-inclusive language be incorporated, a concept that at the time was considered radical and superfluous. Finally, they asked that municipal governments be explicitly charged with promoting projects demanded by women and that gender parity be assured within the oversight committees.[17]

According to Montaño, senior staff of the UPP were ignorant of gender equity issues but receptive to the proposals of the "girls from the gender office," once they had been sensitized to the ideological and political importance of gender equity. The greatest opposition to gender equity issues came from anthropologists in the SNAEGG, the secretariat to which Montaño's office was subordinate. The anthropologists argued that indigenous cultures would be destroyed if any criteria with respect to gender roles in community authority structures or planning practices were imposed on them. This interpretation was the foundation of their position with respect to the autonomy of indigenous communities (a major battle between the anthropologists and the UPP staff), and any wavering on the defense of indigenous customs would weaken that position. Thus, on the LPP and with respect to other legislation and policies, there were constant frictions between the mission of the anthropologists to promote diversity and the mission of the feminists to promote equality. Because of this opposition from within its own secretariat, Montaño and her group had to lobby informally, quietly, and secretly.[18]

A few days before the draft law was to be presented to Congress, Montaño obtained a copy of the current draft. As had happened before, all her proposals had been removed (Montaño 1997). With Urioste's help, Montaño reinserted some of them. As a result, the promotion of gender equity is one of the purposes of the law, and municipalities are directed to promote the participation of women in planning. Gender neutral language was included in a piece of Bolivian legislation for the first time ever—but only in the portions of the LPP on which Montaño was able to work. The law also calls for the promotion of "equitable representation" on the oversight committees, although this was never elaborated in the implementing legislation. Montaño's greatest disappointment was the lack of sanctions in the law or its implementing legislation. In addition, as Aymara congressional deputy Clara Flores (MRTKL) observed, the LPP failed to address the fact that the main subjects of the law—campesino and indigenous organizations—are dominated by men, whereas women's decision-making role is confined to the private sphere of the home or to auxiliary women's organizations. Since only one organization is recognized as representing each territorial community, when leaders are chosen to represent the communities in the oversight committees, these would invariably be men. During the floor debate on the LPP in April 1994, female deputies argued that the LPP still failed to explain how women would participate in the law given their virtual exclusion from OTB leadership and the persistence of gender discriminatory language in most of the text. As indigenous activists would invoke Bolivia's obligations under international conventions on ethnic and indigenous rights in the debate on Article 171, one female deputy reminded the chamber that in 1989 Bolivia had signed the international convention prohibiting discrimination against women and incorporated it at the rank of national law.[19]

Going Public: The LPP Is Presented

On February 20, 1994, Sánchez de Lozada approved the thirty-second draft of the Law of Popular Participation and sent it to Congress. National newspapers published the full text of the draft on February 22. From that time until the LPP was promulgated on April 20, the work of the UPP staff shifted from technical development to traveling around the country promoting the law. Senior officials, including the president, participated in the campaign. Hundreds of meetings were convened and thousands of kilometers traversed to disseminate the benefits of the LPP. Their mission was to create enough public support for the law to achieve its congressional passage not merely along guaranteed party lines but by consensus (Molina M. 1997:230). Government representatives listened to the complaints and suggestions of various corporate groups, social movements, departmental officials, and community leaders. They carried graphs to demonstrate the increased revenue to be distributed to specific localities. And they countered a disinformation campaign propagated by opponents, which included the circulation of fake versions of the law intended to sow opposition.

The government made no major changes to the basic plan concocted in private by the government team, however. Critics contend that not only did the government fail to incorporate the public's suggestions, but the effort of the government to diffuse information about the law was insufficient and left the majority of the public unaware of its nature and of its impact on their lives. The effort was particularly deficient in rural areas, where newspapers and television do not reach, and among non-Spanish-speaking groups. We cannot say with certainty, therefore, that a national dialogue occurred on the LPP, as is claimed by some who were closest to this process.

The government's key sales pitch was purely economic. Instead of flowery language about democracy, the president emphasized the amount of resources to be sent to each municipality and the level of increase over pre-LPP amounts. As the president observed on this occasion, "When money talks, people listen" (Archondo 1997:12). Sánchez de Lozada went on television and radio to explain the complex proposal to the Bolivian people, in particular the mechanism for redistributing resources. Another argument used by members of the UPP propaganda team and supporters of the LPP in the press went like this: If the law was not approved, Bolivia was ripe for a violent Indian-based uprising similar to the one that had rocked the southern Mexican state of Chiapas in January 1994, if not a virulent, entrenched guerrilla movement like the Shining Path in neighboring Peru. They attributed the Chiapas uprising to the failure of the Mexican government to address popular aspirations for participation in social policy and democratic representation.[20] The Chiapas argument backfired, however, when opposition parties and the labor movement accused the MNR of trying to create a clientelist structure like Mexico's hegemonic Institutional Revolutionary Party (PRI).[21]

The Bolivian press devoted a great deal of attention to the public debate on the law, providing space for diverse views and proposed modifications. Most intellectuals, politicians, and interest groups strongly supported the proposal, provided that their suggestions were incorporated. As expected, the greatest opposition came from groups excluded from the drafting process or groups whose interests were threatened—or appeared to be threatened —by the law. The civic committees were among the most vociferous opponents of the law, which thwarted their aspiration to decentralize political power to departmental governments. Opposition political parties warned that the entire LPP scheme was a plot by the MNR to co-opt the entire country through the "MNR-ization" of municipal governments and oversight committees. As authors of the plan that would bring unprecedented fortunes to municipalities throughout the country, the MNR was expected to reap enormous benefits during the 1995 municipal elections. Other sources of opposition were the departmental governments and the municipal government of La Paz, but these were unable to articulate a convincing argument, since they stood to lose privileges that the majority of the country envied. Smaller municipal governments, which were short-changed under the existing arrangement, strongly favored the law.[22]

The LPP also was criticized by leftist intellectuals, who distrusted the government's motives and saw in the plan an effort to co-opt and control autonomous popular organizations—a suspicion fed by the secretive manner in which the government was known to have created the law. Alvaro García Linera suggested that the debate on the LPP was over "how the people participate in their own exclusion and how to institutionalize concretely their marginalization."[23] Others argued that popular participation is only constructive of democracy when it is civil-society driven, rather than the project of a government that convenes civil society to participate under certain specified conditions.[24] NGOs, many of which were criticized for having absorbed international development assistance for many years without producing results, objected to the exclusion of NGOs as subjects of the law (*Hoy*, July 23, 1994, 10). Intellectuals also criticized the restriction of "participation" by the law to the prioritization of local development policies, prohibiting the participation of individuals or groups in decision-making beyond the sphere of local government authority over the provision of basic services and sectoral policy. Rather than provide a sphere for democratic deliberation on public policy among autonomous civil society organizations and the state, the law, they argued, convenes certain specified groups to engage in a prescribed methodology of participation in state-specified public policy matters.

This is not a law of participation. I do not know why they do not speak clearly: it is a law of rural municipalization. Why say that it is participation? Therein lies the trick. They want to make us believe that it is a law of participation when it is something else. It is a law that extends the control of the State over its own space. (Prada 1994)

Provincial and departmental-level labor and campesino organizations marginalized by the LPP registered their vehement opposition. The strident opposition of the CSUTCB and COB led local member organizations to publicly announce their support for the law and to explicitly reject the confrontational stance of the leadership, which had called for protest marches, roadblocks, and hunger strikes to obstruct the law's implementation. Another point of conflict was actually a question of semantics. The law's authors had suggested "OTB" as a generic term to refer to the campesino communities, indigenous communities, and neighborhood committees that were the law's subjects. Leaders of these organizations feared that the government intended to replace existing organizations with their own co-opted organizations, as the MNR had done to the independent campesino syndicates after the 1952 revolution. In fact, sectors of the MNR did want to create new OTBs that could be co-opted by the party (Molina M. 1997:213). Most lower-level campesino organizations, however, recognized in the LPP the fulfillment of long-standing campesino demands.

The secrecy that surrounded the LPP continued in the National Congress. Actors considered to be possible obstacles to the consensual passage of the law were excluded and committee reports analyzing the project closely held. As a senator from the governing coalition complained during the Senate debate, committee reports were signed only by the leadership; members of the opposition and even the governing parties were not allowed to consider the measure or sign the reports. Others complained that less than twenty-four hours had been provided for senators to consider the proposal. Several members of opposition parties were supportive, and some of their suggestions were included. Rather than outright opposition, opposition parties registered their doubts that the proposal could accomplish its lofty goals, along with their resentment that they had not been consulted earlier; and their concern that the MNR would use the innovative new arrangements to co-opt and control community organizations. In response to accusations of secrecy and exclusion, government allies frequently alluded to the fact that the LPP was the concrete expression of the concept of radically improving popular participation in government articulated by the government's electoral platform. As MNR deputy Moscoso Valderrama argued, the LPP had been implied in the Plan de Todos through its municipalization scheme, as well as in the plan's promotion of a "decentralization of the country that would contribute to the strengthening of participatory democracy and the institutions of representative democracy."[25]

Several important modifications were made to respond to congressional opposition. These had to do with which government entity would be authorized to deliver juridical personality (the legal standing to enter into legal and financial relationships), who is authorized to adjudicate disputes with respect thereto, and the proper functioning of the mechanism for freezing co-participation funds in the event of complaints by oversight committees. The most significant changes made at the request of legislators were the lowering of the minimum number of inhabitants for the constitution of a municipality—from ten thousand to five thousand—and the inclusion of mechanisms to channel extra funds to the poorest and least populous departments. Legislators from the departments of Oruro, Potosí, Pando, and Beni had argued that a larger proportion of resources should be distributed to their departments in light of the greater need, as well as the greater expense of providing services to dispersed rural populations. In the end, the population-based mechanism was retained. Poorer and less-populated departments were promised extra help from the central government with infrastructure projects and service delivery.

Following consideration by committees with jurisdiction over its subject matter, the LPP was debated on the floor of the Chamber of Deputies on April 12 and 13, passed on April 13, and was transmitted to the Senate for consideration. The Senate held its debate on April 19 and 20, 1994. The LPP was approved as Law 1551 of 1994 on April 20. Despite the grumbling of opposition politicians that they had not been consulted earlier in the process, analysts noted at the time that it was the first law to be approved during the Sánchez de Lozada administration on which a certain level of consensus had been achieved; other measures had been forced through the legislature using the government's voting majority. Although the modifications were small, they indicated the government's eagerness to negotiate in order to achieve the broad political consensus needed by the LPP for effective implementation. Similarly, even though the president had the votes to force the passage of the Law of Necessity of Constitutional Reform upon assuming office, a conference was convened by the Senate in February 1994 to encourage debate and the creation of consensus on the reforms. The reform package, affecting thirty-five articles of the 1967 Constitution, was finally approved in August 1994.[26]

Principal Aspects of the Law of Popular Participation

The objectives of the LPP are stated in its first article:

> The present Law recognizes, promotes, and consolidates the Popular Participation process by articulating the indigenous, campesino, and urban communities to the juridical, political, and economic life of the country. It strives to improve the quality of life of the Bolivian woman and man with a more just distribution and better administration of public resources. It strengthens political and economic instruments necessary to perfect representative democracy, facilitating citizen participation and guaranteeing equality of opportunity of women and men in the levels of representation.[27]

Article 1 is interesting in two respects. First, we can see the fruits of the efforts of the Gender Subsecretary to insert gender-neutral language and to make the equal representation of women in government an explicit goal of the law. This is the first Bolivian law to do either. Second, this article is conspicuously vague about the nature of the "participation" that the LPP strives to facilitate. According to Rubén Ardaya, the definition of popular participation elaborated by the UPP was omitted from the text of the law to avoid the imposition of a homogeneous vision of participation on a variety of forms of social organization, each with its own democratic culture. For the same reason, procedures for participation were not specified in order to avoid restricting the autonomy of civil society organizations and autonomous municipal governments and the operation of local customs. Although these justifications are valid, the lack of normative specificity deprives citizens of a firm basis upon which to demand their participation rights.

The subjects of the law are the OTBs, comprising an estimated 12,145 campesino and indigenous communities and between 4,000 and 8,000 neighborhood committees (Molina M. 1997:213). By organizing the new system of state-society relations around existing authorities and structures, the new regime was able to share in the substantial legitimacy of indigenous and campesino community organizations and authorities, enabling the state to recuperate some of the legitimacy it had lost through years of neglect of the poor majority, while improving government efficiency and accountability. Moreover, the construction of the new state-society relationship on the foundation of existing, legitimate, collective subjects acknowledges the fact that, in Bolivia, there are two bases for political legitimation: collective and individual. As Lazarte argued years before the popular participation scheme was devised, in Bolivia, ethno-cultural groups function not according to the Liberal, individualistic logic of citizen legitimation but, rather, according to a collective citizenship: "These two principles exist in Bolivian society, the first as a principle of legitimation of the state and the political system, and the second as a principle for legitimation derived from the ethno-cultural groups, whose function is based in the rationality of collective citizenship" (Lazarte 1992:20). The Law of Popular Participation provided an institutional arrangement that derives legitimacy from both sources.

The juridical personality conferred on OTBs is not merely symbolic. It empowers these social organizations to receive donations or loans from governmental or nongovernmental entities or to enter into legal relationships with national or international development agencies. This recognition eliminates the need to have an NGO act as intermediary—long a frustration for indigenous organizations. Article 7 assigns OTBs the following functions:

1. Propose, demand, control and supervise the realization of works and the delivery of public services in accordance with community needs, in the areas of education, health, sports, basic sanitation, irrigation, roads, and urban and rural development.

2. Participate in and promote actions related to the management and preservation of the environment, ecological equilibrium and sustainable development.

3. Obtain the modification of actions, decisions, works or services offered by public entities when these are contrary to the community interest.

4. Propose the change or ratification of educational or health authorities within their territory.

5. Access information about co-participation resources. (Translation by the author)

These rights transform local communities from the objects of development programs prescribed and implemented by others to subjects of and actors in their own development. In exchange, OTBs are required to participate in the execution and administration of public works, to inform their members of their progress, and to assume responsibility for promoting the equitable representation of women.

The territorial basis of the LPP is the municipality, derived from the country's existing urban municipalities and those carved out of provincial sections. To eliminate their traditional urban bias, municipalities were re-districted to include both rural and urban areas. As a result, in 80 percent of municipalities, the rural population outnumbers urban dwellers. The municipality is intended to provide the legal and territorial space for the link between civil society and the state and to serve as the engine for economic and social development (Ardaya 1996:134). Under the LPP, municipalities received expanded responsibilities for the administration of health, education, sanitation, and transportation infrastructure (whose ownership was transferred to municipal governments), as well as for the establishment of sports and cultural programs and economic development projects. Policy direction in these sectors continues to originate in the national government, which also pays the salaries of health and education personnel.

Where indigenous communities exist, municipal governments may designate an indigenous submayor and establish DMIs to ensure the representation of indigenous communities on oversight committees. These districts are supposed to allow a somewhat greater degree of administrative autonomy. Where a sociocultural unity traverses municipal boundaries, the portion of the community in each municipality may petition its municipal government to confer on that portion the status of a municipal district, so that the contiguous districts may be administered jointly. The municipal government, however, is not obligated to spend a certain proportion of the budget on the indigenous districts or to turn over funds to indigenous submayors.

Each municipality has an oversight committee composed of unpaid representatives, chosen annually according to local custom, by the OTBs of each municipal district. The oversight committee is the linchpin of the popular participation scheme because it provides the institutional mechanism through which civil society is articulated with the state and control of civil society over the actions of government is exercised. It has the authority to obtain access to all information regarding the receipt and expenditure of municipal co-participation funds. In the event of suspected mismanagement or corruption, the oversight committee may begin a process of higher-government review that may lead to the suspension of co-participation funds by the Senate.

In addition to their oversight function, oversight committees transmit the priorities of community organizations to the municipal government. Through a process called Participatory Municipal Planning (PPM), each community engages in a diagnostic, prioritization, and planning activity, of which the results are reported by community representatives to the oversight committee, which aggregates and presents them to the municipal government. The oversight committee is responsible for ascertaining the extent to which the municipal government's more technically complex and specific municipal annual operating plan (PAO) and the corresponding municipal budget reflect these societal demands, as well as the extent to which funds have been invested in accordance with the projections stated in the PAO and the budget. The PPM—derived from more than a decade of work by non-governmental development agencies in the Bolivian countryside—establishes the activities through which the communities formulate, prioritize, and express their preferences and participate in the decision-making sphere of the municipal government.

Of government revenues from internal taxes, customs receipts, value-added taxes, and a special tax on hydrocarbons (collectively known as "co-participation funds"), 20 percent is redistributed to the municipalities, of which 85 percent must be invested in social, economic, or cultural development projects. In addition, municipalities have the authority to collect local taxes on property, property transactions, vehicles, and the consumption of *chicha* (an alcoholic beverage)—a privilege previously enjoyed only by the largest cities (Archondo 1997:13). Municipalities also are eligible under certain conditions to receive additional resources from the central government's development funds (Campesino Development Fund, Social Investment Fund, Fund for Rural Development; see Galindo Soza and Medina 1996:79–104).

The new figures of the OTB and oversight committee present a frustrating ambiguity. Under the law these are civil society organizations empowered to assume public functions in their area of competence. But it is unclear whether these autonomous civil society organizations have been converted to public or quasi-public institutions by the LPP. Juan Cristóbal Urioste recalls that the LPP's authors decided explicitly not to confer more expansive jurisdictional and administrative powers on the OTBs in order to maintain the autonomy and non-state character of these organizations.[28] At the level of the oversight committee, which exercises administrative and jurisdictional functions, this nuanced distinction becomes more blurry. It is unclear whether oversight committees are state or civil society entities, or a new hybrid of the two.

The representation and participation of community organizations weakens as we ascend the Bolivian bureaucracy. At the provincial level (between municipalities and departments), accredited, provincial-level communal associations may send a representative to participate in a consultative body presided over by the subprefect. Provincial councils also include representatives of the municipal governments and oversight committees in the province. All three classes of members—communal associations, municipal governments, and oversight committees—may speak and vote in meetings on questions concerning the coordination or direction of provincial development. Since the provinces are not recipients of resources, however, their impact is minimal.

At the departmental level, the activities of the municipalities are coordinated by departmental secretaries of popular participation. The Law of Administrative Decentralization (LDA; Law 1654 of July 1995, in force January 1, 1996), established Departmental Councils composed of a municipal councillor from each province, who is elected by his or her colleagues. According to Henry Oporto, an advisor to Cárdenas, the LDA was devised after the LPP when Sánchez de Lozada realized that a coordinating mechanism was required to control the fragmentation and atomization of municipal development. In addition, the LDA responded to pressure from the civic committees to enhance the powers of the departments, though it failed to include the substantive demands that the committees had been advancing during the previous thirteen years of debate on decentralization (Oporto 1998a :20–25; Laserna 1997:16). The civic committees represent an exception to the rule that the influence of civil society groups lessens as we ascend the Bolivian bureaucracy under the LDA and LPP. They have maintained their role as mediators between departmental elites and departmental government, demonstrating greater visibility, influence, and recognition among the public than departmental councillors (Oporto 1998a:38).

The LDA is more accurately a law of *deconcentration*, since no autonomous policy-making powers were transferred to departments (Oporto 1998a:25). The LDA rationalized the administrative functions of the departmental and national governments to support the municipalization scheme and eliminated the ineffective and corrupt departmental development corporations. The Departmental Council plays a consultative as well as an oversight role. In addition, a Departmental Assembly is composed of the representatives in the National Congress of each department, and the prefect (departmental governor) continues to be named by the president. In this way, the departments integrate the political expression of the local and national levels, rather than create a new sphere of autonomous political expression, as the civic committees had preferred.

Participatory Democracy

During the debate in the Chamber of Deputies, proponents had promoted the LPP as a plan to make democracy more participatory, especially for rural people:

> Through this Law we are going to permit that the people do not simply participate in elections, but rather essentially become an actor. We are going to correct our democracy, which has until now been exclusive, a democracy that has not granted and has not recognized the real participation of the popular classes. Through this Law we vindicate the concept of participatory democracy; through this law each citizen is given the right to participate in the municipality, to participate in the intentions of their development. Never again will thousands of campesinos be marginalized from the making of decisions in our country because they will define their own development and what they must do.[29]

The LPP *even in theory*, however, does not propose a scheme of participatory democracy that would pass the scrutiny of democratic theory. The revised constitution continues to specify the political regime as a "representative democracy," rather than a "participatory democracy," as in the Colombian case. Direct mechanisms of democracy remain prohibited. Even the recall of local mayors, allowed under the new regime, is performed by the municipal council, not voters. Politicians and technical experts involved in the constitutional reform almost universally rejected direct mechanisms of democracy, which were seen to conflict with Bolivia's corporatist tradition.[30] Participatory democrats advocate mechanisms for participation at all levels of government. The LPP explicitly confines participation to the local level, reserving the departmental and national spheres for representative democracy. The Bolivian scheme promotes local participation of communities in development planning far more effectively than the Colombian reforms—by giving political authority and control over resources to the oversight committees. But above the local level, access to decision-making spheres is restricted. Even within the local sphere, citizens are allowed to participate only in decision-making strictly limited to the allocation of municipal co-participation resources to economic development and social investment projects, which occurs solely during community assemblies called for this purpose. Other questions of public policy continue to be debated in the center by politicians and bureaucrats.

Colombian constitution-makers aimed to strengthen civil society organizations. The LPP strengthened certain local organizations while marginalizing higher-level functional and sectoral organizations. This marginalization weakens the local organizations by cutting off channels to national spheres of decision-making and atomizing and isolating them. At the local level, individual participation rights are restricted because the subjects of the law are OTBs rather than individuals. Dissenting minority voices have no channel to express their preferences and no external recourse for their adequate representation in government decision-making spheres. This problem is one of the key concerns raised by Liberals with respect to communitarian policies that privilege the rights and autonomy of the community over those of the individual (Etzioni 1996:156).

Ethnic Recognition and Rights
Taken together, the LPP and the reform of constitutional Articles 1 and 171 represent an attempt to integrate a Western-Liberal state, composed of uni-

form structures and norms, with culturally and socially diverse civil society organizations, most of which are organized according to non-Western, communitarian norms. This is achieved by creating spheres of autonomy below the basic unit of public administration—the municipality—where diverse normative frameworks, modes of production, social organization, and systems of authority are legitimately recognized and empowered to participate in local-level public decision-making.

The 1967 Constitution recognized Bolivia's ethnic diversity for the first time in the 1994 revision of Article 1: "Bolivia, free, independent, sovereign, *multiethnic and pluricultural,* constituted in a unitary Republic, adopts for its form of government representative democracy, founded in the union and solidarity of all Bolivians" (my emphasis). As in Colombia, this recognition is part of a larger project to create a viable national identity to serve as the basis for national integration and development. The construction of national identity is also pursued through the creation of spaces for ethnically and socially organized collectivities to participate in decision-making spheres and in civil society structures that hold government accountable. Article 171 was reformed under Title 3 of the 1967 Constitution, which sets forth the agrarian and campesino regime. The entire text follows:

1. The social, economic, and cultural rights of indigenous peoples who inhabit the national territory, particularly those relating to their original community lands, are recognized, guaranteeing the use and sustainable exploitation of their natural resources, and of their identities, values, languages, customs and institutions.

2. The State recognizes the juridical personality of the indigenous and campesino communities and the campesino associations and syndicates.

3. The natural authorities of the indigenous and campesino communities may exercise functions of administration and application of their own norms as an alternative solution to conflicts, in conformity with their customs and procedures, always providing that they are not contrary to the Constitution and the laws. The law will establish the coordination of this special jurisdiction with the judicial power. (Translation by the author)

The first historic achievement worth noting is the use of the term "indigenous peoples." For the first time, the political regime formally extended recognition to dozens of indigenous cultures as *peoples,* with their own identities and cultures, integrated within Bolivian society as pre-constituted collectivities.

This usage helps to conform the Bolivian constitution to ILO Convention 169, ratified by Bolivia July 11, 1991. In addition to the language rights specified in Article 171, Article 116 of the reformed Bolivian constitution directs the government to provide translation for non-Spanish-speaking Indians in judicial proceedings. Additional linguistic and educational rights for indigenous peoples were provided in the 1994 Educational Reform Law.

Bolivia's recognition of the juridical personality of indigenous and campesino communities resembles the recognition extended to indigenous *cabildo* governments by the 1991 Colombian Constitution. In both countries, the autonomous form of community self-government, the method of choosing authorities, and the functions of these authorities are recognized as legitimate and as a constituent part of the national political system. A zone of political autonomy is delineated around the local ethnic community, from which the state is excluded. The difference is that Colombian *cabildos* have the status of autonomous municipalities, which conveys the right to receive a proportional share of state resources. Bolivia's indigenous communities do not. As in Colombia, recognition of indigenous organizations becomes weaker as we ascend the organization of indigenous peoples past the community level. In Colombia, ethnic organizations may achieve juridical personality if they choose to become social movements or to participate in elections. Regional and national indigenous organizations have the right to participate in various consultative bodies, but no real resources or powers are associated with this right, and individual governments have the power to render this participation meaningless. In Bolivia, individual ethnic groups have relations with the state through the popular participation system to whatever extent the levels of ethnic organization may be compatible with that system. That is, indigenous communities may be incorporated into a municipal indigenous district, or larger groupings may be represented on a provincial or departmental consultative council. All indigenous organizations and other civil society groups may obtain juridical personality for the purpose of receiving resources from national, international, or nongovernmental development agencies. Recognition of these higher-level aggregations of indigenous communities has opened new spaces for dialogue between the state and the Indians. As in Colombia, the extent to which indigenous representatives exercise authority or participate in decision-making, however, depends not on new rights they have attained but, rather, on the discretion of the state, international, and nongovernmental officials that control these spaces. The Bolivian regime does not allow civil society organizations to participate in elections at any level of government, an omission that would be protested later as partisan politics began to permeate indigenous organizations.

The Bolivian constitution is clearly deficient in comparison to the Colombian with respect to territorial rights. Colombian Indians obtained territorial and jurisdictional rights over areas that surpassed community governments—a space potentially comprising roughly 25 percent of the national territory if the ETIs are ever fully implemented. Bolivian Indians gained only property rights—albeit special, inalienable, collective property rights. The only sense in which Indians may exercise jurisdiction is in the administration of indigenous customary law.

Conclusion

In Bolivia, a relatively closed process dominated by the president produced a new relationship between state and society that was codified in the Law of Popular Participation. Although the process of designing the reforms was justly criticized for its closed and secretive nature, the responsiveness of the innovative institutional design to the needs of both economic and state modernization, on one hand, and the long-standing aspirations of popular, especially rural, groups for inclusion in the political system and local development decisions, on the other, earned the LPP widespread legitimacy and popular support. It also earned the Bolivian government international prestige and the commitment of the international donor community to launching the reform with adequate financial backing and technical support.

The unique way in which the LPP recognizes and incorporates a diverse array of ethnic forms of organization, authorities, and political cultures resulted from the collaboration among Sánchez de Lozada's trusted technical advisors and anthropologists and intellectuals familiar with the country's heterogeneous social organization and the aspirations of the campesino and indigenous movements. Incorporating the aspirations of these politically impotent sectors not only garnered popular support for the reform, but it also furthered a number of goals that were among the top priorities of Bolivian elites and the international development community, such as improving the quality of Bolivia's human capital endowment through investment in education and health, integrating rural areas into the national market, developing local productive potential, and extending the presence of the state and the rule of law throughout the territory. In a country as culturally diverse as Bolivia, where homogenizing development and integration schemes had failed repeatedly, policy-makers were ready to gamble on a radical new approach.

7 Implementing the 1994 Bolivian Constitutional Reforms

PRESIDENT SÁNCHEZ de Lozada moved quickly to implement the Law of Popular Participation. The unit in the Human Development Ministry that had been responsible for drafting the law was upgraded to the National Secretariat for Popular Participation (SNPP), and its director, Carlos Hugo Molina, promoted to National Secretary. In addition to Molina, the majority of SNPP officials hired were leftists or political independents who previously had worked in research institutes or the nongovernmental sector, and most senior personnel had worked in the UPP. Initially the SNPP had been transferred to the Sustainable Development Ministry, headed by Luis Lema, an early and active participant in the design of the law and a trusted presidential advisor. Several months later, after Lema resigned following the cabinet crisis of September 1995, his ministry was given to one of the MNR's coalition partners, the Civic Solidarity Union (UCS). In order to keep the government's star program—and the source of politically valuable resources —under the control of the MNR, the SNPP was shifted back to Human Development. This series of adjustments marks the beginning of political conflicts within the governing coalition and the ruling party, which would increasingly challenge the president's ability to manage the implementation of this and other reforms.

The SNPP oversaw all facets of LPP implementation, from designing and implementing norms, to approving co-participation revenue disbursements, to coordinating the dozens of multilateral, private, and foreign government agencies involved in LPP implementation. The SNPP communications program produced numerous training and educational materials for the Bolivian population, as well as more sophisticated analyses of the process aimed at Bolivian and foreign academics, government officials, and development professionals. Unlike in Colombia, where government dissemination of information about the 1991 Constitution ended within a year of its approval, in Bolivia, the Sánchez de Lozada government launched a continuous campaign of boosterism and information. Dissemination of the law was more challenging in Bolivia than in Colombia owing to the greater dispersion of the population, the greater difficulty and cost of transportation, lower literacy rates, and the poorer penetration of communications media. To accommodate low literacy levels, radio programming was developed and pamphlets and posters were printed and disseminated with drawings and diagrams and a minimum of words and technical language. On each anniversary of the approval of the LPP, Sánchez de Lozada sponsored a series of public events, fairs, and ceremonies throughout the country to raise awareness of the benefits of the law. Notwithstanding this activity, it is generally agreed that the reach of the effort was inadequate.[1]

Immediate Implementation Challenges

In Colombia, President Gaviria had prioritized the implementation of judicial reform to protect the new rights regime. In Bolivia, President Sánchez de Lozada's highest priority was to begin transferring money to the municipalities on July 1, 1994, in order to provide some tangible benefits to the population, to justify what opponents considered to be unrealistic expectations of the LPP. This was not only critical to engendering credibility for the new plan; the president expected that this early success would provide him enough popular support to implement reforms on the drawing board that were expected to generate resistance—in particular, the laws of capitalization and educational reform—while creating a large contingent of vested interests in the reforms throughout the country. The amounts of funds transferred are listed in Table 2.

The impact of the distribution of these funds was seen almost immediately in the countryside, since only the country's largest twenty-four mu-

TABLE 2
Distribution of Co-Participation Revenues, in Thousands of Bolivianos

Department	Population	1993 (pre-LPP)	1994	1995	1996	1997
La Paz	1,900,786	110,927	128,666	183,822	233,582	291,269
Santa Cruz	1,364,389	57,302	92,594	131,955	167,673	209,073
Cochabamba	1,110,205	34,220	67,656	107,366	136,429	170,123
Potosí	645,889	1,596	29,975	62,447	79,355	98,973
Chuquisaca	453,756	6,180	22,639	43,869	55,747	69,531
Oruro	340,114	7,011	19,600	32,873	41,774	52,117
Tarija	291,407	4,585	16,116	28,182	35,810	44,654
Beni	276,174	779	12,952	26,700	33,927	42,319
Pando	38,072	111	1,744	3,668	4,664	5,834
	6,420,792	222,116	391,946	620,885	788,966	983,898

Source: Figures from Archondo (1997:11).

Note: During 1997, the exchange rate for bolivianos/dollars was approximately 5/1.

nicipalities previously had received state resources. Results were less visible in urban areas, where entrenched patterns of corruption and politicization remained. In the aggregate, in the first two years of the LPP, municipal public investment tripled and aggregate social investments in education, health, basic sanitation, and urban infrastructure doubled. Three funds established in the mid-1980s—the Social Investment Fund, Campesino Development Fund, and National Fund for Regional Development—supplemented co-participation resources, increasing municipalities' share of public investment from 5 percent prior to the reform to 35 percent in 1995, and reducing the heretofore virtually unlimited discretion of the central government to 25 percent of national spending (Gray Molina 1996:1, 1997; Moe 1997:7).

In the first year of LPP implementation many municipalities spent their new resources on projects considered frivolous in a context of extreme poverty and unmet basic needs—in particular, on visible urban improvements calculated to enhance local politicians' chances in the 1995 municipal elections. However, these projects served an important purpose during the first year of the plan: they provided demonstrable proof that resources were flowing to the municipality while instilling civic pride and providing a public space for building community solidarity. After the first year, spending shifted to social investments—primarily basic sanitation, schools and health posts, and potable water—with a good portion of resources continuing to go toward urban improvements such as sewerage systems. The continued urban spending bias reflects both the better-organized demand of urban elites and the greater ease and quicker results of urban infrastructure projects compared to productive investments, which may require greater technical and managerial capacity than is available (Moe 1997:8; Gray Molina 1997). After 1996, municipal spending patterns shifted again toward productive investment, such as irrigation canals, roads, agricultural assistance, and improved communications. In general, spending continues to be concentrated in urban areas, while indigenous districts are ignored.[2]

In addition to the rapid distribution of funds, other daunting challenges required urgent attention. The government formed an interministerial commission to create a single coherent map of the country's existing provincial sections. Once the new municipal limits had been established, the SNPP turned its attention to resolving approximately ninety-seven conflicts concerning external or internal municipal boundaries; 90 percent of these conflicts were resolved through negotiations before the end of Sánchez de Lozada's term in mid-1997. The international donor community was principally responsible for providing technical assistance in municipal planning, accounting, and resource-management to the new municipal government, while training municipal officials to take on these responsibilities, a task made more difficult by low levels of basic education throughout the country. Meanwhile, the government worked to deliver juridical personality to approximately 20,000 OTBs; by 1997, there were 14,879 OTBs registered (11,585 campesino communities, 2,766 urban neighborhood committees, and 528 indigenous communities). Juridical recognition was prioritized because of the popular support this was expected to generate, since legal recognition was a long-standing demand of ethnic community organizations. The process took place amid a shift in loyalty in highland areas away from syndical structures toward the recuperation of ethnic authorities. This shift complicated the process of juridical recognition, since in some areas two organizations vie for representation of the same population (Ticona, Rojas, and Albó 1995:160; Booth, Clisby, and Widmark 1996:21). In such cases, conflicts were resolved at the municipal level or through local courts. As with territorial disputes, the government avoided imposing a decision in such cases, preferring to promote dialogue and consensus because this is believed to provide for a longer-lasting resolution.

Another immediate priority was the establishment of oversight committees in each municipality. This was achieved in 1996, thanks to a law that made receipt of co-participation revenues contingent upon their establishment. A 1996 SNPP poll found that oversight committees were composed of representatives of the marginalized sectors that the law's authors had hoped to empower. More than half of oversight committee presidents (55.3 percent) spoke a first language other than or in addition to Spanish, and farming was the most common occupation (43.6 percent). One population sector, however, was not well represented: only 3.9 percent of 609 members of the 122 oversight committees surveyed were women, reflecting gender discrimination, women's lower educational opportunities, and the fact that in rural areas women often work in separate organizations and, thus, do not attain leadership positions in the government-recognized OTBs (República de Bolivia/SNPP 1996; Bejarano 1997; Seligson 1998:7).[3]

The proper functioning of oversight committees is crucial to the LPP's goal of enhancing political representation, as it is the key link between civil society and the government. In the few municipalities where OTBs are well organized and recognized as legitimate by their communities, they have been able to pressure oversight committees to fulfill their functions or have established direct relations with the municipal council (*La Razón,* June 29, 1997:6–7). But even the SNPP admitted in 1997 that the committees barely function in most areas—a conclusion confirmed by the Banzer administration in late 1998 (República de Bolivia/VPPFM 1998). Independent observers offer an even harsher view, in the majority of cases calling them a complete failure (see Calla 1998; Orellana 1998). The weakness of the oversight committees is compounded by confusion and disagreement among the public and the government with respect to their rights and obligations under the LPP.

As traditional politicians try to restrict oversight committee powers, the Left and civil society leaders strive to expand them, for example, to include them in decisions on local policy and to make them a functional part of the municipal councils—a proposal clearly not envisioned in the law. Another problem has been municipal governments' resistance to the establishment of oversight committees and, once established, to their intervention in planning. Almost two-thirds of oversight committee presidents polled said that the municipality had failed to provide the oversight committee with an office, as required by law; information with respect to development spending and implementation of projects is not available to oversight committees or the public—or is provided in a coded format impossible for committee members to understand. In some areas, particularly in the Beni, urban elites have created an excessive number of urban municipal districts in order to numerically dominate the oversight committee.[4]

The effectiveness of oversight committees also is impaired by their low legitimacy and lack of autonomous resources and technical capacity. They are new entities and citizens identify more strongly with older community organizations—a problem also found in Colombia with respect to the government-created JALs (Velásquez 1996:41; Jaramillo 1996:51). Unpaid oversight committee members must expend their own non-reimbursable resources to attend numerous meetings, which, in rural areas, may require traveling hundreds of kilometers by mule, foot, or bicycle.[5]

Oversight committee members also lack the technical capacity to perform their jobs. The SNPP estimated that 85 percent of OTB leaders are functionally illiterate. The majority (52 percent) of oversight committee presidents polled said they urgently needed more training in order to examine the annual operating plan (PAO) of their municipality and to judge whether projects were being implemented properly (República de Bolivia/SNPP 1996). They lack resources to hire technical advisers, and most technical assistance provided by the government has gone to municipal governments. The concentration of educational skills and administrative experience in a small segment of society provides further challenges to the representation of marginalized sectors. Indigenous communities, for example, must choose between qualified elites to represent their interests adequately and more "authentic" but less-qualified representatives—a problem that is exacerbated by the practice of rotating leadership positions within indigenous communities, which tends to prevent the accumulation of expertise (Booth, Clisby, and Widmark 1996:28–29).

A further hindrance to the effective representation of civil society is the permeation of the oversight committees by partisan politics: 26.5 percent of oversight committee presidents polled complained that representatives of the government and members of the oversight committee maintained the same political party loyalty.[6] The problem is most severe in the largest municipalities (PNUD 1998:132). As in Colombia, although the oversight committees initially were conceived as a sphere free of partisan conflict, partisan rivalries pervade their operation. The implications of this are mixed. On one hand, the unprecedented territorial penetration of Bolivia's hyper-centralized and personalistic political parties bodes well for the institutionalization of political parties in Bolivia—a major requirement of democratic consolidation. On the other hand, the country's corrupt and personalistic political party culture has permeated indigenous peoples' organizations, generating divisions and diminishing the authority of traditional ethnic authorities (Calla 1998).

In Bolivia, the LPP was implemented swiftly by a series of supreme decrees promulgated by the executive, most of which were written by the government without outside input. The executive decree regulating the subjects of the LPP, however, was influenced by ongoing debates on the proper role of civil society organizations. The decree has a predominantly campesino and indigenous vision, which has resulted in noticeably smoother implementation in rural areas. The contemporaneous political mobilization of the *ayllus* of Norte de Potosí in June 1994 aided the law's authors in their efforts to recognize a multiplicity of forms of indigenous community organization and to keep the wording of the decree flexible enough to allow for its application within a variety of community structures and cultures. In some cases this has backfired. The failure to clearly define the term "indigenous community," for example, enabled municipalities to register indigenous communities as campesino communities, thereby depriving them of rights under Article 171 of the constitution with respect to their community lands, as well as the possibility of forming an indigenous municipal district. There are numerous cases in which municipal authorities denied official recognition of indigenous communities, particularly in the lowlands, where territorial issues are more conflictual (Orellana 1998:16–17). This practice partly explains why, as of mid-1997, only 528 indigenous communities had received their juridical personality.

In early 1995, to stop continuing opposition from the labor movement to LPP implementation, the government negotiated an additional decree to specifically address, among other issues, opposition to the term "OTB." As civil society organizations had feared, in some municipalities elites were organizing the rural population into new OTBs rather than recognizing existing community structures. Civil society leaders charged the government with attempting to replace existing community organizations with government-sanctioned puppets, as the MNR had done following the 1952 revolution. The government agreed to stop using the term and to replace it with "subjects of the Law of Popular Participation." In practice, however, the government continues to use "OTB." The government also failed to fulfill its promise to define the terms "popular participation" and "participatory democracy," arguing that to do so would inhibit the flexible application of the law in distinct cultural settings.

A final challenge in the first year of LPP implementation was preparing for the December 3, 1995, first-ever nationwide municipal elections. Despite predictions by opposition parties that the MNR would contrive to buy the elections through its control over the distribution of co-participation funds, the MNR actually garnered fewer votes than in 1993, prevailing mainly in areas of its historic strength. The autonomy of the LPP mechanisms had equalized the ability of political parties to manipulate the LPP for electoral ends.

Women were the clear losers in the 1995 elections, as the new powers and resources assigned to municipalities attracted more male candidates. In 1993, 229 of 858 municipal councillors were female (26.7 percent); in 1995 only 135 of 1,624 (8.3 percent) were female. Thus, despite the doubling of positions available, and a 31 percent increase in female candidates in the ten largest cities, women lost in relative and absolute terms (Booth, Clisby, and Widmark 1996:11–12). Similarly, the number of female mayors dropped from 19 in 1993 to 11 in 1995, and the number of female departmental *consejeros*, elected from among municipal councillors, dropped in 1995, and again in 1997 when they comprised less than 5 percent of the total.[7] Campesino and indigenous women fared even worse. They won only 22 of 135 female council seats in 1995, and only 2 mayorships.

If women were the clear losers, indigenous and campesino men were clear winners: 464 of 1,624 municipal councillors (28.6 percent) elected in 1995 identified themselves as campesinos or Indians. An estimated half of these indigenous or campesino representatives had close ties to indigenous organizations whom they represented through their candidacy (Iturralde 1997a:356). In 173 municipalities at least one indigenous or campesino council member was elected; in 73 of 311 municipalities, indigenous and campesino members constitute a majority (Gray Molina and Molina S. 1997:9). Staff of the indigenous peoples' unit of the SNPP (API-Danida) expect indigenous and campesino councillors to double their numbers in the 1999 municipal elections, in light of intensive voter registration campaigns conducted in 1996 and 1997. Indians' and campesinos' municipal presence translated into a presence at the departmental level, since each department's municipal councillors elect a councillor to represent each province on the departmental council. On the basis of language information, the government estimates that 26.9 percent of the new departmental *consejeros* are indigenous. The significance of these electoral achievements should not be overestimated because indigenous public officials usually lack experience and education and are easily outmaneuvered by political actors with greater experience, capabilities, and resources. For example, in the heavily indigenous Norte de Potosí area, eight indigenous mayors were elected in 1995. One year later only three remained in office after urban elites created sufficient pressures to remove them.[8]

Indigenous and campesino candidates ran on various party lists since, unlike in Colombia, civil society organizations are prohibited from contesting elections. To lessen the likelihood of indigenous and campesino organizations being politicized by party politics, and to provide opportunities for representation of social groups not well represented by them, anthropologists, sympathetic government officials, and civil society organizations have proposed that the law be amended to allow community associations and OTBs to run their own candidates without requiring affiliation with a registered party, at least at the local level. The Sánchez de Lozada government rejected this option in order to avoid provoking the opposition of political parties—particularly the MNR—to the LPP. During the 1995 municipal elections, indigenous and campesino organizations most often allied with the leftist MBL, because it was less likely than other parties to impose conditions on electoral alliances; more likely to put indigenous candidates in higher slots on the list; and more likely, following elections, to fulfill its commitments to the organizations (Chávez A. 1996:49). They also allied with a new political party founded by mostly Quechua coca growers based in tropical Cochabamba, which swept municipalities in the Chapare region and won a total of ten mayorships and forty-nine councillors in Cochabamba and five councillors in other highland departments (Albó 1997:13; Booth, Clisby, and Widmark 1996:24, 43–47; CSUTCB 1996:15–17). Because the National Electoral Court denied its registration on technical grounds, the Assembly for the Sovereignty of Peoples borrowed the name and registration of the United Left.[9]

Most observers agree that the 1995 municipal elections literally changed the *face* if not the *substance* of politics in Bolivia by making the country's ethnic diversity more visible. Diego Ayo interprets the December 1995 elections as the transformation from a political system dominated by a closed and homogeneous elite to a system governed by a more open and heterogeneous elite, since indigenous and campesino councillors and mayors represent for the most part the sectors of their respective societies that are more integrated into nonindigenous society. The creation of spaces at the local level for nontraditional elites to gain political experience and to acquire technical resource-management skills provides a much needed sphere of apprenticeship for sectors aspiring to national representation. In the past, representatives of marginalized sectors reaching this level were unable to achieve tangible results for their constituencies because they possessed only rhetorical skills in a body of highly educated and skilled professional politicians (Albó 1997:11; Ayo 1997:35–38).

Among the last aspects of the LPP to be defined and established was the mechanism through which communities and individuals—as opposed to their representatives—might participate in local decision-making spheres. Following two years of experimentation in pilot projects, and inspired by more than a decade of NGO-sponsored experimentation, the government codified a single, flexible municipal planning methodology in 1996. The government defines participatory municipal planning (PPM) as "the application of the procedures and methodologies of planning to the municipal context, with an effective participation of civil society organizations in the design and management of their own development" (República de Bolivia/ Sistema Nacional de Planificación 1997:9). In addition to creating spaces for participation, participatory planning is supposed to achieve greater sustainability and equity in municipal development. According to this methodology, OTB authorities organize a community self-diagnostic to ascertain existing levels of services, infrastructure, and investments. Demands then are articulated and prioritized in the near, medium, and long term at two public assemblies. Functional organizations and second-tier associations other than the recognized OTBs are allowed to submit their own planning proposals to the oversight committees. In practice, a variety of local actors participate, including the Catholic Church and NGOs (Gray Molina 1996:8). The demands of each OTB are aggregated by oversight committees into five-year strategic municipal development plans (PDMs), which are delivered to municipal councils for approval. Municipal councils are responsible for ensuring that PDMs are prepared in a participatory fashion and for elaborating detailed annual operating plans (PAOs) that faithfully translate community demands articulated in the PDMs.

According to a government study, the methodology does not operate as envisioned. The finished budgets

> rarely reflect the sectoral and territorial demands expressed during the first [community planning] phase. This is particularly true with rural *municipios*, which consistently identified agricultural, transportation and irrigation needs as predominant during the PDM phase, and typically ended up planning social sector investments at the budget phase. (Gray Molina 1996:9)

A 1996 study of eighty-four PDMs and PAOs concurred that municipal governments tend to ignore the productive investments prioritized by communities in the PDM and to prioritize social investment in the PAOs (Tuchschneider 1995:115).[10] David Tuchschneider attributes this reprogramming of community priorities to the resistance of local—mainly urban—elites, and the greater ease of implementation of social investment projects. Matching-fund incentives offered by the central government also tend to persuade municipalities to channel resources to social investment rather than needs defined by communities.

For reasons described above, the government chose to speed resources to municipalities faster than communities could be trained for effective participation in local development decisions. As a result, in its first two years of operation, the annual operating plans and budgets were prepared mainly by municipal government staff, with intensive support from SNPP technical teams and NGO consultants. In 1996, with World Bank and other donor support, the SNPP provided technical assistance to ninety-eight smaller rural communities in preparing their PDMs. A 1997 study of a sample of sixteen of the municipalities involved found only one case in which respondents even knew what a PDM was.[11] A year later, 82 percent of Bolivian municipalities had prepared a PDM (República de Bolivia/VPPFM 1998:10). A pattern of dependence on external technical support has developed in light of the failure of technical advisors to transfer skills and the slower-than-expected capacity of communities to participate effectively in planning. Involving communities adds weeks if not months to the planning process. Since the government measures the success of the program in terms of the amount of funds sent to municipalities and the number of PAOs delivered on time, rather than the quality of participation or the number of citizens involved in planning meetings, public officials have no incentive to make the effort.

In practice, cultural obstacles have further restricted participation, despite efforts to accommodate implementation in diverse cultural settings. In particular, a disjuncture has been identified between the necessity for decision-making and planning that responds rapidly to evolving needs and the reality of community decision-making processes in which consensus decisions require time to mature. As Rubén Ardaya explains, indigenous communities have a conception of time that cannot produce decisions at the rate that municipal governments require them for timely planning. The municipalities need to make decisions every day, but the communities may only meet together once every two weeks or once a month, and this is just to analyze, not to decide. Other problems emerge with respect to the delegation of representation. Communities may choose representatives, but this does not imply the delegation of the authority to make decisions on behalf of the community, only the responsibility for listening to public officials and reporting back to the community.[12] Women are another group ill-served by the planning methodology. They rarely participate in the community planning process and women's development needs tend not to be included in PDMs. Few municipalities have assigned any budget or programming to train women in management skills or to promote their participation and representation, as required by law.

Since participatory planning is the only activity in which the entire community may participate under the LPP, the fact that a minority of communities are using the methodology is an important indicator of the capacity of the reform to generate participation. The poor results thus far are even more disappointing in light of the restricted scope of the law's vision of participation. The autonomy of municipal participatory planning increasingly is being circumscribed by centralized programs to shape national policy through the development funds and through strategic action plans developed in 1996 to provide resource-matching incentives to municipal and departmental governments to channel investment into centrally defined areas.

Key Actors in the Implementation Process

In marked contrast with the Colombian case, the Bolivian legislature and courts had no significant impact on the implementation of the 1994 constitutional reforms because of the president's voting majority in the former and the failure to implement the judicial reforms during Sánchez de Lozada's term (for reasons discussed below). In their absence, the actors most involved in promoting the development of the new constitutional norms and institutions during this phase were the president, the national secretariats for Popular Participation (SNPP) and Ethnic, Gender, and Generational Affairs (SNAEGG), the ethnic organizations, and the international donor community.

The president closely managed the implementation phase of the constitutional reform, as he had dominated earlier phases. Among the projects in which the president was most intimately involved was implementation of the LPP, which he considered to be the most enduring contribution of his ambitious reform package. Sánchez de Lozada participated directly in the design of norms and mechanisms for the LPP and in the politically delicate decentralization process, which he nestled protectively under the Ministry of the President. His most important role was fending off attempts by traditional MNR politicians to politicize and manipulate the SNPP. The president's "permanent intervention" was necessary to resolve constantly emerging interinstitutional tensions and to enable newly created government entities to assume their proper functions (Medellín 1997:12). By continually confronting party leaders, however, Sánchez de Lozada risked his personal political aspirations. He received little assistance from the vice president, whom Cárdenas's supporters and Sánchez de Lozada himself had hoped would become the critical voice of the people within the government. Interviews with senior government officials indicate that the vice president was too politically cautious to play this role, preferring to consolidate his image as a pragmatic, political moderate and to avoid becoming associated with policy issues that might taint him as radical or provoke accusations of selling out from his campesino constituency.[13]

After 1995 Sánchez de Lozada grew less able to manage the unwieldy process of political reform, to defuse public opposition to his most controversial proposals, and to hold his fragmented party together. His hiring of so many political independents had angered traditional MNR party militants. To maintain support for his programmatic agenda, the president had to put reform within the MNR on the back burner so that the party machine could be harnessed to push the reforms through Congress. As the president's support dropped, his dependence on this machine grew and traditional clientelist interests began to prevail. Independents were increasingly replaced with MNR militants (Molina M. 1997:232). On one such occasion, a coalition of forces successfully intervened. In 1996 the MNR old guard attempted to oust the independent secretary of the SNPP, Carlos Hugo Molina, and give this coveted spot to a party militant who could mobilize the LPP apparatus behind the MNR's 1997 electoral campaign. Molina's replacement had been announced and a going-away party was held. But three important sectors kept Molina in office—the Catholic Church; the military, whose leaders viewed the role of their recruits in the LPP as supportive of the military's goal to maintain a presence throughout the country; and the international donor community, which threatened to cut off foreign aid (Booth, Clisby, and Widmark 1996:17n. 24; Molina S. 1996a:77).[14]

The Role of the SNAEGG and Indigenous Organizations

Not all indigenous and campesino organizations immediately embraced the LPP. Misunderstandings with respect to the term "OTB" and a number of real instances of local officials' attempting to create parallel organizations or to recognize rural unions affiliated with political parties (rather than the traditional *ayllus*) generated pockets of initial resistance in some areas. Although the government successfully negotiated a resolution to most such problems, some indigenous communities continue to refuse to have anything to do with the LPP. The reluctance of many popular organizations to embrace the LPP despite its clear responsiveness to their needs may also be attributed to Sánchez de Lozada's repression of popular protest.[15] Using violence against popular sectors at the same time that the government offered greater popular participation sent an ambiguous message that was compounded by the poor job the government did in articulating the implications of the LPP in terms that ordinary people could understand (Booth, Clisby, and Widmark 1996:34).

The SNAEGG provided an institutional space for the articulation of indigenous and campesino organizations with the implementation process. It established the Consultative Council of Ethnic Affairs, composed of government staff and representatives of regional indigenous and campesino organizations, to develop a strategy for implementing the LPP and other constitutional reforms. Crucial to this partnership between government anthropologists and indigenous leaders was the financial and technical support of international donors, particularly the Danish government, which facilitated the elaboration of programs to enable Indians and campesinos to take advantage of the reforms. International support was vital because the SNAEGG had no office space, equipment, or budget until the United Nations Development Programme (UNDP) provided space within its own building. During the Sánchez de Lozada and Banzer administrations, the SNAEGG—later named the Vice Ministry of Indigenous and Original Peoples Affairs (VAIPO)—and the UNDP shared office space in La Paz, blurring the border between the government and international agencies.[16]

Rather than attempting to weaken the national indigenous organizations, as the Samper administration had done in Colombia, the SNAEGG perceived a government interest in strengthening them. The scale and dispersion of the indigenous population made it far more difficult for the government to form relations with individual communities or ethnic groups, while the approval of CIDOB and other prominent indigenous organizations bolstered the SNAEGG's bargaining position within the government. The SNAEGG channeled international funding to CIDOB for organizational meetings during 1993–1996, which helped the organization consolidate its base, strengthen interorganizational ties, and prepare for the 1995 municipal elections. As a result, CIDOB was actively involved in LPP implementation, through its close relations to SNAEGG and SNPP and through the activities of its militants, since almost all municipalities in its lowland base have at least one CIDOB militant on their oversight committee. Because CIDOB had full access to information with respect to budgetary and technical requirements, it was willing to offer realistic proposals.[17]

The SNAEGG maintained more distant relations with the highland *ayllus* and campesino organizations, owing to a longer tradition of repression or manipulation by, resistance to, and autonomy from the state in the highlands. The national labor and campesino confederations—which dubbed the LPP one of the government's three "accursed laws" *(leyes malditas)*, in addition to the capitalization and educational reforms—maintain a formal position of opposition or indifference toward the LPP as part of a larger strategy of opposition to the government's neoliberal reform policies. Rather than articulating concrete proposals that reflect an understanding of the limitations on government policy, CSUTCB leaders articulate nonnegotiable extreme or abstract demands, or focus on the distribution of government patronage to its militants. The recent emergence of a parallel system of reconstituted *ayllu* authorities, and a concurrent movement to create *ayllu* federations throughout the highlands to replace the old campesino organizations, also constrains the capacity of CSUTCB to articulate itself to the LPP. The experienced campesino network lacks the popular support to mobilize the Andean population; the *ayllu* authorities lack the experience to do so successfully. Confrontations between the two systems of authority divert energies that might be used to mobilize people to appropriate spaces opened by the LPP and demand participation in planning. Despite the formal opposition of their organizations, individual campesino leaders acknowledged the positive benefits of the law and the necessity of the unions to take advantage of the openings it created (Booth, Clisby, and Widmark 1996:20). According to former CSUTCB president Román Loayza, the LPP has benefited campesinos and the campesino confederation itself. The distribution of resources provided education, irrigation, and roads that the CSUTCB never expected to see materialize, while the municipal decentralization enabled the confederation to establish a viable political party for the first time.[18]

The SNAEGG's first priority was to educate the indigenous and campesino populations about their new rights and to train them to take advantage of new spaces for representation and participation. This required translating information into the three major indigenous languages and was mainly accomplished through local radio programming. As in Colombia, an effort was made to explain concepts that did not exist in indigenous languages or which had a different interpretation in indigenous culture, and to stimulate a dialogue on the meaning of the law and encourage the appropriation of its concepts. For a variety of reasons—resistance or lack of interest on the part of communities, incompatibility with local authority structures, poor program design—these training programs produced poor results. To compensate for uneven and inappropriate government and NGO efforts, CIDOB and CPIB developed their own communications and educational programs, although they lack the resources to implement them fully.[19]

Two Danish government–funded agencies—the Proyecto Apoyo Indígena (API-Danida) and Taypi-Danida—took responsibility for assisting indigenous communities to obtain juridical personality, to undertake indigenous voter registration (only 8 percent were registered in 1995), to assist in drawing ethnically coherent boundaries for DMIs, and to train indigenous leaders in resource and municipal management, all of which was conducted in collaboration with CIDOB and other local and regional indigenous organizations during the Sánchez de Lozada government. A great deal of flexibility and negotiation with municipal authorities was required to harmonize the geographic extension and internal organization of the territorially discontinuous *ayllu* with the new system of territorial organization. The establishment of DMIs in the lowlands was even more difficult because ethnic groups there aspire to recognition as indigenous peoples with corresponding territories. The Guaraní, for example, inhabit three departments, six provinces, and twelve municipalities (Booth, Clisby, and Widmark 1996:53). Establishing DMIs fragmented indigenous political representation and technical capacity, weakened the ability of distinct communities to participate in development planning, and weakened the voice of these indigenous organizations at the provincial and departmental levels (Orellana 1998:2–4).[20] DMI status carries no special autonomous capacities, but it does mandate bilingual education suitable for the district, provides a guaranteed representative on the oversight committee, and requires that an indigenous submayor be appointed to oversee the investment of resources in the district. The lack of clear guidelines for the responsibilities of submayors or the allocation of municipal resources for submayoral salaries and expenses has generated conflicts between indigenous submayors and mayors. Only where DMIs are exceptionally well organized have they been able to use this status to achieve greater control over resources and development.[21]

The DMIs were first established and have been most successful in areas where indigenous communities are well organized. But this is a minority of the territory, according to government staff. Frustrated by the impotence of the DMIs, in early 1998, indigenous, campesino, and colonist organizations formally proposed that indigenous municipalities be created to allow ethnically and culturally appropriate forms of democratic representation and participation to develop within the municipal framework. Creating indigenous municipalities would bring Bolivia's scheme closer to Colombia's 1991 Constitution, in which indigenous reserves were recognized as territorial entities comparable to Colombian municipalities.

A key role of the SNAEGG in the first two years of the Sánchez de Lozada government was in inserting ethnicity and gender-sensitive language into the government's ambitious legislative reforms. It was most successful when legislation did not directly conflict with state or private interests in the exploitation of natural resources.[22] The 1996 agrarian reform law (commonly known as the Ley INRA), implements the state's commitment in Article 171 of the constitution to recognize indigenous peoples' inalienable collective property rights in their original community lands and the right to sustainably exploit the renewable natural resources thereon. The law resulted in the titling of 2.3 million hectares of indigenous lands in the last seven months of the Sánchez de Lozada administration; a total of 13.3 million hectares claimed by indigenous groups are expected to be titled by 1999 (Muñoz and Lavadenz 1997:25).[23] The manner in which the indigenous and campesino movements pressured the government to fulfill this commitment demonstrates the continued necessity of strong, sectoral, national-level civil society organizations and massive social mobilization to represent the interests of marginalized sectors of society, notwithstanding the gains in representation secured by the LPP.

The debate on agrarian reform, initiated in the mid-1980s when the CSUTCB first submitted its proposed Fundamental Agrarian Law, reflected a conflict between a neoliberal view of property sponsored by the government and the economic elite and a communitarian view promoted by the peasant and indigenous movements, which emphasized the social function and untradable nature of land. No consensus on this polarized issue could be reached until the Sánchez de Lozada administration began a lengthy process of dialogue on the land issue in 1994. Over the next year and a half, the government engaged in an arduous, at times highly conflictual, dialogue with indigenous organizations and eastern agribusiness interests. The dialogue produced a consensus draft agrarian law in May 1996 and represented the first time all popular rural sectors—the indigenous, campesino, and colonist confederations—had united to work on a common legislative proposal (*Artículo Primero* 1996:3; CSUTCB 1996:19–22; Muñoz and Lavadenz 1997:16).

Consensus on agrarian reform was shattered, however, when the government presented to Congress a version of the law that included changes opposed by rural popular organizations. After a series of demonstrations failed to persuade the government to reintroduce the original agreement, on August 27, 1996, more than two thousand CIDOB militants began a one-thousand-kilometer march from Santa Cruz to La Paz. The next day, the CSUTCB and the CSCB (Syndical Confederation of Bolivian Colonists) joined the march, sending contingents from other departments. The threat to initiate the march—one week prior to the planned meeting in Bolivia of the twelve Latin American presidents of the Rio Group—finally drew the president directly into the negotiations. The three organizations backed a unified platform. As the negotiations proceeded, however, the organizations became divided with respect to tactics. CIDOB suspended its participation in the march in the Santa Cruz town of Samaipata and negotiated an agreement advantageous to its constituency. The final version satisfied a longtime demand of CIDOB by changing the weak, property-restricted definition of original community *lands (tierras comunitarias de origen)* to the more politically potent concept of indigenous *territory,* which implies jurisdiction and sovereignty. The campesino union broke off negotiations and continued the march (Salvatierra 1996:74). More than thirteen thousand campesinos arrived in La Paz between September 24 and 26; an estimated twenty to forty thousand protestors participated in often violent street demonstrations in the following weeks. But the government stood firm. CIDOB and ten campesino organizations signed a final accord with the government on October 4, fracturing the campesino movement and widening the rift between the highland and lowland movements.

The 1994 Educational Reform Law furthers the constitutional commitment to establish a pluricultural, multiethnic, participatory democracy in two ways. First, it creates councils compatible with the new LPP structure to bring together state and civil society actors at the community, municipal, departmental, and national levels to discuss educational curriculum issues. Second, it injects an intercultural and bilingual emphasis throughout the educational system through the establishment of four educational councils —Aymara, Quechua, Guaraní, and Amazonian-multiethnic—to formulate educational policy for indigenous communities. But the impact of this law was diminished by the government's failure to prioritize its implementation. In fact, of all of the Sánchez de Lozada reforms, the educational reform is cited by analysts—including the president himself—as the least implemented of the lot.[24] As the reform initiative that bore the clearest mark of the vice president, an educator and longtime proponent of bilingual intercultural education, its incomplete implementation partially reflects the weakness of Cárdenas vis-à-vis the centralist, pro-labor sector of the MNR bureaucracy.

A third constitutional commitment furthering the realization of a multicultural state is the formal recognition of indigenous customary law and its harmonization with national law. Implementation was still on the drawing board in 1999. The indigenous customary law problematic was part of a larger effort to accommodate Bolivia's formal legal system to the reality of a country where justice is administered mainly in informal, oral, local settings, and to Justice Minister René Blattmann's vision of a more humane system, closer to the people, promoting conciliation and human rights. But within Sánchez de Lozada's ambitious and broad reform agenda, the project was a low priority, despite the existence of international funding. A World Bank–funded Justice Ministry project to document customary legal systems and draft implementing legislation to harmonize these largely oral traditions with positive law only began work in the last eight months of the Sánchez de Lozada administration.[25]

Unlike in Colombia, where the courts have intervened in cases of indigenous customary law that have shocked Western sensibilities (such as the public whipping case in Jambaló), Bolivian courts have not intervened in cases where punishments violate constitutional rights. For example, there was no official government response to a case of reported witch-burning in the Guaraní-Izozeño community of Alto y Bajo Izozog, nor did the state intervene in more than a dozen incidents of expulsion of suspected witches in recent years. One reason for the lack of a state response is that, unlike in Colombia, neither expelled witches nor the families of the executed have sought legal action to protect their constitutional rights. Indigenous communities have maintained solidarity on the issue of customary law in the few cases where they have been challenged by outsiders.[26] Ramiro Molina suggests that one reason there are fewer conflicts than in Colombia between indigenous and Western law is that Bolivian indigenous law has been consistently and autonomously practiced and is well known and understood within the communities. The exercise of judicial authority is rotated among community members, ensuring that punishments are fair and widely accepted. Occasions do not emerge where one sector of elites within the community challenges another's interpretation of indigenous law. In addition, the tradition in the Bolivian countryside is for conflicts to be resolved within communities or appealed to executive authority. In the absence of a civil state presence in most of the country, the administration of justice has been primarily an urban concept, with the exception of some agrarian conflicts that required state mediation, since courts are inaccessible to most of the rural population.[27]

Compared to its efforts to incorporate ethnic organizations into the constitutional implementation process, the government less actively and less successfully promoted the representation and participation of women and women's organizations. The SNPP's Committee on Gender conducted some training seminars for women in conjunction with the Gender Subsecretariat and Units for Gender that were established in departmental governments and a few municipalities. The female mayor of Pucarani credits such seminars, conducted in the first six months of LPP implementation, with preparing and motivating women to run for public office in Pucarani, where the mayor and 40 percent of the municipal council are female. Gender Subsecretariat staff believe that its limited experience demonstrates that targeted programs yield promising results, and that far more resources —and political capital—must be invested in these programs if general progress toward gender equity is to be achieved (Booth, Clisby, and Widmark 1996:25).[28]

Another obstacle to promoting gender equity, according to former Gender Subsecretary Sonia Montaño, was a political backlash against independents in January 1996 following implementation of the Law of Administrative Decentralization (LDA). The MNR and its coalition partners began to fight for their share of power and to push out independents and leftists. Taking advantage of a cabinet crisis, MNR leaders replaced independents with party militants, and departmental gender offices were given to the female relatives and girlfriends of party leaders. At the same time, the SNPP retrenched in response to resistance from the parties to its interference in departmental and municipal governments. As the SNPP lowered its political profile to consolidate administrative and technical aspects of the LPP, its ability to promote gender equity from the center waned. As part of the purge of independents that began in mid-1995, which pushed out Sonia Montaño, in April 1996, SNAEGG Secretary Ramiro Molina, a politically independent anthropologist, was replaced by Nicomedes Sejas, an indigenous congressional deputy representing the MRTKL, the vice president's party. The leadership change in the SNAEGG reduced its operating efficiency and engendered a greater dependency on the administrative capacity of the UNDP. The leadership change also strained the formerly close working relationship between the SNAEGG and CIDOB, since Sejas represented the highland indigenous movement.[29]

The Influence of International Donors
In contrast to the Colombian implementation process, in Bolivia, international development organizations and foreign governments played a deci-

sive role in maintaining the commitment of the government to institutional reform. The special interest of donors in promoting the participation of indigenous peoples and women resulted in funding for programs in this area and helped to maintain government interest. International donors provided crucial technical expertise and financial resources for LPP implementation (approximately 125 million U.S. dollars) in addition to channeling more than 200 million dollars to Bolivia's three national development funds. Their early collaboration, which began prior to congressional approval of the LPP, enabled donors to program crucial start-up funds for implementation in mid-1994, since no money had been earmarked for this purpose in Bolivia's annual budget. During the Sánchez de Lozada administration, major donors such as the UNDP, the World Bank, and the Inter-American Development Bank concentrated on municipal strengthening, which entailed conducting diagnostic studies of each municipality, training government officials, and disseminating information.[30]

Bilateral aid also was generous. In 1993, the U.S. Agency for International Development (USAID) began to develop a strategy to support what were expected to be areas critical to LPP implementation. A twenty-million-dollar Democratic Development and Citizen Participation (DDCP) project became operational in 1996 and was expected to conclude in 2002. Lessons learned in the six pilot municipalities in which USAID was working in 1997 subsequently were expanded to twenty "teaching municipalities." USAID originally intended to expand the project to 100 of the country's 311 municipalities (313 in 1998). But, as of December 1998, the project was planned to end in July 1999. USAID efforts had achieved a 17 percent increase in new registered voters in its six municipalities by 1997. Peace Corps volunteers reported a noticeable change in the local political culture as well as the internalization of their new responsibilities on the part of oversight committee representatives, who have begun to assume a more institutional view of their obligations.[31]

Smaller donors have found niches where targeted but modest efforts can have an impact: The Dutch focus on strengthening community organizations; the Danes target indigenous peoples; Canadians have focused on promoting women's participation. The German, Swedish, Swiss, Belgian, Japanese, and Spanish governments also have sponsored implementation projects, as has the multilateral Indigenous Peoples Fund, which funded a two-hundred-thousand-dollar SNAEGG project to train 120–30 indigenous leaders in resource management. The fund also has sponsored workshops to train indigenous leaders to present project proposals to potential donors.

One problem encountered by all donors was the poor performance of domestic NGOs as executing agencies for most of the international assistance. Virtually all of them flunked a simple test on the basic functions of the LPP given to aspiring NGO subcontractors by USAID's contractor, Chemonics. The donor community had expected national NGOs to provide an adequate level of technical assistance to implement their projects. Instead, resources have had to be diverted to training the NGOs. An additional problem is that many of the larger NGOs are associated with particular political parties, affiliations that may be imposed on the communities where these NGOs work.[32]

The close involvement of foreign governments and organizations in the implementation of the LPP resulted in enormous international prestige for Sánchez de Lozada's reform package, whose centerpiece was the LPP and the capitalization plan. The innovative reforms converted Bolivia from an example of the hemisphere's travails—poverty, inequality, corruption, political instability, illicit coca production—to a laboratory for democratization and state modernization. As the Sánchez de Lozada administration came to an end, the LPP was fêted by the Organization of American States (with which the Bolivian government signed a convention to disseminate the Bolivian experience throughout the Americas), the World Bank, the Atlanta-based Carter Center, and the Brookings Institution. Harvard and Georgetown Universities sponsored special conferences on the reforms. The governments of Colombia, Ecuador, Mexico, Peru, and Venezuela sent observers to study the LPP; and SNPP staff were invited to Argentina, Brazil, Chile, Costa Rica, El Salvador, Guatemala, Mexico, Nicaragua, Spain, Sweden, and Turkey.[33]

Counterreform or Further Reform?

As in Colombia, soon after implementation of the constitutional reforms began, Sánchez de Lozada faced organized opposition from interests vested in the status quo, including forces within his own government. In particular, observers detected a marked tendency toward "clandestine centralism":

the effort by MNR politicians to mitigate the decentralizing advances of the LPP and constitutional reform and to redirect power and control over resources to the center and to departmental governments.[34]

The most blatant effort to stall implementation of the new democratic model was directed against the judicial reform package. This delay postpones the full realization of the democratic aspirations contained in the constitutional reform because it delays the generation of public confidence in the existence of a nondiscriminatory rule of law and in the ability of the state to police its own excesses.[35] The 1994 constitutional reform created three independent judicial institutions, all of which were included in the Colombian reform: the Constitutional Tribunal, the People's Defender (ombudsman), and the Consejo de la Judicatura, an independent body to police the judicial profession. Sánchez de Lozada's minister of justice, René Blattmann, prepared a comprehensive set of laws to modernize the judicial system, but few of the laws drafted under his supervision were sent to Congress, owing to the greater priority placed by Sánchez de Lozada on other aspects of the constitutional reform, the resistance of the MNR to the elimination of political patronage slots in the judiciary, and Sánchez de Lozada's efforts to diminish the growing prestige and popularity of his able justice minister, whom he perceived to be a political rival. Implementing legislation to establish the three new judicial institutions was not prepared until the end of the Sánchez de Lozada administration; it was never sent to Congress. A last-ditch effort to convoke an extraordinary legislative session to approve the reform failed. Sánchez de Lozada did achieve passage of a new penal code, which had been Blattmann's main priority, and which contained provisions important to indigenous peoples.[36]

Civil society organizations tried to push democratic reform further than the president had planned to go. Indigenous organizations, for example, lobbied for greater autonomy for indigenous political structures and authorities. A more threatening challenge came from the departmental civic committees. Departmental elites were furious that their decentralization plan had been superseded by the LPP and LDA. Arguing that the changes would make the political system more democratic, during 1996 and 1997 the civic committees tried to generate public and political support for an extraordinary congress to consider three constitutional reforms: (1) the direct election of departmental prefects, provincial subprefects, and municipal councillors; (2) the separation of the presidential and vice presidential ballot from the congressional ballot, to allow voters to vote for different parties; and (3) the legalization of the popular referendum, legislative initiative, and constituent assembly. To demonstrate that their proposal had popular support, several committees held popular consultations on these and other issues. Senior government officials, including the president, denounced these consultations as illegal, illegitimate, and "political," and denounced the proposed reforms as likely to lead to ungovernability and to revive the polemical issue of federalism.[37]

The political parties also opposed the reforms, which would sharply curtail the prerogatives of the centralized party leadership. Some political analysts opposed the reform proposal because of their suspicions concerning the notoriously self-serving, undemocratic civic committees, as well as their worries that greater political decentralization and direct democracy would generate ungovernability in a country with an equilibrated multiparty system and a tradition of militant populism.[38] Others, however, condemned the political class for rejecting the democratic reforms and continuing to resist institutions of participatory democracy that were instituted in democracies throughout Europe, the Americas, and Africa after World War II, and for clinging to a representative model that is better labeled "oligarchic democracy."[39] The civic committees were unable to achieve their extraordinary congress, which meant that constitutional reform had to await two more legislative terms.

By most all accounts, at the end of his term Sánchez de Lozada had achieved his goal of implementing a dramatic and irreversible reform of relations between state and society (Andrade S. 1996; D'Emilio 1997:46; Moe 1997:ii). No political party proposed the revocation or major restructuring of the LPP during the 1997 presidential campaign, only minor modifications. Although local people continue to complain about the proper mode of implementation and to suggest minor modifications, anyone trying to dismantle the LPP would encounter stiff resistance in rural areas, where the law has brought dramatic improvements in living conditions, if not in political participation. Support is not confined to rural areas. A 1996 independent poll of Bolivia's four largest cities found that 60 percent of Bolivians having an opinion believed the LPP was positive for the country and should not be repealed (20 percent saw the LPP as negative and believed it should be repealed).[40] Of respondents in two 1997 UNDP-sponsored polls, 88 percent believed the LPP and administrative decentralization had improved representation in their municipality; 83 percent believed social services had improved; 76 percent believed municipalities had improved their capacity to respond rapidly to the demands of the people. Even once die-hard labor opponents of the law praise its benefits, while continuing to call for a larger role for upper-tier civil society organizations.

Implementation Under the Banzer Administration

Efforts by the MNR to campaign on the popularity of the LPP failed to garner a win in the presidential election, partly because of the strong direct association of the reforms with Sánchez de Lozada, who was constitutionally prohibited from reelection. The governing party came in second, with 18.2 percent of valid votes (half the party's take in 1993), behind former military dictator Hugo Banzer's ADN, which won 20 percent. The MIR, UCS, and Condepa each earned between 16 and 18 percent. The MNR and MBL were shut out of the government when Banzer formed a "megacoalition" of the four other major parties, comprising 80 percent of seats in Congress, which enabled the new government to legislate virtually by decree and to override the supermajority required for judicial appointments under the constitutional reform. The Banzer government has shown no interest in negotiating with the opposition.[41] Political polarization also was the result in Hungary when one government's supercoalition enabled it to act as a "constitutional dictator" (Elster, Offe, and Preuss, et al. 1998:142).

Despite its congressional majority, the new government faces serious challenges. Banzer has a paper-thin electoral mandate. His "win" actually placed second to the level of abstention (28.82 percent), in a country where voting is obligatory, and barely more than the 19.64 percent garnered in 1989 by Jaime Paz Zamora, who gained the presidency despite finishing third. The megacoalition was formed in part to counter this thin mandate. But the need to maintain a large and programmatically incoherent coalition presents the challenge of evenly distributing political patronage while maintaining the legislative loyalty of parties that oppose each other's economic and social policies. In order to satisfy the patronage demands of the broad coalition, Banzer fulfilled his pledge to purge the government of independents and technical experts and replace them with party militants, reversing Sánchez de Lozada's effort to professionalize the bureaucracy. The division of spoils erupted into open confrontation on the eve of Banzer's inauguration and an ADN-MIR rift has become a feature of the new government (*Presencia*, August 4, 1997, 4). This problem was partially solved when Condepa—the third party in the coalition, and a major source of dissent with respect to ADN policies—dissolved into factional disputes among its deceased founder's political heirs and was expelled from the coalition in August 1998, leaving Banzer with a comfortable majority of 76 seats in the 130-seat lower house and 20 in the 27-seat Senate (EIU 1998a).[42] In order to counter the centrifugal tendency of the broad coalition, key policy decisions have been centralized within the ADN, which holds 8 of 14 cabinet ministries and all 9 prefectures. Policy design is concentrated in the hands of Vice President Jorge Quiroga and a small team of personally loyal advisors. Quiroga is stretched too thin, leaving a vacuum of dynamic leadership outside prioritized economic spheres. The government also has had to deal with embarrassing corruption scandals in which its own militants are implicated, particularly within the Supreme Court (which has not undergone reform), the customs service, and the pension funds (EIU 1998a).[43]

The challenge of holding the coalition together has strained the capacity of the Banzer government in its first eighteen months in office either to promote the implementation of or subvert the original intention of the LPP and the remainder of Sánchez de Lozada's reforms. By the end of 1998, political observers believed the coalition had finally stabilized (EIU 1998a:6).[44] By this time Banzer's intentions with respect to the judicial reform, the decentralization and popular participation projects, and the institutionalization of indigenous rights also had taken shape.

Judicial Reform

Fulfilling a campaign promise, the Banzer administration in its first year in office drafted and achieved passage of legislation implementing the constitution's three new judicial institutions. The judicial reform is part of the Banzer government's effort to rescue Bolivia from its ignominious reputation as the world's second most corrupt country. The potential for the three new institutions to change public attitudes toward the judicial system is endangered by the unrealistically high expectations for these institutions, given the long delay and the hype surrounding their establishment. They are also plagued by partisan appointments, the ambiguous hierarchy of the new tricephalous judicial system, intra-judicial jurisdictional squabbles, and the general incompetence and lack of professionalism among judicial officials.[45]

The Constitutional Tribunal was legally established in April 1998 and began operating in June 1999. In contrast to Colombia's Constitutional Court, which has issued numerous decisions on indigenous constitutional rights, four years following the codification of indigenous rights in the constitution the Supreme Court, which retained jurisdiction over constitutional questions until the establishment of the tribunal, has yet to issue a ruling on these rights, and none are pending before it. Once it begins operating, the tribunal will adjudicate cases involving fundamental rights recognized in the constitution; the fact that many rights of importance to indigenous populations were codified in statutory laws (the LPP and the agrarian and educational reform laws) rather than in the constitution itself limits the capacity of the tribunal to intervene on indigenous rights questions. The tribunal's potential contribution was further restricted by the Banzer government's removal of the citizens' right to appeal directly to the Constitutional Tribunal from the implementing legislation for this institution, a decision that Blattmann-era Justice Ministry official Bernardo Wayar believes violated the constitution. Instead, citizens must bring complaints to a local judge, whose prerogative it is to decide whether to refer the complaint to the tribunal.[46]

Banzer's Justice Ministry set aside the project prepared by the Sánchez de Lozada administration to harmonize indigenous legal systems with state courts and started from scratch. The technical difficulty of the task is increased by the ambiguity of Article 171, which may recognize an indigenous jurisdiction that is entirely separate from the national system or one that is subordinated to it. As in Colombia, it is unclear whether Indians or communities have the right to choose indigenous jurisdiction, whether indigenous jurisdiction is mandatory, whether indigenous communities have broad powers to apply their own justice systems, or whether their powers are strictly limited to internal, cultural matters not regulated by the state. In 1999 Banzer's team was leaning toward identifying the constitution as the only limit, since international conventions are not well integrated into Bolivian law, as they are, for example, in Argentina, Colombia, and Costa

Rica. For this reason, the work of the Constitutional Tribunal is potentially important. A heated debate is expected among anthropologists and indigenous activists over whether indigenous cultures are organic wholes that may not be altered externally without destroying them, or whether like modernized cultures they can tolerate a great deal of dynamic change, generated from both within and without.[47]

The bright spot in the implementation of the three new judicial institutions is the People's Defender, which began operating in October 1998. All subjects interviewed, including those critical of the Banzer administration's judicial reform efforts, were impressed by the office's achievements in less than three months of operation. This positive assessment is attributable to the appointment of a prominent and well-respected independent journalist, Ana María Romero de Campero. Romero de Campero has taken up controversial issues, such as the long-standing claim of coca growers that their human rights are being violated by the government's forced eradication campaign in the Chapare, and has been an outspoken government critic. As in Sweden, the office's power to scold is its main weapon. Although some government ministers have criticized her actions, there is no indication that the government has interfered with any of her investigations. On December 4, 1998, just two months after the office opened, she issued her first two rulings—against the police and the customs service. Among the People's Defender's greatest challenges in the next few years will be to avoid the inevitable onset of public disappointment with the results of the office, given the enormous demand for justice and the office's limited competencies. It already has been besieged by numerous complaints outside its competency. Even in Sweden, where the rule of law is beyond reproach, only 10–15 percent of complaints result in some type of criticism.[48]

Indigenous grievances are among the more than seven hundred complaints received thus far. There is no special delegate for ethnic rights, as in Colombia. The law requires the office to hire translators when necessary, and its staff includes speakers of indigenous languages. In an effort to encourage complaints from vulnerable groups and to design a strategy for redressing their grievances, the office has initiated a series of roundtables with civil society organizations. In their first session, indigenous and campesino organizations identified some of their greatest frustrations with respect to constitutional reform implementation as areas for urgent action by the

People's Defender. These include administration of justice, the implementation of the agrarian reform law, the protection of territorial and natural resource rights, and defense against excessive force used by the armed forces against coca growers in the Chapare—some of the most conflictual issues in the country. Indigenous organizations participating in the roundtable committed themselves to creating positions within their organizations to work directly with the office.[49]

Decentralization and Popular Participation

During its first year, the Banzer administration alternately ignored and attacked the popular participation program because of its association with Banzer's political rival, despite campaign promises that the program would be maintained and expanded. Most of the staff of the SNPP were fired or resigned; the remainder are working on short-term contracts. The secretariat itself was downgraded to a low-priority vice ministry in the Ministry of Sustainable Development and placed under the direction of the NFR, a coalition partner with a regional base in Cochabamba. According to USAID staff, the SNPP is politically isolated and lacks technical capacity. The Banzer government's attacks on municipal decentralization and the LPP drew criticism from former staff and international donors. By late 1998, international and domestic pressures, as well as a reevaluation of the intrinsic political and economic merits of the scheme, had convinced the government to adopt the program as its own, although it is nothing like the showcase it had been in the previous administration.[50]

The popular participation plan has been adapted by the Banzer government as a tool for the alleviation of poverty—the principal theme of the current administration. Although government documents continue to cite the deepening of democracy as a main goal of the program, there are no actual policies in place to facilitate the participation of marginalized civil society actors—individuals or community organizations—in municipal or departmental government. In fact, the participation of privileged political actors—national political party leaders, departmental elites represented by the civic committees—has been enhanced at the expense of marginalized and local actors. The Banzer government's adoption and reorientation of the LPP have entailed a number of important changes.

First Banzer reorganized and downsized the popular participation office, eliminating vital programs like community strengthening and special assistance to indigenous peoples and leading the World Bank to cite among future "issues" the "lack of support for the development of the stakeholders of decentralization."[51] Other functions were distributed to three separate ministries, threatening the fluid coordination of rural, urban, and institutional development. Departmental offices of popular participation have been downgraded in the departmental hierarchy. Professionalism and institutional continuity have been sacrificed to political patronage: Staff turnover attributable to the change of government—in the national as well as departmental offices—has been compounded by turnover since then, in response to pressure for patronage jobs from megacoalition members.

Banzer also shifted the emphasis of the program from the municipal to the departmental level. The motivation for this is obvious: ADN militants hold all nine departmental prefectures, but the party is weak at the municipal level. Greater resources and responsibilities have been shifted to this level of government to enhance the ADN's future electoral chances and to facilitate the proportional distribution of patronage jobs among coalition partners. It also indicates a response to pressure from the civic committees, which are closer to the ADN than to the MNR. Sánchez de Lozada had marginalized the departmental governments because of their reputation for corruption and inefficiency, greater distance from common people, and greater susceptibility to capture by regional elites. The LDA provided no direct mechanism for representation or accountability within departmental governments that would siphon legitimacy or authority away from the central or municipal levels. Prefects do not even have the authority to name their senior staff members (Laserna 1997:18–19). Banzer has promised the civic committees, which had been marginalized by Sánchez de Lozada, that he would change the constitution to allow the direct election of prefects. What the shift in emphasis does not represent is a response to the aspirations of Bolivians: in a 1998 poll, 40 percent advocated giving more responsibility to municipal governments, and an additional 21 percent preferred more municipal responsibility if it can be administered more effectively (Seligson 1998:176). According to Ardaya, although the government is not doing anything to strengthen municipalities, it has thus far refrained from trying to weaken them. The government has pulled out of efforts to strengthen civil society organizations at the municipal level; USAID is working with the

Dutch and Swiss development agencies to continue a limited amount of this work.[52]

Immediately after taking office Banzer issued a decree internally restructuring the prefectures. The restructuring exacerbated confusion, turnover, and weakness within the departments and was done

> only in the interest of indicating differences from the previous government and to introduce substantive modifications without a basis in technical studies with regard to what these might correct and modify, hurriedly, and was done under the influence of political pressures, which have nothing to do with rationality and do not respond to a serious policy of institutional development. (Oporto 1998a:51; translation by author)

Henry Oporto blames the Banzer government for increasing the influence of political party competition and clientelism at the departmental level, which has produced a decrease in professionalism and technical competence and in coordination within the prefecture among rival parties (1998a :52).

In early 1999, Congress was debating reforms of the Law of Municipal Organization (LOM), including the modification of the article allowing municipal councils to remove mayors through annual censure votes (this also requires a constitutional reform of Article 201).[53] In practice, the censure vote has led to excessive turnover of mayors and widespread corruption as mayors dole out patronage to maintain council support. After the first year of the mayoral term in office following the 1995 elections, 29 percent of the country's mayors had been replaced; the following year 25 percent of mayors were ousted (Rojas Ortuste 1998:14). The greatest instability appears to occur where there is greatest fragmentation among the political parties represented on the council—where, for example, five or six parties are represented—requiring mayors to form coalitions to secure office. A 1998 study (Rojas Ortuste) found that the mayoral changes occurred in a clear pattern: In 1997 and 1998 the ADN and MIR nearly doubled their complement of mayors while the MNR, which had been the most dominant party at the local level, lost 12 percent. Case studies of individual censure votes indicate that national political leaders are pressuring local militants to unite against opposition parties (Rojas Ortuste 1998). ADN prefects also have used their influence to secure ruling coalition representation on departmental councils, which are elected from among municipal councillors in each province

(Oporto 1998a:39). Although some advocate changing the law to require censured mayors to be replaced by the second-most-popular candidate, or to provide for the direct election of mayors, the momentum to abolish the constructive censure appears to be overwhelming.

The new draft LOM also proposes to improve municipal efficiency by increasing the minimum population for municipalities to five thousand, a change that would affect ninety-five municipalities. This change would diminish indigenous communities' opportunity for political representation in municipal government and would increase competition for resources among indigenous and nonindigenous districts. The government rejected indigenous organizations' proposal to create indigenous municipalities, as well as the idea that the territorial organization of the country should be based on the distribution of ethnic groups, as organizations like CIPCA have suggested. Aside from creating "ethnic ghettos," government representatives argue, this would permit excessive intervention by civil society organizations into state functions and would disrupt the universal system of collective citizenship established by the LPP. There is also no plan to increase the autonomy of indigenous districts within the municipality, which would have helped address the skewed investment of municipal resources in rural areas.[54]

International donors have been quiet about changes to the LPP because of positive steps by the Banzer government on issues of greater importance to donor governments, like economic reform and coca eradication. In light of weak government support for a municipality-based popular participation program, USAID now plans to shift funding to newly formed departmental associations of municipal governments and subassociations to enable them to provide technical support to their members. Those associations are opposing Banzer's proposed reforms to the municipalities law.[55]

Indigenous Rights
The promotion of ethnic diversity as a major theme of government lost centrality and coherence in the Banzer government. There is no evidence of a continuing state discourse on multiculturalism outside the policy documents published for international consumption by the indigenous affairs office. The state discourse on indigenous peoples has shifted from an emphasis on multiculturalism, participation, and human development to an

emphasis almost exclusively on reducing poverty, which is one of the four pillars of the government's policy program (República de Bolivia/VAIPO 1998:11). The main tool the government proposes to use in the fight against poverty is to dramatically enhance the availability of private micro-credit for low-income sectors (EIU 1998a).[56] The emphasis on poverty, in itself, is salutary, since 70 percent of the entire population, 95 percent of the rural population, and nearly all of the indigenous population, is considered poor or indigent (see República de Bolivia/Vicepresidencia 1998:13–15). The problem is that, as anthropologist Ricardo Calla observes, "ethnicity has become an economic concept" and Indians are no longer a cultural group but, rather, a segment of the rural poor. The government no longer alludes to rights or to culture, but only to the economy of indigenous communities as productive units."[57]

As the MNR had done after the 1952 revolution, the ADN's neoliberal policy team discursively converted the majority indigenous population into an ethnically neutralized economic class of individualized "micro-entrepreneurs." It remains to be seen whether Calla's suspicion—that this discourse is intended to clear the way for the de-collectivization of indigenous Original Community Lands—is correct. Some indigenous leaders themselves appear to have adapted to this emphasis. Many have become disillusioned by the lack of improved material circumstances resulting from their new constitutional rights. Indians themselves are facilitating the illegal and clandestine sale of timber on indigenous lands in violation of the forestry law secured by their organizations during the Sánchez de Lozada government.[58]

The first indication of this shift in discourse was the lack of multicultural symbolism in the Banzer government's inaugural ceremonies—a marked contrast to the participation of traditional indigenous leaders, speeches in indigenous languages, and the exchange of Aymara ceremonial objects that had heralded the beginning and the end of the Sánchez de Lozada–Cárdenas administration. Banzer has eliminated multicultural symbolism from state occasions. No representatives of the indigenous majority hold senior positions in the government, not even in the new vice ministry devoted to this population.

Although the indigenous affairs office was given a higher status in the state hierarchy, in practice it has become less active and influential. It was shifted to the newly named Ministry of Sustainable Development and Planning and separated from the gender and generational portfolios. VAIPO is controlled by the MIR, which is using its control over resources to forge closer ties with the major indigenous organizations in order to improve its chances in the December 1999 municipal elections. Critics contend that the office is trying to move MIR sympathizers into leadership positions within indigenous organizations. This politicization of the indigenous affairs office is indicative of tendencies throughout the government as each party jockeys for position before the 1999 municipal and 2002 national elections. Intense partisan competition, combined with the lack of ideological and policy consensus within the governing coalition, has resulted in two dynamics that make progress on indigenous rights issues difficult: a lack of coherence in general on social policy, since this has been ceded to the weaker partners in the ADN-led alliance, and a tendency for ministries that had worked cooperatively in the previous government on multi-sectoral ethnic issues to act competitively and antagonistically. These dynamics not only isolate the indigenous affairs office (whose MIR director is knowledgeable about and committed to indigenous rights issues), but it also makes a transversal approach to accommodating ethnic and cultural diversity in public policy nearly impossible.[59]

Indigenous issues also have lost their saliency because of a shift in the base of power of the Banzer government relative to previous governments. Whereas previous Bolivian administrations had their political and financial basis in western, highland mining interests (an economic sector in decline), the Banzer government ushers in a new era where politics is dominated by a rising national bourgeoisie comprised of lowland economic elites based in the eastern departments of Santa Cruz and Beni. Banzer himself owns extensive holdings in the lowlands. The economic interests of these agroindustrialists, ranchers, and timber exporters (many of whom are Brazilian) clash directly with the interests of the indigenous population, because the expansion of their landholdings is constrained by the indigenous territorial frontier. This shift in the dominant political class has coincided with, and partly generated, a decline in the fortunes of both highland and lowland indigenous movements. The CSUTCB has declined as a national movement alongside the fortunes of its state interlocutors—the MNR, MBL, and MRTKL—which were the big losers in the 1997 elections.[60]

The CSUTCB organization also faces an attack on the syndical system of organization in the highlands, which is being challenged by the recuperation of *ayllus* and traditional community authorities. The CSUTCB has disintegrated as a regional movement and is now reduced to its most dynamic subgroup, the militant coca growers, who are locked in a losing battle against the government's forced coca-eradication policy. The coca growers continue to be the most militant and politically prominent sector of the campesino movement, but their public support has declined, and they have been unable to extract substantive concessions from the Banzer government (EIU 1998a:10). Meeting U.S. coca eradication targets is among Banzer's highest priorities, since it was under his military government in the late 1970s that the expansion of export coca production occurred, including the development of the Chapare as a coca export center. Nevertheless, in the absence of dynamism elsewhere in the indigenous movement, the coca growers' congressional representatives are the only interlocutors representing indigenous and campesino interests at the highest levels of the state. They have monopolized the campesino rights agenda along with the government's energy with respect to indigenous and campesino demands.

The lowland organization CIDOB was decimated by the 1997 elections, in which its leader, Marcial Fabricano, ran as vice president on the presidential ticket of the leftist MBL. On the basis of their 1995 municipal election success, Indians had been predicted to win 8–9 percent of directly elected congressional seats (Iturralde 1997a:358). The CIDOB-MBL ticket won less than 4 percent of the vote, garnering not a single representative. The involvement of much of CIDOB's leadership in election campaigns during 1997 left the Sánchez de Lozada government's ethnic affairs office with no major partner as it fought unsuccessfully to accommodate the government's proposed mining code to indigenous constitutional rights and ILO Convention 169. The electoral defeat not only left CIDOB without representation or allies in the government. It also lost them the critical political and financial support of domestic and international nongovernmental and government agencies, which were turned off by the organization's entry into partisan politics. The 1997 electoral disaster also generated severe divisions within the organization itself, which has fragmented into the five largest local organizations it represents. By late 1998, Fabricano had been somewhat rehabilitated and was elected vice president of the organization. Both regional movements are reportedly riddled with corruption by the easy money flowing from political parties, state agencies, and NGOs.[61]

Like the Colombian indigenous organizations, the CSUTCB and CIDOB are suffering the growing pains of maturing social movement organizations while trying to reconcile often contradictory roles as grassroots organizations, interest groups, and electoral machines. As Dugas argues with respect to the student movement in Colombia, the establishment of permanent movement organizations has both positive and negative effects on the achievement of social movement goals. Although they contribute to the endurance and consolidation of the movement, they also tend to distance leaders from their base and provide tempting opportunities for co-optation and corruption of leaders, which in turn tends to reduce constituency support (Dugas 1998:9).

The political dynamics described above have slowed or stopped the implementation of Sánchez de Lozada–era reforms that were vitally important to indigenous organizations. This is most notable with regard to the agrarian and educational reform laws. The distribution of indigenous-claimed land has come to a standstill. In Santa Cruz, in the first two years the agrarian reform has been in effect, not a single land title has been delivered to an indigenous community. Indigenous organizations blame political parties, which have interfered in the National Agrarian Reform Institute and have had local police imprison indigenous community leaders who defend their land from incursions.[62] The failure to deliver the promised Original Community Lands is a serious setback in the construction of indigenous citizenship, because it is through secure attachment to a territory that indigenous communities "generate political discourses and construct identities" (Paz Patiño 1998:128). As Paz Patiño argues, in the 1980s, through their collective struggles over territory, lowland indigenous people have constructed an identity as indigenous citizens:

> The Original Community Lands do not only present in a programmatic sense a concession or granting of lands by the State. Rather—and fundamentally—they express in a subjective sense the constitution of indigenous citizenship as a function of territory, which is projected at the level of the general society, generating relations not only between the State and the Indians, but also among Indians and "others". . . . [C]itizenship is not just a juridical cate-

gory, but a practice and a textual reality that has discourses and symbols that design identities. (Paz Patiño 1998:126)

Indigenous communities' own governing systems are linked intimately to the territories in which those systems are embedded. Complete state recognition of indigenous authorities requires official recognition and legal security of those territories.

Ironically, then, although financial resources from international donors for programs targeting the indigenous population are now more available than in previous governments, the government is hesitant to move forward on them.[63] On the other hand, the greater openness of the Banzer government to establishing corporatist relations with selected groups provides an opening for the indigenous and campesino movements to reconstitute themselves at the provincial and departmental levels, where they had been marginalized by the municipality-focused LPP. Banzer's policy documents on indigenous rights and the LPP call for the creation of consultative councils at the provincial and departmental levels that would include representatives of civil society groups (República de Bolivia/VAIPO 1998:31, 41; República de Bolivia/VPPFM 1998). This provides an institutional space in the LPP system at levels where indigenous and campesino organizations are stronger and less atomized. In early 1999, however, there was no evidence that meaningful discussions were being held at these levels with any groups other than the departmental civic committees.

Conclusion

As in Colombia, politicians and civil society organizations have proposed a number of additional constitutional reforms. In late 1998 the Bolivian Congress defeated proposals to legalize popular consultation mechanisms like the referenda and plebiscites and to directly elect the remaining 50 percent of congressional deputies (EIU 1998a). The influential vice president is determined to eliminate economic and social policy from the constitution. Sánchez de Lozada's policy institute is working on its own set of reforms. An emerging civil society movement is focusing on ethics and anticorruption in political issues, as well as institutional reforms to increase government accountability and transparency.[64]

The implementation of the recent reforms—along with the negotiation of new ones—is severely strained by the absence of elite consensus, specifically among the three largest parties, on the Sánchez de Lozada-era reforms. This is revealed in the cosmetic and substantive efforts of the current government, led by Sánchez de Lozada's political rivals, to undo or distort them. As in Colombia, the momentary consensus that Sánchez de Lozada was able to construct in order to pass his reform agenda did not last once the urgent crisis they were devised to address had passed. The Banzer government's second wave of institutional reforms has added to the confusion, instability, and ineffectiveness of all levels of the government. Equally important, it has generated the public impression that institutional reforms are all about control of political power and not about improving the responsiveness and effectiveness of government (Oporto 1998b). As in Colombia, thus, a key dilemma with regard to implementing the spirit of the new model of democracy is the difficulty of democratizing the political party system when political parties are unwilling to democratize themselves or limit their prerogatives.

Part III

A State which is incompetent to satisfy different races condemns itself; a State which labours to neutralize, to absorb, or to expel them, destroys its own vitality; a State which does not include them is destitute of the chief basis of self-government.

—Lord Acton, 1862

8 The Impact of the Reforms and Prospects for Constitutional Transformation

A T THE OUTSET, I had proposed that the end result of constitutional reform would be a transformation of both countries' exclusionary states and regimes. Political leaders would be drawn from a larger social base and more channels would exist "for the expression of popular demands and interests" (Remmer 1985–1986:80). Once this transformation had occurred, the regime would have a greater likelihood of becoming a consolidated democracy. But how are we to know whether this transformation has occurred?

It is too early in the implementation process to provide a definitive answer to this question. Although most of the institutions created by constitution-makers have been established formally, it is too soon to expect the norms and values that imbue these institutions to have been fully internalized by political elites and citizens. Constitution-makers themselves expected this might take a generation. Nevertheless, a review of such indicators as are available concerning the impact of the reforms will allow us to assess the extent to which a transformation might have begun. These indicators are divided into two sets: those relating to increased or improved political representation and participation and those indicating the effect of special measures to recognize and extend special rights to previously marginalized ethnic groups. A final section will look at two additional factors (inequality and violence), which, to a large degree, affect the chances that the first two sets of indicators of transformation may endure, improve, or be reversed.

Measures of Improved Political
Representation and Participation

Bolivian and Colombian constitution-makers believed that their constitutional reforms would legitimate democratic institutions and that this would
lead to increased voter registration and reduced abstention. Data from both
countries are inconclusive. In Colombia, voter abstention actually increased
after 1991. This may reflect either greater voter discontent or the increase in
voter registration since the ANC, which reversed a downward trend (Taylor
1995a:table 1).[1] Ex-delegate María Teresa Garcés attributes increased voter
abstention to the failure of the constitution to re-legitimate democratic institutions because of the excessive commitments to the traditional political
class made by the Gaviria government. Manuel José Cepeda, however, attributes the increase to the dismantling of the clientelist system, which removed material incentives for voters; the reluctance of traditional parties to
mobilize voters in the absence of clientelist controls; and the continued low
public opinion of politicians.[2]

In Bolivia, increased voter registration, attributable mainly to the en-
franchisement of eighteen-, nineteen-, and twenty-year-olds, also coincided
with increased abstention.[3] In light of this increase, the widespread support
for the Law of Popular Participation (LPP), and the fact that voting is *obligatory* in Bolivia (it is not in Colombia), the 28.82 percent abstention rate of
registered voters in the 1997 national elections is puzzling and disturbing. It
continues a steady increase in abstention during presidential elections since
the transition to democracy in 1982: from 18.3 percent in 1985, to 26.34 in
1989, to 27.8 percent in 1993. In fact, abstention in 1997 far exceeded the percentage of valid votes gained by the winning candidate (20.88) in the presidential elections. Political analysts had hoped that the incorporation of
directly elected congressional representatives (half the lower chamber, pursuant to the 1994 constitutional reform) would reduce voter apathy induced
by the inability to choose among candidates under the party-list system.
They attribute the unexpected increase in abstention to a persisting breach
between the political class and the rest of the population, as well as a continued distrust of political parties and of government.[4]

Despite these aggregate declines, in both countries the indigenous population increased its levels of registration and voting. The 1991 National Con-

stituent Assembly and the subsequent process of education about their rights inspired many more Colombian Indians to seek voter registration cards than had wanted them in the past. The government made a special effort to register indigenous voters after Indians in the department of Vichada had been unable to obtain documents prior to the 1994 elections because the government underestimated demand. In early 1997 Colombia's indigenous affairs office estimated that no more than six thousand indigenous adults desiring voter registration cards were without them.[5] Similarly, in Bolivia, indigenous people were among the groups targeted by the government for intensive voter registration in 1996 and 1997.

Constitution-makers in both countries aimed to improve representation along two dimensions: improving the accountability of representatives to their constituents and improving access to public office for previously excluded groups. Among the mechanisms used in both countries was municipal decentralization. Municipal decentralization brings the state and its remedial powers closer to the local sphere, whose parochialism is the main source of violations of civil and human rights (Elster, Offe, Preuss, et al. 1998:103). In addition to improving representation, accountability, and access to state protection, municipal decentralization was expected to improve the efficiency and availability of government services and to alleviate poverty, particularly in rural areas. Ultimately, decentralizers expect that the greater proximity, responsiveness, and efficiency of government will increase the legitimacy of government, particularly in socially heterogeneous societies where the state's exclusion of and discrimination against certain groups are more likely (Laserna 1997:18).

In Colombia, although local government spending has increased dramatically since 1990, results have been meager. Municipal decentralization efforts begun in 1986 failed to reduce poverty or improve service delivery, owing to the weak institutional capacity of local and departmental governments (World Bank 1994:139–45; Orjuela E. 1998:59). This problem is exacerbated where decentralizing authority has the perverse effect of increasing the power of paramilitary bands, guerrillas, and drug dealers, who sponsor their own candidates for municipal office. Rather than being accountable to voters, mayors are under greater pressure to appease local armed groups, who routinely assassinate, kidnap, and threaten local government officials (Kline 1999:179). In other localities, decentralization has strengthened local elites whose interests clash with those of the poor and indigenous populations (Roldán 1997:247).

In Bolivia, a number of reforms were aimed at improving accountability, including the municipalization of the territory, the election of municipal government, the staggering of elections to weaken the hegemony of central party leaders, and the direct election of half the Chamber of Deputies, which Bolivians overwhelmingly favored over the party-list format in a 1998 poll (Seligson 1998:11). The most important new mechanism designed to increase government accountability was the municipal oversight committee. Independent observers, both Bolivian administrations, and international donors agree that oversight committees have yet to become an effective check on municipal governments or a space for dialogue between society and state. The most important reasons for this are the domination of the committees by political parties and the insufficient resources and technical support provided to civil society organizations. When local pressure fails, oversight committees may appeal to the central government. But higher government intervention occurs only ex post facto, and slowly, averaging seven months for the consideration of complaints, although oversight committees may immediately publicize infractions and mobilize local public opinion against the government. In the first eighteen months of implementation of the LPP, eighty-six complaints were filed by oversight committees, eight of which resulted in the suspension of co-participation revenues by the Senate. This number is somewhat misleading, since the government has preferred to negotiate with oversight committees, particularly when government-party municipalities are involved, in order to avoid scoring an "own goal" against the ruling party.[6]

Another measure of increased municipal government accountability in Bolivia is polling on public trust in government. A 1997 Catholic University poll of the four major cities found that 29 percent of respondents trusted municipal government "a lot"; an additional 36.25 percent trusted municipal governments "a little"; 31.50 percent trusted them "not at all." This compares favorably with far lower levels of trust in the National Congress, which respondents trusted "a lot" (12.75 percent), "a little" (33.5), or "not at all" (44 percent). A 1998 poll of urban and rural areas in all nine departments found the level of support for Bolivian institutions to be strongest for the Catholic Church, indigenous authorities, municipal government, and

OTBs (in that order), and weakest for political parties, police, courts, Congress, and the central government (also in that order; see Seligson 1998).[7]

Both countries have been somewhat successful in improving access to public office for marginalized groups. In Colombia, a trend toward voter preference for independent candidates began prior to the ANC in 1988, when nontraditional candidates first broke the 10 percent mark for local and departmental office (Hoskin 1991:30–31; Fals Borda 1992:308). Nontraditional parties comprised roughly one-third of the Congress in 1991, but their representation declined considerably in 1994. The same tendency is observed at the municipal and departmental levels (Taylor 1995a:table 4). The 1998 congressional elections demonstrated the strength of several new progressive political organizations and alliances that may bode well for nontraditional parties in the future. In Bolivia, representation of local elites, rural voters, and Indians improved dramatically after implementation of the LPP and other constitutional reforms. This is attributable mainly to the creation of elective municipal offices.

In both countries, the indigenous population improved its representation in elected office. In Colombia, newly created indigenous political parties have taken advantage of campaign financing and media access for political parties and movements made available pursuant to the constitutional reform. Although, in 1994 indigenous congressional representation declined, in 1997 a reconsolidated indigenous movement gained three senators and two deputies. In these elections, CRIC leader Jesús Piñacué, representing ASI within a progressive opposition coalition, finished fifteenth in a field of more than three hundred national candidates. ASI also picked up two national representatives in the majority-indigenous departments of Guainia and Vaupés and came in second in the governors' races in Cauca and Vaupés.[8]

Indians also made gains at the local and departmental levels (see table 3), a result of the tremendous increase in the number of candidates proposed, as well as the successful mobilization of indigenous and nonindigenous voters. In 1997, ASI won the first governorship for an indigenous party, in the majority indigenous department of Guainia, and indigenous parties increased their mayoral wins to twelve. In Antioquia, ASI assembly deputy Eulalia Yagary won reelection with the most votes of any candidate, twice as many as her closest competitor. In the heavily indigenous department of

TABLE 3
Colombian Indigenous Political Parties' Representation in Public Office

	1991–1992	1994–1995	1997–1998
Senators (total 102)	3	2	3
Representatives (total 161)	2	1	2
Departmental governors	0	0	1
Departmental assembly	5	11	12+[a]
Mayors	0	8	12
Municipal councillors	23	175	–[b]

Notes: [a]My estimate of 12+ is based on votes received by indigenous candidates and
    my estimate of departmental population.
  [b]Figures not available from Colombian Registrar's office.

Cauca, the base of two of the indigenous parties, ASI has become the third force, behind the Liberal and Conservative parties; it finished second, ahead of the Conservatives in the 1997 governors' race. Traditional parties and the Left have courted indigenous leaders in an effort to capitalize on the popularity of indigenous candidates, placing more Indians in office, but leading to further fragmentation of the movement and the dispersal of leadership.

For the most part, these impressive electoral achievements have not been translated into substantive change in state policy. According to ASI Cauca assembly deputy Claudia Piñeros, the indigenous movement has gained a voice in departmental government and the respect of the other political parties, and it has forced the departmental government to channel more resources to indigenous communities, for example, supporting the communities' bilingual education programs and traditional medicine. She also observes a change in the political culture: people assert their rights as citizens and criticize public functionaries, citing particular laws that correspond to their rights. ASI Cauca President Jesús Avirama argues that, although the scarcity of resources has prevented rapid results, the brief experience of political participation has taught the communities that they must participate more actively in the allocation of the budget and invest more in long-term productive projects. Avirama sees the main obstacle to participation by indigenous representatives in government to be the continued centralization of decision-making authority. Local and departmental spaces for indigenous organizations to participate in policy-planning in diverse state agencies have opened up since the constituent assembly, but the proposals and preferences of the indigenous representatives are generally not taken into account by state decision-makers, and decisions continue to be made at the national level. As a result of their frustration, many indigenous leaders have abandoned these spaces.[9]

Indians' lack of satisfaction with indigenous political representatives is partly attributable to a different understanding of the concept of representation among indigenous cultures. Indigenous communities and organizations tend to confer less authority on their representatives and expect greater subservience to the articulated will of the community or ethnic group than is implied by a Liberal-democratic interpretation of representation. Hanna Pitkin refers to this distinction as the "mandate-independence controversy" (1967:215). Most Western observers would argue that representatives are free to determine the best interests of their constituency and to balance this determination with the interests of the public as a whole (the "independence" position); indigenous voters and communities, however, expect their representatives to adhere to decisions made by consensus in the community or by traditional community authorities, and to defend their particular interests against those of the wider society (the "mandate" position).

The improved representation of Colombia's black population is difficult to measure, since blacks were represented in appointive and elective office in the decades preceding the ANC. Afro-Colombian political parties have not been formed on the scale seen in the indigenous movement. A major setback was the failure of the Samper administration to reinstate the two seats reserved for Pacific Coast blacks in the lower house of Congress, which existed only during the 1994–1998 term. Pacific Coast blacks' most effective legislative representative, Zulia Mena, lost her Senate race in 1998.

In Bolivia, representation of ethnic minorities improved dramatically as a result of the municipalization of the country and the election of municipal councillors. Of 1,624 municipal councillors elected in 1995, 464 (28.6 percent) identified themselves as campesinos or Indians, which translated into 26.9 percent of the new departmental *consejeros*. The lowland indigenous organization CIDOB took full advantage of the 1995 municipal elections via alliances with locally strong parties that brought many CIDOB militants into public office. All ten parties contesting the 1997 congressional elections included indigenous candidates on their lists.[10] That year the

Quechua coca-growers' party ASP won four directly elected seats in the lower Chamber. Controversial leader Evo Morales received among the greatest number of votes of all single-member district candidates.[11] Although they remain a small minority in the lower house, in the context of extreme party fragmentation, small parties have the potential of making substantive legislative gains through strategic alliances.

In both countries constitutional reform failed to improve the representation of women. In Colombia, despite some high-profile cabinet appointments, women are underrepresented in public office, comprising only 5.3 percent of mayors elected in 1992 (Archila 1995:286). In Bolivia, women are *less* visible in electoral office and civil society leadership since the 1994 constitutional reform because of the greater resources and prestige now accruing to local office. In addition, Bolivia gained its first female cabinet minister in 1997, the same year a major party ran a female presidential candidate for the first time (CONDEPA's Remedios Loza finished third). In 1998, the high-profile position of People's Defender went to a woman. Women's organizations have disappeared or grown weaker owing to their marginalization under the new popular participation regime. The only good news for women was a slight increase in congressional representation because of the new law requiring parties to reserve 30 percent of their lists for female candidates, a measure recently introduced in Argentina and Uruguay. The number of female senators remained the same (one), and the number of female deputies increased from ten to twelve, increasing women's representation from 7 percent to 8 percent (even though the number of female candidates almost doubled in order to comply with the new law, since women mainly were placed at the bottom of the lists). In Argentina, by contrast, use of the 30 percent quota resulted in a 27 percent female congressional body.[12] Representation of indigenous women has improved since the LPP as a result of efforts by the government to sensitize indigenous communities to gender equity as well as efforts of indigenous women since 1990 to demand representation and participation and to establish their own organizations.

Creating spaces for citizens to participate in decision-making apart from periodic voting was one of the chief goals of both constitutional reforms. In Colombia, the main strategy for increasing citizen participation was the legalization of direct mechanisms of democracy. Effective exercise of these mechanisms has been impeded by congressional restrictions. A study by the NGO Procomún found that, where excessive regulations raise the short-term cost of participation, people are likely to forgo long-term benefits in favor of abstaining. Moreover, excessive regulations coexist in some areas with a less cumbersome, alternative system of decision-making by non-state entities, such as guerrillas, narco-traffickers, and landowners. Participating in tedious decision-making fora does not appear worthwhile if decisions will ultimately be made by informal powers.[13]

On three occasions citizens collected sufficient signatures to present a legislative initiative to Congress. One initiative, a measure to strengthen kidnapping laws, became law.[14] The right to recall, limited to mayors and governors, has been used mainly in small municipalities. Five times in 1996 citizens brought the recall of the mayor to a public vote. Even though in all five "yes" outnumbered "no" votes, insufficient votes were cast to effect a recall. This is an example of the impact of excessive restrictions on the use of direct democracy mechanisms. Legislation implementing the recall requires that 60 percent of voters approve the recall and that the number of voters participating be no less than 60 percent of those voting in the election in which the mayor or governor was elected—an excessive level of participation given traditional levels of abstention in Colombia, as a minority of the Constitutional Court argued upon review of this statutory law (Sentencia C-180/94, cited in Gaitán and Bejarano 1994:31). The popular consultation twice has been used unsuccessfully at the local level (Procomún 1997:17). At the national level, the Gaviria government began the process for a popular consultation on the criminalization of the personal use of drugs, which the Constitutional Court ruled in 1994 was unconstitutional under the fundamental right of personal autonomy. The Samper administration chose to refer the matter to Congress rather than pursue a referendum. President Samper proposed a popular consultation on the continuation of his term after the explosion of the drug-money scandal that implicated his presidential campaign. This idea was dropped after the Liberal-dominated Congress exonerated him in 1996. A citizens' movement for a referendum on the removal of Samper, Colombians for the Referendum, failed to collect the required 10 percent of the national electoral census. Eighteen referenda were held during 1995–1996 on the creation of new municipalities, seventeen of them on the Atlantic Coast. Most of these passed, although abstention averaged 50 percent (Procomún 1997:17). The Colombian government has no system to document whether the mandated *cabildos abiertos* (town meetings) are functioning or to promote their establishment. Anecdotal evidence suggests that the *cabildo abierto* has had greater support from municipal governments controlled by nontraditional forces. Such an example is Pasto, under the mayoralty of ADM-19 leader and former ANC copresident Antonio Navarro Wolff.[15]

Ironically, the new participatory mechanisms created by the 1991 constitution have marginalized the community action juntas (JACs) and failed to integrate them into the framework of the new statutory legislation. Rather than providing space for these established and experienced civic committees to participate in decision-making, local administrations tend to promote parallel, competing public spaces, perhaps in an effort to neutralize their influence (Procomún 1997:21, 67). According to Jorge Jairo Posada, a specialist in municipal government at the Universidad Javeriana, from the beginning of the decentralization effort in 1986 to the present, the government has convoked community participation in fragmented, disorganized social and political spaces rather than those preferred by social movements.

Decentralization creates the opportunity for collective community action and democratic participation, but the latter does not follow from the former unless organized collective actors are able to act voluntarily to define their own needs and design solutions to them (Posada E. 1998:154–55, 163). In Colombia, where citizen participation occurs, it is generally confined to committees to monitor the design and implementation of a particular public works or services project, and citizens usually lack the technical capacity and access to information to have their opinions taken into account. Planning continues to be performed by municipal authorities, often with external advisors, and usually without community participation. Participation is most likely to occur where it is clearly linked to material benefits. There are no legal sanctions for officials who fail to establish public spaces for citizen participation or a legal means through which citizens can demand that they do so. Despite the existence of funds in their budgets for the promotion and training of citizen participation, none of the nine municipalities studied by Procomún had elected to use them for this purpose (Procomún 1997:4, 66).[16]

Humberto de la Calle argues that the key to the development of Colombia's new democratic model is the transformation of the culture and habits of the people. But the government cannot by itself create new citizens, even if it were willing to do so (Gaitán and Bejarano 1994:39–41).[17] Colombian civil society has not assumed that vital role, for the reasons noted above and also because of the habit of social organizations of demanding state action rather than seizing the initiative, and the tendency of existing opposition political forces to maintain an adversarial attitude toward the state rather than to work constructively to promote consensus on viable alternatives (Gaitán and Bejarano 1994:40). In addition, social movements and NGOs have allowed themselves to be co-opted and their objectives subordinated to political party alliances. They are overly bureaucratic and generally undemocratic in their internal operations (FESCOL 1996a:11).

In Bolivia, the establishment of municipalities throughout the country increased space for citizen participation by creating multiple, decentralized public spheres. The development-planning methodology, implemented only in 1996, provides in theory a space for every citizen to participate in decision-making activities on vital local issues. In its three years of implementation, Bolivia's LPP has been touted by the country's most skeptical analysts as the most revolutionary reform since the 1952 revolution. Admirers laud its "historic," profound, and lasting impact, which has brought democracy and development for the first time to the rural poor.[18]

Anecdotal reports and the assessments of donor institutions indicate a wide range of variation in the ability of citizens to take advantage of these new spaces. Studies by external auditors find that participation is among the weakest aspects of LPP implementation. Communities are not consistently consulted in the design or implementation of development plans. Government efforts to address the lack of community participation by requiring the preparation of municipal development plans or the establishment of oversight committees sometimes have backfired, as more elite, educated members of communities are pushed forward to fulfill these tasks and dependence is increased upon technical advisers, who resist transferring their skills to communities (Moe 1997:19).

Women's participation is even more of a problem. USAID project director Rubén Ardaya observes that women normally do not participate in the participatory planning process, except on "women's projects." Women may attend meetings, but they rarely speak. The problem of women's participation runs throughout the country, but it is most severe in indigenous communities, where customs may limit the role of women: "And this is a significant problem, in that the law says that there must be equal representation of women and men in governing and also that we must respect the communities' 'usos y costumbres.' Well, the usos y costumbres are that women are in the kitchen." Given this discriminatory culture, Ardaya believes that addressing the lack of women's participation will require legislation similar to the congressional female quota law.[19]

A variety of explanations for the lack of participation under the LPP have been offered: the resistance of powerful local interests and efforts of political parties to exclude communities that do not support them; lack of access to information about the LPP and the rights and duties of communities; the lack of community capacity and technical assistance; the overly complicated and technical nature of the planning methodology; the lower priority placed on participation by the central government; the government's failure to undertake a major effort to inculcate a culture of participation among the Bolivian people (Molina M. 1997:231; Vadillo 1997a). In addition, the basis upon which the LPP was to have been built—Bolivia's dense network of rural and urban community organizations—was not as supportive as had been hoped. A UNDP-sponsored poll of Bolivia's four major cities found that 78 percent of respondents belonged to a civil society organization. However, the actual level of participation in sporting and social clubs, political parties, unions, and community organizations was low. In urban neighborhood committees, for example, few members actually vote in elections and participation is dominated by upper-income men over thirty years of age (PNUD 1998:117). In the countryside, traditional community organizations tend to be gender-based and to discourage the articulation of competing interests in favor of the maintenance of consensus and the fostering of a "community interest." Despite the hyperbole of anthropologists with respect to "ethnic democracy" in rural communities, USAID found them to be hierarchical, with community leaders hesitant to pass along information obtained during training sessions to community members, especially to women, who typically receive no information about their rights or responsibilities. Highland campesino organizations, in particular, are organized according to rigid, vertical, patron-client relations. These are not the type of dense, horizontal, civil society relations that Robert Putnam found to underpin a civic culture in northern Italy (Putnam 1993:101–05).[20]

The lack of citizen and community participation in the participatory planning methodology is mainly due, in my view, to the higher priority that both post-reform Bolivian governments have given to the efficient distribution of resources and the technically adequate production of annual operating plans, relative to the effort to foster citizen participation. Technical staff in municipal and departmental governments are under greater pressure to produce their PAOs and to implement development projects in a timely and efficient manner than they are to ensure that citizens participate in these tasks. Quantitative measures of implementation have been stressed to the detriment of qualitative ones. Participation also was impeded by the Sánchez de Lozada government's conceptualization of the problem of popular participation as the inability of clients to affect the abysmal quality and accessibility of public services. The extension of the opportunity to participate in certain decisions with respect to the provision of public services, and the resulting more efficient and ample delivery of these services, is intended to support democracy by building, among the citizens, more confidence in the effectiveness and responsiveness of government to public demands. But the end toward which the whole popular participation concept is heading is economic and social development, rather than democratic aspirations such as greater freedom, self-fulfillment, or communal solidarity. This client-centered conceptualization justifies confining participation to the control of users over the provision and administration of public services. In practice, this is further circumscribed to the prioritization of certain services with respect to others and the location of the services within the municipality. The decentralization of public service delivery to the municipal level justifies the geographical confinement of participation to that level. The marginalization of the higher-tier organizations from the political conjuncture, the co-optation and distraction of local organizations by the cumbersome municipal planning process, and the state's repression of popular protest all diminish the capacity of autonomous civil society organizations to mobilize effectively in favor of political change (Booth, Clisby, and Widmark 1996). In sum, the activity of participation is conceptualized as instrumental for satisfying needs and not as intrinsically beneficial or transformative.[21]

In both Bolivia and Colombia, a long-term investment in basic education, technical training, and democratic values is required for the inculcation of a participatory culture and for the creation of a citizenry capable of participating effectively in available spheres of monitoring and decision-making. As Will Kymlicka argues:

> The health and stability of a modern democracy depends, not only on the justice of its basic institutions, but also on the qualities and attitudes of its citizens: e.g., their sense of identity, and how they view potentially competing forms of national, regional, ethnic, or religious identities; their ability to tolerate and work together with others who are different from themselves; their desire to participate in the political process in order to promote the public good and hold political authorities accountable; their willingness to show self-restraint and exercise personal responsibility in their demands, and in personal choices which affect their health and the environment, and their sense of justice and commitment to a fair distribution of resources. (Kymlicka 1995:175)

Unlike the Colombian government, which heeded the mandate of the 1991 Constitution to promote the study of the new charter in the country's schools, the Bolivian government has done virtually nothing to promote the formation of citizen or democratic values. The importance of educational levels and political culture to the success of institutional reform projects is one reason it is so difficult to predict the long-term results of constitutional change (Banting and Simeon 1985a:6).[22]

Despite the problems in the new participatory model just noted, on balance I concur with an independent study commissioned by the UNDP in 1997 that Bolivia today is more democratic than it was prior to the institutional reforms begun in 1993 (PNUD 1998:135). A greater diversity and number of Bolivians have access to government decision-making spheres, are registered to vote, are represented in public office, and receive public services. Elected officials are more *vertically* accountable than before, at least at the local level, where civil society organizations are better able to monitor the performance of municipal government. Horizontal accountability remains impaired by the hegemony of the government coalition in Congress and its ability to appoint justices without opposition approval. On balance, Bolivians had better success implementing their new participatory model of democracy than did Colombians because of the lack of generalized violence in the country, the more focused and consistent effort by Sánchez de Lozada to supervise reform implementation, the ability of the government to draw on the expertise and financial resources of international donors, and the en-thusiasm with which Bolivians appropriated the new participation mecha-nisms. In addition, Bolivia's new democratic model was less ambitious than Colombia's. Its scope was restricted to facilitating popular participation in local development-planning and the prioritization and delivery of public services. The area in which Colombia had relatively greater success was in the establishment of independent judicial institutions to curb the excesses of the executive and legislative branches of government, to define, develop, and protect fundamental constitutional rights, and to confer legitimacy and credibility on the constitution as a whole. The Banzer administration con-tributed to this goal by promulgating the judicial reform; it remains to be seen whether the government will use its legislative majority to perpetuate the politicized administration of justice.

Several obstacles to implementation of the new democratic model in Bolivia remain. These include the extreme deficit of municipal manage-ment capacity and infrastructure throughout the country, which is com-pounded by a basic educational deficit that will take a generation to fill; continued confusion among the public with respect to the purpose of the LPP and their new rights and responsibilities; popular organizations' pro-found mistrust of government and of any proposal emanating therefrom, with a corollary tendency to blindly legitimate acts of resistance; and the tight grip on politics maintained by the country's undemocratic, unrepre-sentative political parties (Laserna 1996:105). Development experts at the Indigenous Peoples Fund expect that it will take a generation to see results from the reforms, on the basis of the contrasting experience in Ecuador, where participatory planning is being implemented by newly elected in-digenous mayors—in defiance of the country's municipal legislation. The difference in Ecuador is its educational system, which delivers a far higher level of basic education and literacy than Bolivia's, as well as the fact that Ecuadorian rural elites traditionally have invested public capital in roads, communications, transportation, and other infrastructure. In contrast, in Bolivia, the mining class and other rural elites extracted the wealth and left an enormous deficit in public infrastructure. Thus, while results should be apparent within five years in Ecuador, they may take twenty-five years in Bolivia.[23]

Indicators of Recognition of Ethnic Rights

The greatest achievement of ethnic groups in both countries has been symbolic rights: formal state recognition of indigenous customs, traditions, authorities, and forms of political organization. The topics of cultural identity, collective rights, and indigenous authorities are now mainstream political issues. Indigenous leaders and political candidates have a high profile and are courted by major parties. In Colombia, the constitutional discourse on diversity and tolerance has become an object of national pride, and Indians have gained enormous "symbolic capital" through their role in the constitutional reform struggle and in subsequent disputes with the state (Gros 1997:46). In Bolivia, the discourse on the "multicultural state" that began in the late 1980s has become a fixture of mainstream political discourse and has made ethnic difference more visible and more accepted as inherently Bolivian than ever before (Booth, Clisby, and Widmark 1996:8; Molina S. 1996a:78). As Bolivian activist Lucia D'Emilio observes:

> The discursive position of the State with respect to indigenous peoples has changed radically, moving away from homogenizing conceptions and the negation of the cultural and linguistic uniqueness of indigenous cultures to a perspective more respectful of difference. . . . Ethnic pluralism is being converted into an enriching factor for the idea of the "State," for the notion of democracy itself, and a challenge for any proposals of change. (D'Emilio 1997:43)

Even the Banzer government's attempts to exclude ethnicity from state discourse and policy cannot diminish the salience of ethnic identity in mainstream politics. In both countries, the constitution's recognition of state and society as "multiethnic and pluricultural" is located at the beginning of the charter as a defining principle of the state, as a supreme value governing the political community, requiring its development through all state laws, policies, and structures (Vadillo 1997b:340). Although elite and public acceptance of this value cannot be decreed, and it will take time for its symbolic meaning to be reflected in reality, the high rank given to this principle is salutary and juridically significant.

Both constitutions created spaces for representatives of indigenous organizations to "participate" in decision-making on public policy directly affecting them. The crucial question remains how terms such as "participation" and "consultation" are defined. Indigenous leaders complain that the government defines participation as the passive attendance by indigenous representatives at a series of meetings in which their proposals are not given meaningful consideration. Decisions are made elsewhere and do not incorporate the priorities expressed by indigenous representatives. Indigenous peoples' organizations tend to define participation and consultation as requiring their explicit consent. It has been impossible to forge a mutually acceptable definition of or procedure for participatory, intercultural deliberations. In the absence of intellectual consensus on these points, indigenous organizations and communities have achieved the greatest control over resources and local policy issues where they enjoy strong community support, where Indians are numerically significant, and where local municipal authorities have incentives to be responsive to them.

In Colombia, pressure from indigenous representatives in local policy-making spheres produced measurable gains in access to health care and other public services. There are anecdotal accounts of Indians achieving unprecedented responsiveness from government. For example, through their representatives on the departmental assembly of Antioquia, Indians obtained departmental funds to title indigenous lands and access to departmental mass media (Valencia 1997:258). Resource transfers to *resguardos* have generated income-producing projects that allow for the accumulation of savings. But the state has failed to remove nonindigenous mayors as intermediary recipients of the funds, as required by the constitution, and there have been insufficient efforts made to ensure that the resources are invested wisely by providing *cabildo* authorities with intensive training in development planning and management (Roldán 1997:241). The possibility of political participation also has been foreclosed by the fierce resistance of governmental personnel at all levels to decentralizing power and to relinquishing control over decision-making to civil society organizations. This is demonstrated by the failure of the state to include civil society participation in the National Development Plan, as required by law. Indians and black communities living in northwestern Colombia have been excluded from debate on the construction of highways through their territories to close the Darien Gap on the Colombian-Panamanian border or to connect the Caribbean and Pacific coasts (Valencia 1997:257). Political participation has been most elusive for the smaller and more remote indigenous communities, who are more subject to abuses and pressures and have little access to agencies that might assist them (Roldán 1997:238).

Political participation also has had negative effects. According to Elizabeth

García, an indigenous woman from the Sierra Nevada de Santa Marta, in her community the new political openings have resulted in conflict between older authorities and younger political officeholders, resulting in community fragmentation and a decline in the value of traditional authority. Indigenous municipal council members in her community resigned their positions after fruitless attempts to obtain information about the functioning of the council and the destination of resources owed to indigenous reserves. The lack of political experience among indigenous politicians has been a grave problem, as they are unable to compete on an equal playing field with more experienced players with greater resources.[24]

The realization of substantive benefits from the reforms in both countries would require a comprehensive overhaul of ordinary legislation at all levels. This process has been slow, has lacked coordination among the ministries handling issues that affect indigenous peoples most (Interior, Environment, and Agriculture), and in some cases has included language detrimental to indigenous rights. The process is complicated by a parallel process of bilateral and multilateral treaty negotiations that have powerful impacts on indigenous peoples—for example, with respect to intellectual property rights. Because these treaties deal mainly with commercial and foreign policy matters, Interior Ministry staff, who coordinate indigenous policy, are commonly excluded and are thus unable to contribute their knowledge of the possible impact on the indigenous population. Indians also have difficulty gaining access to these fora. The proliferation of norms concerning indigenous peoples, at so many levels and concerning so many issues, immensely complicates the challenge of participating in their formulation. Even where access to these fora is facilitated, indigenous organizations lack the battalions of technically trained representatives required to participate continuously and effectively and must balance these activities with other pressing social movement activities (Valencia 1997:261–62, 266).

The realization of substantive rights has been uneven. The rights to use indigenous languages and to bilingual, intercultural education have been difficult to implement in both countries, mainly because of a lack of state resources for education, in general, and the organized resistance of teachers' unions and the education bureaucracy. Implementation of indigenous customary law is far advanced in Colombia but remained on the drawing board in Bolivia in 1999. Territorial rights were among the most important substantive issues on the indigenous constitutional rights agenda. Although the Colombian Congress has yet to establish the ETIs envisioned by the constitution, the state has established more than 260 new indigenous *resguardos* since 1991. In Bolivia, the 1994 reform of Article 171 recognized inalienable, collective property rights on "original community lands." The 1996 agrarian reform law resulted in the distribution of titles for ten million hectares of land to three hundred indigenous communities and rhetorically upgraded original community lands to the status of territories. Future progress during the Banzer administration, however, appears unlikely.[25]

The least progress in both countries has been achieved with respect to the realization of the most important and ambitious constitutional goal of indigenous peoples: the establishment of extensive autonomous regions under indigenous authority, with horizontal relations between independently constituted indigenous peoples and the state. Indigenous activists, like communitarian theorists, argue that recognition of individual rights alone is not sufficient to protect the rights of indigenous individuals to cultural membership, to facilitate the equal representation of members of minority cultures in the state, or to allow the free development of indigenous culture within a society dominated by an alien culture. Autonomy regimes create parallel public spheres closer to and dominated by indigenous cultures where indigenous individuals can speak in their own voice and recognize themselves in the face of government. They are usually established within a larger scheme of decentralization. When they function properly, they fulfill not only the aspirations of subaltern cultural groups, but national aspirations for social integration and unity.

> What makes autonomy so valuable in the contemporary era is the common recognition of a society of optimum solidarity and the more solid sociopolitical integration *of the nation* that can be achieved by satisfying the regional and local aspirations of certain collectivities. Autonomy is, thus, the maximum "congruence between plurality and unity in political integration." (Díaz Polanco 1991:153; translation by author)[26]

The "pluricultural, multiethnic" state composed of diverse, autonomous human collectivities and territorial units remains more an indigenous frame and an aspirational ideal than a short-term state project.

The realization of more substantive ethnic-rights achievements depends upon the resolution of two problems. First, governments continue to resist institutionalizing state-indigenous relations, leaving them to the goodwill of particular administrations. This is demonstrated by the great variation in relations between indigenous organizations and communities and the state when we compare governments in the same country. For example, in Colombia, whereas the Gaviria government had maintained cooperative relations with indigenous organizations and established a number of mechanisms to facilitate interethnic dialogue, the Samper administration dismantled these mechanisms and marginalized the national organizations. In Bolivia, the Sánchez de Lozada administration had established the first Office of Ethnic Affairs and given ethnic diversity a high profile within his administration; the Banzer administration downgraded the institutional space for indigenous-state relations and subordinated it to political party control. If ethnic rights are to become consolidated in a new multicultural democratic regime, mechanisms for relations between the state and indigenous organizations and communities must be institutionalized so that a dialogue on interethnic relations may be made a permanent part of governance. If such spaces are left to the discretion of individual governments, they will not be able to generate a sustained dialogue.

The institutionalization of relations between ethnic organizations and the state raises important questions, however. As Steven Vertovec found with respect to ethnic organizations and the state in England, the creation of state committees or councils to provide a channel for dialogue and to address the material demands of ethnic minorities had the perverse effect of justifying the state's exclusion of the concerns of ethnic minorities from the government's main agenda on the assumption that these concerns belong in specially designated fora. By creating separate policy "ghettos" for ethnic minorities, well-meaning states may be unwittingly confining ethnic political demands to defined spaces, and thus excluding them from "meaningful parts of the public domain" (Vertovec 1996:60). In addition, such arrangements tend to empower more institutionalized and less confrontational organizations regardless of their representativity. Vertovec argues that such arrangements are based on culturalist, essentialist conceptions of ethnic minorities that ignore the actual heterogeneity within ethnic communities and the degree to which leadership and shared cultural meanings are contested. They also tend to favor more oligarchic, patriarchal sectors and leaders at the expense of individuals and more democratic sectors (Vertovec 1996:52–53).

In England, institutionalizing relations between the state and ethnic organizations was based on two assumptions, promoted by states and ethnic organizations themselves, that are commonly asserted but often wrong: (1) that there are insurmountable differences and boundaries between ethnic minorities and the greater society that require special collective representation by (often) self-appointed representatives apart from the political party system; and (2) that these boundaries are permanent and unresolvable and thus require permanent intermediaries between state and ethnic group (Vertovec 1996:55–56). If we are to take the multicultural constitutional aspirations of Bolivians and Colombians at face value, the creation of spaces within the state for regular, continuous interethnic dialogue and the channeling of ethnic group demands that otherwise would have no fora should be conceived not as an end in itself but, rather, as a means to facilitate meaningful democratic representation for ethnic minorities. The long-term goal is the construction of a more representative and more participatory democracy, where legitimate and accountable democratic institutions and a prevailing political culture of tolerance, respect for difference, and the protection of rights provide sufficient guarantees and mechanisms for the recognition of all identities and the representation of all claims. The key, as Vertovec cautions, is to generate "multiple modes of minority representation" and multiple spaces for interethnic dialogue within a range of democratically elected representatives of ethnic minority communities as well as common individuals (Vertovec 1996:66).

A second obstacle is the hesitancy of ethnic organizations to acknowledge that rights and recognitions codified in constitutions or other binding legislation as a result of brinkmanship or other forms of extreme temporary pressure are difficult to implement since, as Banting and Simeon observe: "Constitutional provisions inconsistent with underlying political forces will eventually be by-passed or subverted" (1985a:27). For example, territorial rights for indigenous and black communities were inserted in the 1991 Colombian Constitution, at the last minute, to persuade indigenous delegates to sign. There was no consensus within the ANC or among the Colombian public on the necessity for these rights and little understanding within or outside the ANC on their practical implications. In Bolivia, the Paz Zamora and Sánchez de Lozada administrations made promises under duress in order to end lengthy, disruptive demonstrations by indigenous organizations. These promises represent neither a public consensus nor a permanent shift in political power toward indigenous organizations. Similarly, in Spain, deep conflicts persist among the major ethno-nationalist subaltern groups with respect to the functioning of autonomous ethnic regions established in 1978 pursuant to the Spanish constitutional reform. In this case as well, ambiguities and disagreements papered over in the interest of expediency and tolerance during the constitutional reform erupted into conflict during the implementation process (Clark 1989:17).

Indigenous organizations may be justified in expecting governments to fulfill their promises, but they should not expect commitments made under duress to be implemented in a sustained fashion over time. Brinkmanship is more suited to extracting promises that can be delivered by the executive immediately and unilaterally. Similarly, although independent, strong judicial institutions play an important role in developing and defending the rights of subordinate groups (particularly when such rights are newly established), rights are not derived solely from the legal system or the courts, but also from the power of groups to defend themselves politically (Díaz Polanco 1991:231). The long-term satisfaction of rights claims depends mainly on the ability of indigenous organizations to achieve internal political unity, to forge alliances with nonindigenous sectors, and to maintain at least passive support from the public.

Throughout this study indigenous peoples' movements have been treated as independent variables. It is important, however, to assess the impact of the constitutional reform process on these movements themselves in order to assess their ability to continue defending their constitutional gains. In the positive column, we can place the valuable experience gained by a generation of indigenous leaders through the social movement struggles of the 1980s and the formal political experience gained rapidly in the 1990s. These experiences garnered for the movement influential elite supporters, generally favorable public opinion, and a broad set of rights codified in international, constitutional, and ordinary law (Roldán 1997:250). However, some negative impacts also have been observed. Gros notes the greater saliency of ethnic boundaries, which may lead to lesser rather than greater social integration (Gros 1997:46–47). As noted above, participation by Indians in formal politics has impaired the strength and legitimacy of traditional indigenous authorities. Ironically, although the goal of the indigenous movement during Colombia's constituent assembly was to assert the autonomous authority of traditional leaders, the salaried political opportunities generated by the constitution may provide a more enticing alternative to the younger generation of indigenous activists and may thus threaten the authority of traditional leaders. This type of conflict is endemic in traditional cultures where authorities are less likely to speak Spanish or have contact with Western culture and are prized for their knowledge of the community's internal reality, whereas knowledge of Spanish and Western ways are considered more desirable in political candidates or those selected to participate in spaces opened by the state for the negotiation of policy (Padilla 1995:148–49).

The Colombian indigenous movement's progress has been impeded by its internal fragmentation, the growing distance between its acculturated leaders and the majority of the indigenous population, and the temptations and fractious rivalries engendered by sudden access to salaried jobs and control over resources (Archila 1995:278–79; Rappaport and Dover 1996:39–40). Frictions always have existed within the indigenous movement, but conflicts have become more open and divisive, and once-unified organizations have split over electoral competition. Fierce political competition in areas where two or more indigenous parties run against each other, such as occurred between AICO and ASI in the Cauca assembly elections and between MIC and ASI in the Vichada assembly elections, has weakened the movement locally. There is no better example of this than the Jambaló case, which resulted from an intra-indigenous political rivalry. Resources flowing to *cabildo* authorities pursuant to the constitution have generated intense rivalries over management of the funds, accusations of fraud and incompetence, and the same type of clientelism in which traditional parties engage. There also has been a sharpening of inequalities between indigenous communities that are integrated into national politics and those that lack political representation. As indigenous leaders become more involved in election campaigns and political activities, they are enticed into making political pacts with local and national actors opposed to their material interests, and they tend to devote less time to consolidating the movement's precarious gains in territory, education, and health.[27]

Given these problems within the indigenous movement, some Colombian anthropologists question whether indigenous peoples have benefited or lost from their new constitutional rights. Esther Sánchez argues that the integration of the indigenous population into the political system has hampered the possibility of their surviving as peoples, since groups on the margins are better able to maintain their autonomy.[28] Guillermo Padilla concurs that indigenous communities are now more likely to suffer the intrusion of the state and its ideology into their internal affairs. The new rights regime has increased the dependence of indigenous communities on nonindigenous advisors and on nontraditional forms of organization, leadership, and resistance. New political opportunities have reduced the numbers of protests and marches and have distracted indigenous leaders and their organizations from the important task of constructing ethnic identity (Padilla 1995:141–42, 146–48). These concerns should be balanced with Judith Adler Hellman's observation that the incorporation of a grassroots movement within a broader political movement or party, or into state-governed spaces of political decision-making, is commonly bemoaned by social scientists and activists as a loss of autonomy, rather than seen as progress in the achievement of movement demands or the construction of a broader alternative political formation (1992:59).

In Bolivia, the indigenous movement was in some disarray in early 1999, in the wake of the disastrous participation of CIDOB and its former president in the 1997 elections. Organizational progress achieved as a result of technical and financial support during the first three years of the Sánchez de Lozada government was reversed when CIDOB's electoral alliance with the MBL failed to deliver the congressional representation militants had expected. The Banzer government's dismantlement of government- and quasi-governmental agencies devoted to assisting indigenous and campesino communities to implement their constitutional rights has deprived the indigenous movement of financial and technical support.

In order to realize their aspirations for self-determination, indigenous organizations and communities face the challenge of shifting from strategies of resistance to the state to strategies for the assumption of administrative and political powers formerly monopolized by the state. Their ability to assume these powers has been impeded by their generally low levels of education and technical capacity to design, plan, implement, and evaluate development projects without relying on outside experts, who may have their own agendas. Indigenous authorities who were heretofore answerable only to their constituencies chafe at state reporting requirements with respect to the management of public funds; at gender equity laws requiring equal participation of women in public roles; and at national juridical norms that limit the leeway of authorities in judging and punishing indigenous defendants. The experience of the Bolivian and Colombian indigenous movements confirms the findings of social movement theorists that "political party activity is always potentially divisive of social movements at the local and community level in Latin America" (Foweraker 1995:84). Political parties fracture the fragile consensus and unity forged by social movements through common experience and inject a contrary logic into movement activities, in that the representative, state-oriented logic of political parties tends to erode the directly participatory and autonomous logic of effective social movements (ibid.).

The Problems of Worsening Inequality and Increasing Violence

Democratic theorists draw an empirical and conceptual link between the more equitable distribution of resources and prospects for democratization. In unequal societies, large sectors of the public lack the political resources necessary to exercise political autonomy and citizenship rights. Widespread and severe poverty and stark inequality tend to foster what O'Donnell calls "patterns of authoritarian relations" between the privileged, who rule, and all others, who are ruled, inhibiting the ability of the former to recognize the autonomy and equality of the latter (1997a:5, 25). Moreover, the visibility of socioeconomic inequality generates what Elizabeth Jelin and Eric Hershberg call a "double discourse":

> a discourse of participation and a nondiscourse of economic exclusion. Under such conditions, the historically constructed "threshold of humanity" is threatened. Since those who are marginalized and excluded do not become individual and/or collective subjects in the newly emerging public and political sphere, they may refuse to accept the rules of the democratic game or accept them only partially. They may resist and protest, and/or they may retreat into a universe of violence, acting out instead of participating. (Jelin and Hershberg 1996b:218)

To what extent has inequality lessened since the reforms?

In Colombia, three-quarters of the nation's economic activity remains concentrated in the hands of a few conglomerates owned by a few families. Inequality, which had declined during the 1970s and the first half of the 1980s, increased steadily between 1988 and 1994, despite an increase in social spending from 7.8 percent to 9.0 percent between 1990 and 1994. During the Gaviria administration, the percentage of Colombians below the extreme poverty line grew slightly, driven by an increase in rural poverty attributable to short-term problems in the agricultural sector and the failure of the Gaviria administration to adequately address these difficulties (Mejía and Vos 1997:appendix; Sarmiento 1995:312–15, 329; World Bank 1994:6; UNDP 1995:5). The Samper government's antipoverty plan faltered as the weak and discredited government lost the ability to negotiate with the opposition or to challenge the expanding military budget. The political crisis spread quickly to the economy, engendering low growth, decreasing productivity, and increasing inflation, unemployment, and the fiscal deficit (Bernal Medina 1997:3). A December 1997 study concluded that inequality increased sharply in 1995 and 1996 as a direct result of stalled growth and growing unemployment linked to the Samper scandal. After less than a year in office for the Pastrana government, its fiscal austerity measures appeared to be having a stabilizing impact on macroeconomic indicators, but further cuts in social spending appear likely.[29]

Observers point out a basic contradiction between the emphasis of the 1991 Constitution on improving the quality of democracy and the neoliberal economic reform that accompanied the charter's implementation. The constitution calls for government policies to promote more equitable distribution of political and socioeconomic resources, whereas the economic model of the Gaviria, Samper, and Pastrana governments, the continuing economic recession, and the decision to allocate scarce government funds to the military rather than to antipoverty and social investment programs all exacerbate socioeconomic inequality (Orjuela E. 1998). The extreme inequality in the distribution of resources impedes the disempowered majority from exercising their new rights to participation. There is no state actor to defend the rights of the poor, since the Constitutional Court has been reluctant to rule on questions of policy.[30]

The only redistributive effects of the constitutional reform are transfers to indigenous *resguardos,* which began receiving funds in 1994. That year about US$ 12 million were distributed to 364 recognized *resguardos,* where 439,267 Indians are settled. Roughly US$ 15.5 million were transferred in 1995 (Cepeda 1995a:11). As a result of the creation of additional *resguardos* pursuant to the constitution, by March 1997 there were 460 *resguardos* receiving transfers of approximately US$ 61,000 per reserve. The number of *resguardos* exceeds the 450 that experts estimate existed at the time of independence from Spain (Roldán 1998:52). Still, 20 percent of Colombian indigenous communities lack land, have insufficient land, or lack legal title to it, and approximately 60 percent of *resguardos* are partially occupied by nonindigenous intruders. Many of these intruders cultivate illegal crops and introduce pernicious values and activities into indigenous communities or exploit natural resources on indigenous lands in environmentally destructive ways (Roldán 1997:243). Pending the establishment of ETIs, municipal authorities receive the *resguardo* funds and disburse them to the *cabildos* for specific projects. In most of the country, the funds are getting to the indigenous population, but problems have emerged because of the lack of experience of indigenous authorities in managing such large sums and the malfeasance of nonindigenous mayors (Cepeda 1995a:11). In addition to *resguardo* transfers, pursuant to Article 143 of the Constitution, 2 percent of social and environmental spending is to be allocated to the indigenous population, which was reflected in the 1997 national budget.[31]

In Bolivia, one of the major goals of the LPP was to reduce poverty, particularly in rural areas, where extreme poverty exceeded 69 percent in 1992 (República de Bolivia/Vicepresidencia 1998:14). An immediate and tangible redistributive impact has been the generation of local employment opportunities linked to development projects funded by co-participation funds: 24,000 jobs were generated in 1994, 52,000 in 1995, and 55,000 in 1996. In addition, 16,722 permanent municipal employees were hired, not including elected officials (Ardaya 1998:3). Jobs and resources, however, are not necessarily flowing to the most needy. In fact, they appear to be reinvigorating a provincial elite that had been in decline since the 1952 revolution (Calla 1998:8). Clearly, municipal decentralization will not empower marginalized groups if it enhances the power of their local exploiters. Still, increased rural employment has furthered a key goal of the LPP: slowing rapid, unplanned urban migration and the corresponding depopulation of the countryside.

The redistribution of social and productive investment funds from the center to rural municipalities under the LPP should show up in rural poverty indicators in a few years. Per capita spending in rural areas increased from twenty-eight U.S. dollars in 1993 to seventy-seven dollars in 1996. In urban areas, a measurable impact on poverty alleviation should result from the existing tendency toward public investments in education, health, sanitation, and urban development, which jumped from 1.72 percent of GNP in 1993 to 3.61 percent in 1995 (Gray Molina 1996:3). A 1997 government survey of eight major cities determined that poverty diminished from 51.2 percent to 44.2 percent between 1992 and 1996 (Ardaya 1998:4). Improvements also are measurable in maternal and child health. Since 1996, municipalities have been required to spend 3 percent of co-participation resources on this. According to the government, maternal mortality decreased by 20 percent and child mortality by 25 percent in the plan's first year of operation.[32]

Bolivia's real GDP growth rate has been much stronger than Colombia's and is expected to remain so. The rate fluctuated between 4 percent and 5 percent between 1993 and 1997 and is expected to reach 6 percent in the year 2000. Inflation only broke the 10 percent barrier twice since 1993 and is expected to remain below 7 percent through 2000. These are promising macroeconomic indicators that enhance the government's ability to address the problem of poverty, which the Banzer government has prioritized as a vital national goal. The key obstacles to increased redistribution and social investment spending are large fiscal and current account deficits, which were 4.1 percent and 8 percent of GDP, respectively, in 1998. A major reason for the fiscal problem is the commitment made to the elderly under Sánchez de Lozada's pension reform, which absorbs 1.8 percent of GDP and kept the Banzer government from registering a surplus in 1998. The government attributes its inability to keep its electoral promise to increase the amount of co-participation resources, as well as the proportion going to poor municipalities, to the fiscal constraint caused by the pension fund commitment (EIU 1998a).[33] The LPP's population-based resource-distribution formula, and the unequal ability of municipalities to raise their own taxes, may actually increase inequality among municipalities and departments. If the Banzer government adjusts the methodology to provide a more progressive distribution of state resources, as it promised to do during the 1997 campaign, the trend may be reversed.

The principal impediment in both cases to achieving significant redistribution through constitutional reform was the necessity of securing support from political elites for radical political reform by protecting the material interests of well-organized business sectors, who otherwise might have opposed the entire democratic project. Both reforms strengthened the neoliberal model. In Colombia, this was because of the majority wielded by the traditional parties representing the business elite on the commission addressing economic issues, as well as the desire of the principal opposition party, the ADM-19, to consolidate the movement as a moderate alternative by postponing a struggle for radical economic change. In Bolivia, following the disastrous economic policies of the leftist UDP government (1982–1985), there has been broad consensus among the political class on the necessity to maintain the structural adjustment and liberalization begun by the MNR-ADN government in 1985. The two forces advocating more populist, labor-friendly economic and social policies (the political party CONDEPA and the labor movement) were marginalized from the constitutional reform debate.

Similarly, neither constitutional reform significantly touched the armed forces. This may have been a mistake in Colombia, where the continued impunity of the military with respect to human rights violations continues to drain legitimacy from the state and perpetuate the cycle of violence the constitutional reform was intended to halt. The constitution hinders the prosecution of the armed forces for human rights violations by confirming the jurisdiction of military courts over crimes committed by the military or police (Arnson and Marcus 1995:40–41). In Bolivia, this was less important, since the armed forces already had been gravely weakened by the tumultuous transition to civilian rule and the series of judicial retributions against the military that followed.

Reducing violence was an explicit goal of Colombia's National Constituent Assembly. The 1991 Constitution was intended to heal violent conflicts among warring factions of Colombian society and to reduce the impunity and injustice to which many attributed the spiraling violence. The staggering statistics on violence in Colombia since the ANC demonstrate the failure to reach that goal. In 1997, UNICEF reported that there were more people internally displaced by multiple forms of violence in Colombia than in Rwanda, Burundi, and Congo combined, and twice the number of internally displaced in the former Yugoslavia—a total of 920,000 Colombians, or 2.5 percent of the population.[34] Colombia's homicide rate has held steady since 1988; 15 percent of homicides, ten per day, are considered politically motivated. Scholars of Colombian political violence attribute 35 percent of these to the guerrillas and the remainder to the state and paramilitary groups (Arnson and Marcus 1995:23–29). Although efforts by the Gaviria and Samper administrations to crack down on the drug cartels were partially successful, negotiations with the FARC and ELN guerrillas failed. With an estimated combined guerrilla force of twenty thousand combatants, the government cannot defeat the guerrillas militarily (EIU 1998b:10) and they have had little incentive to disarm. The guerrillas' income from drug trafficking, extortion, and kidnapping grew from an estimated US$ 592 million in 1994 to US$ 790 million in 1997, and they have much to fear from demobilization, since the government is incapable of protecting demilitarized soldiers from assassination.[35] The EPL, which disarmed to take part in the 1991 Constituent Assembly, lost 274 former militants to assassination between 1991 and 1994 (Arnson and Marcus 1995:3).

The Conservative Andrés Pastrana government, which took office on August 7, 1998, made peace talks with the guerrillas a priority. Pastrana must overcome opposition from the military but has strong backing from a sector of the business elite. The first serious government-guerrilla peace talks since 1992 began tentatively, pursuant to a February 1998 accord negotiated between the Spanish government and the ELN that opens the possibility for the convocation of another National Constituent Assembly. Exploratory talks with the government stalled in April 1999. Talks in Germany with representatives of civil society, begun in July 1998, are expected to continue through 1999. Talks with the FARC are even less promising. Pastrana granted the FARC guerrillas de facto political status in October 1998 and, in a controversial move, pulled the army out of five southeastern municipalities (EIU 1998b:10). Formal talks begun on January 7, 1999, were suspended after a FARC commander murdered three American indigenous rights activists in February 1999 (Tate 1999:1–6). Further clouding the prospects for peace is the fact that neither guerrilla group has offered a coherent set of negotiable demands. Political and financial resources required for reconstruction following a major earthquake on January 25 have been diverted away from the peace process.

Since the ANC, guerrilla violence is fueled by a dramatic increase in violence by paramilitary organizations, which have exploited the vacuum of authority generated by the corruption scandal to expand their territorial control and consolidate their network. In the late 1990s, paramilitaries transformed themselves from local amateur self-defense units, tolerated by or coordinating with local army units, into professional armies with offensive capabilities, a national coordinating structure, and a coordinated strategy "to concentrate land holdings and secure control of all strategic regions of the country" (WOLA 1997:25). In 1998, twelve hundred Colombian civilians were killed in massacres attributed mainly to right-wing paramilitaries—a 16 percent increase over 1997.[36] Indigenous communities and leaders continue to be among the groups targeted by all forms of violence: particularly on the part of paramilitaries and guerrillas, who target indigenous leaders and hamper the construction of effective leadership and organization, and on the part of drug traffickers, who violently attack the indigenous struggle to maintain or assert territorial rights (Roldán 1997:249). Since the constitutional reform hundreds of indigenous leaders have been murdered, with complete impunity (Valencia 1997:265).

In addition to contributing to the climate of terror and the weakening of state legitimacy, paramilitaries and guerrillas have attacked the democratization process at its roots by targeting local government officials, the unarmed Left, and civil society leaders, including many indigenous leaders. Attacks against the country's 1,062 mayors increased in the 1995–1997 period, when 22 were assassinated; 3 more resigned following death threats. In 1996 alone, 67 mayors were violently attacked or kidnapped by guerrilla or paramilitary units. In order to consolidate their power in zones they occupy, paramilitaries and guerrillas impeded voter registration and participation in the 1997 municipal elections (La Razón, May 2, 1997:4A). Violence against candidates and voters resulted in more than 30 election-related fatalities (WOLA 1997:11). This actually represents an improvement over pre-ANC levels of electoral violence: 140 local candidates were assassinated in 1988 (Hoskin 1991:30). In response, 800 candidates withdrew their names from the ballot, leaving no candidates in 1 percent of the country's municipalities. In the weeks prior to the 1998 congressional races, guerrillas kidnapped 10 mayors and increased attacks against state security forces to intimidate voters and candidates.[37] The military also continues to attack civil society leaders with impunity. In 1996 a Colombian NGO brought a charge of genocide against the Colombian government before the Organization of American States (OAS) Inter-American Commission on Human Rights, alleging that the military had a plan to liquidate the nearly extinct leftist political party Patriotic Union, whose members were being assassinated at a rate of one every two days (WOLA 1997:22).

The 1991 constitution resulted in the creation of an impressive human rights bureaucracy, but the government failed to provide the resources or the environment of security necessary for its own human rights work. As a result, the human rights situation in Colombia has worsened, threats of and attacks on governmental and nongovernmental human rights workers have increased since 1995, and several local human rights committees in the most conflictive zones have been virtually exterminated. Threats against Amnesty International's personnel caused the organization to close its Colombian office in February 1998. The previous year, in response to a four-year campaign by Colombian human rights organizations, the UN High Commissioner for Human Rights established a permanent office in Colombia to monitor human rights and assist the government with policies for their protection—a distinction Colombia shared that year only with Yugoslavia.

Prospects for Future Consolidation of the Reforms

The constitutional reforms are in a delicate stage in both Colombia and Bolivia. The consensus underpinning the multicultural aspects of the reforms was fragile and a backlash is possible, as is occurring in Australia, which was also once touted as an international model (Forbes and Uhr 1998:23). The initial euphoria surrounding the deconcentration of administrative and political power has waned and attention is focused on the shortcomings of the new democratic regime. This phenomenon is not unique to our cases. Putnam and Clark report similar euphoria among local and regional elites in Italy and Spain, respectively, who expected decentralizing political and administrative institutions alone to lead to radical political transformation and later became disappointed with the results (Putnam 1993:21; Clark 1989:21). Although Bolivian and Colombian reformers decentralized to the municipal rather than the regional level in order to prevent the type of political struggles that occurred in southern Europe, many of the same problems did emerge. As in Italy, the resistance of center-based elites, national bureaucrats, and centralized political parties resulted in a political struggle between local and regional elites and the center. Public management problems stemming from a lack of competent, trained personnel and an entrenched clientelist system of public employment stalled the expected improvement of government efficiency. The exacerbation of interregional inequalities generated interregional conflict (Putnam 1993:49–61). Central and eastern European constitutional reforms that were intended to decentralize politics and administration to municipalities also have failed to meet expectations of greater citizen participation and government responsiveness because they have been unable to break entrenched centralized structures mired in bureaucratic inertia, and because localities remain dependent upon the center for resources and policy direction (Regulska 1993:138).[38] Similarly, although we may be disappointed that Bolivians and Colombians have been unable or unwilling thus far to appropriate new democratic rights, this is to be expected. Despite the inclusion of mechanisms for direct democracy and participation rights in the new constitutions of eastern and central Europe, voter turnout and the exercise of these rights remains low. Although this passivity has been attributed to the problems of establishing participatory democracy in post-communist societies (Regulska 1993:156), the presence of this phenomenon in Latin America may indicate a more universal phenomenon.

Whereas the effects of poorly designed institutions are always visible, it is more difficult for new social institutions to have a noticeable positive impact on political behavior, no matter how well designed and well intentioned. This is partly because of the path dependency of existing "national and sectoral institutional orders," which often precludes the development of preferable alternatives and makes new social institutions difficult to design and implement (Offe 1996:51–52). But we can recognize the challenges of constitutional transformation without dismissing constitutions as impotent rhetoric. In the worst case scenario, where states ignore or attack the new constitutional vision, the new rights continue to interact with and nourish the heightened political consciousness and organizational capacity of social movements in the post-constitutional conjuncture (Roldán 1996:7). According to Roldán this is especially the case with constitutional rights, "because the Constitution lends solidity and influence to [political] decisions and because it presumes some solidarity and national support for them" (1993:7; translation by the author). Rather than the result of past political mobilization by disadvantaged groups, rights should be viewed as a resource for counter-hegemonic mobilization by dominated groups (Sieder 1997:14). The demand for citizenship rights from disadvantaged and marginalized groups is a "promising democratic impulse" and, as such, "worthwhile in itself" because a society in which people claim rights is a necessary, albeit insufficient, condition for a society in which citizens empower themselves to exercise them (O'Donnell 1998:21; Foweraker 1995:98). In Colombia and Bolivia, as in post-communist Europe, the mere fact that constitutions matter—that they are the subject of intense political struggles—"is in itself already a major achievement in the transition process" (Elster, Offe, Preuss, et al. 1998:63).

Perhaps the most important indicator that ethnic rights will make a meaningful long-term impact on the status of indigenous peoples vis-à-vis state and society is that virtually all states in the region have felt impelled to include them in their own constitutions during the 1990s or are contemplating doing so now (Roldán 1996:7). In an earlier era (roughly the 1920s through 1970s), all Latin American states embraced *indigenismo,* a policy of forced assimilation for indigenous peoples. Today, *"neo-indigenismo,"* the mode of indigenous-state relations exemplified by Colombia and Bolivia, has become a regional approach to a common problem.[39]

9 Multicultural Constitutionalism

A Comparative Analysis

T HE CONSTITUTIONAL treatment of indigenous peoples has changed dramatically since the 1970s, when references to this population began to creep back into the region's constitutions. Integrationist and paternalistic approaches have been replaced by language negotiated with indigenous peoples' representatives that is derived from the inherent rights of pre-constituted, autonomous indigenous communities (Dandler 1996:14). In country after country,

> what was once simply a sociological reality that was systematically rejected and denied (undoubtedly due to the negative perception held of human groups who are differentiated from the national community by virtue of their "cultural backwardness"), was translated into a new normative order. (Gros n.d.:9; translation by the author)

These constitutional reforms are part of a regional effort to reconstitute relations between the state and society on the eve of the millennium. As in Bolivia and Colombia, they are part of a larger democratic project to decentralize the state and open new spheres for popular participation (Gros n.d.:10). Half a dozen states—beset by crises of legitimacy, representation, and participation that evoke those described here—have adapted parts of the multicultural constitutional frameworks developed by Bolivians and Colombians.

Although it remains to be seen how this is to be implemented, Ecuador currently has the broadest and strongest regime of protection for indigenous and black rights in Latin America. Ecuadorian Indians participated in the 1998 constituent assembly and have held seats in the National Congress since 1996. They even achieved the constitutional incorporation, in Spanish and Quichua, of the old Inca code of conduct—don't lie, don't steal, don't be lazy (art. 97). In Guatemala, a broad spectrum of constitutional reforms affecting indigenous rights, based on the March 1995 government-guerrilla Accord on the Identity and Rights of Indigenous Peoples, were approved by Congress in 1998. These were nullified when Guatemalan voters narrowly rejected (50.63%) the entire constitutional reform package in a May 1999 referendum in which less than 20 percent of eligible voters participated.[1]

As this book goes to press, Guyana's parliament is considering a report submitted by the country's Constitutional Reform Commission on July 17th that contains a number of recommendations concerning indigenous rights. A representative of indigenous peoples' organizations appointed to the Commission, Jean La Rose, later named its vice-chair, facilitated the introduction of indigenous rights issues, which were among the most hotly debated by the Commission. Parliament is expected the debate the provisions, after which a newly drafted constitution must be approved by Parliament and by referendum prior to January 2001.[2] In Mexico a set of constitutional reforms based on the 1996 San Andrés accord on indigenous rights negotiated between the government and indigenous rebels awaits action by the Mexican government. Negotiations with the rebels are deadlocked, partly over the failure of the government to implement the accord, as a national debate on the questions of democracy, diversity, participation, representation, and legitimacy rages on in the run-up to the 2000 elections.

Perhaps the most important case on the horizon, because of the country's size and the singular backwardness of its constitution with respect to indigenous rights, is Venezuela. Indigenous organizations battled successfully to include 3 indigenous representatives, elected by the country's indigenous population, in the 131 seat constituent assembly installed on August 3, 1999. Venezuelan Indians had available the constitution of the state of Amazonas to use as a model for national constitutional rights. This state constitution recognizes the multiethnic and pluricultural nature of the state population, the existence of indigenous autonomous regions, and other important indigenous rights (Smith 1999:50). Parallels to neighboring Colombia—the small size of the indigenous population; the possibility that ILO Convention 169 will be signed during the proceedings; the emphasis of national constitutional debates on restoring the moral authority of political institutions, strengthening the rule of law, and adjusting formal institutions to social reality; the fragmentation of the political party system; the choice of a constituent assembly—present an interesting opportunity for comparative analysis.

It is important to remember that in no country was the demand by ethnic organizations for special rights and recognition the most important reason for the decision to radically revise or replace the political constitution. In many cases, political elites, international experts, and common citizens perceived states to be overly centralized and inefficient. In others, persistent institutional stalemates between branches of government required constitutional adjustments. In all cases, judiciaries were weak and politically compromised, contributing to a deepening legitimacy crisis. As in the contemporaneous post-communist European constitutional reforms, Latin American constitution-makers were influenced by the international discourse on rights in the late twentieth century (Howard 1993:10). And they were as susceptible as their European counterparts to the transmission of an "international political culture," its absorption with political reconstruction, and its marked preference for a narrow range of constitutional models (Arjomand 1992:73).

The groundwork for elite acceptance of indigenous rights was laid decades earlier. As in Bolivia and Colombia, indigenous movements emerged in most countries of the region in the 1970s to respond to a variety of new threats (Assies 1998; Bengoa 1994; Gros 1997; Stavenhagen 1992; Van Cott 1994; Wade 1997; Yashar 1996, 1998). Indians gained access to formal education in unprecedented numbers during the decade, enabling a generation of future indigenous leaders to form a consciousness of indigenous peoples as an excluded and oppressed group, and as one of many groups subordinated by a hegemonic, monoethnic state (González and Roitman 1996:15). In this era, indigenous organizations formed to assert rights and demand participation, often in alliance with other popular groups struggling for democracy. As part of this collective mobilization and framing process, the category "people" itself passed from being a vague reference to the popular—more or less broadly defined—to being a concept whose content unleashed a political and social force capable of presenting a hegemonic democratic project that is present in the entire struggle against globalizing and transnational capitalism. Moreover, the category of people became combined with that of indigenous peoples. The new democratic project puts into question the asymmetric relations of exploitation in Latin America. The impulse given by the rich hegemony of the people and of indigenous peoples purports to rupture old conceptions of a political, economic, social, ethnic, and cultural vanguard. Indigenous peoples join working people, and also citizens and their political and social organizations. (González and Roitman 1996:16; translation by the author)

Indigenous peoples' unprecedented political mobilization coincided with an international effort to codify social, economic, and cultural rights. Many Latin American countries enacted statutory laws during the 1970s referring to indigenous people, most of which concerned the agrarian regime and language rights, and some of which were detrimental to their interests, such as Brazil (1973), Chile (1979), Costa Rica (1977), Guyana (1977), Paraguay (1981), Peru (1974). The fundamental principle upon which most national laws concerning disadvantaged groups was based remained that of equality, nondiscrimination, and the protection of individual rights. The legislation was intended to transform Indians into undifferentiated citizens, not to recognize a distinctive status (Roitman Rosenmann 1996:49).

By the mid-1980s, indigenous social movements had coalesced into a single or a few permanent national-level organizations in most countries. As in Bolivia and Colombia, the origins of these contemporary social movements lie in the agrarian struggles of the 1960s and 1970s; the dismantlement of agrarian reform and support programs by heavily indebted states in the 1980s; the decline of leftist parties and labor movements, which created space for ethnic themes to orient oppositional politics; neoliberal reforms that threatened collective property rights and deepened indigenous poverty; and the defensive reaction of forest-dwelling tribes to unprecedented intrusions by the state and private enterprises. The expansion and institutionalization of indigenous organizations in the 1980s and 1990s may be attributed to political liberalization at the national level; the greater receptivity to the concepts of collective rights, cultural diversity, and "sustainable development" in international fora (Gros n.d.); and the construction of "transnational advocacy networks" in support of indigenous rights (Keck and Sikkink 1998; Tarrow 1998:188–89). The variation in political opportunity structure in each country explains the variance in the maturity and institutionalization of these movements. National movement organizations are most consolidated in Ecuador and Colombia, followed by Bolivia and Chile. In Venezuela and Peru, they are weaker (Iturralde 1997b:83). In Mexico and Guatemala, multiple indigenous organizations compete for the loyalty of a diverse indigenous population, although they are capable of brief moments of unity.

Within each country, and in a variety of international fora, diverse indigenous organizations have participated in more than a decade of discussion of their common problems and goals and, as a result, have converged on a common platform of grievances. These discussions not only helped aggregate and articulate a common set of demands. They enabled the inter-American indigenous movement to frame new categories of grievances, such as autonomy and self-determination, and invent new terms, such as "indigenous nationality" and "the pluricultural and multiethnic state," which are geared toward success in national as well as global fora, since these categories and concepts are linked to international discourses on self-government and democracy in multiethnic states (Iturralde 1997b:83; González Casanova and Roitman Rosenmann 1996:16). Through this process of vetting a common platform, indigenous organizations came to articulate their grievances in terms of rights. Magdalena Gómez (cited in Iturralde 1997a:84), calls this process the *juridización* of indigenous demands, or the framing of these demands in terms of constitutional and legal reforms. Juridization, which is common to moments of profound social change as challenging groups seek to formally regulate "hitherto informally regulated social situations" (O'Donnell 1998:7, citing Habermas), enabled indigenous peoples to construct a new identity as people with rights, or citizens.

> This identity is above all the consciousness of difference and the situation of disadvantage that this has implied historically, and the will to overcome this precisely through the reinforcement of the practices that make them distinct, such as language, their forms of organization, traditions, etc. (Iturralde 1997b:85; translation by the author)

The codification of indigenous collective identities through national and international discourses on rights and human rights law tends to produce "essentialized, idealised and atemporal" indigenous identities that do not necessarily correspond to the complex realities they purport to represent, but which indigenous leaders may perceive as tactically necessary to secure collective rights (Sieder and Witchell forthcoming).

Within the context of widespread dissatisfaction with the democratic model in the late 1980s and 1990s, the discourse of the indigenous rights movement provided a conceptual framework for political elites to question the quality of the democracies they were consolidating, particularly with respect to the persistence of inequalities and political exclusion. Indigenous organizations offered an alternative vision of citizenship that incorporates collective rights and new modes of individual and collective participation —a vision that was nurtured by and framed within the contemporary international discourse on rights. In gaining acceptance for their claims, indigenous organizations have benefited from the earlier example of legislative and policy revision in industrialized countries, particularly Australia and Canada, where aboriginal organizations pressed for self-government and treaty rights in the 1970s and 1980s (Plant 1998).

The decision of the ILO to revise its 1957 convention on indigenous peoples (ILO 107) was even more important. The new version eliminated its predecessor's assimilationist and paternalist language and emphasized the responsibility of states to ensure that policies affecting indigenous peoples are devised through a process of consultation and participation, although the precise meaning of these terms is contested by governments and indigenous organizations. Indigenous organizations had wanted language requiring indigenous peoples' *consent* to policies affecting them and indigenous *control* over natural resources on their land (Schulting 1997:10).

The impact of the completion of this instrument in 1989 (ILO Convention 169, in force September 5, 1991) on the emergence of a multicultural model of constitutional reform in Latin America cannot be overstated. The new convention provided a concrete instrument for indigenous organizations to use in demanding a revision of state-indigenous relations; it also provided a model for those revised relations. As Margaret Keck and Kathryn Sikkink argue, public commitments to specified principles enable social movement organizations to embarrass governments by "expos[ing] the distance between discourse and practice" (1998:24). According to a prominent organ of the Latin American indigenous rights movement:

The idea that a true democracy must be pluricultural is beginning to take hold in a number of Latin American countries. More than any other international document, the International Labor Organization's Convention 169 represents this shift in attitude from an assimilationist perspective to one that respects and values Indigenous cultures.[3]

As this passage suggests, a country's ratification of the convention and its adoption of the multicultural constitutional model described below are both effects of larger processes at the national and international levels, rather than one being the cause of the other. As table 4 (pp. 266–68) demonstrates, in some cases the international convention came first; in others it followed constitutional reform. Nevertheless, evidence from the Bolivian, Colombian, Ecuadorian, Guatemalan, Mexican, and Paraguayan cases demonstrates that the ratification of the convention provided a useful tool for indigenous organizations to mobilize around the set of rights contained in that convention and to achieve their codification at the constitutional level (Sieder and Witchell forthcoming).[4]

The year that ILO Convention 169 was approved, the OAS Inter-American Commission on Human Rights began work on an American Declaration of the Rights of Indigenous Peoples. Representatives of member states and indigenous peoples' organizations met in Washington in February 1999 to review what OAS staff considered to be a nearly final version prior to its consideration at the 2000 OAS General Assembly. The current draft recognizes the pluricultural nature of Latin American societies and contains interesting preamble language recognizing the roots of some of the region's democratic institutions in indigenous institutions and the potential contribution of Indians' participatory authority and decision-making systems to democratization of the state. The declaration could potentially be applied to other social groups, for example, black communities whose "social, cultural and economic conditions distinguish them from other sections of the national community, and whose status is regulated wholly or partially by their own customs or traditions or by special laws or regulations" (art. 1).

Representatives of indigenous peoples' organizations attending the Washington meeting rejected the OAS draft declaration, which they argue is not as strongly worded as a draft United Nations declaration produced in 1995 by a Commission on Human Rights working group. Indigenous representatives had a more direct role in drafting the UN declaration through more than a decade of participation in the working group, and they achieved the inclusion of explicit, unqualified recognition of an indigenous right to self-determination. As a result, the UN draft declaration has unanimous support from indigenous representatives—but not a single article has been approved by the commission since the draft was approved four years ago because of the objection of some states (particularly the United States, Brazil, Japan, and France) to self-determination language. Indigenous representatives are angry that the OAS document does not recognize the territoriality or right of self-determination of indigenous peoples the way the UN document does. They appear equally angry about their more consultative and less participatory role, since among the goals of international indigenous organizations is status comparable to that of states in international fora. The opposition of indigenous organizations to the OAS draft and the drafting process itself led to the decision of the Permanent Council to form a working group of states' and indigenous organizations' representatives to consider the declaration further rather than send it forward for ratification by the General Assembly.[5]

Despite the international climate favoring indigenous rights, conflicts between states and indigenous peoples over these legal instruments are to be expected, since indigenous organizations explicitly challenge the prerogatives of states. Some indigenous organizations reject the sovereignty of states and their claim to exclusive jurisdiction over territory. All insist that rights recognized in national or international legal documents are inherent to indigenous peoples and not a revocable grant generated by the momentary goodwill of states. They argue that any satisfactory "re-constitution" of indigenous-state relations must be based on the free will of indigenous communities to join the political community (Assies 1994:42–43). Indigenous and state representatives disagree over the use of the term "indigenous peoples," which both agree would lend strength to indigenous organizations' claim that international law currently recognizes a right of indigenous peoples to self-determination—including the external version, secession. The draft OAS declaration and ILO Convention 169, which substituted "peoples" for "populations" in its 1989 revision, deal with the issue by explicitly stating that the term "shall not be construed as having any implications as regards the rights which may attach to the term under international law." Indigenous organizations participating in the February OAS meeting insisted that the declaration must not qualify self-determination to exclude the possibility of secession, because to do so would deny Indians rights enjoyed by other peoples. As Chilean Mapuche leader Aucan Huilcaman put it, states must live with the risk of indigenous secession because keeping indigenous people oppressed is a greater risk.[6]

There are valid arguments to be made in international law both for and against the application of the right to self-determination to indigenous peoples. What is clear is that the self-determination issue is an obstacle to the adoption of a UN or an OAS declaration of indigenous rights acceptable to the most radical and internationalized indigenous organizations.[7] This is unfortunate since most indigenous organizations in Latin America seek not the full independence that a minority insist must be codified as a legal alternative but, rather, a sphere of autonomy within the state and a greater role in decision-making that affects them.

The Emerging Multicultural Regional Model

Although they vary on a number of dimensions, nine of the new constitutions share at least three of five elements of what I call the "multicultural model":

- rhetorical recognition of the multicultural nature of their societies and the existence of indigenous peoples as distinct, substate social collectivities;
- recognition of indigenous peoples' customary law as official, public law;
- collective property rights protected from sale, dismemberment, or confiscation;
- official status or recognition of indigenous languages;
- a guarantee of bilingual education.

Only one constitution replaced in this decade (Uruguay) lacks at least three elements of the model.[8] In addition, by ratifying ILO Convention 169, Costa Rica and Honduras incorporate the model at the rank of constitutional law. (The components of the model are illustrated in table 4.)

Eight Latin American constitutions contain language, usually near the beginning of the document, that recognizes the multiethnic, pluricultural, and/or multilingual nature of their societies. For example, Bolivia's first article begins, "Bolivia free, independent, sovereign, multiethnic and pluricul-

TABLE 4

Latin American Constitutions and Indigenous Rights

Country	ILO 169/ year	Rhetorical Recognition of Multi-culturalism	Recognition of Customary Law	Collective Property Rights	Official[1] Language Recognition	Bilingual Education	Autonomy Regime
Argentina 1994[a]	yes,[b] 1998	indirect/weak	no	yes	no	yes	no
Bolivia 1994	yes, 1991	yes	yes	yes	no	yes	no
Brazil 1988[c]	no	no	no	no	no	yes	no
Chile 1989, 1997[d]	no	no	on a limited basis, by statute	no	no	no	no
Colombia 1991	yes, 1991	yes	yes	yes	in indigenous territories	yes	yes, municipal
Costa Rica 1949/1997[e]	yes, 1993	no	no	no	no	no	no
Ecuador 1998	yes, 1998	yes	yes	yes	in indigenous territories	yes	yes, sectional
El Salvador 1982	no	no	no	no	no	no	no
Guatemala 1985/1998	yes, 1996	yes	yes	yes	no	no	no
Guyana 1980 reform under way[f]	no	no	no	no	no	no	no
Honduras 1982[g]	yes, 1995	no	no	yes	no	no	no

TABLE 4

Country	ILO 169/year	Rhetorical Recognition of Multi-culturalism	Recognition of Customary Law	Collective Property Rights	Official[1] Language Recognition	Bilingual Education	Autonomy Regime
Mexico 1917, 1994, 1995	yes, 1990	yes	government commitment pursuant to 1996 San Andrés Accord	yes	promised	promised	unclear what will result from accord
Nicaragua 1987[h]	no	yes	yes	yes	in multiethnic regions	yes	yes, multiethnic regions
Panama 1972/1983, 1994	no	no	yes	yes	no	no	yes, four indigenous comarcas established in 1953, 1983, 1996 and 1997.
Paraguay 1992[i]	yes, 1993	yes	yes	yes	Guaraní is official	yes	no
Peru 1993[j]	yes, 1994	yes	yes	yes	in own zones	no	no
Uruguay 1999	no	no	no	no	no	no	no
Venezuela 1961[k] Constituent Assembly scheduled for 1999	no	no	no	no	no	no	no

TABLE 4

Notes:

[a] In Argentina, indigenous rights are also addressed by Law 23,302 (1985), which declares the protection of indigenous communities to be a "national interest."

[b] The Argentine Congress ratified ILO 169 in 1992 but failed to deposit the ratification documents with the ILO. Argentine Indians' complaint before the Supreme Court aimed to force the government to deposit the documents, but the Court denied the request, arguing that this is a presidential prerogative (Frites 1998).

[c] In Brazil, a 1973 Indian Statute (Law 6.001/73) is still in effect. Landowners and legislators from Amazonian states have attacked the 1988 indigenous constitutional rights regime and effectively resisted its implementation.

[d] Chile's constitution, inherited from the Pinochet dictatorship, contains no provisions targeting the indigenous population. In 1993 the Chilean Congress passed an Indigenous Statute (no. 19.253) containing a set of indigenous rights and establishing a National Indigenous Development Board with indigenous representation (Smith 1999:22–23).

[e] Costa Rica has an indigenous law (6172 of 1977), which mainly has to do with protecting indigenous reserves. A 1993 law (Law 22072) promotes the progressive development of bilingual education. In 1999, a Law on the Autonomous Development of the Indigenous Peoples of Costa Rica awaited congressional attention (Smith 1999:27).

[f] In Guyana, a 1977 Amerindian Act is still in force (Smith 1999:36).

[g] In Honduras, Article 346 makes it the duty of the state "to adopt measures to protect the rights and interests of the indigenous communities" (1999:28).

[h] In Nicaragua, indigenous rights are protected also by the 1987 Autonomy Statute establishing the Atlantic Coast Autonomous Regions. Indigenous representatives participated in the constituent assembly.

[i] In Paraguay, the state designated four Indian representatives without votes, and one was elected with voting rights in the 1991 constituent assembly. (See Bareiro [1996:274–75] for an insider's account of the assembly.)

[j] In Peru, a 1974 law (20653) accompanying the agrarian reform recognized the legal existence of "native communities" (Smith 1999:46). A comprehensive law protecting the rights of campesinos and lowland indigenous peoples and organizations was presented in 1998 and was under consideration in the Peruvian Congress in 1999 (Interview, Javier Aroca, Ombudsman for Native Communities, Zurich, April 30, 1999).

[k] In Venezuela, all constitutional references to indigenous peoples are contained in Article 77, which promotes the integration of Indians into society.

tural"; Ecuador's first article begins, "Ecuador is a pluricultural and multi-ethnic state." The Colombian and Peruvian constitutions declare the state's duty to recognize and protect the ethnic and cultural diversity of the nation (articles 7 and 2, respectively). The Nicaraguan and Paraguayan constitutions use this type of language in more than one instance. The Mexican constitution recognizes the pluricultural nature of its people, which is based in the preexistence of indigenous peoples (art. 4). Argentina's charter, while not explicitly recognizing the ethnic diversity of its population, acknowledges the "ethnic and cultural preexistence of indigenous peoples" (art. 75).

Equally important to indigenous organizations is explicit recognition of indigenous peoples as distinct substate entities with their own forms of social and political organization. In Argentina, Bolivia, Brazil, Colombia, and Peru, constitutions recognize the juridical personality of indigenous communities, which provides communities the legal standing to sue in courts or enter into private or public contracts. The Guatemalan and Mexican governments are committed by peace accords to recognizing the right of indigenous communities to use their own forms of social and political organization; the Ecuadorian and Nicaraguan constitutions already do.

This type of symbolic rhetoric is cheap and may appear meaningless to those who are unfamiliar with the region or the aspirations of its indigenous populations. But it is in reality an astounding development. Prior to the incorporation of these sentiments, official rhetoric throughout the region declared the homogeneous nature of Latin American societies, based on the assumption that the distinctive cultural traits and identities existing in colonial Latin America had been integrated into a new hybrid type through racial mixing and social integration (Bengoa 1994:20; García Canclini 1992; Klor de Alva 1995:247–50; Stavenhagen 1992:422, 428; Wade 1997:12–13, 32). The demand for official recognition of their existence as distinct peoples has been a prominent revindication of the indigenous movement in Latin America. For a movement that is as much about dignity and identity as it is about the improvement of material circumstances, symbolic recognition is an important achievement. This symbolic recognition also has practical implications. In Colombia, what many considered to be mere rhetoric has been interpreted by the nation's Constitutional Court as a mandate of higher rank than most other constitutional rights. Elsewhere, this official recognition of social diversity provides a legal basis for the state to enact legislation that differentiates among groups in society for the purpose of avoiding discrimination, and to "sacrifice formal equality in favor of real equality" (Comisión Andina de Juristas 1994:13).

The rhetorical recognition of the linguistic, ethnic, and cultural diversity of states in the region is an important step toward the elusive goal of national unity, which is among the most important goals of constitutions in countries with communal cleavages (Murphy 1993:9). The enduring significance of this recognition will depend on how states follow up. As Jorge Dandler suggests: "The new constitutional recognition of the multi-ethnic or multi-cultural composition of the national society presupposes that the State now has the challenge to develop legislation, regulations, policies and administration of justice that indeed reflect *cultural diversity*" (Dandler 1996:14). Several constitutions (Bolivia, Colombia, Ecuador, Mexico, Nicaragua, Panama, Peru) extend this symbolic recognition to explicitly recognizing and guaranteeing the existence of indigenous forms of social organization. Bolivia and Colombia go one step further by recognizing the public and authoritative nature of these forms of organization. In Ecuador and Guatemala, decentralization and territorial reorganization schemes that are being designed in conjunction with constitutional reforms affecting indigenous peoples provide for this practical possibility, since they allow local jurisdictions to be created according to ethnicity and language. States that allow for the incorporation of ethnically defined social and territorial units rupture the uniformity and universality of public administration at the local level.

As in post-communist countries, the constitutional debates in Bolivia and Colombia centered on the lack of fit between formal, legal guarantees of citizenship and a reality in which many are unable to exercise their citizenship or access mechanisms to redress their grievances (Rapaczynski 1993:105). In addition to the new regime of ethnic rights discussed here, most Latin American countries also have overhauled their judicial systems in ways that are similar to contemporaneous reforms in post-communist Europe—for example, the adoption of constitutional courts, human rights ombudsmen, and independent councils to police the judicial profession (García Belaunde 1996a:30).[9] These efforts are being supported by a fourteen-country Inter-American Development Bank judicial reform project (Jarquín and Carrillo 1998:152–53). According to the bank's specialist on judicial reform, the seventeen "constitutional reforms now underway in the region aim, almost without exception, to strengthen the judiciary and uphold citizens' rights" (Carrillo, in Jarquín and Carrillo 1998:453). Among the most important reforms for indigenous peoples are those to the codes of criminal procedure, which regulate Indians' access to and treatment by police and the justice system. Bolivia, Guatemala, and Paraguay—countries of the region where language and illiteracy are major barriers to access— are undergoing reforms to incorporate orality and translation into court proceedings.[10]

The recognition of customary law, thus, is part of a larger effort to address the problem of weak judiciaries, the impunity of public officials, and the inaccessibility of the justice system to the poor and disadvantaged groups. Formalizing customary law protects indigenous people from the discriminatory application of nonindigenous law in a context of extreme power inequalities while compensating for the inaccessibility and weakness of state justice administration (Zanotta Machado 1994:80). It also extends the reach of the rule of law. The Andean Commission of Jurists observes that indigenous systems of justice administration have high legitimacy and efficacy and fill gaps where the state has no presence. To deny them legality would deprive society of the benefits of their problem-solving capacity (Comisión Andina de Juristas 1994:21).

Six Latin American states (Bolivia, Colombia, Ecuador, Nicaragua, Paraguay, and Peru) recognize constitutionally the official and public nature of indigenous customary law and the jurisdiction of indigenous authorities over internal community affairs. Others recognize customary law by statute or through their ratification of ILO Convention 169. The scope of this recognition varies from the recognition of juridical pluralism in Colombia, to an exceptional regime with circumscribed application within a monist system in Chile's statutory law (Comisión Andina de Juristas 1994:26). In all cases, the scope of indigenous jurisdiction is limited by the constitution. In effect, the new constitutions formally recognize what has been the practice in the region since colonial times, when the weak presence of the state in rural areas left a legal vacuum in which indigenous communities have been relatively free to resolve internal disputes. Even in modern times, indigenous communities that retain their traditional authority structures commonly handle internal matters themselves and refer serious crimes, or those involving outsiders, to state courts, where these are available. The innovation here is that indigenous authorities are given a public character and their decisions are recognized as public law. Formal recognition has required that some mechanism of coordination be created between legal systems, usually to be determined by a subsequent statutory law.

Eleven Latin American countries recognize the right of indigenous communities to own property in common (Argentina, Bolivia, Colombia, Ecuador, Guatemala, Honduras, Mexico, Nicaragua, Panama, Paraguay, and Peru). In some cases this right was retained from colonial times; in others it was restored or reinforced by revolutionary governments. In most cases, constitutions prohibit the alienation of the collective title through mortgaging, nonpayment of taxes, or sale. The Mexican and Peruvian governments went against the current trend by weakening these protections in 1992 and 1993, respectively.[11] Brazilian Indians have the right only to collective use of their traditional lands, which remain the property of the federal government. In many cases, collective property or even territorial rights are weakened by the inability of indigenous communities to exercise control over the exploitation of natural resources on their property/territory. Throughout the region, where legal systems were adapted from French and Roman law, subsoil rights are retained by the state. Although many states are bound by ILO Convention 169 and constitutional provisions to consult with indigenous communities about the exploitation of these resources or other development activities on indigenous territories, this is almost never accomplished to the satisfaction of the communities, as we found in the Bolivian and Colombian cases. In 1998, for example, the Chilean government violated its own legislation (the 1993 Indigenous Statute), which confers effective veto power over such activities on the National Indigenous Development Board, which includes indigenous representation. The government argued that the nation's need for the electricity to be generated by a proposed dam that would flood the lands of a dozen Mapuche families outweighs the right of Indians to those lands (Smith 1999:23). This is the same argument the Colombian government makes with respect to drilling for oil in U'wa territory.

The recognition of language rights actually precedes the emergence of the multicultural constitutional model in the 1990s. In the 1970s and 1980s Brazil, Colombia, Guatemala, Mexico, Nicaragua, Panama, Paraguay, and

Peru provided some recognition of indigenous languages and culture (Iturralde 1997b:89). The mere recognition of indigenous culture and language did not encounter much resistance from the legal and political establishment. Elites resisted more strongly the attainment of official status for indigenous languages, which did not come until the 1990s. Only in Paraguay does an indigenous language enjoy nationwide official status comparable to Spanish.[12] (Peru rescinded official status for Quechua in the 1993 Constitution.) In Colombia, Ecuador, Nicaragua, and Peru, indigenous languages are official in zones where their speakers are settled. In Ecuador and Guatemala indigenous organizations are negotiating to redraw administrative borders according to linguistic criteria in order to foster more participatory and culturally appropriate public service delivery and development planning.

The recognition of language rights facilitated the recognition of the right to bilingual education (Iturralde 1997b:89). Six constitutions (Argentina, Bolivia, Colombia, Ecuador, Nicaragua, and Paraguay) guarantee bilingual education. Guatemala and Mexico are committed by peace accords to incorporating this right into their pending reforms. (Other countries provide some bilingual education without a constitutional mandate.) This right also may be construed from ILO Convention 169, part 6. The main problems in implementing it have been the lack of funding for education; the scarcity of qualified, bilingual teachers; and the opposition of teachers' unions to changes that affect their ability to dictate the availability and terms of employment.

In addition to the five rights enumerated above, the new constitutions incorporate a number of other special provisions affecting the indigenous population. These include a range of exemptions from the duties of citizens (paying taxes, military service) as well as special treatment that other citizens are not legally entitled to, such as free health care or education. All of these are included in the Colombian constitution. These types of collective rights are less feasible when the population approaches a majority. In addition, some constitutions create administrative-territorial autonomous regimes for indigenous peoples. Two such regimes predate the current wave of constitutional reform. Panama recognized a large region of indigenous self-government *(comarca)* for the Kuna in 1953. The state recognized three additional *comarcas* for other indigenous groups in 1983, 1996, and 1997

(Huerta 1998:40). The creation by Nicaragua of two multiethnic autonomous regions in 1987 (following five years of warfare between the Sandinista government and Miskitu Indians, backed by the United States) inspired indigenous organizations throughout the hemisphere to press for autonomous territories.

In the 1980s, autonomy became the defining claim of indigenous movements and the centerpiece for their project to build "multiethnic, pluricultural" states. It articulates the dual nature of their demand for the voluntary reconstitution of relations with the states and societies in which they live: the desire to preserve a territorial sphere into which the state and nonindigenous society cannot intrude while integrating more effectively and participatively into the state and larger society. As in other countries challenged by claims by communal groups for territorial autonomy, this claim becomes more difficult to operationalize as indigenous populations increasingly become more urbanized and territorially integrated with nonindigenous groups.[13] Constitution-makers must choose between conferring autonomy upon territorial entities where Indians constitute a majority (indirect consociation) or upon population groups (direct consociation), exemplified by Colombia's special indigenous senatorial district, by Chile's statutory National Indigenous Development Board, and by the Saami parliaments created recently in Sweden and Norway (Assies 1994:45–47). The concept of autonomy becomes more difficult where Indians constitute a majority. How can a state foster national unity and solidarity if a majority of the population and territory is autonomous of the state and nonindigenous society, or if the majority of the territory is organized into "exceptional" or anomalous administrative units (Plant 1998)? The realization of the ideal of autonomy is impeded also by the lack of consensus among indigenous organizations within specific countries over the shape autonomy regimes should take, that is, whether they should be confined to culture or take on a territorial shape (Bengoa 1994:38); if the latter, whether they should be constructed at the community, municipal, or a higher administrative level; and whether they should be mono- or multiethnic.

Autonomy regimes are under active discussion in Ecuador, Guatemala, and Mexico; Venezuelan Indians have included indigenous autonomous regions in their constitutional proposal. The 1998 Ecuadorian constitution allows for the creation of indigenous and Afro-Ecuadorian administrative districts with powers comparable to autonomous sectional governments (art. 228). It remains to be seen how or whether this will be implemented. Both Guatemala's 1995 Indigenous Accord and Mexico's 1996 San Andrés Accord on Indigenous Rights recognize the right of indigenous communities to political autonomy, but there is no consensus within the indigenous movements in either country over the appropriate administrative unit for this autonomy. Both governments are attempting to hold autonomy below the level of a government unit with meaningful powers (namely, the municipality). Indigenous organizations are split on whether autonomy should be exercised at the community (submunicipal) level, the municipal level, or across more extensive multiethnic regions. Canada's creation of an autonomous indigenous region called Nunuvut in April 1999 may provide a positive model for future indigenous claims to autonomy, since the Nicaraguan regime, once viewed as a regional model, is now considered a failure.[14]

The indigenous movements' demands for political autonomy are facilitated by the shift in the new constitutions—and throughout Latin America —toward greater decentralization of administrative and political powers to municipal levels. This is indeed a global phenomenon, promoted by the multilateral development banks and international NGOs, whose experts view decentralization as a means toward greater responsiveness, efficiency, and accountability of government, while also promoting democratic participation and values (Assies 1998; O'Neill 1998). For these reasons and others, local-government decentralization was launched in all the post-communist constitutions (Regulska 1993:133–61). As in eastern and central Europe, however, Latin Americans have been disappointed by the results of the much ballyhooed decentralizations. Recentralization efforts, resistance by central elites to relinquishing policy-making powers, and corruption and incompetence at the local level have limited the benefits. The success of decentralization is important for indigenous movements aspiring to greater political autonomy, since effective decentralization is a necessary, albeit insufficient, condition for local autonomy.

Autonomy regimes remain an exception to the model described here, since they typically encounter stiff resistance, particularly from provincial elites who dominate politics in rural areas and who view indigenous political autonomy as encroaching upon their prerogatives. Given the way that indigenous groups are currently settled, and the resistance of elites to creating geographically extensive territories, it is likely that future experiments in indigenous autonomy (such as those being negotiated in Ecuador, Guatemala, and Mexico) will be located at the municipal level.

For many reasons (discussed above with respect to the Colombian case), communities of African descent in Latin America have been less inclined to mobilize in favor of, or to achieve, special constitutional language or laws recognizing a distinct black identity or set of rights. Following the abolition of slavery in the nineteenth century, blacks lacked any special legal status or rights apart from the wider society. The exception to this rule is the case of some Maroon (runaway slave) communities, which enjoyed a distinct, semi-autonomous legal status through treaties with colonial powers. The successor states to colonial powers have tended to ignore these treaties and to resist demands by Maroon organizations to recognize constitutionally a distinct status based on historical treaty rights.[15] In practice, blacks endured social discrimination, were underrepresented in political office, and were trapped in rural or urban poverty. For the most part, where blacks have mobilized politically as a group it has been to demand equality, rather than recognition as a distinct group.

Despite this unpromising social and legal context, two constitutions recently recognized blacks as distinct cultural communities. The first to do so was Colombia's. The 1998 Ecuadorian constitution includes a broader scope for Afro-Ecuadorian rights than its Colombian predecessor, although these rights are still less ample than those of indigenous peoples. This may be because blacks are a much smaller proportion of Ecuador's population (less than 5 percent) and are concentrated mainly in the province of Esmeraldas.[16] Thus, as in Bolivia, their conceptualization as "peoples" is more innocuous. Chapter 5 of the 1998 Ecuadorian Constitution, on collective rights, includes a section on "indigenous peoples and blacks or Afro-Ecuadorians," which contains the charter's most important statement with respect to ethnic rights. Article 83 recognizes that "indigenous peoples, which identify themselves as nationalities of ancestral roots, and black peoples or Afro-Ecuadorians, form part of the Ecuadorian State." This language is interesting in that blacks are identified as "peoples," a designation usually used by indigenous activists to distinguish Indians from "ethnic minorities." In Article 84, a set of fifteen collective rights are recognized and guaranteed to indigenous peoples, including, but not limited to, the following: the right to develop and strengthen their identity and spiritual, cultural, linguistic, social, political, and economic traditions; to conserve their inalienable communally owned lands, which are exempt from taxes; to be consulted with respect to plans to exploit natural resources on those lands and to participate in the benefits of that exploitation; to conserve their forms of social organization and authority; to retain intellectual property rights over their ancestral knowledge; and to receive intercultural, bilingual education. Article 85, which concludes this section, states that the foregoing rights enunciated for the indigenous population shall apply to black peoples or Afro-Ecuadorians "to the extent they are applicable." This language leaves the application of the indigenous rights regime to Afro-Ecuadorians open to the interpretation of those with the power to do so in the years to come. In addition to this section on collective rights, the chapter on the administrative divisions of the country allows for the creation of special territorial units encompassing indigenous and Afro-Ecuadorian populations. Provinces, municipalities, parishes, and the "organs of administration of" indigenous and Afro-Ecuadorian districts are to have autonomous functions, as determined by law. Again, the devil is in the details. Ecuadorean indigenous and black organizations were preparing draft statutory legislation implementing their constitutional rights as this book went to press.[17]

The mere insertion of the broad array of multicultural recognition and rights enumerated above is impressive and signifies the reawakening of state and society to a long-forgotten and ignored population and its grievances. But this insertion alone is far from achieving Pogany's "constitutional transformation." In most cases legislation and policy implementing the more substantive provisions have been scarce (Dandler 1996:14–15), and this is crucial in cases, such as Ecuador's 1998 charter, where much is left to future legislation. In the most recent cases, implementing legislation has not yet been produced; in some of the oldest, notably Brazil and Nicaragua, central and regional governments have resisted implementation or even overturned specific provisions. Indigenous peoples have had particular difficulty inserting provisions developing their constitutional rights in the "avalanche" of laws with respect to democratization and economic modernization, which have accompanied constitutional reform, particularly with respect to forestry, penal codes, and nonrenewable natural resources (Dandler 1996: 14–15).

Prospects for the future faithful implementation of the new multicultural constitutional model in Latin America are encouraged by "positive externalities" in the international community—the existence of international human rights instruments and the monitoring efforts of international governmental and nongovernmental organizations. They are also fostered by positive developments internal to states in both regions, such as the creation of constitutional courts and human rights ombudsmen, the attention of the independent media, and the existence of organized civil society groups willing and able to mobilize against efforts to curtail newly won constitutional rights. As Pogany argues with respect to post-communist Europe, the impact of these external and internal variables varies and "their importance within a particular society will depend on a range of factors including the history of the country in question, its economic circumstances, the prevailing social and political culture and the presence of potentially divisive elements, such as sizeable national, ethnic, religious or linguistic minorities" (1996a:575). The presence of such diversity, however, need not be divisive. Latin American constitution-makers have wagered that ethnic diversity may instead promote national unity by drawing attention to the problem of political exclusion, emphasizing the importance of rights to democracy, and infusing the political culture with the values of participation, inclusion, and tolerance. Conceding spheres of autonomy to the peoples that constitute the state—indigenous and nonindigenous—is a strategy for strengthening the state itself, by increasing its capacity to dispense justice and protect rights.

Conclusion

Multicultural constitutional debates underscore the fact that the principles upon which the Western tradition of "universal" individual human rights rests sometimes cannot be reconciled with claims for autonomy by groups outside this tradition. Some autonomy claims and identity conflicts are not negotiable, and some particularly isolated and alienated groups are unable to participate autonomously in intercultural dialogues (Santos 1997:208). The question is, how do states resolve or manage conflicts of values and interests when they arise without imposing Western values on non-Western groups or permitting groups to treat their members in ways that members of the dominant culture consider unfair or cruel? One option is to develop institutionalized procedures for the reconciliation of claims by ethnic minorities, such as the hierarchy of values formulated by the Colombian Constitutional Court with respect to the harmonization of indigenous customary law and national law. The difficulty is to construct a procedure that does not measure the claims of culturally subordinated groups against Western standards of justice, since principles of justice are not culturally neutral and even procedural rules reflect the political principles of the dominant culture (Mouffe 1992:12; Tully 1995; Walzer 1983). The challenge is to balance a view of law as a value-free system for resolving disputes among subjects with conflicting rights with a view of the political community in which the law is embedded as governed by common norms, specifically with respect to fundamental human rights. This challenge is complicated by the ambiguity and lack of consensus among indigenous organizations in the hemisphere with respect to the application of international human rights norms to their cultures.

Another option is to negotiate each conflicting claim politically through the operation of democratic institutions. Although this surely is the long-term goal, until fragile democratic institutions are fully operational, continual negotiation of incompatible claims may inject a constant source of social conflict into the political system. It also skirts the key goal of the constitutional reforms: the establishment and protection of rights. The protection of rights reduces interethnic conflict by providing guarantees to ethnic minorities that their vital interests are protected. But rights can only be protected if they are consensually defined and mutually understood. Incompatible expectations and understandings can be papered over with vague and ambiguous language during the creative phase of constitution-making, but they become open conflicts when claimants attempt to assert rights.

The new multicultural constitutions should not be viewed as perfectly embodying the resolution of intercultural normative conflicts. Instead, we should see them as establishing a framework for a permanent intercultural dialogue, or a continuing process of mutual adjustment.[18] This option provides less security to ethnic minorities, but it may be a more realistic way to build a durable multicultural state. Ultimately, Indians will have to decide whether being an integral part of the state and the wider political community is worth compromising cultural and political autonomy. Some communities and individuals, no doubt, will opt to sacrifice material gains and withdraw into a cocoon of marginality.

This does not mean that the constitutional reform processes discussed here failed. As Banting and Simeon argue, constitution-making processes have three possible outcomes. In "negative outcomes," participants fail to reach agreement, a new order is not created, and the political system continues to lack legitimacy. In "mixed outcomes," underlying issues and conflicts are not completely resolved, but they are channeled into the political process through new mechanisms and spaces created by constitutional agreement. This is to be expected in the case of "categorical conflicts" concerning belonging and identity that are often nonnegotiable (Elster, Offe, Preuss, et al. 1998:147). Contesting and challenging groups may be unsatisfied with the results, but they have attained a "constitutional niche in the system," which provides a platform to press for further advances. Constitutional issues are now ripe for resolution through ordinary politics (Banting and Simeon 1985a:22). In "creative outcomes," competing constitutional projects are reconciled or compromised, and "both the process and the result [create] the basis for a redefinition of the polity and of the relationships among the groups within it. If this is achieved, then the changes may become a kind of template, establishing a set of principles and understandings which can serve as a model for resolving future issues" (Banting and Simeon 1985a:22–23).

The cases of Bolivia and Colombia exhibit the achievements of the mixed outcome. Constitutional questions of importance to marginalized groups have been incorporated into mainstream politics in both countries. Although serious challenges remain to the consolidation of both transformations, supportive developments in the international political environment give reason to hope that the consensus reached on a subset of contested principles, and the partial understandings reached on certain issues, can provide a model for future accommodations and transformations.

Notes

Chapter 1

1. A commonly cited definition of the term "indigenous peoples" is that of the United Nations Subcommission on the Prevention of Discrimination and Protection of Minorities: "Indigenous communities, peoples and nations are those which, having a historical continuity with pre-invasion and pre-colonial societies that developed on their territories, considered themselves distinct from other sectors of the societies now prevailing in those territories, or parts of them. They form at present nondominant sectors of society and are determined to preserve, develop and transmit to future generations their ancestral territories, and their ethnic identity, as the basis of their continued existence as peoples, in accordance with their own cultural patterns, social institutions and legal systems" (United Nations 1986: para. 379).

2. The "rule of law" is the nondiscriminatory application of legal standards to all social actors according to preestablished and transparent procedures (O'Donnell 1997b :6).

3. Hart distinguishes between the former, "internal acceptance," and the latter, "external acceptance" (1994:91).

4. The term "multiculturalism" was coined in Canada in the 1960s to describe both the ideals of a democracy that values cultural diversity and the policies necessary to realize these goals (Forbes and Uhr 1998:1).

5. As Douglas Dion argues, when we are looking for "necessary conditions" for the presence of a phenomenon, a "most different systems" design (where the small number of cases studied share a dependent variable) is most appropriate, particularly when we know very little about the phenomenon under study. In such cases, choosing on the dependent variable advances political theorizing by reducing the number of possibly irrelevant factors from the data set (Dion 1998).

6. According to Venezuelan constitutional scholar Ricardo Combellas, whose 1992 book is cited on the Venezuelan government's official "Constituyente" web site.

7. Chávez polled 56 percent, his closest opponent 40 percent. *El Universal Digital,* February 21, 1999. Unless otherwise noted, all translations from the original text provided in this book are my own.

8. Other than Bolivia and Colombia, the following countries have ratified ILO 169: Argentina, Costa Rica, Denmark, Ecuador, Fiji, Guatemala, Honduras, Mexico, the Netherlands, Norway, Paraguay, and Peru.

9. In the absence of an English equivalent, I use the Spanish term throughout.

Chapter 2

In the part epigraph, Iván Orozco Abad is cited in a debate published in *Análisis Político* 10 (May–August 1990):72; Norberto Bobbio (1987:120).

1. Interviews, Miguel Eduardo Cárdenas, February 1997; Libardo Sarmiento, January 30, 1997. All interviews in chapters 2–4 took place in Colombia unless otherwise noted.

2. A 1991 poll indicated that 49 percent of Colombians did not identify with a traditional party; a 1994 poll found 33 percent identified with a nontraditional party or with none at all (Taylor 1995b :3).

3. The largest language group is the Wayúu in the eastern part of the country (22 percent), followed by the Páez in the southwest (16 percent), and the Emberá in the Pacific littoral (9 percent) (CONAPI 1992:2–3).

4. The indigenous "reserve" was created in the 1960s to set aside land for mainly Amazonian Indians. The reserve does not possess the same legal standing as *resguardos*, in that no actual title was recognized or rights given to indigenous governments thereon. Between 1965 and 1986, 158 reserves comprising an area of 12,400,000 hectares were created to sustain 128,000 Indians (Jimeno 1996:229).

5. Important black grassroots organizations include the Integral Campesino Organization of the Atrato (ACIA) and the Organization of Popular Barrios (OBAPO), both founded in 1984. Among the most prominent elements of the urban *negritudes* movement were the organization Cimarrón, the National Movement for the Human Rights of Black Communities, formed in 1982, and the Center for the Investigation of Black Culture (Wade 1993a:332–33, 352).

6. Colombia ranks fourth among Latin American countries in unequal income distribution (Santana Rodríguez 1996:56).

7. Petition cited in Dugas (1997).

8. Additional unsuccessful constitutional reform proposals were promoted by members or parties in Congress and civil society organizations.

9. The Colombian case confirms Banting and Simeon's observation that "[r]ecourse to alternative channels [of constitutional reform] is usually a sign of weakness or intense internal division within the dominant elite. Challenging elites are likely to assert the uniqueness of the constitutional questions and argue for a greater role of special forums" (Banting and Simeon 1985a:17–18; see also Martínez-Lara 1996:9).

10. The silence was intended to convey the seriousness of the students and the end of an era when students kept silent about political affairs (Dugas 1998:26).

11. There were two main student groups: We Can Still Save Colombia took its name from the petition published in *El Tiempo*, which ended with this slogan; and the Student Movement for a Constituent (Assembly), which broke off from the first group.

12. During the 1988 campaign alone, 46 of 140 UP candidates were assassinated. *Semana*, October 30, 1990, 23–29.

13. Jaramillo was gunned down by a teenage hit man wielding a machine gun at

Bogotá's El Dorado International Airport. Pizarro was shot fifteen times on a plane at fifteen thousand feet. His killer was immediately shot dead by Pizarro's bodyguards. Miraculously, none of the shots fired pierced the cabin of the plane, and it landed safely (Echeverri de Restrepo 1993:56–60).

14. The movement was named after a Páez leader who led indigenous land struggles in the 1920s and 1930s.

15. Interview, Manuel José Cepeda, January 28, 1997.

16. Echeverri de Restrepo (1993:229–241).

17. Interview, Alfonso López Michelsen, *Semana*, October 16, 1990, 25.

18. See, for example, Cepeda (1992b:258, 1995a); Echeverri de Restrepo (1993:28); García D. (1991:35); Valencia Villa (1990a:76, 1990b:85–86), and President Gaviria's address before the ANC on April 22, 1991.

19. Interview, Raúl Arango, January 30, 1997.

20. Of the Colombians polled, 46 percent believed that the low voter turnout placed in doubt the legitimacy of the constituent assembly. Poll by Napoleon Franco, February 1991, with 2,132 respondents. *El Tiempo,* December 10, 1990, 1A, 3A, 6A.

21. *El Tiempo,* December 10, 1990, 6A.

22. The four parties to the August accords shared 50 percent of the free television time allotted to ANC candidates, divided according to each party's share of congressional seats. The Colombian government also guaranteed private bank loans to candidates for their campaigns and provided campaign financing at the rate of three hundred pesos for each vote obtained, paid after the elections. The four main parties received the lion's share of funds (Buenahora 1991:345–57; Echeverri de Restrepo 1993:434–35).

23. Carrillo led the list for We Can Still Save Colombia. After entering the ANC, he was loyal to President Gaviria and is commonly counted among the Liberal Party delegates (Dugas 1998:5).

24. *Semana,* October 16, 1990, 17.

Chapter 3

1. The title of this chapter comes from ex-president Alfonso López Pumarejo, who referred to the constitutional reform process as "la liquidación amistosa del pasado . . . [la] cancelación cordial del peso abrumador de rencores y prejuicios que requería la Nación para ser próspera y pacífica" ("the friendly liquidation of the past . . . the cordial cancellation of the overwhelming weight of rancors and prejudices that the Nation would require to be prosperous and peaceful"). Cited in Cepeda (1992a:374).

2. According to Gaviria's minister of government, the Coordinadora Guerrillera Simón Bolívar negotiating on behalf of the FARC and ELN demanded eight seats, which would have been more than 10 percent of the ANC's seats (Kline 1999:88). It had earlier demanded twenty seats.

3. Another reason that the neoliberal economic model was strengthened was the

absence of opposition from the ADM-19. The party's leader, Navarro Wolff, hoped to use the ANC to consolidate the ADM-19 as a moderate political alternative and to erase the memory of its violent seizure of the Palace of Justice in 1985, which had resulted in the deaths of one hundred people, including eleven of twenty-four Supreme Court justices (Dugas 1997:333).

4. Formal negotiations took place between the Gaviria government and Coordinadora on May 15 and 16, 1991, in Arauca, Colombia. They were continued in Caracas, Venezuela, in June and extended into July, after the new constitution had been signed. Talks also occurred in Caracas in September and October 1991. See Kline (1999:ch. 6).

5. Dugas attributes the high degree of consensus to a variety of auspicious factors. The end of the cold war removed some barriers to compromise between the Left and the Right; there were common interests to be achieved, such as peace, the expansion of rights, and the modernization of the state; and there was a sense of solidarity within the ANC, encouraged by frequent informal meetings among delegates as well as criticism from the outside—in particular from members of Congress and former president López Michelsen, head of the Liberal Party. Consensus also was encouraged by the culture of pragmatism that characterizes Colombian political parties, the positive flip side of a tradition of clientelism (Dugas 1993a).

6. In the absence of an English equivalent, I use the Spanish term.

7. Two issues led to controversy within the ranks of all the parties: the popular election of departmental governors and the conversion of the "region" into the "territorial entity." Consensus also was reached only narrowly on the preamble over the issue of the invocation of God. Related to this debate was the question of the relationship between the state and the Catholic Church. In the end, the conservatives were defeated and the invocation of God that had long marked Colombian constitutions was removed, as was the prohibition on divorce (Ramírez Ocampo 1991:4). After a highly conflictual debate, in November 1997 the Colombian Congress lifted the six-year constitutional ban on extradition. It cannot be applied retroactively.

8. The spirit of reconciliation was not to last. Alvaro Gómez was assassinated on November 2, 1995.

9. The two turned down offers to head those committees, citing their lack of political experience. Rojas Birry also was appointed to the Codifying Commission, which was composed of delegates with legal training, and the post-ANC legislative commission. Both Rojas Birry and Muelas were named to the twelve-member ad hoc commission created to receive proposals from active guerrilla organizations—principally the FARC and ELN.

10. See El Tiempo, December 9, 13, 1990; El Espectador, December 7, 9, 1990.

11. Interview, Cepeda, January 28, 1997. Among the black candidates were traditional politicians as well as intellectuals active in social-movement organizations, such as Otilia Dueñas and Carlos Rosero. Juan de Dios Mosquera, president of Cimarrón, was included on a list launched by popular organizations allied with the UP (Wade 1993b:179–80, 1994:10–11; Sánchez, Roldán, and Sánchez 1993:184; Rosero n.d.).

12. *El Tiempo*, July 7, 1991, 3B; *El Espectador*, June 9, 1991, 7A.

13. Interview, Fernando Carrillo, Washington, September 18, 1997.

14. *Semana*, July 9, 1991, 24; Napoleon Franco poll, with 2,085 respondents, May–June 1991.

15. Interview, César Gaviria, Washington, December 16, 1996. See the Gaviria administration's reform proposal, published in *El Tiempo*, November 19, 1990, 8A; his address to the Constituent Assembly, April 17, 1991; and his speech upon the closing of the ANC, published in national newspapers on July 5, 1997.

16. This theory also has been proposed by Christian Gros and Virginie Laurent of the University of Paris. Personal communication, Bogotá, February 1997. Gaviria's team relied on the national Office of Indigenous Affairs to interpret the indigenous constituents' proposals. Its director, Luis José Azcárate, acted as a "bridge" between the indigenous constituents and the government, participating in many of the ANC's subcommissions, where he provided documents and educational materials on the situation of Indians and policy alternatives in sectoral areas, such as health and education. Interview, Luis José Azcárate, January 22, 1997.

17. Interview, Myriam Jimeno Santoyo, February 6, 1997.

18. Interview, Humberto de la Calle, February 20, 1997.

19. Interview, Zulia Mena, Washington, October 19, 1996.

20. Tarrow defines "political opportunities" as changes in the political environment that "lower the costs of collective action, reveal potential allies, show where elites and authorities are most vulnerable, and trigger social networks and collectivities into action around common themes" (1998:20). Political opportunities typically are measured across four dimensions, all of which were present during the ANC: a sudden opening of the political system through an unusual ANC electoral process, which favored minorities; the instability of elite alignments over procedural and substantive issues; the presence of elite allies; and the absence of state repression against indigenous organizations during the ANC (McAdam 1996:24–27).

21. Interview, Luis José Azcárate, January 22, 1997.

22. Other nontraditional forces in the ANC and many Liberal and Conservative delegates also supported a popular referendum, for diverse reasons. Interview, Manuel José Cepeda, January 28, 1997.

23. *Semana*, July 9, 1991, 20–22, 26–27.

24. These citations from the 1991 Colombian Constitution, and the ones to follow, are taken from the English language version published by the U.S. Information Agency as a Daily Report Supplement to its Foreign Broadcast Information Service series on Latin America (FBIS-LAT-91-170-S, September 3, 1991).

25. According to Lane (1996:154), about half of all Latin American countries now recognize referendum rights in their constitutions.

26. A 1993 government census counted 2,508,877 members of JACs, organized in 43,582 juntas throughout the country (Archila 1995:271), of which 70 percent were in rural areas, although Medófilo Medina observes that they have been most active in

poor urban neighborhoods. According to Medina, the JACs thrived since the 1960s because their system of organization was compatible with the mode of co-optation inherent in the bipartisan clientelist system, which was able to use the juntas to channel patronage and mobilize voters, although in some areas the JACs were able to foster autonomous participation (1996:28–29).

27. The exact amount of resources distributed is determined by the central government. The constitution only stipulates that it is scheduled to "increase annually from 14 percent [of total government revenues] in 1993 to a minimum of 22 percent in 2002."

28. Interview, Manuel José Cepeda, January 28, 1997.

29. Interviews, Manuel José Cepeda, January 28, 1997; Francisco Rojas Birry, February 24, 1997.

30. Constitutional courts or tribunals have been established also in Chile, Ecuador, Guatemala, and Peru. Supreme Courts confined to the consideration of constitutional questions exist in Argentina, Brazil, Mexico, and Venezuela. These courts do not function in the manner of the U.S. Supreme Court, that is, through judicial review.

Chapter 4

1. Because of the vast difference in the understandings of political and legal concepts between Western and indigenous cultures, the translation project was not simply a question of word substitution and syntax but also an interactive process of reflection on the meaning of the new constitution. The project was most challenging for groups with little contact with the West—such as the Cubeo, who translated "constitution" as "tree of sustenance," and the Iku, who translated "law" as "that which encompasses goodness." The most difficult concepts to translate were the philosophical ones: law, rights, duties, society, person, liberty. The concepts of territoriality and exploitation of natural resources were particularly difficult, since indigenous peoples tend not to separate geographical space from what it contains (Padilla 1995). Interviews, Jon Landaburu, March 17, 1997; Lorenzo Muelas, March 4, 1997.

2. Napoleon Franco polls, July 1992, March–April 1993, October 1993, June 1994.

3. As noted earlier, in the absence of an English equivalent, I use the Spanish term.

4. Interview, Fernando Carrillo, Washington, September 18, 1997.

5. Interview, María Teresa Garcés Lloreda, March 20, 1997.

6. Interview, Inés de Brill, February 12, 1997.

7. In August 1993, Senator Gabriel Mujuy Jacanamejoy, who represented ONIC in the Senate from 1991 to 1994, founded a new party, the Indigenous Movement of Colombia (MIC). Mujuy needed a new electoral vehicle to secure reelection as an indigenous senator, after ONIC renounced its party registration and retired from electoral politics to focus on its social movement role.

8. Interviews, Héctor Riveros, January 27, 1997; César Gaviria, Washington, December 1996.

9. Interviews, Luis José Azcárate, January 22, 1997; Héctor Riveros, January 27, 1997.

10. Libia Grueso, Carlos Rosero, and Arturo Escobar define the two distinct tendencies in terms of their aspirations for relations with the wider society: "If integrationist approaches seek the incorporation of black communities into national life, ethno-cultural approaches construct the relation between national and minority cultures and their corresponding projects as problematic." The integrationist tendency tends to base black identity on skin color and historical discrimination, whereas the ethno-cultural tendency tends to emphasize shared cultural expression and the process of constructing collective cultural identity (Grueso, Rosero, and Escobar 1998:206).

11. Delegate Orlando Fals Borda, who participated in the drafting of the article, later wrote that the rights were intended to correspond specifically to a geographically isolated and culturally distinct sector of the black population concentrated in the Pacific Coast and in similar culturally distinct outposts along rivers located elsewhere in the country, and not to the diversity of black cultural expression that can be found throughout the country. In a memorandum to the Special Commission drafting Law 70 of 1993, the statute that would implement Transitory Article 55, Fals Borda warned of the danger of mixing in one piece of legislation rights specifically created for a minority of the Afro-Colombian population with those of the entire population of African descent protected elsewhere in the constitution through language pertaining to the rights of ethnic groups (Fals Borda 1993:224).

12. Interview, Piedad Córdoba, February 19, 1997. Article 176 authorized Congress to create a special circumscription of five seats in the Chamber of Representatives for ethnic groups and Colombians residing outside the country. Constitutional Court Magistrate Eduardo Cifuentes Muñoz subsequently ruled that the creation of a special district for two black representatives is supported constitutionally.

13. The first black collective land titles were not delivered until March 1997—four years after the promulgation of Law 70. According to Mena, the Samper government wanted the first five titles delivered in December 1996 but encountered resistance from functionaries in the Chocó's agrarian reform agency, who tend to favor indigenous communities over blacks. Interviews, Piedad Córdoba, February 19, 1997; Zulia Mena, February 3, 1997.

A thirteen-candidate field vied for the two black House seats in 1994. Zulia Mena won easily (forty thousand votes) with support from the Organization of Popular Barrios of the Chocó (OBAPO) and an alliance with the indigenous-movement-based party ASI, allowing the latter to maintain state support as a congressionally represented party when its indigenous candidates lost. She gained more votes than the other black candidates combined, all of whom represented traditional parties. Conservative candidate Augustín Valencia, a wealthy intellectual, won the other seat (Asher 1998).

14. Polling from *Semana*, January 7, 1992, 44–45.

15. The *cabildo abierto*, or consultative public assembly, is defined in Article 9 of

Law 134 of 1994 as "the public meeting of the district councils, municipalities, or local administrative juntas, in which the inhabitants are able to participate directly with the purpose of discussing affairs of interest to the community."

16. For example, citizens organizing a referendum or legislative initiative must collect signatures from five of every thousand voters inscribed in the corresponding electoral district; this means eighty-five thousand signatures for the national level. Once brought to a vote, citizen-sponsored plebiscites and referenda require an unlikely level of voter participation in a country with traditionally high abstention. Referenda passing these strict tests may be overturned by Congress, a factor that tends to discourage the great investment of time and resources required to mount a successful referendum. Other restrictions on participation not envisioned by the constitution include the confinement of the recall to cities with more than thirty thousand inhabitants, and the further restriction of the subject matter and agents of legislative initiatives (Velásquez 1992b:65; Gaitán and Bejarano 1994; Muñoz Losada 1993:44–56). Interviews, María Teresa Garcés, March 20, 1997; Inés de Brill, February 12, 1997.

17. For example, Title 10 of the law that establishes the new Environment Ministry (Law 99 of 1993) includes mechanisms for the participation of indigenous and black community representatives, environmental NGOs, and the wider community and establishes public audiences on environmental policy. The education and decentralization laws also incorporate mechanisms for public participation, particularly at the municipal level. Interview, María Teresa Garcés, March 20, 1997.

18. Interview, Inés de Brill, February 12, 1997.

19. The electoral setback has been attributed to disunity in the movement, the exhaustion of movement rank and file after several years of intense mobilization, and the failure of indigenous parties to work with other social sectors to reach consensus on their party platforms prior to the elections, as the indigenous parties had done in 1991.

20. Interviews, Luis José Azcárate, January 22, 1997; Héctor Riveros, January 27, 1997; Roque Roldán, February 20, 1997. The author was unable to obtain an interview with ONIC president Abadio Green, who failed to appear for four scheduled appointments.

21. Interviews, Gladys Jimeno, January 29, 1997; Diego Iturralde, Sergio Delgado, La Paz, Bolivia, May 20, 1997.

22. Interview, Lorenzo Muelas, March 4, 1997. The absence of the ETI legislation affects the amount of resource transfers reveived by indigenous *resguardos*. Under Law 60 of 1992, *resguardos* established prior to the constitutional reform receive resource transfers on a par with nonindigenous municipalities. The ninety or so indigenous communities that lack this status receive smaller transfers. In addition to the territorial issue, the Indians were protesting a recent wave of violence against indigenous leaders and communities, and the government's failure to comply with recommendations of the Inter-American Commission on Human Rights with respect to recent massacres in the Cauca. They also condemned the government's failure to

prosecute the diversion of indigenous *resguardo* funds by nonindigenous mayors; to spend the budget available for purchasing lands for indigenous communities; and to consult with indigenous communities on development projects that affect them. Interviews, Luis José Azcárate, January 22, 1997; Gladys Jimeno, January 29, 1997; Hildur Zea Sjoberg, January 1997.

23. As Córdoba observes, the Office of Indigenous Affairs also has never had an indigenous director, let alone a representative of the indigenous movement. Interviews, Piedad Córdoba, February 19, 1997; Jenny de la Torre Córdoba, Yamil Alberto Arango Hurtado, February 27, 1997.

24. Interview, Piedad Córdoba, February 19, 1997.

25. Interviews, Yamil Alberto Arango Hurtado, February 27, 1997; Piedad Córdoba, February 19, 1997. Decree 1745 expanded the scope of Transitory Article 55 to incorporate the more urban and assimilated population of the Atlantic Coast.

26. Polling by Napoleon Franco, June 13, 15, 30, October 6, November 27, 1996. In October 1998 after the inauguration of Samper's rival, Andrés Pastrana, the Supreme Court "opened procedures" against 111 members of Congress who had absolved Samper (EIU 1998b:13).

27. "Crisis Política: la sociedad civil en la jugada," *CAJA de Herramientas* 5, 37 (May 1996):1.

28. "Vice presidente a la derecha," *CAJA de Herramientas* (September 1996):1.

29. Interview, Humberto de la Calle, February 20, 1997.

30. Since 1991, the Constitutional Court has overturned two states of exception: one imposed by the Gaviria administration, which immediately complied; the other imposed by the Samper government, which complied under protest.

31. *El Tiempo,* March 19, 1997, 1A; February 16, 1997, 9A.

32. Interview, María Teresa Garcés, March 20, 1997. Nontraditional parties comprised 35.71 percent of the ANC and gained 31.29 percent of the House seats and 36.2 percent of the Senate seats in 1991. In 1994 their number declined to 21.47 percent and 35.49 percent, respectively. The ADM-19 failed to match its electoral success in the ANC and failed to become the third force that analysts had expected. It won only thirteen House and nine Senate seats in the 1991 elections, and these were reduced to one seat in the House and none in the Senate in 1994. For an analysis of the failure of opposition parties in the post-ANC conjuncture, see Taylor (1995a, 1995b) and Boudon (1995).

33. Its most controversial decisions promoting equality and pluralism in civil society involved the promotion of religious pluralism by revoking many of the privileges enjoyed by the Catholic Church and its followers (Cepeda 1995b).

34. Ninety-five of the first one thousand writs of protection were conceded; 11.5 percent of sentences challenged were overturned. *Semana,* June 30, 1992, 31.

35. The number of rulings is greater than the number of cases, since some cases include multiple decisions.

36. In the memorandum, dated March 10, 1997, Perafán advises Piñacué that there is no evidence of intellectual authorship, but only of *tardecer*—a legal concept in Páez

law attributing guilt to a prior act that may have inspired a later outcome, although no causal link can be proved. In this instance, the crime of *tardecer* consists of the seven defendants' lying about Betancur in a public meeting during a bitter election campaign lost by Gembuel. Those lies were judged to have inspired the ELN to murder Betancur. Perafán also notes that in Páez law, the expulsion of a community member is never applied as a punishment for the first offense, as it was applied against Gembuel and his associates.

37. Interview, Constitutional Court Magistrate Eduardo Cifuentes Muñoz, March 17, 1997.

38. In 1996 alone, the Supreme Court ruled on 2,076 writ of protection claims, mostly negatively, impeding the Court's ability to address the more than 3,000 ordinary claims awaiting consideration. *El Tiempo,* March 16, 1997, 4A, 12A; March 19, 1997, 1A; March 18, 1997, 7A.

39. Written presentation of the Swedish Parliamentary Ombudsman to the Latin American Defenders of the People, August 21, 1998, La Paz, Bolivia.

40. Internet message received from the Association of Cabildos and Traditional Authorities of the U'wa and the executive committee of ONIC, dated February 4, 1999. Decree 1320 requires the government to hold a meeting with indigenous and black communities affected by a natural resource exploitation or other development project. The purpose of the meeting is to discuss how the project might affect these communities and what alternatives exist for mitigating harm. The government retains the right to decide whether and how the project goes forward.

41. Oral presentation, Universidad de los Andes, Bogotá, September 12, 1996, from the notes of Beatriz Sánchez.

42. Interview, Fernando Carrillo, Washington, September 18, 1997.

43. *El Tiempo,* March 20, 1997, 1A; *El Tiempo,* March 5, 1997, 1A.

44. Colombia's current account deficit was 5.8 percent of GDP as Pastrana took office. Reuters reports dated June 21 and 22, 1998.

Chapter 5

In the part epigraph, Nino cited from Nino (1996:221). Sánchez de Lozada is frequently heard to use the expression cited in the epigraph, which conveys his pragmatic and technocratic disinterest in political ideology.

1. Interview, Miguel Urioste, July 11, 1997. All interviews in chapters 5–7 occurred in Bolivia, unless otherwise noted. Other supporters of a constituent assembly were the United Left (IU), the National College of Bolivian Lawyers, and the Confederation of Professionals. The populist United Civic Solidarity (UCS) favored a popular referendum on constitutional reform.

2. Interview, Carlos Toranzo, May 20, 1997.

3. Interview, Ramiro Molina Rivero, May 6, 1997.

4. Interview, Miguel Urioste, July 11, 1997.

5. Interview, Gustavo Fernández, June 9, 1997.

6. Ibid.

7. Linz had worked on the Spanish constitution; Nino had been constitutional adviser to Argentine President Raúl Alfonsín. The other international consultants were Brazilian Bolivar Lamounier; Uruguayan Carina Perelli; and Arturo Valenzuela, of Georgetown University. In early 1991 Sánchez de Lozada had sought Valenzuela's advice on how the Bolivian constitution could be reformed to allow a second-round presidential election and thereby improve his chances of winning the presidency. Interview, Arturo Valenzuela, Washington, October 15, 1996.

8. Interviews, Juan Cristóbal Urioste, April 25, May 2, 1997. Arturo Valenzuela's files on the project.

9. The 1992 accord committed the parties to work on judicial reform, electoral reform, educational reform, decentralization, constitutional reform, election of the Fiscalía General, the trial of ex-dictator García Meza, a law on industrialization of coca, and a law of political parties. Despite Oblitas's efforts, the Supreme Court would play a marginal role in the deliberations on constitutional reform in Bolivia because it lacked both the jurisdiction to issue any formal decisions on the reform process and the political weight to intervene on the content or scope of the reforms. Interviews, Fernando Aguirre, May 8, 1997; Arturo Valenzuela, Washington, October 15, 1996.

10. Letter dated August 10, 1992, pp. 2–3. The same letter was addressed to multiple recipients of the document. Files of Arturo Valenzuela.

11. The MIR's main reform goals were judicial reform; restoring confidence in the electoral regime; and establishing and strengthening independent state institutions to control the power of the executive, such as the Constitutional Court and People's Defender. Juan Cristóbal Urioste, who attended the meetings as technical adviser to Sánchez de Lozada, recalls that the only reform in which ADN chief Banzer was interested was the extension of the presidential term to five years and the maintenance of the ban on reelection. He would agree to anything else provided there was agreement on these two issues. Interviews, Juan Cristóbal Urioste, April 25, May 2, 1997; Gustavo Fernández, June 9, 1997; Luis Vásquez Villamar, June 1997.

12. Interview, Gustavo Fernández, June 9, 1997.

13. Interview, Ivan Arias, June 3, 1997.

14. Interviews, Juan Cristóbal Urioste, April 25, 1997; Carlos Hugo Molina, May 26, 1997.

15. *Ultima Hora,* March 24, 1993, 9; *La Razon,* March 24, 1993, 8.

16. Interview, Carlos Hugo Molina, May 26, 1997.

Chapter 6

1. Interviews, Víctor Hugo Cárdenas, May 8, 1997; Juan Cristóbal Urioste, April 25, 1997; Luz María Calvo, May 9, 1997. The Sánchez de Lozada government passed three other major reform laws. The 1994 Law of Educational Reform aimed to improve the

overall quality and reach of education while making it more respectful of local, especially rural, linguistic diversity and creating mechanisms for the participation of communities in its design and implementation to accommodate local social realities. The 1995 Law of Capitalization provided for private international investment funds to "capitalize" half of the stock of public enterprises. Funds taken in by the initial sale of the enterprises were used to create an old-age pension fund for Bolivians born at the time of the sale (distributed for the first time in 1997). (The Law of Agrarian Reform, approved in late 1996, is discussed in chapter 7.)

2. Remarks by Sánchez de Lozada, cited in Molina M. (1997:157n35).

3. Interviews, Miguel Urioste, July 11, 1997; Walter Guevara Arze, May 6, 1997.

4. Interview, Horst Grebe, May 30, 1997.

5. Interviews, Rubén Ardaya, May 12, 1997; Verónica Balcazar, June 9, 1997.

6. Interview, Horst Grebe, May 30, 1997.

7. The smallest territorial unit, the canton, was deemed too small and too numerous (1,500) to become the basis of the scheme, while provinces (of which there were an estimated 112) were deemed too large to facilitate the expression of diverse local organizations and cultures. Another advantage of choosing the provincial section was the absence of an existing public authority or private institution with vested interests at this level, allowing the UPP team a freer hand in creating new institutions (Urioste and Baldomar 1996:32–33).

8. Interviews, Horst Grebe, May 30, 1997; Diego Iturralde, Sergio Delgado, May 20, 1997.

9. Interview, Luis Lema, June 9, 1997.

10. According to Horst Grebe, the core group of participants consisted of himself, Carlos Hugo Molina, Fernando Romero, Javier Torres Goitia, and Molina's senior staff. Víctor Hugo Cárdenas was a frequent, but not regular, participant. The subministers for health and education attended frequently because these sectors were the first to be decentralized under the LPP. Interviews, Horst Grebe, May 30, 1997; Rubén Ardaya, May 12, 1997.

11. For example, while the president did not sit down with the COB executive committee, Carlos Camargo, a member of that committee, was invited to participate in several meetings of the president's working group. Interviews, Rubén Ardaya, May 12, 1997; Carlos Camargo, June 16, 1997; Rodolfo Erostegui, April 21, 1997; Esteban Ticona, May 15, 1997.

12. Rather than taking advantage of an opportunity to build a viable indigenous political party, Cárdenas also distanced himself from the MRTKL congressional delegation and worked to solidify his position as the most prominent indigenous politician in the country. He did not allow the party to participate in the 1996 elections, in which he was not eligible to run for president. Interviews, Iván Arias, June 3, 1997; Ramiro Molina R., April 28, 1997.

13. Interview, Ivan Arias, June 3, 1997.

14. Interviews, Alcides Vadillo Pinto, May 20, 1997; Luz María Calvo, May 9, 1997; Ramiro Molina R., April 28, 1997.

15. Interviews, Alcides Vadillo Pinto, May 20, 1997; Rubén Ardaya, May 12, 1997; Ramiro Molina R., April 28, 1997; Marcial Fabricano, July 1997.

16. Interviews, Sonia Montaño, June 10, 1997; Verónica Balcazar, June 9, 1997.

17. Interview, Sonia Montaño, June 10, 1997.

18. Ibid.

19. Interview, Clara Flores, May 21, 1997. Statement of Deputy Zabala, April 12, 1994 (cassette no. 9).

20. See, for example, an interview with Carlos Hugo Molina in the *Christian Science Monitor,* February 16, 1995.

21. *La Razón* (economía), February 22, 1994, 2; *Presencia,* January 27, 1994; *El Diaro,* May 8, 1994.

22. Key supporters of the new law were the Catholic Church, which applauded the effort to ameliorate poverty and improve democratic participation, and the Bolivian Confederation of Private Entrepreneurs (CEPB), which viewed it as a vehicle for improving the distribution of income while modernizing the state. *Los Tiempos* (Cochabamba), February 25, June 3, 1994. The Association of Autonomous Municipal Governments was concerned that municipalities might not receive sufficient resources to cover the expense of maintaining the newly transferred health and education infrastructure. Although the association was disappointed that only three of its suggestions were incorporated, this was far more than was accomplished by most critics of the law. *Hoy,* April 19, 1994; *La Razón,* June 10, 1994, 10A. Interview, Horst Grebe, May 30, 1997.

23. *La Razón,* January 30, 1994.

24. Interview, José Enrique Pinelo, June 17, 1997.

25. Congressional comments are from published transcripts of the Senate debate, April 19–20, 1994, p. 292, and from unpublished transcripts of the Chamber of Deputies debate, April 12, 1994. *Presencia,* February 22, 1994, 7; *La Razón,* February 22, 1994, 8–9A.

26. *La Razón,* April 13, 1994.

27. This paragraph was modified in 1996 to appease the demands of indigenous, campesino, and other sectoral organizations with respect to the term "OTB," which led many to fear that the government was trying to replace the autonomous organizations with a homogeneous government-controlled entity, as the MNR government had done in the 1950s. Law 1702 (1996) specifies more explicitly that the term "OTB" means "Indigenous Communities, Indigenous Peoples, Campesino Communities and Neighborhood Juntas."

28. Interview, Juan Cristóbal Urioste, May 2, 1997.

29. Deputy Kukoc, transcript of debate on LPP in Chamber of Deputies, April 12, 1994, translation by the author.

30. Interview, Javier Torres Goitia, June 11, 1997.

Chapter 7

1. The World Bank (1996a) estimates illiteracy among Bolivians over fifteen years of age at 17 percent; female illiteracy is estimated to be 24 percent. Newspaper circulation is fifty-seven per thousand in Bolivia, far below the Latin American and Caribbean average of eighty-six, and the average for lower-middle-income countries such as Bolivia (World Bank 1996b); about 90 percent of the population has access to radio, whereas only 30 percent has access to television.

2. Interviews, Maryann Minutillo, May 6, 1997; Tony Cauterruci, May 15, 1997; Lucio Mendez, July 2, 1997. Beginning in 1996, municipalities were required by law to channel 3 percent of the invested portion of co-participation funds to the National Security for Maternity and Childhood program. Only 10 percent of co-participation resources, later changed to 15 percent, may be spent on administrative costs. In December 1998, the Banzer administration was trying to change this to 20 percent.

3. A 1997 survey found that only 11 percent of leadership positions in OTBs were held by women, and most of these were as community treasurers or as heads of women's committees (Bejarano 1997). In order to respond in individual cases to the need for greater representation of certain community sectors, especially women, in practice, the government recognized a variety of functional organizations. Interview, George Gray Molina, June 12, 1997.

4. Comments by SNPP staff at July 8–9, 1997, seminar on LPP implementation, La Paz; Interviews, Diego Iturralde, Horst Grebe, December 1998.

5. On the last day of his administration, Sánchez de Lozada authorized the distribution of funds to oversight committees to reimburse members for travel and expenses required for meetings or other duties, to be disbursed beginning in 1998. The Banzer administration ignored the decree (*Presencia*, August 6, 1997; Calla 1998:6).

6. SNPP poll, July 30, 1996.

7. Oral presentation by SNPP staff, July 8–9, 1997, seminar on LPP implementation, La Paz.

8. Xavier Albó argues that indigenous and campesino councillors may actually have gained more seats than the SNPP data suggest, since, according to a poll conducted by the SNPP—given to 35 percent of the total number of mayors and municipal councillors, with geographical emphasis in the three major cities (cited in Albó 1997:9)—half the new municipal councillors speak an indigenous language, and two-thirds report belonging to a campesino organization. It is difficult to interpret these results simply as a preference among voters for indigenous or campesino candidates, since all candidates are presented on party lists: ballots contain only the logo and name of the party, not the particular candidates that correspond thereto. In many cases it is not known on election day by the parties themselves which persons would be elected on a particular party's list. Interviews, Ivan Arias, June 3, 1997; Wigberto Rivero, May 5, 1997; Xavier Albó, May 28, 1997; Mario Arrieta, May 14, 1997.

9. Interviews, Marcial Fabricano, July 8, 1997; Xavier Albó, May 28, 1997; Ivan Arias, June 3, 1997; Florencio Antuñi Sánchez, June 26, 1997.

10. A 1996 SNPP survey of 122 oversight committee presidents found that only 18.9 percent reported participating in the elaboration of a PDM; 80.3 percent reported not participating at all and/or not even knowing what a PDM was. More than twice as many (49.2 percent) reported participating in the preparation of the 1996 PAO. In the same survey, 61.5 percent of oversight committee presidents said that they did not exercise any control over the management and distribution of co-participation resources (Bejarano 1997). These figures are disappointing, since these municipalities are receiving special technical assistance and encouragement with respect to the PPM. As of mid-1997, only 134 of the country's municipalities had produced PDMs. Interview, Mauricio Lea Plaza, July 15, 1997.

11. Interview, George Gray Molina, June 12, 1997.

12. Interviews, Mauricio Lea Plaza, July 15, 1997; Rubén Ardaya, May 12, 1997.

13. Interview, Walter Guevara, May 6, 1997; Confidential interviews. It is widely believed that Cárdenas was preparing for a presidential run in 2002.

14. Interviews, Carlos Toranzo, May 20, 1997; Sergio Molina, May 5, 1997; Walter Guevara, May 6, 1997.

15. In particular, campesino leaders cite the December 1996 massacre of ten protesting Quechua miners in Amayapampa (D'Emilio 1997:45).

16. Interview, Ramiro Molina R., April 28, 1997.

17. Interviews, Wigberto Rivero, May 5, 1997; Ramiro Molina R, April 28, 1997.

18. Interviews, Esteban Ticona, May 15, 1997; Wigberto Rivero, May 5, 1997; Diego Iturralde, Sergio Delgado, May 20, 1997; Ramiro Molina R., April 28, 1997; Ricardo Calla, June 3, 1997; Román Loayza, June 21, 1997.

19. Interviews, Sergio Molina, May 5, 1997; George Gray Molina, June 12, 1997; Marcial Fabricano, July 8, 1997; José Gabriel Guasebe, July 2, 1997.

20. Interview, Esteban Ticona, May 15, 1997.

21. Interview, Luz María Calvo, May 9, 1997.

22. Interviews, Ramiro Molina R., May 6, 1997; Xavier Albó, May 28, 1997; Marcial Fabricano, July 8, 1997. The last change made to Article 171 prior to its congressional approval was the modification of "guaranteeing the use and sustainable exploitation of *their* natural resources" to "guaranteeing the use and sustainable exploitation of *the* natural resources"—in order to weaken claims of ownership by indigenous groups of resources on their "original community lands" (Marinissen 1995:96).

23. *Presencia* (economía), May 16, 1997, 9.

24. The delay is attributable to the resistance of the teachers' unions, which stand to lose control over teacher appointments, salaries, and government patronage; the lack of an adequate government communications policy to convey the importance of the reform; and the more long-term nature and expectations of the reform. It will take years to train the teachers necessary to implement the new pedagogy, a task made more difficult by the uncooperative posture and traditional mentality of the teachers and their union. Only the slowness of congressional action prevented approval of a counterreform drafted by the teachers to restore privileges and prerogatives to the

union. Government officials (including Sánchez de Lozada) also attribute the stalled implementation of the educational reform to the lack of political support from and direct supervision of the president in the face of recentralizing tendencies in the government and the counterreform efforts of the MNR and MBL, which staffed the educational secretariat with managerially and technically incompetent party militants. *La Razón*, June 29, 1997, 5A.

25. Interviews, Silvina Ramírez, May 7, 1997; René Orellana Halkyer, July 18, 1997.

26. In 1991, the aunt of Capitán Grande Bonifacio Barrientos (later the first indigenous submayor of an indigenous municipal district) and her husband—both declared to be witches and expelled from the community of Cuarirenda—were shot and their bodies burned upon returning to the community. Municipal authorities of Charagua sent the police to arrest the perpetrators, but when the entire community claimed responsibility for the murder, the police left without making an arrest. A nearby army post also attempted to intervene but was rebuffed. Interviews, Ramiro Molina R., May 6, 1997; Silvina Ramírez, May 7, 1997; René Orellana Halkyer, Isabelle Combes, July 18, 1997.

27. Interviews, Ramiro Molina R., May 6, 1997; Jorge Luis Vacaflor, May 13, 1997; Silvina Ramírez, May 7, 1997.

28. Interviews, María Aida Luzán de Cabrera, mayor of Pucarani, June 26, 1997; Raquel Romero, May 26, 1997.

29. Interviews, Sonia Montaño, June 10, 1997; J. Roberto Rozo, April 29, 1997.

30. Interviews, Verónica Balcazar, June 9, 1997; Sonia Montaño, June 10, 1997; José Antonio Nava, May 28, 1997; Gerardo Berthín, May 22, 1997; Alberto Nogales, May 27, 1997. Financial information from confidential U.S. government documents.

31. Interview, Maryann Minutillo, May 6, 1997. I could not obtain an explanation from USAID with respect to the decision to end the DDCP project prematurely.

32. Interviews, Walter Guevara, May 6, 1997; Tony Cauterruci, May 15, 1997.

33. The Bolivian government also signed conventions to provide technical assistance to seven countries.

34. The term was coined by Tony Cauterruci of Chemonics. Interview, May 16, 1997.

35. Interviews, Carlos Toranzo, May 20, 1997; Carlos Hugo Molina, May 26, 1997; Gustavo Fernández, June 9, 1997; Luis Vásquez Villamar, June 17, 1997; Marcial Fabricano, July 8, 1997. Fernando Aguirre (interview, May 8, 1997), one of the key authors of the judicial reforms, disagrees that the failure to implement the judicial reforms in any way affects the exercise of new rights, or of indigenous rights in particular.

36. Confidential interviews, former justice administration officials. Interviews, Luis Vásquez, June 17, 1997; Gustavo Fernández, June 9, 1997; Ramiro Molina R., May 6, 1997. *La Razón*, October 11, 1996, 2A. In addition, Congress approved laws abolishing imprisonment for debts to the state, allowing defendants awaiting trial who were unable to post bail to enjoy provisional liberty, and providing for the release of defendants held for more than 180 days. Interview, Bernardo Wayar, December 17, 1998.

37. The Santa Cruz civic committee achieved 79 percent public approval for their reform proposals in polling conducted on May 21–23, 1997, with 184,105 Santa Cruceños responding. *Presencia,* May 27, 1997, 1, 3B. Of 10,000 Potosinos polled on July 10, 1997, 89 percent supported the direct election of prefects and other offices; 74 percent supported the separation of ballots; 82 percent supported the legalization of the referendum; and 89 percent opposed the capitalization law. *Presencia,* July 19, 1997, 3B. These results are consistent with a 1993 Bolivian government survey, which found that 71 percent of Bolivians polled favored the direct election of departmental prefects (Moe 1997:6). Politicians' comments from *La Razón,* May 22, 1997, 21A; *Presencia,* May 22, 1997, 3B; *Presencia,* May 24, 1997, 6B.

38. Interview, Fernando Mayorga, June 24, 1997.

39. Pablo Dermizaky, *Presencia,* May 27, 1997, 5A.

40. Poll of four hundred adults in La Paz, El Alto, Cochabamba, and Santa Cruz, on October 26, 1996, performed by the Universidad Católica Boliviana.

41. The ADN won forty-three congressional seats, the MIR thirty, the UCS twenty-three, and CONDEPA twenty-two. The governing coalition also includes some regional parties, such as the NFR (New Republican Force), whose base is in Cochabamba.

42. Each of the nine departments elects three senators. Half of the Chamber of Deputies is directly elected; the other half is indirectly elected through party lists, which are usually determined by party leaders.

43. Confidential interviews, December 1998.

44. Interview, Gerardo Berthin, December 1998.

45. Interviews, Jorge Quiroga, Fernando Aguirre, Nardy Suxo, Bernardo Wayar, December 1998. *Presencia,* December 18, 1998, A8; December 17, 1998, A2.

46. Interviews, Jorge Luis Vacaflor, May 13, 1997; Bernardo Wayar, December 17, 1998.

47. Interviews, Silvina Ramírez, May 7, 1997; Lorena Ossio, December 18, 1998; Ivan Arias, December 16, 1998.

48. Interviews, Fernando Aguirre, Marisol Sanjinez, Bernardo Wayar, December 17, 1998; Nardy Suxo, December 18, 1998. Written comments of the Swedish Ombudsman at a presentation in La Paz in 1998.

49. Interview, Marisol Sanjinez, December 17, 1998. A separate office was also established to mediate complaints that do not fall under the jurisdiction of the People's Defender.

50. According to Rubén Ardaya (interview, December 16, 1998), at the April 1998 Paris Club meetings international donors obligated the Banzer government to incorporate the popular participation program into their development planning as a state policy. Previously, the government's plan had included no mention of the program.

51. November Mission Preliminary Findings: Public Expenditure Review, Decentralization and Popular Participation, November 1998. Draft.

52. In a poll of 3,576 Bolivians in all nine departments, in urban and rural areas,

representing all ethnic, gender, and income levels, 24 percent advocated more responsibility for the central government; 15 percent advocated no change. The departmental option was not among the choices. Other observers describe the shift away from the municipal level as a lack of focus, owing to the interplay of strong centralizing and decentralizing forces within the ADN, emanating from the traditional and technocratic wings, respectively. Interviews, Carlos Mollinedo, December 14, 1998; Horst Grebe, December 15, 1998; Gerardo Berthin, Ricardo Calla, Jorge Quiroga, Diego Iturralde, Rubén Ardaya, December 1998; Confidential interviews, December 1998.

53. Under the current law, votes to remove a mayor must not occur within a year of the beginning or end of his or her term, must receive a three-fifths majority of municipal council votes, and must coincide with an election of a replacement by the council (Rojas Ortuste 1998:13). Departmental councils also have the right to censure prefects, but this has never been used (Oporto 1998a:33).

54. The government also plans to revise the LOM to raise the proportion municipal governments may spend on current expenditures from 15 to 20 percent. Interview, Ericka Brockman, December 16, 1998.

55. Interviews, Gerardo Berthín, Washington, December 22, 1997; Rubén Ardaya, December 16, 1998.

56. Interview, Jorge Quiroga, December 1998.

57. Interview, Ricardo Calla, December 16, 1998.

58. Interviews, Ivan Arias, Ricardo Calla, December 16, 1998; Diego Iturralde, December 18, 1998. According to Arias, all eight leaders of CIDOB have signed clandestine contracts with timber companies; a total of fifteen such clandestine contracts exist between indigenous leaders and timber companies.

59. Interviews, Ivan Arias, Ricardo Calla, December 16, 1998; Diego Iturralde, December 18, 1998.

60. Interview, Diego Iturralde, December 18, 1998.

61. Some regional and local indigenous organizations rejected the CIDOB strategy and formed alliances with locally strong parties. Interviews, Ramiro Molina R., April 28, 1997; Wigberto Rivero, May 5, 1997; Ivan Arias, June 3, 1997, December 16, 1998; Luz María Calvo, May 9, 1997; René Orellana Halkyer, July 18, 1997; Ricardo Calla, December 16, 1998; Diego Iturralde, December 18, 1998.

62. *Presencia* (Santa Cruz), December 18, 1998, 2.

63. Interview, Diego Iturralde, December 18, 1998.

64. Interviews, Jorge Quiroga, December 14, 1998; Gerardo Berthin, December 17, 1998.

Chapter 8

The part epigraph is from Lord Acton, *Essays on Freedom and Power* (Glencoe, Ill.: The Free Press, 1948; cited in Hans Kohn, *Nationalism: Its Meaning and History* [Malabar, Fla.: Robert E. Krieger Publishing, 1982], 125).

1. The number of registered voters decreased between 1986 and 1990, from sixteen to thirteen million; then it increased between 1991 and 1994, from thirteen to seventeen million. Abstention in presidential elections increased from 57 percent in both 1986 and 1990, to 66 percent in the 1994 first round of presidential voting.

2. Interviews, María Teresa Garcés, March 20, 1997; Manuel José Cepeda, January 28, 1997.

3. Bolivia's National Electoral Court registered 630,101 new voters between the 1995 municipal and 1997 national elections.

4. *Presencia,* April 19, 1997, 2; April 9, 1997, 2.

5. In Andean regions, voter registration offices are accessible to the majority of indigenous adults. The problem there has been caused by efforts of the local personnel to deny services to Indians, claiming, for example, that they are out of paper. The process has been more difficult in thinly populated, less accessible areas where much of the indigenous population lives. In these areas, the problem is the lack of resources. In some far-flung regions it can cost as much as two or three thousand U.S. dollars to provide documents for forty or fifty people. To address this problem, some indigenous communities are using their *resguardo* transfer funds to offset the cost of registration. Interviews, Gladys Jimeno, Doris Aristizabal, February 26, 1997; Jesús Avirama, March 10, 1997.

6. Oral presentation by SNPP staff, June 25–26, 1997, Cochabamba.

7. A December 1998 World Bank study of the popular participation and decentralization plan found many positive achievements, among them: further consolidation of oversight committees; the establishment of a state presence at the local level; an appropriate focus of expenditures on basic needs and local development; and some anecdotal improvements in public service delivery. Among the "issues" identified by the World Bank are significant local tax evasion and a tendency to grant tax amnesties and exemptions; a lack of connection between municipal income and development planning strategies; central government impingement of municipal autonomy with respect to development priorities and other re-centralizing tendencies; high staff turnover and disproportionate (excessive) growth of personnel; administrative corruption; lack of professional incentives; weak monitoring, evaluation, and control systems; lack of coordination between municipal and departmental development planning; and confusion about the distribution of responsibilities at the various levels of government (Ardaya 1998). See also Oporto (1998a:50–56).

8. Free media time is allotted according to the number of seats a party currently holds in Congress. Each indigenous party with juridical personality currently is allocated two minutes of television time every forty-five days; traditional parties are allocated more time and can afford to purchase additional spots. Interviews, Luis Carlos Osorio, February 26, 1997; Jesús Avirama, March 10, 1997; oral presentation by Virginie Laurent, February 14, 1997.

9. According to Piñeros, the change in political culture began not with the constitution, but in 1987 with the government's National Rehabilitation Plan, which brought

professionals to organize and mobilize communities to work on local development projects. Interviews, Claudia Piñeros, March 9, 1997; Jesús Avirama, March 10, 1997.

10. Inter-Press Service, April 9, 1997, cited in Smith (1999:17).

11. Prior to 1997, Indians had little or no congressional presence as representatives of indigenous organizations. In the 1993–1997 Congress there were ten ethnic Indians, but these did not identify with the indigenous movement, according to Wigberto Rivero Pinto (interview, May 5, 1997).

12. The quota law does not apply to single-member-district seats, 90 percent of which were contested by men. In some cases, because of provisions in the new electoral law, women winning seats by virtue of their position on party lists were displaced by men winning single-member-district seats, which were given preference in the final calculation of votes. Interviews, Xavier Albó, May 28, 1997; Sonia Montaño, June 10, 1997. *La Razón* (ventana), July 6, 1997, 8–9, and June 29, 1997, 12A, 15A; *Presencia*, June 4, 1997, 4; *Bolivian Times*, September 19, 1996, 5.

13. Interview, Carlos Alviar, February 18, 1997.

14. Other efforts to exercise the legislative initiative failed to secure sufficient signatures. Interview, Manuel José Cepeda, January 28, 1997; Procomún (1997:17).

15. Interview, Antonio Navarro Wolff, February 13, 1997.

16. Interview, Carlos Alviar, March 1997.

17. Interview, Humberto de la Calle, February 20, 1997.

18. *La Razón*, June 22, 1997, 6A.

19. Although USAID has no specific programs geared to reaching women, they have provided training sessions conducted by female project staff for women's groups that have requested women-only meetings. On one such occasion, it took more than an hour to get the meeting started because male community leaders refused to leave, fearing that the meeting was subversive. Interview, Tony Cauterruci, May 15, 1997.

20. A 1997 Harvard study of "social capital" in Bolivia found that "the high density of local organizations [...] improves performance only when coupled with indigenous inclusion in local politics. The density of civic organization actually hurts performance in divided societies" (O'Neill and Gray Molina 1998:1).

21. A team of Swedish analysts concluded that the model tended to promote an instrumentalized version of participation linked conceptually to municipal planning. The channeling of social mobilization into projects (dubbed "projectism" by the Swedes) may cause the homogenization and denaturation of community demands, while disaggregating social action that could be mobilized behind a more comprehensive reform agenda. Alternatively, this may be only a phase in a learning process that leads communities toward becoming autonomous engines of democratization (Booth, Clisby, and Widmark 1996:viii).

22. Interviews, Ricardo Calla, June 3, 1997; Juan Carlos Nuñez V., July 14, 1997.

23. Interview, Sergio Delgado and Diego Iturralde, May 20, 1997.

24. Interview, Claudia Piñeros, March 9, 1997; oral remarks, Elizabeth García, February 14, 1997.

25. Interview, Gladys Jimeno, January 29, 1997; *Bolivia Multiétnica* 1, 2 (February 1997):1.

26. Quotation is cited from Eduardo L. Llorens, *La autonomía en la integración política* (Madrid: Editorial Revista de Derecho Privado, 1932), 24.

27. Interviews, Virginie Laurent, March 11, 1997; Jesús Avirama, March 10, 1997; Claudia Piñeros, March 9, 1997; Myriam Jimeno Santoyo, February 6, 1997; Roque Roldán, February 20, 1997; oral presentation, Virginie Laurent, February 14, 1997.

28. Interview, Esther Sánchez, February 3, 1997.

29. In 1997 urban unemployment reached a ten-year high of more than 14 percent. "Gap between Colombian rich and poor said widening," Reuters, Bogotá, December 16, 1997. At the beginning of the 1980s, the richest 20 percent of Colombians received 49 percent of national income, while the poorest 20 percent received 6.6 percent. In 1996 the first group's portion increased to 54 percent of income, while the latter's portion fell to 6 percent (Orjuela E. 1998:60). Pastrana figures from *Financial Times of London,* March 12, 1999, 7.

30. Cepeda observes that this tendency prevails among constitutional courts even in countries, like Germany, where the court is explicitly empowered to do so (Cepeda 1995b:23).

31. Pursuant to Law 60 (1993), *resguardos* are considered municipalities for the purpose of resource transfers, which are determined by population. The corresponding municipality or departmental government, depending on the location of the *resguardo,* holds the money corresponding to the indigenous population and establishes a convention with *resguardo* authorities pursuant to which the money is to be spent solely on social investment projects chosen by *cabildo* authorities. Once the ETIs are established, the money is to go directly to the authorities. In the Guajira, twelve of the department's thirteen mayors' offices were investigated for corruption and illicit enrichment, including the diversion of funds destined to indigenous *resguardos* (*El Tiempo,* March 9, 1997, 8A). Interviews, Raúl Arango, January 30, 1997; Diego Iturralde, May 20, 1997; Claudia Piñeros, March 9, 1997; Jesús Avirama, March 10, 1997.

32. *Presencia* (social), July 1, 1997, 2; *La Razón,* June 19, 1997, 3B.

33. Interview, Jorge Quiroga, December 14, 1998.

34. *El Tiempo,* March 22, 1997, 9A.

35. "Colombian rebels' finances are booming," Infobeat internet news service. Source cited is July 5, 1998, issue of *Cambio 16* magazine, which cites a confidential official security report. Message received July 6, 1998.

36. Associated Press, via internet, February 19, 1999.

37. *Washington Post,* March 1, 1998, A22; March 8, 1998, A26.

38. On the failure of local decentralization to improve public service delivery and promote democratization in Nigeria in the decade leading up to the coup, see Wunsch and Olowu (1996–1997:66–82).

39. This term is used by Gros (n.d), Iturralde (1997b), and others. Bengoa prefers the term "postindigenism" (1994:15).

Chapter 9

1. According to Plant, the Guatemalan government has shown interest in Bolivia's popular participation model. Mayan groups and their allies, however, have criticized the Bolivian scheme for its top-down development approach and the "limited recognition of indigenous institutions and structures at the local level" (1998).

2. Information from *Amazon Update* #49, August 15, 1999.

3. Editorial, *Abya Yala News* 10.4 (1997):3. The entire issue is devoted to the impact of ILO 169 in the hemisphere. See also Dandler (1996:3–5).

4. Four non–Latin American countries (Denmark, Fiji, the Netherlands, and Norway) have ratified the document. Twenty-seven countries ratified ILO Convention 107. In Mexico, indigenous organizations used the convention as a bargaining instrument to reach consensus with the government on the San Andrés accord.

5. Report of the Committee on Juridical and Political Affairs on the Proposed Declaration on the Rights of Indigenous Populations, March 29, 1999.

6. Interview with Huilcaman, "UN Still at Odds over Indigenous Rights," Interpress Service, December 14, 1998.

7. I would place in this group the Washington-based Indian Law Resource Center and the Chilean Mapuche organization Council of All the Lands. Representatives of both groups participated in both OAS and UN fora and have voiced the most critical comments. North American indigenous organizations also are usually among this group. They tend to equate self-determination with sovereignty based on the history of treaty relations in the United States (Zanotta Machado 1994:77).

8. At independence, Uruguay had approximately four thousand or five thousand Indians. These were soon exterminated or expelled to Paraguay (Regueiro Elam 1995).

9. Latin American countries with constitutional courts include Bolivia, Chile, Colombia, Ecuador, Guatemala, and Peru. In Argentina, Brazil, Mexico, and Venezuela, existing supreme courts have been confined to considering constitutional questions (García Belaunde 1996a:30). On the effectiveness and importance of constitutional courts in post-communist Europe, see Schwartz (1993:163–207), Pogany (1996a:576–79, 581–83), and Elster, Offe, Preuss et al. (1998:102–05).

10. I have not done a complete survey of the region, but I am aware of major reforms to codes of criminal procedure in Bolivia, Guatemala, and Paraguay in the last two years, which attempt to make the codes more accessible to indigenous peoples.

11. A 1995 law confined the privatization and sale of indigenous and campesino community lands to the coastal peasant population, whose communal landholding practices are relatively recent. Interview, Javier Aroca, ombudsman for native communities, Zurich, April 30, 1999.

12. For unique historical reasons, although Indians comprise less than 5 percent of the population, there is a large rural nonindigenous population that speaks only Guaraní: 40 percent of the country is monolingual in a standardized Guaraní, 5 percent speak only Spanish, 45 percent are bilingual (Bareiro 1996:262–63).

13. For an introduction to the global literature on ethnic autonomy, see Hannum (1996) and Lapidoth (1997).

14. The most important reasons for this are the Nicaraguan government's resistance to relinquishing power; conflicts of interest among social groups in the regions; recent cataclysmic natural disasters that strain the capabilities of all levels of government; a failing national economy; and the hegemonic pretensions of the Miskitu. See Van Cott (1999).

15. On this issue in Suriname and Jamaica, see Pakosie (1996) and Zips (1996), respectively.

16. Information from web site: abyayala.nativeweb.org/cultures/ecuador/afro/.

17. Interviews, Quito, Ecuador, July–August 1999.

18. This possibility was suggested by Colombian anthropologist Esther Sánchez, with respect to the harmonization of indigenous and national justice systems. Interview, February 3, 1997.

Bibliography

Adler, Judith Hellman. 1992. "The Study of New Social Movements in Latin America and the Question of Autonomy." In *The Making of Social Movements in Latin America*, ed. Arturo Escobar and Sonia Alvarez, 52–61. Boulder: Westview Press.

Albó, Xavier. 1994. "And from Kataristas to MNRistas? The Surprising and Bold Alliance Between Aymaras and Neoliberals in Bolivia." In *Indigenous Peoples and Democracy in Latin America*, ed. Donna Lee Van Cott, 55–82. New York: St. Martin's Press.

———. 1996a. "Making the Leap from Local Mobilization to National Politics." *Report on the Americas* 29, 5 (March/April):15–20.

———. 1996b. "Nación de muchas naciones: Nuevas corrientes políticas en Bolivia." In *Democracia y estado multiétnico en América Latina*, coord. Pablo González Casanova and Marcos Roitman Rosenmann, 321–66. México: UNAM/La Jornada.

———. 1997. "Alcaldes y concejales campesinos/indígenas: La lógica tras las cifras." In *Indígenas en el poder local*, 7–26. La Paz: Ministerio de Desarrollo Humano, SNPP.

Albó, Xavier, and Josep M. Barnadas. 1990. *La Cara india y campesina de nuestra historia*. La Paz: UNITAS/CIPCA.

Alvarez, Sonia E., and Arturo Escobar. 1992. "Conclusion: Theoretical and Political Horizons of Change in Contemporary Latin American Social Movements." In *The Making of Social Movements in Latin America: Identity, Strategy, and Democracy*, ed. Arturo Escobar and Sonia E. Alvarez, 317–329. Boulder: Westview Press.

Alvarez, Sonia E., Evelina Dagnino, and Arturo Escobar, eds. 1998. *Cultures of Politics/Politics of Cultures: Revisioning Latin American Social Movements*. Boulder: Westview Press.

Andrade S., Lupe. 1996. "A Quiet Revolution." *Hemisfile* 7, 5 (September–October): 1–2, 12.

Angarita Barón, Ciro. 1994. *Soberanía del pueblo y poder constituyente*. Bogotá: Escuela de Liderazgo Democrático, Corporación Viva la Ciudadanía.

———. 1998. "Colombia: Comunidades indígenas y constitución de 1991." In *Seminario Internacional de Administración de Justicia y Pueblos Indígenas*, 95–117. La Paz: República de Bolivia.

Angel, Jaime Giraldo. 1993. "La reforma constitucional de la justicia." In *La constitución de 1991: Un pacto político viable?* comp. John Dugas, 97–133. Bogotá: Universidad de los Andes.

Archila Neira, Mauricio. 1995. "Tendencias recientes de los movimientos sociales." In *En busca de la estabilidad perdida,* comp. Francisco Leal Buitrago, 251–302. Bogotá: TM Editores, IEPRI–Universidad Nacional, Colciencias.

Archondo, Rafael. 1997. *Tres años de participación popular: Memoria de un proceso.* La Paz: Ministerio de Desarrollo Humano, SNPP.

Ariana, Mónica Pérez. 1996. "Participación de la comunidad negra del Chocó en el marco de la Ley 70 de 1993." Trabajo de grado. Bogotá: Universidad de los Andes.

Arjomand, Said Amir. 1992. "Constitutions and the Struggle for Political Order: A Study in the Modernization of Political Traditions." *Archives Européennes de Sociologies* 33, 1:39–82.

Arnson, Cynthia, and Jane Marcus. 1995. *Colombia: Human Rights and the Peace Process.* Working paper no. 212. Washington, D.C.: Woodrow Wilson International Center for Scholars.

Ardaya Salinas, Rubén. 1991. *Ensayo sobre municipalidad y municipio.* La Paz: Instituto de Investigaciones y Desarrollo Municipal.

———. 1996. "El fortalecimiento municipal para la participación popular." In *Apre(he)ndiendo la participación popular,* 125–144. La Paz: Programa de las Naciones Unidas para el Desarrollo/SNPP.

———. 1998. "Primer censo de gobiernos municipales: La fuerza de la nueva realidad." Unpublished remarks.

Arocha, Jaime. 1992a. "Afro-Colombia Denied." *Report on the Americas: The Black Americas, 1492–1992* 25, 4.

———. 1992b. "Los negros y la nueva constitución colombiana de 1991." *América Negra* 3 (June):39–54.

Arocha, Jaime, and Nina S. de Friedemann. 1993. "Marco de referencia histórico-cultural para la ley sobre derechos étnicos de las comunidades negras en Colombia." *América Negra* 5 (June):155–71.

Artículo Primero. 1996. "Editorial." *Artículo Primero,* año 1, no. 2 (October–December): 3–12.

ASI. 1995. *Proyecto político joven con una historia cultural milenaria.* Bogotá: ASI.

Asher, Kiran. 1998. "Constructing Afro-Colombia: Ethnicity and Territory in the Pacific Lowlands." Ph.D. dissertation, University of Florida.

Assies, Willem. 1994. "Self-Determination and the 'New Partnership': The Politics of Indigenous Peoples and States." In *Indigenous Peoples' Experiences with Self-Government,* ed. Willem Assies and A. J. Hoekema, 31–71. IWGIA doc. no. 76. Copenhagen: University of Amsterdam.

———. 1998. "Pueblos indígenas y reforma del estado en América Latina." Paper prepared for the workshop on Indigenous Peoples and Reform of the State, Amsterdam, October 29–30.

Assies, Willem, and A. J. Hoekema, eds. 1994. *Indigenous Peoples' Experiences with Self-Government.* IWGIA doc. no. 76. Copenhagen: University of Amsterdam.

Avirama, Jesús, and Rayda Márquez. 1994. "The Indigenous Movement in Colombia."

In *Indigenous Peoples and Democracy in Latin America*, ed. Donna Lee Van Cott, 83–106. New York: St. Martin's Press.

Ayo, Diego. 1997. "La elección del tres de diciembre de 1995: Análisis de las 464 autoridades indígenas y campesinas elegidas." In *Indígenas en el poder local*, 27–41. La Paz: Ministerio de Desarrollo Humano, SNPP.

Banting, Keith G., and Richard Simeon. 1985a. "Introduction: The Politics of Constitutional Change." In *Redesigning the State: The Politics of Constitutional Change in Industrial Nations*, ed. Keith G. Banting and Richard Simeon, 1–29. Toronto: University of Toronto Press.

———, eds. 1985b. *Redesigning the State: The Politics of Constitutional Change in Industrial Nations*. Toronto: University of Toronto Press.

Barber, Benjamin R. 1984. *Strong Democracy: Participatory Politics for a New Age*. Berkeley and Los Angeles: University of California Press.

Barco Vargas, Virgilio. 1990. "Intervención del Señor Presidente de la República Doctor Virgilio Barco Vargas, en la instalación de la Comisión Preparatoria para el Proceso de Reforma Institucional, febrero 25 de 1988." In *Una constituyente para la Colombia del futuro*. Bogotá: Universidad de los Andes, FESCOL.

Bareiro Saguier, Rubén. 1996. "Paraguay: Estado pluricultural, multiétnico y bilingue." In *Democracia y estado multiétnico en América Latina*, coord. Pablo González Casanova y Marcos Roitman Rosenmann, 261–292. México: UNAM/La Jornada.

Baynes, Kenneth. 1992. "Liberal Neutrality, Pluralism, and Deliberative Politics." *Praxis International* 12, 1 (April):50–69.

Bejarano, Nilse. 1997. "Diagnóstico de situación de organizaciones territoriales de base, comités de vigilancia, asociaciones comunitarias y listado de organizaciones funcionales." Preliminary document. La Paz: SNPP.

Bellamy, Richard, and Dario Castiglione. 1996. "Introduction: Constitutions and Politics." *Political Studies* XLIV, 413–416.

Bengoa, José. 1994. "Los indígenas y el estado nacional en América Latina." *Anuario Indigenista* 33:13–40.

Benhabib, Seyla, ed. 1996. *Democracy and Difference: Contesting the Boundaries of the Political*. Princeton: Princeton University Press.

Bernal Medina, Jorge Arturo. 1996. "Cinco años de la nueva carta política." *CAJA de Herramientas* (July):18.

———. 1997. "No hay clima para pactar." *CAJA de Herramientos* (February):3.

Betancourt, Ana Cecilia, and Hernán Rodríguez. 1994. "After the Constitution: Indigenous Proposals for Territorial Demarcation of Colombia." *Abya Yala News* 8, 1–2 (summer):22–23.

Bobbio, Norberto. 1987. *The Future of Democracy: A Defence of the Rules of the Game*. Translated by Roger Griffin. Edited and introduced by Richard Bellamy. Cambridge, Mass.: Polity Press.

Booth, David, Suzanne Clisby, and Charlotta Widmark. 1996. "Empowering the Poor Through Institutional Reform? An Initial Appraisal of the Bolivian Experience." Working paper no. 32. Development Studies Unit, Department of Social Anthropology, Stockholm University.

Borón, Atilio. 1993. "Latin America: Constitutionalism and the Political Traditions of Liberalism and Socialism." In *Constitutionalism and Democracy: Transitions in the Contemporary World*, ed. Douglas Greenberg et al., 339–353. New York: Oxford University Press.

Boudon, Lawrence. 1995. "Party Failure amid Party Crisis: The Case of Colombia's M-19 Democratic Alliance." Paper prepared for delivery at the 1995 meeting of the Latin American Studies Association, Washington, D.C., September 28–30.

Buenahora Febres-Cordero, Jaime. 1991. *El proceso constituyente: De la propuesta estudiantil a la quiebra del bipartidismo*. Bogotá: Cámara de Representantes/Pontificia Universidad Javeriana.

————. 1995. *La democracia en Colombia: Un proyecto en construcción*. Bogotá: Controlaria General de la República.

Bushnell, David. 1993. *Colombia: A Nation in Spite of Itself*. Berkeley: University of California Press.

Calderón, Fernando. 1987. "Nación, movimientos sociales y democracia en Bolivia." In *Repensando el país*. La Paz: Movimiento Bolivia Libre.

Calderón, Fernando, Alejandro Piscitelli, José Luis Reyna. 1992. "Social Movements: Actors, Theories, Expectations." In *The Making of Social Movements in Latin America: Identity, Strategy, and Democracy*, ed. Arturo Escobar and Sonia E. Alvarez, 19–36. Boulder: Westview Press.

Calla Ortega, Ricardo. 1992. "Introducción al tema." In *Diversidad étnica y cultural*, comp. Carlos Toranzo, 47–54. La Paz: ILDIS.

————. 1993. "Hallu hayllisa huti: Identificación étnica y procesos políticos en Bolivia." In *Democracia, etnicidad y violencia política en los países andinos*, comp. Carlos Ivan Degregori. Lima: IEP Ediciones.

————. 1998. "El ayllu andino y la participación popular (Bolivia)." Paper prepared for the Workshop on Indigenous Peoples and Reform of the State, Amsterdam, October 29–30.

Carrillo Flórez, Fernando. 1994. "La historia de la séptima papeleta o la victoria sobre la apatía electoral." In *De una agenda con futuro: Testimonios del cuatrienio Gaviria*. Bogotá: Presidencia de la República.

Castañeda, Jorge G. 1996. "Democracy and Inequality in Latin America: A Tension of the Times." In *Constructing Democratic Governance: Latin America and the Caribbean in the 1990s*, ed. Jorge I. Domínguez and Abraham F. Lowenthal, 42–63. Baltimore: Johns Hopkins University Press.

Caycedo Turriago, Jaime. 1996. "La reforma olvido a la oposición." *CAJA de Herramientas* (September):5.

CEDIB. 1994. *Participación popular: Ley y comentarios*. Serie dossier no. 2 (June). La Paz: Centro de Documentación e Información.

Cepeda Espinosa, Manuel José. 1992a. *Introducción a la constitución de 1991: Hacia un nuevo constitucionalismo*. Bogotá: Presidencia de la República.

————. 1992b. "La polémica sobre la Acción de Tutela." *Revista Foro* 17 (April):32–33.

————. 1993. *La constituyente por dentro: Mitos y realidades*. Bogotá: Presidencia de la República.

———. 1994. *La constitución que no fue y el significado de los silencios constitucionales.* Bogotá: Ediciones Uniandes/El Ancora Editores.

———. 1995a. "Constitutional Reform as a General Peace Treaty: The Colombian Case." Paper prepared for the conference Federalism Against Ethnicity? Institutional, Legal, and Democratic Instruments to Prevent or Resolve Violent Minority Conflicts, Swiss Peace Foundation, Basel, September 27–29.

———. 1995b. "Democracy, State and Society in the Colombian Constitution: The Role of the Constitutional Court." Unpublished manuscript.

———. 1995c. "Ethnic Minorities and Constitutional Reform in Colombia." In *Ethnic Conflict and Governance in Comparative Perspective,* 100–138. Working paper no. 215. Washington, D.C.: Woodrow Wilson International Center for Scholars.

———. 1997. "Contrareforma, al borde del naufragio." *CAJA de Herramientas* (February):15.

———. 1999. "Colombia multiétnica: El papel del derecho constitucional en la promoción de la diversidad y la construcción de la convivencia pacífica." Documento preparado para el Taller "Multiethnic Nations in Developing Countries: Colombia as a Latin American Case." Institute of Federalism, Fribourg, Switzerland.

Chalmers, Douglas, et al., eds. 1997. *The New Politics of Inequality in Latin America: Rethinking Participation and Representation.* Oxford: Oxford University Press.

Chambers, Ian. 1997. "Comentario." In *Derecho indígena,* coord. Magdalena Gómez, 123–136. México: La Jornada/UNAM.

Chávez A. 1996. "Municipios, participación popular y pueblos indígenas (entrevistas a dirigentes indígenas)." *Artículo Primero,* año 1, no. 1 (January–March):42–59.

CIDOB. 1992. "Proyecto de ley indígena: Confederación indígena del oriente boliviano." La Paz: CIDOB.

———. 1996. "La marcha indígena y el papel de CIDOB: Un balance necesario." *Artículo Primero,* año 1, no. 2 (October–December 1996):88–92.

CIPCA. 1991. *Por una Bolivia diferente: Aportes para un proyecto histórico popular.* Cuadernos de investigación no. 34. La Paz: CIPCA.

Clark, Robert. 1989. "Spanish Democracy and Regional Autonomy: The Autonomous Community System and Self-Government for the Ethnic Homelands." In *Ethnoterritorial Politics, Policy, and the Western World,* ed. Robert J. Thompson and Joseph Rudolph Jr., 15–44. Boulder: Lynne Rienner.

Comisión Andina de Juristas. 1994. "Derechos de los pueblos indígenas y constitucionalidad." Lima: Comisión Andina de Juristas.

Cohen, Jean L. 1985. "Strategy or Identity: New Theoretical Paradigms and Contemporary Social Movements." *Social Research* 52, 4 (winter):663–716.

CONAPI. 1992. "Política con los pueblos indígenas." Discussion paper. Bogotá: Consejo Nacional de Política Indigenista.

Consejo Regional Indígena del Cauca. 1981. *Diez años de lucha: Historia y documentos.* Bogotá: CINEP.

———. 1983. *Como nos organizamos.* Cartilla del CRIC no. 2. November.

———. 1991. "Cabildos indígenas en la constituyente." *Unidad Alvaro Ulcue* (September):5.

Correa Rubio, François. 1992. "Lo 'Indígena' ante el estado colombiano: Reflejo jurídico de su conceptualización política." In *Antropología jurídica,* ed. Esther Sánchez, 71–101. Bogotá: Sociedad Antropología de Colombia, VI Congreso Nacional de Antropología.

CPIB. 1996. "Movimiento y territorios indígenas en el Beni: Resumen histórico, 1987–1995." Mimeo. Trinidad: CPIB.

CSUTCB. 1983. "Tesis política 1983." La Paz: CSUTCB.

———. 1996. *VII Congreso CSUTCB: Documentos y resoluciones.* La Paz: CSUTCB.

CSUTCB and CIDOB. 1992. *Convocatoria: Primera asamblea de Naciones Originarios y del Pueblo.* Encuentro histórico andino amazónico en la cumbre marcha indígena. La Paz: CSUTCB and CIDOB.

Dandler, Jorge. 1996. "Indigenous Peoples and the Rule of Law in Latin America: Do They Have a Chance?" Paper prepared for the Academic Workshop on the Rule of Law and the Underprivileged in Latin America, Kellogg Institute for International Studies, University of Notre Dame, November 9–11.

De Dios Mosquera, Juan. N.d. *Las comunidades negras de Colombia: Pasado, presente y futuro.* Bogotá: Cimarrón.

De la Cruz Willka, Juan. 1992. "Propuesta para la discusión en las bases." In *Convocatoria: Primera asamblea de Naciones Originarios y del Pueblo.* La Paz: CSUTCB and CIDOB.

De Tocqueville, Alexis. 1988. *Democracy in America.* George Lawrence, translator, J.P. Mayer, editor. New York: Perennial Library.

"Del ovido surgimos para traer nuevas esperanzas": La jurisdicción especial indígena. 1997. Bogotá: Ministerio de Justicia, CRIC, Ministerio Interior.

D'Emilio, Lucia. 1997. "Processes of Change and Indigenous Participation." *Cultural Survival Quarterly* 21, 2 (summer):43–46.

Democracia y participación popular. 1996. La Paz: Universidad Mayor de San Simon, ILDIS, SNPP.

Deruyttere, Anne. 1997. *Indigenous Peoples and Sustainable Development: The Role of the Inter-American Development Bank.* Washington, D.C.: Inter-American Development Bank.

Diamond, Larry, Marc F. Plattner, Yun-han Chu, and Hung-mao Tien, eds. 1997. *Consolidating the Third Wave Democracies.* Baltimore: Johns Hopkins University Press.

Díaz Polanco, Héctor. 1991. *Autonomía regional: La autodeterminación de los pueblos indios.* México: Siglo Veintuno Editores.

Dion, Douglas. 1998. "Evidence and Inference in the Comparative Case Study." *Comparative Politics* (January):127–45.

Domínguez, Zulema. 1997. "Colombia descertificada en derechos humanos." *CAJA de Herramientas* (February):21.

Dugas, John C. 1993a. "El desarrollo de la Asamblea Nacional Constituyente." In *La constitución de 1991: Un pacto político viable?* comp. John Dugas, 45–76. Bogotá: Universidad de los Andes.

———. 1993b. "La constitución de 1991: Un pacto político viable?" In *La constitución de 1991: Un pacto político viable?* comp. John Dugas, 15–44. Bogotá: Universidad de los Andes.

———. 1995. "Structural Theory and Democratization in Colombia: The Role of Social Classes, Civil Society, and the State in the 1991 Constitutional Reform." Paper prepared for delivery at the nineteenth meeting of the Latin American Studies Association, Washington, D.C., September 28–29.

———. 1997. "Explaining Democratic Reform in Colombia: The Origins of the 1991 Constitution." Ph.D. dissertation, Indiana University.

———. 1998. "The Origin, Impact, and Demise of the 1989–1990 Colombian Student Movement: Insights from Social Movement Theory." Paper prepared for delivery at the 1998 annual meeting of the Latin American Studies Association, Chicago, Illinois, September 24–26.

Dugas, John C., comp. 1993c. *La constitución de 1991: Un pacto político viable?* Bogotá: Universidad de los Andes.

Echeverri de Restrepo, Carmenza. 1993. *Conflicto social y constituyente.* Cali: Biblioteca Jurídica Diké/Universidad Libre.

Echeverri de Restrepo, Carmenza, and Libardo Orejuela Díaz. 1995. *La constitución de 1991 ante la crisis de legitimidad institucional.* Cali: Biblioteca Jurídica Diké/Universidad Libre.

Echeverri Uruburu, Alvaro. 1990. "Acuerdo de Convivencia y reforma constitucional." In *Constitucionalistas ante la constituyente*, ed. Luis Carlos Sachica et al., 13–34. Bogotá: Editorial Temis.

EIU Country Report. 1998a. *Bolivia.* Fourth quarter 1998. London: Economic Intelligence Unit.

———. 1998b. *Colombia.* Fourth quarter 1998. London: Economic Intelligence Unit.

Elazar, Daniel J. 1985. "Constitution-Making: The Pre-Eminently Political Act." In *Redesigning the State: The Politics of Constitutional Change in Industrial Nations,* ed. Keith G. Banting and Richard Simeon, 232–48. Toronto: University of Toronto Press.

Elster, Jon, and Rune Slagstad, eds. 1988. *Constitutionalism and Democracy.* Cambridge: Cambridge University Press.

Elster, Jon, Claus Offe, Ulrich K. Preuss, et al. 1998. *Institutional Design in Post-Communist Societies: Rebuilding the Ship at Sea.* Cambridge: Cambridge University Press.

Escobar, Arturo. 1992. "Culture, Economics and Politics in Latin American Social Movements: Theory and Research." In *The Making of Social Movements in Latin America: Identity, Strategy, and Democracy,* ed. Arturo Escobar and Sonia E. Alvarez, 62–88. Boulder: Westview Press.

Etzioni, Amitai. 1996. "A Moderate Communitarian Proposal." *Political Theory* 24, 2 (May):155–71.

Fals Borda, Orlando. 1992. "Social Movements and Political Power in Latin America." In *The Making of Social Movements in Latin America: Identity, Strategy, and Democracy,* ed. Arturo Escobar and Sonia E. Alvarez, 303–316. Boulder: Westview Press.

———. 1993. "Constituyentes de 1991 también defendimos a los afrocolombianos." *América Negra* 6 (December):221–25.

———. 1995. "La accidentada marcha hacia la democracia participativa en Colombia." In *La democracia en América Latina: Actualidad y perspectivas,* coord. Pablo González Casanova and Marcos Roitman Rosenmann, 361–84. México: La Jornada/UNAM.

Fals Borda, Orlando, and Lorenzo Muelas Hurtado. 1991. "Pueblos indígenas y grupos étnicos." *Gaceta Constitucional* 40, April 8, pp. 2–8.

Faúndez, Julio. 1993. "Constitutionalism: A Timely Revival." In *Constitutionalism and Democracy: Transitions in the Contemporary World,* ed. Douglas Greenberg et al., 354–360. New York: Oxford University Press.

FESCOL. 1996a. *Estado y autonomía de la sociedad civil.* debate laboral. Bogotá: Fundación Friedrich Ebert de Colombia.

———. 1996b. *Nuevas formas de participación política.* Debate político. Bogotá: Fundación Friedrich Ebert de Colombia.

Findji, María Teresa. 1992. "From Resistance to Social Movement: The Indigenous Authorities Movement in Colombia." In *The Making of Social Movements in Latin America,* ed. Arturo Escobar and Sonia E. Alvarez, 112–33. Boulder: Westview Press.

Forbes, H. D., and John Uhr. 1998. "Multiculturalism and Political Community: Australia and Canada." Paper prepared for delivery at the annual meeting of the American Political Science Association, Boston, Mass., September 4.

Foro de ICAN. 1993. "Conceptos sobre identidad cultural en las comunidades negras." *America Negra* 6 (December):173–80.

Foweraker, Joe. 1995. *Theorizing Social Movements.* London: Pluto Press.

Franco, Cristina, and Juan Andrés Valderrama, eds. 1990. *Una constituyente para la Colombia del futuro.* 2nd ed. Bogotá: Universidad de los Andes, FESCOL.

Friede, Juan. 1976. *El indio en lucha por la tierra.* Bogotá: Editorial Punta de Lanza.

Friedemann, Nina S. 1992. "Negros en Colombia: Identidad e invisibilidad." *America Negra* 3 (June):25–35.

Friedemann, Nina S., and Jaime Arocha. 1995. "Colombia." In *No Longer Invisible: Afro-Latin Americans Today,* ed. Minority Rights Group, 47–76. London: Minority Rights Group.

Frites, Eulogio. 1998. "La experiencia Argentina." In *Seminario Internacional de Administración de Justicia y Pueblos Indígenas,* 125–29. La Paz: República de Bolivia.

Fundación Milenio. 1997. *Proyecto de reforma a la constitución política del estado, 1991–1992.* La Paz: Fundación Milenio.

Gaitán Pavia, Pilar, and Ana María Bejarano. 1994. "Posibilidades y límites de la participación política en Colombia." Bogotá: Consejería Presidencial para la Modernización del Estado.

Galindo de Ugarte, Marcelo. 1991. *Constituciones bolivianas comparadas, 1826–1967*. La Paz: Editorial "Los Amigos del Libro."

Galindo Soza, Mario, and Fernando Medina Calabaceros. 1996. "Ley de participación popular: Aspectos económico-financieros." In *Apre(he)ndiendo la participación popular*, 79–104. La Paz: PNUD/SNPP.

Gamarra, Eduardo A. 1991. *The System of Justice in Bolivia: An Institutional Analysis*. Monograph 4. Miami: Center for the Administration of Justice, Florida International University.

———. 1997. "Goni's Unsung Swan Song." *Hemisfile* (May/June):1–2, 12.

Gamarra, Eduardo A., and James M. Malloy. 1995. "The Patrimonial Dynamics of Party Politics in Bolivia." In *Building Democratic Institutions: Party Systems in Latin America*, ed. Scott Mainwaring and Timothy R. Scully, 399–433. Stanford: Stanford University Press.

García Belaunde, Domingo. 1996a. "Constitutional Processes in Latin America." In *Contemporary Constitutional Challenges*, ed. César Landa and Julio Faúndez, 25–33. Lima: Pontificia Universidad Católica del Peru, Fondo Editorial.

———. 1996b. "The New Peruvian Constitution: The Judiciary and Constitutional Guarantees." In *Contemporary Constitutional Challenges*, ed. César Landa and Julio Faúndez, 35–65. Lima: Pontificia Universidad Católica del Peru, Fondo Editorial.

García Canclini, Néstor. 1992. *Culturas híbridas: Estrategias para entrar y salir de la modernidad*. Buenos Aires: Editorial Sudamericana.

García D., Ricardo. 1991. "Constituyente y recomposición política." *Revista Foro* 14 (April):27–35.

Gaviria Díaz, Carlos. 1997. "Alcances, contenidos y limitaciones de la jurisdicción especial indígena." In *"Del olvido surgimos para traer nuevo esperanzas": La jurisdicción especial indígena*, 159–173. Bogotá: Ministerio de Justicia, CRIC, Ministerio de Interior.

———. 1998. "Liberales y comunitarios: La jurisdicción penal indígena." In *Seminario Internacional de Administración de Justicia y Pueblos Indígenas*, 133–136. La Paz: República de Bolivia.

Gaviria Trujillo, César. 1991. "Tenemos la obligación de mantener el espíritu consensual en los temas que serán cimiento de la nueva constitución." *Gaceta Constitucional* 56, April 22, pp. 2–7.

Geddes, Barbara. 1996. "Initiation of New Democratic Institutions in Eastern Europe and Latin America." In *Institutional Design in New Democracies: Eastern Europe and Latin America*, ed. Arend Lijphart and Carlos H. Waisman, 15–41. Boulder: Westview Press.

Ghai, Yash. 1993. "The Theory of the State in the Third World and the Problematics of Constitutionalism." In *Democracy: Transitions in the Contemporary World*, eds. Douglas Greenberg et al.

González Casanova, Pablo. 1996. "Las etnias coloniales y el estado multiétnico." In *Democracia y estado multiétnico en América Latina*, coord. Pablo González Casanova and Marcos Roitman Rosenmann, 23–36. México: UNAM/La Jornada.

González Casanova, Pablo, and Marcos Roitman Rosenmann. 1996. "Introducción." In *Democracia y estado multiétnico en América Latina,* coord. Pablo González Casanova and Marcos Roitman Rosenmann, 11–20. México: UNAM/La Jornada.

Gray Molina, George. 1996. "Determinants of Social Investments Under Popular Participation in Bolivia." Draft. La Paz: Ministry of Human Development, HIID-UDAPSO.

———. 1997. "Adónde fue la plata de la participación popular?" *La Razón* (ventana), May 25, p. 10.

Gray Molina, George, and Carlos Hugo Molina Saucedo. 1997. "Popular Participation and Decentralization in Bolivia: Building Accountability from the Grassroots." Paper prepared for a seminar to evaluate the Bolivian reforms organized by the Harvard Institute for International Development, Cambridge, Mass., April 30.

Greenberg, Douglas, et al. 1993. *Constitutionalism and Democracy: Transitions in the Contemporary World.* New York: Oxford University Press.

Gros, Christian. 1988. "Una organización indígena en lucha por la tierra: El consejo regional indígena del Cauca." In *Indianidad, etnocidio, indigenismo, en América Latina,* ed. Françoise Morin, 235–56. México: Instituto Indigenista Interamericano, Centre d'Etudes Mexicaines et Centraméricaines.

———. 1991. *Colombia indígena: Identidad cultural y cambio social.* Bogotá: CEREC.

———. 1993. "Derechos indígenas y nueva constitución en Colombia." *Análisis Político* 19 (May–August):8–23.

———. 1997. "Indigenismo y etnicidad: El desafío neoliberal." In *Antropología en la modernidad,* ed. María Victoria Uribe and Eduardo Restrepo, 15–58. Bogotá: Instituto Colombiano de Antropología.

———. N.d. "Ser diferente por (para) ser moderno, o las paradojas de la identidad." Unpublished manuscript.

Grueso, Libia, Carlos Rosero, and Arturo Escobar. 1998. "The Process of Community Organizing in the Southern Pacific Coast Region of Colombia." In *Cultures of Politics/Politics of Cultures: Revisioning Latin American Social Movements,* ed. Sonia Alvarez et al., 196–219. Boulder: Westview Press.

Grueso C., Libia R. 1995. "Cultura política y biodiversidad en el proceso de comunidades negras del pacífico colombiano." Paper prepared for presentation at the Twenty-First International Congress of the Latin American Studies Association, Washington, D.C., September 28–30.

Gunther, Richard. 1985. "Constitutional Change in Contemporary Spain." In *Redesigning the State: The Politics of Constitutional Change in Industrial Nations,* ed. Keith G. Banting and Richard Simeon, 42–70. Toronto: University of Toronto Press.

Gunther, Richard, P. Nikiforos Diamandouros, and Hans-Jurgen Puhle, eds. 1995. *The Politics of Democratic Consolidation: Southern Europe in Comparative Perspective.* Baltimore: Johns Hopkins University Press.

Gurr, Ted Robert. 1993. *Minorities at Risk: A Global View of Ethnopolitical Conflicts.* Washington, D.C.: U.S. Institute of Peace.

Gutmann, Amy, ed. 1994. *Multiculturalism: Examining the Politics of Recognition.* Princeton: Princeton University Press.

Habermas, Jurgen. 1996. *Between Facts and Norms: Contributions to a Discourse Theory of Law and Democracy.* Trans. William Rehg. Cambridge: MIT Press.

———— 1994. "Struggles for Recognition in the Democratic Constitutional State." Translated by Shierry Weber Nicholsen. In *Multiculturalism: Examining the Politics of Recognition,* ed. Amy Gutmann, 107–48. Princeton: Princeton University Press.

Haggard, Stephan, and Robert Kaufman. 1992. "Institutions and Economic Adjustment." In *Politics of Economic Adjustment: International Constraints, Distributive Conflicts and the State,* ed. Stephan Haggard and Robert Kaufman, 3–40. Princeton: Princeton University Press.

————. 1995. *The Political Economy of Democratic Transitions.* Princeton: Princeton University Press.

Hahn, Dwight R. 1992. "Indigenous-State Relations in Bolivian Politics." Paper prepared for delivery at the Twenty-Seventh Congress of the Latin American Studies Association, Los Angeles, September 24–27.

————. 1996. "The Use and Abuse of Ethnicity: The Case of the Bolivian CSUTCB." *Latin American Perspectives* 23, 2 (spring):91–105.

Hannum, Hurst. 1996. *Autonomy, Sovereignty, and Self-Determination.* Revised edition. Philadelphia: University of Pennsylvania Press.

Harb, Benjamin Miguel, and Edgar Moreno Morales. 1996. *Constitución política del estado reformada: Comentada, concordada y con referencias.* 2nd ed. La Paz: Editorial "Los Amigos del Libro."

Hart, H. L. A. 1994. *The Concept of Law.* 2nd ed. Oxford: Clarendon Press.

Hartlyn, Jonathan. 1988. *The Politics of Coalition Rule in Colombia.* Cambridge: Cambridge University Press.

Hellman, Judith Adler. 1992. "The Study of New Social Movements in Latin America and the Question of Autonomy." In *The Making of Social Movements in Latin America,* ed. Arturo Escobar and Sonia Alvarez, 52–61. Boulder: Westview Press.

Higley, John, and Richard Gunther, eds. 1992. *Elites and Democratic Consolidation in Latin America and Southern Europe.* Cambridge: Cambridge University Press.

Hochstetler, Kathryn. 1997. "The Evolution of the Brazilian Environmental Movement and Its Political Roles." In *The New Politics of Inequality in Latin America: Rethinking Participation and Representation,* ed. Douglas Chalmers et al., 192–216. Oxford: Oxford University Press.

Honneth, Axel. 1995. *The Struggle for Recognition: The Moral Grammar of Social Conflicts.* Translated by Joel Anderson. Cambridge: Polity Press.

Hoskin, Gary. 1991. "La democracia colombiana: Reforma política, elecciones y violencia." In *Crisis y transición democrática en los paises andinos,* comp. Diego Cardona, 25–36. Bogotá: Programa Democracia, Departamento de Ciencia Política, Universidad de los Andes, CEREC.

Howard, A. E. Dick, ed. 1993. *Constitution Making in Eastern Europe*. Washington, D.C.: Woodrow Wilson Center Press.

Huerta G., Héctor. 1998. "La aplicación de los convenios internacionales en la administración de justicia en casos que afecten los intereses: Caso de Panamá." In *Seminario Internacional de Administración de Justicia y Pueblos Indígenas*, 40–43. La Paz: República de Bolivia.

Huntington, Samuel J. 1991. *The Third Wave: Democratization in the Late Twentieth Century*. Norman: University of Oklahoma Press.

Hurtado Mercado, Javier. 1995. "Comportamientos políticos del campesinado 1978/1995." *Opiniones y Análisis* (May):127–54.

Iturralde Guerrero, Diego A. 1997a. "Comentario de Diego Iturralde." In *Derecho indígena*, coord. Magdalena Gómez, 356–360. México: La Jornada/UNAM.

———. 1997b. "Demandas indígenas y reforma legal: Retos y paradojas." *Alteridades* 7 (14):81–98.

Izko, Xavier. 1993. "Etnopolítica y costumbre en los andes bolivianos." In *Derecho, pueblos indígenas y reforma del estado*, by various authors, 183–206. Quito: Abya Yala.

Jacinta Lizarazo, María. 1996. "La reforma es pura hojarasca." *CAJA de Herramientas* (November).

Jackson, Jean E. 1991. "Being and Becoming an Indian in the Vaupes." In *Nation-States and Indians in Latin America*, ed. Greg Urban and Joel Sherzer, 131–55. Austin: University of Texas Press.

———. 1995. "Culture, Genuine and Spurious." *American Ethnologist* 22, 1 (February):3–27.

———. 1999. "Contrasting Discourses in Colombian National Indigenous Politics: The Occupations of the Summer of 1996." Paper prepared for the Conference on Indigenous Movements, Self-Representation, and the State in Latin America, Cambridge, Mass.

Jaramillo, Ana María. 1996. "Panorama reciente de la participación política en Medellín (1960–1995)." In *Nuevas formas de participación política*, 47–59. Bogotá: FESCOL.

Jarquín, Edmundo, and Fernando Carrillo, eds. 1998. *Justice Delayed: Judicial Reform in Latin America*. Washington, D.C.: Inter-American Development Bank.

Jelin, Elizabeth, and Eric Hershberg, eds. 1996a. *Constructing Democracy: Human Rights, Citizenship, and Society in Latin America*. Boulder: Westview Press.

———. 1996b. "Convergence and Diversity: Reflections on Human Rights." In *Constructing Democracy: Human Rights, Citizenship, and Society in Latin America*, ed. Elizabeth Jelin and Eric Hershberg, 215–24. Boulder: Westview Press.

———. 1996c. "Introduction: Human Rights and the Construction of Democracy." In *Constructing Democracy: Human Rights, Citizenship, and Society in Latin America*, ed. Elizabeth Jelin and Eric Hershberg, 1–12. Boulder: Westview Press.

Jimeno Santoyo, Myriam. 1996. "Pueblos indios, democracia y políticas estatales en Colombia." In *Democracia y estado multiétnico en América Latina*, coord. Pablo

González Casanova and Marcos Roitman Rosenmann, 223–236. México: UNAM/La Jornada.

Karl, Terry Lynn. 1990. "Dilemmas of Democratization in Latin America." *Comparative Politics* 23, 1 (1990):1–21.

Keck, Margaret E., and Kathryn Sikkink. 1998. *Activists Beyond Borders: Transnational Advocacy Networks in International Politics.* Ithaca: Cornell University Press.

Klein, Herbert. 1969. *Parties and Political Change in Bolivia, 1880–1952.* Cambridge: Cambridge University Press.

———. 1992. *Bolivia: The Evolution of a Multiethnic Society.* 2nd ed. Oxford: Oxford University Press.

Kline, Harvey F. 1994. "Colombia: Building Democracy in the Midst of Violence and Drugs." Paper prepared for delivery at the Inter-American Dialogue Conference on Democratic Governance, Washington, D.C., December 11–12.

———. 1999. *State Building and Conflict Resolution in Colombia, 1986–1994.* Tuscaloosa: University of Alabama Press.

Klor de Alva, J. Jorge. 1995. "The Postcolonization of the (Latin) American Experience: A Reconsideration of 'Colonialism,' 'Postcolonialism,' and 'Mestizaje.'" In *After Colonialism,* ed. Gyan Prakash, 241–75. Princeton: Princeton University Press.

Kymlicka, Will. 1989. *Liberalism, Community, and Culture.* Oxford: Clarendon Press.

———. 1995. *Multicultural Citizenship.* Oxford: Clarendon Press.

Landa, César. 1996. "Effectiveness of the Constitution in Latin America." In *Contemporary Constitutional Challenges,* ed. César Landa and Julio Faúndez, 13–23. Lima: Pontificia Universidad Católica del Peru, Fondo Editorial.

Landa, César, and Julio Faúndez, ed. 1996. *Contemporary Constitutional Challenges.* Lima: Pontificia Universidad Católica del Peru, Fondo Editorial.

Lane, Jan-Erik. 1996. *Constitutions and Political Theory.* Manchester: Manchester University Press.

Lapidoth, Ruth. 1997. *Autonomy: Flexible Solutions to Ethnic Conflicts.* Washington, D.C.: U.S. Institute of Peace.

Laserna, Roberto. 1996. "Modernización, democracia y participación." In *Democracia y participación popular.* La Paz: UMSS, ILDIS, SNPP.

———. 1997. [Untitled essay.] In *Bolivia hacia la modernidad: Balance de la descentralización administrativa.* La Paz: República de Bolivia/Ministerio de la Presidencia.

Lazarte, Jorge. 1991. "Partidos políticos, problemas de representación e informalización de la política (el caso de Bolivia)." *Revista de Estudios Políticos* 74 (October–December):579–614.

———. 1992. "Introducción al tema." In *Diversidad étnica y cultural,* comp. Carlos Toranzo, 9–20. La Paz: ILDIS.

Le Bot, Yvon. 1988. "Extranjeros en nuestro propio país: El movimiento indígena en Bolivia durante los años 70." In *Indianidad, etnocidio, indigenismo en América Latina,* ed. Françoise Morin. 221–234. México: Instituto Interamericano Indigenista and Centre d'Etudes Mexicaines et Centraméricaines.

Lijphart, Arend, and Carlos H. Waisman, eds. 1996. *Institutional Design in New Democracies: Eastern Europe and Latin America.* Boulder: Westview Press.

Linz, Juan, and Alfred Stepan. 1997. "Toward Consolidated Democracies." In *Consolidating the Third Wave Democracies,* ed. Larry Diamond et al., 14–33. Baltimore: Johns Hopkins University Press.

Lleras de la Fuente, Carlos, et al. 1992. *Interpretación y génesis de la constitución de Colombia.* Bogotá: Cámara de Comercio.

Lleras Restrepo, Carlos, et al. 1988. *Hacía una reforma constitucional.* Medellín: El Mundo, Universidad de Medellín.

Lynch, Nicolás. 1997. "New Citizens and Old Politics in Peru." *Constellations* 4, 1 (April):124–40.

Macdonald, Theodore, S. James Anaya, and Yadira Soto. 1997. "Observaciones y recomendaciones sobre el caso del Bloque Samoré: Proyecto en Colombia de la organización de los Estados Americanos y la Universidad Harvard." Washington, D.C.: OAS.

Malloy, James M., and Eduardo A. Gamarra. 1988. *Revolution and Reaction: Bolivia, 1952–1982.* New Brunswick: Transaction Books.

Mainwaring, Scott. 1992. "Transitions to Democracy and Democratic Consolidation: Theoretical and Comparative Issues." In *Issues in Democratic Consolidation: The New South American Democracies in Comparative Perspective,* ed. Scott Mainwaring, Guillermo O'Donnell, and J. Samuel Valenzuela, 294–342. Notre Dame: University of Notre Dame Press.

Mainwaring, Scott, and Timothy Scully, eds. 1995. *Building Democratic Institutions: Party Systems in Latin America.* Stanford: Stanford University Press.

Mainwaring, Scott, Guillermo O'Donnell, and J. Samuel Valenzuela, eds. 1992. *Issues in Democratic Consolidation: The New South American Democracies in Comparative Perspective.* Notre Dame: University of Notre Dame Press.

Marinissen, Judith. 1995. *Legislación boliviana y pueblos indígena: Inventario y análisis en la perspectiva de las demandas indígenas.* Santa Cruz: SNV-Bolivia, CEJIS.

Martínez-Lara, Javier. 1996. *Building Democracy in Brazil: The Politics of Constitutional Change, 1985–1995.* New York: St. Martin's Press.

MBL. 1987. *Repensando el pais.* La Paz: MBL.

McAdam, Doug. 1996. "Conceptual Origins, Problems, Future Directions." In *Comparative Perspectives on Social Movements,* ed. Doug McAdam et al., 23–40. Cambridge: Cambridge University Press.

McAdam, Doug, John D. McCarthy, and Mayer N. Zald. 1996. *Comparative Perspectives on Social Movements.* Cambridge: Cambridge University Press.

McWhinney, Edward. 1981. *Constitution-Making: Principles, Process, Practice.* Toronto: University of Toronto Press.

Medellín Torres, Pedro. 1997. "The Role of Central Governments in Strengthening Processes of Decentralization, Local Government and Citizen Participation: Contributions of the Bolivian Model of Decentralization." Washington, D.C.: Organization of American States, Unit for the Promotion of Democracy.

Medina, Medófilo. 1996. "Condiciones Históricas de lat Participación Política en Colombia." In Nuevas Formas de Participación Política. Bogotá: FESCOL.

Mejía, José Antonio, and Rob Vos. 1997. "Poverty in Latin America and the Caribbean: An Inventory, 1985–1995." Washington, D.C.: Inter-American Development Bank.

Mejía Quintana, Oscar, and Maritza Formisano Prada. 1998. "Hacía una asamblea constitucional como instrumento de democratización ciudadana y herramienta de paz en Colombia." *Dossier: Revista de Estudios Sociales* (Bogotá) (August):61–65.

Mesa Gisbert, Carlos D. 1993. *De cerca: Una decada de conversaciones en democracia.* La Paz: ILDIS.

MIC. N.d. "Origen, antecedentes y situación actual." Bogotá: MIC.

Moe, Judith A. 1997. "Implementing Bolivia's Laws on Popular Participation and Administrative Decentralization: Progress and Challenges." Draft. Washington, D.C.: Inter-American Development Bank.

Molina, Sergio, and Ivan Arias. 1996. *De la nación clandestina a la participación popular.* Informe especial. La Paz: CEDOIN.

Molina García, Oscar Alberto. 1996. "Cronología de la reforma." *CAJA de Herramientas* (August):3–5.

Molina Monasterios, Fernando. 1997. *Historia de la participación popular.* La Paz: Ministerio de Desarrollo Humano, SNPP.

Molina Saucedo, Carlos Hugo. 1994. *La descentralización imposible y la alternativa municipal.* 2nd ed. Santa Cruz: Ediciones el Pais.

———. 1996a. "Comentario." In *Democracia y participación popular.* La Paz: UMSS, ILDIS, SNPP.

———. 1996b. "Decisiones para el futuro." In *Apre(he)ndiendo la participación popular.* La Paz: PNUD, SNPP.

Montaño Virreira, Sonia. 1997. "Participación popular: Una historia incompleta." *El Comunitario,* May 18, p. 7.

Montesquieu, Charles de Secondat. 1989. *The Spirit of the Laws.* Trans. and ed. Anne M. Cohler et al. Cambridge: Cambridge University Press.

Mosquera de Meneses, Luz Stella. 1997. "Conflicto entre la JEI y la jurisdicción ordinaria." In *"Del olvido surgimos para traer nuevas esperanzas": La jurisdicción especial indígena.* 272–286. Bogotá: Ministerio de Justicia, CRIC, Ministerio de Interior.

Mouffe, Chantal. 1992. "Introduction: Democratic Politics Today." In *Dimensions of Radical Democracy: Pluralism, Citizenship, Community,* ed. Chantal Mouffe, 1–14. London: Verso.

MNR-MRTKL. 1993. *El plan de todos.* La Paz: MNR-MRTKL.

Munck, Gerardo L. 1998. "The Peculiarities of Latin America's Experience with Democracy: A Conceptual Synthesis and Empirical Reassessment of Regime Analysis." Paper prepared for presentation at the American Political Science Association Annual Meeting, Boston, September 3–6.

Muñoz, Jorge A., and Isabel Lavadenz. 1997. "Reforming the Agrarian Reform in Bolivia." Paper prepared for the Harvard Institute for International Development seminar on the Bolivian reforms, Cambridge, Mass., April 30.

Muñoz Losada, María Teresa. 1993. "La participación política sin participación social." *Revista Foro* 21 (September):44.

Murrillo Castaño, Gabriel. 1993. "Prólogo." In *La constitución de 1991: Un pacto político viable?* comp. John Dugas, 9–14. Bogotá: Universidad de los Andes.

Murrillo Castaño, Gabriel, and Elisabeth Ungar. 1996. "The Struggle for the Implementation of Participatory Democracy in Colombia." In *Colombia: A Rich and Unknown Country.* Bogotá: Universidad de los Andes.

Murphy, Walter F. 1993. "Constitutions, Constitutionalism, and Democracy." In *Constitutionalism and Democracy: Transitions in the Contemporary World,* ed. Douglas Greenberg et al., 3–25. New York: Oxford University Press.

Needler, Martin. 1967. *Latin American Politics in Perspective.* Princeton: D. Van Nostrand Company.

Nino, Carlos Santiago. 1996. "Hyperpresidentialism and Constitutional Reform in Argentina." In *Institutional Design in New Democracies: Eastern Europe and Latin America,* ed. Arend Lijphart and Carlos H. Waisman, 161–74. Boulder: Westview Press.

OAS. 1999. "Resultados de la reunión de expertos gubernamentales sobre la declaración americana sobre los derechos de los pueblos indígenas." Washington, D.C.: OAS.

O'Donnell, Guillermo. 1994a. "Delegative Democracy." In *Comparative Politics: Notes and Readings,* ed. Bernard E. Brown and Roy C. Macridis, 115–24. 8th ed. Belmont: Wadworth Publishing.

———. 1994b. "The State, Democratization, and Some Conceptual Problems (A Latin American View with Glances at Some Post-Communist Countries)." In *Latin American Political Economy in the Age of Neoliberal Reform: Theoretical and Comparative Perspectives for the 1990s,* ed. William C. Smith, Carlos H. Acuña, and Eduardo A. Gamarra, 157–80. Coral Gables: North-South Center.

———. 1997a. "Illusions About Consolidation." In *Consolidating the Third Wave Democracies,* ed. Larry Diamond et al., 40–57. Baltimore: Johns Hopkins University Press.

———. 1997b. "Polyarchies and the (Un)Rule of Law in Latin America." Paper prepared for delivery at the annual meeting of the American Political Science Association, Washington, D.C., August 28–31.

———. 1998. "Reflexiones adicionales a 'Polyarchies and the (Un)rule of Law in Latin America.'" Paper prepared for delivery at the meetings of the Latin American Studies Association, Chicago, Ill., September 24–26.

O'Donnell, Guillermo, Philippe Schmitter, and Laurence Whitehead, eds. 1986. *Transitions from Authoritarian Rule: Tentative Conclusions About Uncertain Democracies.* Baltimore: Johns Hopkins University Press.

Offe, Claus. 1996. *Modernity and the State: East, West.* Cambridge, Mass.: Polity Press.

———. 1998. "'Homogeneity' and Constitutional Democracy: Coping with Identity Conflicts Through Group Rights." *Journal of Political Philosophy* 6, 2:113–41.

O'Neill, Kathleen. 1998. "Understanding the Great Power Give-Away: Decentralization in the Andes." Paper prepared for delivery at the annual meetings of the American Political Science Association, Boston, Mass., September 3–6.

O'Neill, Kathleen, and George Gray Molina. 1998. "Social Capital in a Multi-Ethnic Society." Paper prepared for delivery at the annual meetings of the American Political Science Association, Boston, Mass., September 3–6.

ONIC. 1995. *Derechos indígenas en Colombia: Material básico de consulta.* Bogotá: ONIC.

Oporto Castro, Henry. 1996. "Comentario." In *Democracia y participación popular.* La Paz: UMSS, ILDIS, SNPP.

———. 1998a. *El difícil camino hacia la descentralización.* Descentralización y participación no. 2. La Paz: Friedrich Ebert Stiftung/ILDIS.

———. 1998b. "La problemática de la institucionalidad política: Ideas y propuestas para su revitalización, reforma y consolidación." Cochabamba: FUNDAPPAC.

Orellana Halkyer, René. 1997. "Un derecho sobre muchos derechos: Sistemas jurídicos indígenas y derecho oficial." *Artículo Primero,* año 2, no. 3 (January–April 1997):11–30.

———. 1998. "Municipalización de pueblos indígenas en Bolivia, impactos y perspectivas." Paper prepared for the Workshop on Indigenous Peoples and Reform of the State, Amsterdam, October 29–30.

Orjuela E., Luis Javier. 1993. "Aspectos políticos del nuevo ordenamiento territorial." In *La constitución de 1991: Un pacto político viable?* comp. John Dugas, 134–61. Bogotá: Universidad de los Andes.

———. 1998. "El estado colombiano en los noventa: Entre la legitimidad y la eficiencia." *Dossier: Revista de Estudios Sociales* (Bogotá) (August):56–60.

Pabón Tarantino, Elvyra Elena. 1993. "Colombia y su revolución pacífica: La nueva constitución del 5 de julio de 1991; inicio de un marco institucional dentro de un contexto político pluralista." *Revista de Estudios Políticos* 29 (January–March):161–208.

Padilla, Guillermo. 1994–1995. "La tutela, la expansión del estado y los pueblos indígenas." *Consolidación de la Región Amazónica* 1 (December–February):5–9.

———. 1995. "That Which Encompasses Goodness: Law and the Indigenous People of Colombia." In *Ethnic Conflict and Governance in Comparative Perspective,* 139–53. Working paper no. 215. Washington, D.C.: Woodrow Wilson International Center for Scholars.

———. 1996. "La ley y los pueblos indígenas en Colombia." *Journal of Latin American Anthropology* 1, 2 (spring):78–97.

Pakosie, André R. M. 1996. "Maroon Leadership and the Surinamese State (1760–1990)." *Journal of Legal Pluralism* 37–38:263–77.

Palma Capera, Alfonso, and Oskar Benjamin Gutiérrez. 1994. "Special Indian Districting: Unresolved Political Problems in Colombia." *Abya Yala News* 8, 3 (summer):14–15.

Pardo-Rojas, Mauricio. 1994. "Ethnic and Territorial Struggle in the Colombian Pacific." Paper prepared for delivery at the Eighteenth International Congress of the Latin American Studies Association, Atlanta, Georgia, March 10–12.

Pastrana Borrero, Misael. 1991. *Desde la ultima fila.* Bogotá: Fundación Simon Bolivar.

Pateman, Carol. 1970. *Participation and Democratic Theory.* Cambridge: Cambridge University Press.

Paz Patiño, Sarela. 1998. "Los territorios indígenas como reivindicación y practica discursiva." *Nueva Sociedad* 153 (January–February):120–29.

Perafán Simmonds, Carlos César. 1995. *Sistemas jurídicos páez, kogi, wayúu y tule.* Bogotá: Instituto Colombiano de Cultura.

Pérez Ariana, Mónica. 1996. "Participación de la comunidad negra del Chocó en el marco de la Ley 70 de 1993." Trabajo de grado. Bogotá: Universidad de los Andes.

Peruzzotti, Enrique. 1997. "Civil Society and the Modern Constitutional Complex: The Argentine Experience." *Constellations* 4, 1 (April):94–104.

Pinzón, William Alvis. 1993. "La tutela en Colombia: Hacía la vigencia de los derechos fundamentales." *Revista Foro* 21 (September):28–43.

Pitkin, Hanna Fenichel. 1967. *The Concept of Representation.* Berkeley and Los Angeles: University of California Press.

Plant, Roger. 1998. "Indigenous Rights and Latin American Multiculturalism: Lessons from the Guatemalan Peace Process." Paper prepared for workshop on Indigenous Peoples and Reform of the State, Amsterdam, October 29–30.

PNUD. 1998. *Desarrollo humano en Bolivia, 1998.* La Paz: Programa Naciones Unidas de Desarrollo.

Pogany, Istvan. 1996a. "Constitution Making or Constitutional Transformation in Post-Communist Societies?" *Political Studies* 44, special issue, 568–91.

———. 1996b. "History, Human Rights and Constitutional Convergence in Eastern Europe." In *Contemporary Constitutional Challenges,* ed. César Landa and Julio Faúndez, 207–35. Lima: Pontificia Universidad Católica del Peru, Fondo Editorial.

Political Studies. 1996. [Special issue, Vol. 44]. "Constitutionalism in Transformation: European and Theoretical Perspectives."

Posada, Juan Carlos. 1996. "Aperatura palabras." In *Comunidades negras, territorio y desarrollo,* 12–13. Bogotá: República de Colombia, Ministerio de Gobierno.

Posada E., Jorge Jairo. 1998. "Desarrollo y participación de la comunidad." *Revista Javieriana* (Bogotá) no. 647, tomo 131, año 66 (August):149–66.

Prada Alcoreza, Raúl. 1994. "El territorio como espacio de dominación." In *Certezas e incertidumbres de la participación popular,* 15–16. La Paz: CIDES-UMSA.

Prentice Hull, Adrian. 1999. "Comparative Political Science: An Inventory and Assessment Since the 1980s." *PS* 32, 1 (March):117–24.

Presidencia de la República (Colombia). Consejero Presidencial para Desarrollo Constitucional. 1993. *Constitución política de 1991: Visión latinoamericana.* Bogotá: Presidencia de la República.

Preuss, Ulrich K. 1995. *Constitutional Revolution: The Link Between Constitutionalism and Progress.* Trans. Deborah Lucas Schneider. New Jersey: Humanities Press.

Procomún. 1997. *El poder local: Aplicación de los mecanismos de participación ciudadana en los municipios colombianos.* Bogotá: Procomún/Fundación Konrad Adenauer.

Programa de las Naciones Unidas para el Desarrollo. 1996. *Apre(he)ndiendo la participación popular: Análisis y reflexiones sobre el model boliviano de descentralización.* La Paz: PNUD, SNPP.

———. 1998. *Desarrollo Humano en Bolivia 1998.* La Paz: PNUD.

Przeworski, Adam. 1991. *Democracy and the Market: Political and Economic Reforms in Eastern Europe and Latin America.* Cambridge: Cambridge University Press.

Psacharopoulos, George, and Harry Anthony Patrinos, eds. 1994. *Indigenous People and Poverty in Latin America: An Empirical Analysis.* Washington, D.C.: World Bank.

Putnam, Robert D. 1993. *Making Democracy Work: Civic Traditions in Modern Italy.* Princeton: Princeton University Press.

Ramírez de Jara, María Clemencia. 1997. "Indigenous Peoples Six Years After the New Colombian Constitution." *Cultural Survival Quarterly* 21, 2 (summer):40–46.

Ramírez Ocampo, Augusto. 1991. "Ponencia para segundo Debate de la Nueva Constitución Política de Colombia." *Gaceta Constitucional* 112, July 3.

Rapaczynski, Andrzej. 1993. "Constitutional Politics in Poland." In *Constitution Making in Eastern Europe,* ed. A. E. Dick Howard, 93–132. Washington, D.C.: Woodrow Wilson Center Press.

Rappaport, Joanne, and Robert V. H. Dover. 1996. "The Construction of Difference by Native Legislators." *Journal of Latin American Anthropology* 1, 2 (spring):22–45.

Regueiro Elam, Helen. 1995. "El indio ausente y la identidad nacional unguaya." In De Palabra y obra en el nuevo mundo, eds. J. Jorge Klor de Alva, et al. Madrid:Siglo XXI.

Regulska, Joanne. 1993. "Self-Governance or Central Control? Rewriting Constitutions in Central and Eastern Europe." In *Constitution Making in Eastern Europe,* ed. A. E. Dick Howard, 133–61. Washington, D.C.: Woodrow Wilson Center Press.

Remmer, Karen. 1985–1986. "Exclusionary Democracy." *Studies in Comparative International Development* 20 (winter):64–85.

República de Bolivia. Ministerio de Desarrollo Humano. Secretaría Nacional de Participación Popular. 1995. *Debate nacional sobre la ley de participación popular.* La Paz: Unidad de Comunicación, SNPP.

———. 1996. "Un análisis sobre el Comité de Vigilancia en base a un sondeo de opinión." Unpublished manuscript. La Paz: Ministerio de Desarrollo Humano, SNPP, Unidad de Investigación y Análisis, July 30.

República de Bolivia. Ministerio de Desarrollo Sostenible y Medio Ambiente. VAIPO. 1998. *Desarrollo con identidad: Política nacional indígena y originaria.* La Paz: VAIPO.

————. VPPFM. 1998. *Profundización del proceso de participación popular y descentralización administrativa: Estrategia de acción.* La Paz: VPPFM.

República de Bolivia. Sistema Nacional de Planificación. 1997. *Norma de la planificación participativa municipal.* La Paz: Ministerio de Desarrollo Sostenible/Ministerio de Desarrollo Humano.

República de Bolivia. Vicepresidencia. 1998. *Propuesta contra la pobreza: Grupo de trabajo para el diálogo nacional.* La Paz: Vicepresidencia.

República de Colombia. 1991a. "Discurso del Presidente César Gaviria Trujillo al recibir los informes de las Comisiones Preparatorias." *Propuestas de las comisiones preparatorias.* Bogotá: Presidencia de la República.

————. 1991b. *Estadísticas finales de propuestas de reforma constitucional presentadas a las comisiones/subcomisiones preparatorias y mesas de trabajo a nivel nacional.* Bogotá: Presidencia de la República, Centro de Información y Sistemas para la preparación de la ANC, February 8.

————. 1996a. *Comunidades negras: Territorio y desarrollo.* Bogotá: República de Colombia, Ministerio de Gobierno.

————. 1996b. Documento CONPES. *Promoción de la participación de la sociedad civil: Del derecho a participar a la participación efectiva.* Bogotá: Ministerio de Interior.

Restrepo, Eduardo. 1997. "Afrocolombianos, antropología y proyecto de modernidad en Colombia." In *Antropología en la modernidad,* ed. María Uribe and Eduardo Restrepo, 279–318. Bogotá: Instituto Colombiano de Antropología.

Restrepo, Luis Alberto. 1991. "Asamblea nacional constituyente en Colombia: Concluirá por fin el Frente Nacional?" *Análisis Político* 12 (January–April):52–60.

Restrepo Londoño, Diego. 1996. "Estado, movimientos sociales y organizaciones civiles." In *Estado y autonomía de la sociedad civil,* 27–42. Bogotá: FESCOL.

Revista Foro. 1991a. Editorial. "El tamaño de la democracia colombiana." *Revista Foro* 14 (April):1–4.

————. 1991b. Editorial. "La batalla por el nuevo país." *Revista Foro* 15 (September):1–4.

————. 1992a. Editorial. "El proyecto democrático en Colombia: Entre la reforma y la contrarreforma." *Revista Foro* 19 (December):1–5.

————. 1992b. Editorial. "Entre la modorra y la esperanza." *Revista Foro* 18 (September):1–4.

Rivera Cusicanqui, Silvia. 1986. *Oprimidos pero no vencidos: Luchas del campesinado aymara y quechua de Bolivia, 1900–1980.* Geneva: UNRISD Programa de Participación.

————. 1987. "Luchas campesinas contemporáneas en Bolivia: El movimiento katarista (1970–1980)." In *Bolivia hoy,* comp. René Zavaleta Mercado, 129–68. 2nd ed. México: Siglo 21 Editores.

————. 1990. "Democracia liberal y democracia del ayllu: El caso del norte de potosi, Bolivia." In *El difícil camino hacia la democracia,* ed. Carlos F. Toranzo Roca, 9–51. La Paz: ILDIS.

————. 1991. "Aymara Past, Aymara Future." *NACLA Report on the Americas* 25, 3:18–23.

Roitman Rosenmann, Marcos. 1996. "Formas de estado y democracia multiétnica en América Latina." In *Democracia y estado multiétnico en América Latina*, coord. Pablo González Casanova and Marcos Roitman Rosenmann, 37–62. México: UNAM/La Jornada.

Rojas Birry, Francisco. 1991a. "Los derechos de los grupos etnicos." *Gaceta Constitucional* 67, May 4, pp. 14–21.

————. 1991b. "Proyecto de reforma a la constitución política de Colombia. No. 119." *Gaceta Constitucional* 29, March 30.

Rojas Birry, Francisco, Orlando Fals Borda, and Hector Piñeda Salazar. 1991. "De las entidades territoriales: Proyecto de acto reformatorio de la constitución política. No. 104." *Gaceta Constitucional* 25, March 21.

Rojas Ortuste, Gonzalo. 1992. "El movimiento étnico-campesino en Bolivia: Retos y posibilidades en la democracia en 1992." Paper prepared for delivery at the Seventeenth International Congress of the Latin American Studies Association, Los Angeles, September 24–27.

————. 1995. *La participación popular: Avances y obstáculos.* La Paz: Grupo DRU, Unidad de Investigación y Análisis, SNPP.

————. 1996. "Comentario." In *Democracia y participación popular.* La Paz: UMSS, ILDIS, SNPP.

————. 1998. *Censura constructiva, inestabilidad y democracia municipal.* Descentralización y Participación no. 1. La Paz: Friedrich Ebert Stiftung/ILDIS.

Rojas Ortuste, Gonzalo, and Luis Verdesoto Custode. 1997. *La participación popular como reforma de la política: Evidencias de una cultura democrática boliviana.* La Paz: Ministerio de Desarrollo Humano, SNPP.

Rojas Ortuste, Gonzalo, and Moira Zuazo Oblitas. 1996. *Los problemas de representatividad del sistema democrático boliviano.* debate político no. 1. La Paz: ILDIS.

Roldán, Roque. 1996. "El reconocimiento de los derecho indígenas: Un asunto de incumbencia global." In *Derechos de los pueblos indígenas en las constituciones de América Latina*, comp. Enrique Sánchez, 5–12. Bogotá: Coama/Disloque Editores.

————. 1997. "El régimen constitucional indígena en Colombia: Fundamentos y perspectivas." In *Derecho indígena*, coord. Magdalena Gómez, 233–251. México: Instituto Nacional Indigenista.

————. 1998. "Los convenios de la OIT y los derechos territoriales indígenas, en las políticas de gobierno y en la administración de justicia en Colombia." In *Seminario Internacional de Administración de Justicia y Pueblos Indígenas*, 47–63. La Paz: República de Bolivia.

Rosero, Carlos. 1996. "Reflexiones sobre el concepto de desarrollo entre comunidades negras." In *Comunidades negras, territorio y desarrollo*, 180–81. Bogotá: República de Colombia, Ministerio de Gobierno.

————. N.d. "El Pacífico: Frontera cultural." *Autodescubrimiento de nuestra América: Camino de identidad.* Boletin informativo. Bogotá.

Rout, Leslie B. 1976. *The African Experience in Spanish America, 1502 to the Present Day.* Cambridge: Cambridge University Press.

Rustow, Dankwart. 1970. "Transitions to Democracy: Toward a Dynamic Model." *Comparative Politics* 2, 3 (April).

Salvatierra, Hugo. 1996. "Ley INRA: Entre la realidad del latifundio y la necesidad del cambio social en el mundo agrario boliviano." *Artículo Primero,* año 1, no. 2 (October–December):73–77.

Sánchez, Enrique, comp. 1996. *Derechos de los pueblos indígenas en las constituciones de América Latina.* Bogotá: Disloque Editores.

Sánchez, Enrique, Roque Roldán, and María Fernanda Sánchez. 1993. *Derechos e identidad: Los pueblos indígenas y negros en la constitución política de Colombia de 1991.* Bogotá: Disloque Editores.

————. N.d. *Bases para la conformación de las entidades territoriales indígenas.* Bogotá: Departamento Nacional de Planeación.

Sánchez, Esther. 1997. "Conflicto entre la JEI y la jurisdicción ordinaria." In *"Del olvido surgimos para traer nuevas esperanzas": La jurisdicción especial indígena,* 287–292. Bogotá: Ministerio de Justicia, CRIC, Ministerio Interior.

Sánchez de Lozada, Gonzalo. 1994. "Inauguración." *Reflexiones sobre la ley de necesidad de reforma de la constitución política del estado.* La Paz: ILDIS, Senado Nacional, Fundación Milenio.

Sanjinés, Javier. 1992. "Introducción al tema." In *Diversidad étnica y cultural,* comp. Carlos Toranzo, 75–86. La Paz: ILDIS.

Santana Rodríguez, Pedro. 1996. "Las ONGs, los movimientos sociales, y las organizaciones civiles." In *Estado y autonomía de la sociedad civil,* 43–58. Bogotá: FESCOL.

Santos, Boaventura de Soussa. 1997. "Pluralismo jurídico y jurisdicción especial indígena." In *"Del olvido surgimos para traer nuevas esperanzas": La jurisdicción especial indígena,* 201–211. Bogotá: Ministerio de Justicia, CRIC, Ministerio de Interior.

Sarmiento Anzola, Libardo. 1995. "Reformas y desarrollo social en los noventa." In *En busca de la establidad perdida,* comp. Francisco Leal Buitrago, 303–31. Bogotá: TM Editores, IEPRI–Universidad Nacional, Colciencias.

Schmitter, Philippe, and Terry Lynn Karl. 1991. "What Democracy Is . . . and Is Not." *Journal of Democracy* 2, 3 (summer):75–88.

Schulting, Gerard. 1997. "ILO Convention 169: Can It Help?" *Abya Yala News* 10, 4 (fall):10–31.

Schwartz, Herman. 1993. "The New East European Constitutional Courts." In *Constitution Making in Eastern Europe,* ed. A. E. Dick Howard, 163–207. Washington, D.C.: Woodrow Wilson Center Press.

Seligson, Mitchell. 1998. "La cultura política de la democracia en Bolivia, 1998." Study prepared for USAID. La Paz: Bolivia.

Senado Nacional (Bolivia). 1994. *Reflexiones sobre la ley de necesidad de reforma de la constitución política del estado.* La Paz: Senado Nacional, Fundación Milenio, ILDIS.

Serpa Uribe, Horacio. 1991a. "El liberalismo en la constituyente le cumplió al pueblo colombiano." *Gaceta Constitucional* 114, July 7, p. 33.

————. 1991b. "La constituyente es el escenario para hacer la gran transformación política de Colombia." *Gaceta Constitucional* (no number), March 4, p. 3.

————. 1997. "Introducción: Justicia, diversidad y jurisdicción especial indígena." In *"Del olvido surgimos para traer nuevas esperanzas": La jurisdicción especial indígena,* 17–23. Bogotá: Ministerio de Justicia, CRIC, Ministerio de Interior.

Sieder, Rachel. 1997. *Customary Law and Democratic Transition in Guatemala.* London: Institute of Latin American Studies.

————. 1999. "Rethinking Democratisation and Citizenship: Legal Pluralism and Institutional Reform in Guatemala." *Citizenship Studies* 3, 1: 103–18.

Sieder, Rachel, and Jessica Witchell. Forthcoming. "Advancing Indigenous Claims Through the Law: Reflections on the Guatemalan Peace Process." In *Culture and Rights,* ed. Jane Cowan, Marie Dembour, and Richard Wilson. Cambridge: Cambridge University Press.

Smith, Michael Addison. 1999. "Indigenous Law and the Nation-States of the Latin American Region." University of Texas, School of Law/Mexican Center, working draft, March 12.

Spinner, Jeff. 1994. *The Boundaries of Citizenship: Race, Ethnicity, and Nationality in the Liberal State.* Baltimore: Johns Hopkins University Press.

Stavenhagen, Rodolfo. 1992. "Challenging the Nation-State in Latin America." *Journal of International Affairs* 34, 2 (winter).

————. 1996. "Indigenous Rights: Some Conceptual Problems." In *Constructing Democracy: Human Rights, Citizenship, and Society in Latin America,* ed. Elizabeth Jelin and Eric Hershberg, 141–60. Boulder: Westview Press.

Ströbele-Gregor, Juliana. 1996. "Culture and Political Practice of the Aymara and Quechua in Bolivia: Autonomous Forms of Modernity in the Andes." *Latin American Perspectives* 23, 2 (spring):72–90.

Tamir, Yael. 1993. *Liberal Nationalism.* Princeton: Princeton University Press.

Tarrow, Sidney. 1995. "Mass Mobilization and Regime Change: Pacts, Reform, and Popular Power in Italy (1918–1922) and Spain (1975–1978)." In *The Politics of Democratic Consolidation: Southern Europe in Comparative Perspective,* ed. Richard Gunther, P. Nikiforos Diamandouros, and Hans-Jurgen Puhle, 204–30. Baltimore: Johns Hopkins University Press.

————. 1998. *Power in Movement: Social Movements and Contentious Politics.* 2nd ed. Cambridge: Cambridge University Press.

Tate, Winifred. 1999. "Prospects for Peace in Colombia." *Cross Currents* (Newsletter of the Washington Office on Latin America) 1, 1 (January):1–6.

Taylor, Steven L. 1995a. "Colombian Parties and Political Change: Evaluating the Impact of Electoral Reform in the 1991 Constitution." Unpublished manuscript.

————. 1995b. "Third Party Activity in Colombia." Paper prepared for delivery at the Nineteenth International Conference of the Latin American Studies Association, Washington, D.C., September 28–30.

Thévoz, Laurent. 1995. "La participación popular bajo presión." *Autodeterminación* 13 (July):35–77.

Ticona Alejo, Esteban. 1996. *CSUTCB: Trayectoría y desafíos.* Informe especial. La Paz: CEDOIN.

Ticona Alejo, Esteban, Gonzalo Rojas O., and Xavier Albó. 1995. *Votos y Wiphalas: Campesinos y pueblos originarios en democracia.* Cuadernos de investigación no. 43. La Paz: Fundación Milenio/CIPCA.

Triana, Adolfo. 1993. "Constitución geopolítica y pueblos indígenas." In *Derecho, pueblos indígenas y reforma del estado,* ed. Juan Carlos Ribadeneira, 151–72. Quito: Biblioteca Abya-Yala.

Tuchschneider, David. 1995. "Una visión desde la planificación participativa municipal." In *La participación popular: Avances y obstáculos,* comp. Gonzalo Rojas O., 105–25. La Paz: Grupo DRU, SNPP.

Tully, James. 1995. *Strange Multiplicity: Constitutionalism in an Age of Diversity.* Cambridge: Cambridge University Press.

Turriago, Jaime Caycedo. 1996. "La reforma olvidó a la oposición." *CAJA de Herramientas* (1996):5.

Ungar, Elisabeth Bleier. 1995. "El congreso en la nueva realidad: Modernización o retroceso?" In *En busca de la estabilidad perdida: Actores políticos y sociales en los años noventa,* comp. Francisco Leal Buitrago, 93–134. Bogotá: TM Editories, IEPRI/Universidad Nacional, Colciencias.

UN. 1986. "Study of the Problem of Discrimination Against Indigenous Populations." New York: UN Sub-Commission on the Prevention of Discrimination and Protection of Minorities. UN doc. E/Cn.4/Sub.2/1986/7Add.4.

UNDP. 1995. "Pobreza, políticas sociales y desarrollo en Colombia." Bogotá: PNUD.

USAID. 1995. "Democratic Development and Citizen Participation." Project paper. Unclassified. Washington, D.C.: USAID.

Urban, Greg, and Joel Sherzer, eds. 1991. *Nation-States and Indians in Latin America.* Austin: University of Texas Press.

Urcullo Reyes, Jaime. 1993. *Proceso democrático, situación jurídica y reforma constitucional en Bolivia.* La Paz: Empresa Editora "Urquizo" S.A.

Urioste, Miguel. 1990. *Proyecto: Ley de comunidades campesinas e indígenas.* La Paz: Movimiento Bolivia Libre.

Urioste, Miguel, and Luis Baldomar. 1996. "Ley de participación popular: Seguimiento crítico." In *La participación popular: Avances y obstáculos,* 29–57. La Paz: Grupo DRU, SNPP.

Urueña, Jaime. 1994. "La idea de heterogeneidad racial en el pensamiento político colombiano: Una mirada historica." *Análisis Político* 22 (May–August):5–25.

Vacaflor Gonzales, Jorge Luis, comp. 1997. *Legislación indígena: Compilación 1991–1997.* La Paz: Vicepresidencia de la República.

Vadillo, Alcides. 1997a. "Avances y peligros para la participación popular." *ProCampo* 77, 14–15.

———. 1997b. "Constitución política del estado y pueblos indígenas: Bolivia, país de mayoría indígena." In *Derecho indígena,* coord. Magdalena Gómez, 268–272. México: Instituto Nacional Indigenista.

Valencia, María del Pilar. 1997. "Desarrollo de los derechos indígenas en Colombia." In *Derecho indígena,* coord. Magdalena Gómez, 252–267. México: Instituto Nacional Indigenista.

Valencia Villa, Hernando. 1990a. "El constituyente de 1990 y la constituyente de 1991." *Análisis Político* 11 (September–December):70–76.

———. 1990b. "Por una asamblea constituyente democrática." *Análisis Político* 9 (January–April):82–86.

———. 1993. "Los derechos humanos en la constitución de 1991." In *La constitución de 1991: Un pacto político viable?* comp. John Dugas, 208–25. Bogotá: Universidad de los Andes.

Valencia Villa, Hernando, and Manuel Barreto Soler. 1992. "La Tutela: O la lucha por los derechos." *Revista Foro* 17 (April):24–31.

Van Cott, Donna Lee. 1994. "Indigenous Peoples and Democracy: Issues for Policymakers." In *Indigenous Peoples and Democracy in Latin America,* ed. Donna Lee Van Cott, 1–27. New York: St. Martin's Press.

———. 1996. "Unity Through Diversity: Ethnic Politics and Democratic Deepening in Colombia." *Nationalism and Ethnic Politics* 2, 4 (winter):523–49.

———. 1999. "'Toward the Pluricultural State': Ethnic Autonomy Regimes in Latin America." Unpublished manuscript.

Vásquez, Miguel. 1994. *Las caras lindas de mi gente negra.* Bogotá: PNR/PNUD/ICAN.

———. 1996. "Reflexiones sobre autoridad y poder en comunidades negras." In *Comunidades negras: Territorios y desarrollo,* 205–06. Bogotá: República de Colombia, Ministerio de Gobierno.

———. 1997. "Antecedentes sobre la aplicación de la jurisdicción especial indígena." In *"Del olvido surgimos para traer nuevas esperanzas": La jurisdicción especial indígena,* 251–64. Bogotá: Ministerio de Justicia, CRIC, Ministerio de Interior.

Vega, Juan Enrique. 1996. "Participación popular y gobernabilidad democrática." In *Democracia y participación popular,* 43–58. La Paz: UMSS, ILDIS, SNPP.

Velásquez C., Fabio E. 1992a. "La democracia participativa: Algo más que una ley." *Revista Foro* 19 (December):77–84.

———. 1992b. "Participación ciudadana y modernización del Estado." *Revista Foro* 17 (April):56–67.

———. 1996. "Una mirada desde Cali." In *Nuevas formas de participación política,* 34–46. Bogotá: FESCOL.

Vertovec, Steven. 1996. "Multiculturalism, culturalism and public incorporation." *Ethnic and Racial Studies* 19, 1 (January):49–69.

Vilas, Carlos M. 1997. "Participation, Inequality, and the Whereabouts of Democracy." In *The New Politics of Inequality in Latin America: Rethinking Participation and Representation,* ed. Douglas Chalmers et al. Oxford: Oxford University Press.

Wade, Peter. 1993a. *Blackness and Race Mixture: The Dynamics of Racial Identity in Colombia*. Baltimore: Johns Hopkins University Press.

———. 1993b. "El movimiento negro en Colombia." *América Negra* 5 (June):173–91.

———. 1994. "The Cultural Politics of Blackness in Colombia." Paper prepared for delivery at the Eighteenth International Congress of the Latin American Studies Association, Atlanta, Georgia, March 10–12.

———. 1997. *Race and Ethnicity in Latin America*. London: Pluto Press.

Walzer, Michael. 1983. *Spheres of Justice*. New York: Basic Books.

———. 1992. "The Civil Society Argument." In *Dimensions of Radical Democracy: Pluralism, Citizenship, Community*, ed. Chantal Mouffe, 89–107. London: Verso.

WOLA. 1997. *Losing Ground: Human Rights Advocates Under Attack in Colombia*. Washington, D.C.: Washington Office on Latin America.

Wheeler, Harvey. 1975. "Constitutionalism." In *Handbook of Political Science*, ed. Fred I. Greenstein and Nelson W. Polsby, 1–91. Reading, Mass.: Addison-Wesley.

Wiarda, Howard. 1992. *American Foreign Policy Toward Latin America in the 1980s and 1990s*. New York: New York University Press.

Wiarda, Howard, and Harvey F. Kline. 1990. *Latin American Politics and Development*. 3rd ed. Boulder: Westview Press.

Wirpsa, Leslie. 1992. "Taking Responsibility: In Colombia, Electoral Politics and Grassroots Activism Complement One Another." *Cultural Survival Quarterly* (fall):49–52.

World Bank. 1994. *Poverty in Colombia*. A World Bank Country Study. Washington, D.C.: World Bank.

———. 1996a. *Social Indicators of Development 1996*. Washington, D.C.: Johns Hopkins University Press.

———. 1996b. *Trends in Developing Economies, 1996*. Washington, D.C.: World Bank.

———. 1998. *World Development Report, 1998*. London: Oxford University Press.

Wunsch, James S., and Dele Olowu. 1996–1997. "Regime Transformation from Below: Decentralization, Local Governance, and Democratic Reform in Nigeria." *Studies in Comparative International Development* 31, 4 (winter):66–82.

Yashar, Deborah. 1996. "Indigenous Protest and Democracy in Latin America." In *Constructing Democratic Governance: Latin America and the Caribbean in the 1990s*, ed. Jorge I. Domínguez and Abraham F. Lowenthal, 87–105. Baltimore: Johns Hopkins University Press.

———. 1998. "Indigenous Movements and Democracy in Latin America." *Comparative Politics* 31, 1 (October):23–42.

Young, Crawford. 1976. *The Politics of Cultural Pluralism*. Madison: University of Wisconsin Press.

Young, Crawford, ed. 1993. *The Rising Tide of Cultural Pluralism: The Nation-State at Bay?* Madison: University of Wisconsin Press.

Young, Iris Marion. 1990. *Justice and the Politics of Difference*. Princeton: Princeton University Press.

Zanotta Machado, Lia. 1994. "Indigenous Communitarianism as a Critique of Modernity and Its Juridical Implications." In *Indigenous Peoples' Experiences with Self-Government*, ed. Willem Assies and A. J. Hoekema. 73–91. IWGIA doc. no. 76. Copenhagen: University of Amsterdam.

Zips, Werner. 1996. "Laws in Competition: Traditional Maroon Authorities Within Legal Pluralism in Jamaica." *Journal of Legal Pluralism* 37–38:279–305.

Interviews Conducted in Colombia (in Bogotá, unless otherwise noted)

Carlos Alviar, Procomún

Miriam Amparo Espinosa, Universidad del Cauca (Popayán, Cauca)

Raúl Arango, National Department of Planning

Doris Aristizabal, DGAI Samper administration

Jesús Avirama, ASI-Cauca (Popayán, Cauca)

Luis José Azcarate, DGAI Gaviria administration

Ana María Bejarano, Universidad de los Andes

Miguel Eduardo Cárdenas, FESCOL

Manuel José Cepeda, counselor for constitutional affairs, Barco and Gaviria administrations

Eduardo Cifuentes, magistrate, Constitutional Court

Piedad Córdoba, senator, Liberal Party

Inés de Brill, Colombian Federation of NGOs

Humberto de la Calle, minister of interior, Gaviria administration; vice president, Samper administration

Jenny de la Torres, Office of Black Communities

Blanca Lucía Echeverry, delegate for ethnic minorities, People's Defender

María Teresa Garces Lloreda, ex-constituent, National Constituent Assembly

Zheger Hay Harb, Citizen Participation Fund

Víctor Jacanamejoy, MIC

Gladys Jimeno Santoyo, DGAI Samper administration

Miriam Jimeno, Universidad Nacional

Jon Landaburu, Universidad de los Andes

Virginie Laurent, IHEAL, University of Paris

Fernando Londoño, Interinstitutional Participation Committee

César Marulanda, CINEP

Alvaro Mejia, CRIC (Popayán, Cauca)

Zulia Mena, deputy, Chamber of Deputies

Lorenzo Muelas, senator, ex-constituent, National Constituent Assembly

Gabriel Murrillo, Universidad de los Andes

Antonio Navarro Wolff, copresident, National Constituent Assembly, mayor of Pasto (Pasto, Nariño)

Luis Carlos Osorio, ASI

Roberto Pineda, Universidad de los Andes

Claudia Piñeros, deputy, Cauca Assembly (Popayán, Cauca)

Gabriel Eduardo Riveros, ESAP

Héctor Riveros, vice minister of interior, Gaviria administration

Francisco Rojas Birry, ex-constituent, National Constituent Assembly

Roque Roldán, CECOIN

Esther Sánchez, Colombian Institute of Family Welfare

Libardo Sarmiento, S.O.S.–Viva la Ciudadana

María Lucia Sotomayor, Colombian Institute of Anthropology

Segundo Tombé, Guambiano leader, Indigenous Authorities of Colombia (Silvia, Cauca)

Elisabeth Ungar, Universidad de los Andes

Hildur Zea, Colombian Institute of Anthropology

Interviews Conducted in Bolivia (in La Paz, unless otherwise noted)

Fernando Aguirre, consultant, Fundación Milenio

Xavier Albó, CIPCA

Florencio Antuñi Sánchez, president, vigilance committee, Charagua, Santa Cruz (Cochabamba)

Rubén Ardaya Salinas, Unidad de Participación Popular

Ivan Arias, API-Danida

Mario Arietta, ILDIS

Oscar Bakir, president, Comité Pro-Cochabamba (Cochabamba)

Verónica Balcazar, director of international cooperation, SNPP

Roberto Barbery, subsecretario, SNPP

Carmen Barragan, Vice Ministry of Popular Participation

José Barriga, vice minister of Popular Participation, Banzer administration

Gerardo Berthín, United Nations Development Programme–La Paz

Ericka Brockman, senator

Fernando Calderón, United Nations Development Programme–La Paz

Ricardo Calla, TAYPI-Danida

Carlos Camargo, MBL

Luz María Calvo, subsecretary of ethnic affairs, SNAEGG

Victor Hugo Cárdenas, vice president (1993–1997)

Tony Cauterruci, Chemonics–La Paz

Juan Antonio Chahin Lupo, vice minister of justice, Banzer administration

Isabelle Combes, Capitanía de Alto Bajo Izozog (Santa Cruz)

Sergio Delgado, Indigenous Peoples Fund
Rodolfo Eróstegui, ILDIS
Marcial Fabricano, CIDOB
Gustavo Fernández Saavedra, presidential minister, Paz Zamora administration
Clara Flores, MRKTL deputy, National Congress
Horst Grebe, Fundación Milenio
José Gabriel Guaseve, CPIB (Trinidad, Beni)
Walter Guevara Arze, USAID
Diego Iturralde, Indigenous Peoples Fund
Mauricio Lea Plaza, subsecretary of participatory municipal planning, SNPP
Luis Lema, MNR senator, Minister of Sustainable Development
Román Loayza, CSUTCB/ASP
María Aida Luzan de Cabrera, mayor, Pucarani, La Paz (Cochabamba)
Rosa Machaca, Federation of Women–Bartolina Sisa
Fernando Mayorga Ugarte, Centro de Estudios Superiores Universitarios–Universidad Mayor de San Simon (Cochabamba)
Lucio Mendez, departamental secretary of popular participation–Beni (Trinidad, Beni)
Maryann Minutillo, Peacecorps
Carlos Hugo Molina, national secretary, SNPP
George Gray Molina, Harvard Institute for International Development
Ramiro Molina R., SNAEGG/Justice Ministry
Sergio Molina, Communications Unit, SNPP
Carlos Armondo Mollinedo, World Bank
Sonia Montaño, subsecretary for gender
J. Antonio Moreno, Federation of Neighborhood Juntas, La Paz
Javier Ernesto Muñoz, Vice Ministry of Indigenous and Original Peoples Issues
José Antonio Navia, Inter-American Development Bank
Alberto Nogales, World Bank
Juan Carlos Nuñez, Episcopal Pastoral Social Commission
René Orellana Halkyer, CEJIS (Santa Cruz)
Lorena Ossio, Justice Ministry, Banzer administration
José Enrique Pinelo, Semilla
Jorge Quiroga, vice president (1997–2002)
Silvina Ramírez, Justice Ministry
Wigberto Rivero Pinto, API-Danida
Julio Rodríguez, Comité Cívico de Tarija (by telephone)
Raquel Romero, subsecretary for gender
Gonzalo Rojas, Research Unit, SNPP

J. Roberto Rozo, United Nations Development Programme
Carmen Beatríz Ruiz, Office of the People's Defender
Marisol Sanjinez, Office of the People's Defender
Nicomedes Sejas, SNAEGG
Javier Seaone, SNPP
Gonzalo Simbron, departmental secretary of popular participation–La Paz
Rodolfo Siñani, departmental secretary of popular participation–Cochabamba (Cochabamba)
Selwyn Suarez, Beni Civic Committee (Trinidad, Beni)
David Tejada, UNICEF
Esteban Ticona, TAYPI-Danida
Carlos F. Toranzo Roca, ILDIS
Javier Torres Goitia, senator, MNR
Diana Urioste, women's coordinator
Juan Cristóbal Urioste, Fundación Milenio
Miguel Urioste, MBL
Jorge Luis Vacaflor, Vice President's Office
Alcides Vadillo Pinto, SNAEGG/SNPP
Luis Vásquez Villamar, MIR deputy, National Congress
Bernardo Wayar, Justice Ministry, Sánchez de Lozada administration

Interviews Conducted in Washington, D.C.

Gerardo Berthín, UNDP
Fernando Carrillo, ex-constituent, National Constituent Assembly, minister of justice, Gaviria administration
César Gaviria, president of Colombia (1990–1994)
Zulia Mena, deputy, Colombian National Congress
Arturo Valenzuela, Georgetown University

Interviews Conducted in Zurich, Switzerland

Javier Aroca, ombudsman for native communities, Peru

Index

Abella, Aida, 69
Acción de tutela. *See* Writ of protection
Agrarian reform, 260; in Bolivia, 127, 129; in Colombia, 46–47. *See also* Ley INRA
Afro-Bolivian population, 18, 126
Afro-Colombian population, 18, 43, 47; activities surrounding ANC, 61, 76–77; constitutional rights, 86, 95; racial/ethnic identity, 43–44, 47, 76, 96–97, 110, 117, 287*n*10; representation in ANC, 68–69; representation in political office, 97, 110, 229, 287*n*13; social movement organizations, 47, 282; territorial rights discussed in ANC, 66, 76, 77. *See also* Transitory Article 55
Aguirre, Fernando, 296*n*35
Albó, Xavier, 294*n*8
Amnesty International, 64, 114, 254
Arango, Raúl, 162
Ardaya, Rubén, 152, 158, 169, 191, 211, 234
Argentine constitution, 269, 272–73
Arias, Ivan, 159, 160
Armed forces: of Bolivia, 34, 131, 193, 251; of Colombia, 248, 251, 252–54
Autonomy regimes, 273–77
Avirama, Jesús, 228
Azcarate, Luis José, 285*n*16

Balcazar, Verónica, 162
Banzer, Hugo, 127, 131, 139, 143, 206, 291*n*11; administration of, 206–07, 297*n*50; decentralization/recentralization policies of, 210–13, 299*n*7; indigenous rights policies of, 194, 213–18, 242, 246
Barco, Virgilio, 41, 46, 51–52, 55–56, 74
Barrientos, Bonifacio, 296*n*26
Barrientos, René, 132
Betancur, Belisario, 46, 50–53
Black constitutional rights, 276–77
Blacks. *See* Afro-Colombian population, Afro-Bolivian population
Blattmann, René, 199, 204
Bobbio, Norberto, 59

Bolivian campesino movement, 126–28, 234; attitude of toward LPP, 161, 167, 194–96. *See also* Bolivian Unitary Syndical Peasant Workers Confederation
Bolivian civil society, quality of, 234–35, 300*n*20
Bolivian Communist Party, 131
Bolivian Confederation of Private Entrepreneurs (CEPB), 132, 142, 293*n*22
Bolivian constitution (1967), 132–33, 135
Bolivian constitution (1995 reformed): article (1), 175–76; article (60), 143, 224, 226; article (90), 143; article (171), 160, 162, 175–77, 187, 197, 208, 241, 295*n*22; influence of Colombian constitution on, 145, 162
Bolivian constitutional history, 132
Bolivian indigenous legislation, 135
Bolivian indigenous movement, 127, 246; promotes multicultural state, 133; role of in constitutional reform, 125, 162. *See also* Katarista movement
Bolivian indigenous population, 125–26; constitutional rights of, 143, 175–78, 210; representation of in public office, 188–89, 227, 229–30, 300*n*11; territorial rights of, 162, 178, 187, 197, 198, 210, 241; voting behavior of, 224–25
Bolivian labor movement, 126, 128–29, 131, 158, 206, 251; opposition of to LPP, 158, 165, 187, 195
Bolivian population, 126
Bolivian Revolution (1952), 126, 167
Bolivian transition to democracy, 130–31, 138, 224, 251
Bolivian Unitary Syndical Peasant Workers Confederation (CSUTCB), 128, 129, 150, 196, 198–99, 215–17; proposal of for multicultural state, 135–37; opposition of to LPP, 161, 167
Bolivian Workers Central (COB), 126–28, 150, 167
Botero, Fernando, 106

335

Brazilian constitution, 16, 269, 272; and 1987–1988 constituent assembly, 20, 141

Cabildos, 45, 177, 245
Calvo, Luz María, 159
Calla, Ricardo, 214
Capitalization law, 292*n*1, 297*n*37
Cárdenas, Víctor Hugo, 136, 146–48, 159, 160, 199; political aspirations of, 193, 292*n*12, 295*n*13; role of in drafting LPP, 151, 153, 159, 292*n*10
Carranza, María Mercedes, 69
Carrillo, Fernando, 54, 62, 91–92, 111
Catholic Church: Bolivian, 34, 190, 193, 226, 293*n*22; Colombian, 284*n*7, 289*n*33
Cepeda, Manuel José, 52, 108, 224
Chávez, Hugo, 28, 281*n*7
Civic committees, 131–32, 155, 157, 158, 162, 173–74, 210, 218; constitutional reform campaign of, 204–05, 297*n*37; opposition of to LPP, 166; support of for departmental decentralization, 146, 211, 297*n*37
Clark, Robert, 254
Coca growers, 189, 209–10, 216, 230
Collective rights, 8, 12–13, 15, 238, 260, 262, 273; in Colombia, 45, 84, 85, 112; in Ecuador, 276–77
Colombian civil society, quality of, 41, 233
Colombian Communist Party, 55
Colombian Constitution of 1886, 39, 51, 61, 89
Colombian Constitution of 1991: implementing legislation for, 100–101; public opinion of, 91
Colombian Constitutional Court, 33, 35, 66, 70, 98, 248, 289*n*30; and protection of human rights, 111–18; establishment of, 91–92; rulings on indigenous rights, 84–85, 88, 112–16, 119, 120; rulings on Afro-Colombian rights, 84–85, 98, 116–17; rulings on participation of civil society, 10, 231; rulings on special indigenous jurisdiction, 113, 115; efforts of others to reduce its powers, 107–08, 118
Colombian constitutional history, 39–40, 50–51
Colombian Fiscalía General, 33, 35, 66, 80, 91–92, 109, 121

Colombian indigenous movement, 72, 77, 245–46. *See also* Colombian National Indigenous Organization; Indigenous Authorities of Colombia; Regional Indigenous Council of the Cauca
Colombian indigenous population, 44–45, 249; legislation concerning, 45; representation of in political office, 110, 227–29; territorial rights of, 66, 75, 77, 85–94, 103, 241; voting behavior of, 224–25. *See also* Indigenous territorial entities
Colombian National Indigenous Organization (ONIC), 46, 67, 90, 103, 104; electoral experience of, 94, 102, 286*n*7
Colombian population, 18, 43
Colombian Supreme Court, 50, 51, 52, 55, 64, 118, 119; ruling on Decree 927, 56, 58–59; ruling on Decree 1926, 58–59; ruling on legality of 1957 plebiscite, 51; rulings on writs of protection, 290*n*38
Communitarianism, 87–88, 112, 175, 198, 241
Conscience of the Fatherland (CONDEPA), 129, 142, 158, 230, 251; alliance of with ADN, 206–07; support of for municipal decentralization, 138, 146
Conservative party (Colombia), 39, 41, 42, 49, 52, 65. *See also* Social Conservative Party
Constitutionalism, 1, 12, 15, 37
Constitutional Courts: in Latin America, 87, 270, 278, 286*n*30, 302*n*9; in postcommunist Europe, 34, 270. *See also* Colombian Constitutional Court
Constitutional reform, alternative processes compared, 19–23
Constitutions, study of, 11–13
Córdoba, Piedad, 96–97, 104
Corruption: in Bolivia, 130, 203, 207, 212, 218, 299*n*7; in Colombia, 49, 79, 92, 107, 122, 301*n*31

Dandler, Jorge, 270
De Brill, Inés, 93
Decentralization, 35, 151, 225, 257, 275; benefits CSUTCB, 196; Bolivian debate on, 137–39, 142, 146, 157–58, 173; Bolivian municipal decentralization, 153–54, 193, 226, 229, 235, 249; in Colombia, 50, 81, 108, 156, 225, 239; in

Ecuador, 270; in Fundación Milenio proposal, 143; in Guatemala, 270; in Plan de Todos, 168; supported by international advisors, 151; under Banzer administration, 210–13
Decree 927, 56, 58
Decree 1926, 57–58, 85
De Dios Mosquera, Juan, 284n11
De la Calle, Humberto, 70, 77, 101, 106, 232–33
Democratic Alliance M-19 (ADM-19), 55, 251, 289n32; participation of in ANC, 62, 65–66, 68, 71–72, 75, 284n3
Direct democracy mechanisms, 80, 91, 93, 100, 111, 285n25; exercise of in Colombia, 23–32, 288n16; in post-communist European constitutions, 255; proscribed in Bolivia, 133, 142, 175, 205, 218
Drug cartels, 122, 225, 252; attacks on Colombian state, 48, 53, 55, 91; attacks on civil society and media, 48, 54, 55
Dueñas, Otilio, 284n11

Ecuadorian constitution, 258, 269–76; and 1998 constituent assembly, 16, 33, 258
Educational reform law, 161, 177, 181, 195, 199, 217, 291n1, 295n24
Escobar, Pablo, 99, 109
Extradition issue, 48, 53, 65–67, 284n7

Fabricano, Marcial, 130, 161, 162, 216
Fals Borda, Orlando, 69, 287n11
Fernández Saavedra, Gustavo, 140–41
Flores, Clara, 164
Free Bolivia Movement (MBL), 129, 133, 142, 147, 206, 215; electoral alliance with indigenous organizations, 189, 216, 246; state reform proposal of, 137–38, 147, 154
Fundación Milenio, 141–46

Gaitán, Jorge Eliécer, assassination of, 39
Galán, Luis Carlos, assassination of, 53
Garces Lloreda, María Teresa, 69, 93, 224
García Meza, Luis, 131, 140, 291n9
Gaviria Trujillo, César, 30, 52, 53, 56–58; attempts to control ANC, 63, 69–70; policies of toward ethnic rights, 74, 94, 242; implements constitution reform, 33, 91–92, 95; leadership of in ANC,

69–71, 78; negotiates with guerrillas, 64, 69, 99, 284n4; public opinion of, 99
Gómez, Alvaro, 62, 63, 67, 284n8
Gómez, Magdalena, 261
Governability crisis, 2, 13, 27; in Bolivia, 133–34; in Colombia, 48–49
Grebe, Horst, 154, 292n10
Green, Abadio, 103, 288n20
Group rights. See Collective rights
Guatemalan constitution, 272; 1999 attempt to reform, 16–17, 33
Guerrilla movements, 39, 41, 91, 122, 225, 231, 252; attacks on Colombian ANC, 64; in Bolivia, 144; peace talks with, 56, 60, 62, 64, 66; relations with Indians, 46; role in ANC, 62, 72; violence against civil society, 253. See also Revolutionary Armed Forces of Colombia; National Liberation Army; Popular Liberation Army, M-19, Quintín Lame
Guyanese constitutional reform, 17

Hellman, Judith Adler, 246
Herrán, Helena, 69
Hershberg, Eric, 247
Honduran constitution, 272
Huilcaman, Aucan, 265
Human rights, 32, 72, 91, 225, 278; in Bolivia, 200, 209; in Colombia, 254; in Colombian constitution, 60, 87; in Latin American constitutions, 16; violations by Colombian government/ military, 42, 48–49, 66, 251
Human rights ombudsman, 16, 270, 278. See also People's Defender

Indigenismo, 256
Indigenous Authorities of Colombia (AICO), 46, 67, 94, 245
Indigenous Confederation of Eastern Bolivia (CIDOB), 129, 161, 195–96, 201, 216–17, 229, 246; proposes indigenous law, 136, 161
Indigenous customary law, 74, 75, 208–09, 240, 265, 271–72; exercised in Bolivia, 199–200, 296n26; exercised in Colombia, 113–16; in Bolivian constitution, 135, 176, 178; in Colombian constitution, 85. See also Special Indigenous Jurisdiction